DIGGING FOR HISTORY

EDWARD BACON

Digging For History

ARCHAEOLOGICAL DISCOVERIES THROUGHOUT

THE WORLD, 1945 TO 1959

WITH AN INTRODUCTION BY *William Foxwell Albright*
PROFESSOR EMERITUS, JOHNS HOPKINS UNIVERSITY

The JOHN DAY Company   *New York*

Library of Congress Catalogue
Card Number: 61-5680

MANUFACTURED IN THE UNITED STATES OF AMERICA

Dedicated to

SIR BRUCE INGRAM, O.B.E., M.C.,

Editor of
The Illustrated London News
since 1900

In acknowledgement
of all he has done for
the World of Archaeology
and in gratitude for
his introducing the author to it

CONTENTS

LIST OF PLATES

Following page 54.

ACKNOWLEDGEMENTS

IT must be obvious that the author of a book like this is indebted to a very great number of people. He is, after all, the reporter; they are the doers. It can in fact be said that I owe a debt of gratitude to every person whose name is mentioned in the pages of the book and this I gladly acknowledge. Without them my life would have been duller and this book could never have existed. I would, however, like to acknowledge certain other debts. I have received considerable help from a number of foreign Embassies in London; and I should like to mention especially the Swedish Institute and the Cultural Attachés of Bulgaria, the Sudan and Yugoslavia. I wish to thank most heartily Mr Maurice Michael for the germinal idea; the Editor of *The Illustrated London News* and my colleagues in that paper for their interest, encouragement and help; Mr Bray of the London Electrotype Agency for his cheerful pertinacity in hunting out elusive photographs; and finally, and most important of all, I must most willingly thank my wife for her stimulus, encouragement and forbearance.

For permission to reproduce the illustrations in the book, I am indebted as follows:—

Plates 1 and 45a: Miss Theresa Goell and the Nemrud Dagh-Arsameia expedition. Plate 4: Central Press Photos, Ltd. Plates 2, 3, and 16: *The Illustrated London News.* Plate 5 and the illustration on the dust-cover: M. René Joffroy. Plate 6: The Bulgarian Academy of Sciences. Plate 7: Professor Juan de M. Carriazo. Plate 8: Dr Dino Adamesteanu. Plate 9: Professor G. V. Gentili. Plate 11: Dr Libero d'Orsi. Plates 12 and 13: Professor Paolo Enrico Arias. Plates 14 and 15: The Superintendent of Antiquities of Rome I, Professor Giulio Jacopi. Plates 17, 18a, c, d, and e, and 19a and b: the American School of Classical Studies at Athens. Plates 18b and 19c: Mr M. S. F. Hood and the British School of Archaeology at Athens. Plate 20: The Mycenae Excavations and Miss Elizabeth Wace. Plates 21 and 23b and c: Professor Carl W. Blegen. Plate 22: Professor Sp. Marinatos. Plate 23a: Mr Nicholas M. Verdelis. Plate 24: Professor Oscar Broneer and the University of Chicago. Plate 25: Professor John L. Caskey and the American School of Classical Studies at Athens. Plate 26: Professor George E. Mylonas and the Archaeological Institute of America. Plates 27 and 28: Professor Doro Levi and the Italian Archaeological School at Athens. Plate 29: Professor L. Bernabo Brea. Plate 30: Dr P. Dikaios and the Department of Antiquities, Cyprus. Plates 31 and 32: Professor Claude F. A. Schaeffer. Plate 33: Mr James B. Pritchard. Plates 34 and 46b: The Department of Antiquities, Hashemite Kingdom of Jordan. Plate 35: Dr Kathleen M. Kenyon and the Jericho Excavation Fund. Plate 36a: Dr N. Avigad, the Israel Exploration Society and the Hebrew University, Jerusalem. Plate 36b: Professor Robert Braidwood and the Iraq Petroleum Company. Plate 37: Dr Yigael Yadin, the James A. de Rothschild Expedition at Hazor and the Hebrew University, Jerusalem. Plate 38: Professor G. E. Bean. Plate 39: Professor Franz Miltner and the Austrian Archaeological Institute. Plates 40, 41, and 58b: Professor Rodney S. Young and the University Museum, Philadelphia. Plate 42a, c, and d: Mr Seton Lloyd and the British Institute of Archaeology at Ankara. Plates 42b and 44: Professor D. Storm Rice. Plate 43: Professor Dr Helmuth Th. Bossert. Plate 45b: Dr F. K. Doerner, Director of the Arsameia Excavations. Plate 46a: The late Sir Leonard Woolley. Plate 47: Professor Dr R. Ghirshman and C. J. B. (Iran). Plate 48: Professor M. E. L. Mallowan and the British School of Archaeology in Iraq (copyright reserved). Plates 49 and 50: Directorate General of Antiquities of Iraq (copyright reserved). Plate 51: Professor W. B. Emery. Plate 52: The Abbé Henri Breuil and the Trianon Press. Plate 53: Commander Michael Parker, R.N. (Retd.). Plates 57a and c: Mr Kermit Goell and the Arsameia Excavations. Plate 57b: Statens Historiska Museum, Stockholm. Plate 56: Fondazione Ing. C. M. Lerici. Plates 58a and c: Mr Anthony Clark, Mr John Martin, the Instrumentation Laboratory of the Distillers Company and Messrs F. A. Hughes, Ltd.

CHAPTER ONE

INTRODUCTION

ONE of the most remarkable facts in journalism is the widespread public interest in archaeology. Thanks to such recurrent sensations as the discovery of the tomb of Tutankhamen and the Dead Sea Scrolls, students of the press often rate archaeology as second only to sex in popular appeal. Rich tombs, lost cities, hoards of priceless manuscripts, galleys submerged with their cargoes — these are the stuff of which the romance of archaeology is made. And the first popular journal to grasp the possibilities of archaeology was the *Illustrated London News,* whose brilliant editor, Bruce Ingram, made it the foremost organ for the publication of exciting new finds in world archaeology nearly sixty years ago. It is a happy idea on the part of Mr. Edward Bacon to collect and edit choice samples of the archaeological material which has appeared in the *News* since the beginning of the century.

Archaeology is one of the most recent of sciences. It is true that antiquarian interest may be traced back to the third millennium B.C. and that the Babylonian king Nabonidus, in the sixth century B.C., ordered soundings to be made under ruined temples in order to recover the names of their builders. It is true that Israelite and Hellenic historians collected information from old documents and the memories of men as early as the tenth and the fifth centuries B.C., respectively. The Roman emperor Hadrian was an avid collector of art objects. Yet archaeology was one of the latest major scholarly disciplines to be organized according to the methods of inductive reasoning.

Historically the lag of archaeology is easy to explain. No study can become scientific until it is based on systematic observation and experiment — in other words, on inductive logic. (Mathematics occupies a special place.) Even the study of ancient books and manuscripts could not become scientific until philology was placed on an inductive basis by Newton's friend Richard Bentley, and his successors in the eighteenth and nineteenth centuries. The development of historical philology greatly facilitated the development of archaeology, but there could be no real archaeology until there was systematic digging. The accidental discovery of Herculaneum under the ashes of the eruption of Vesuvius (A.D. 79) was quickly followed by the first archaeological excavation in 1738. When, a century later, the French started to excavate the capitals of ancient Assyria, modern world archaeology was born.

Today there is scarcely a country where archaeological activities are not organized under some sort of national or academic control. Both East and West have taken up the challenge of the past, and archaeology is nowhere more popular than in the Soviet Union. Turkey, Iran and the leading Arab countries have well-established departments of antiquities. Notable progress has been made in India and Pakistan. Though China has been slow in undertaking excavations and foreign scholars have difficulty in obtaining information, Japan is already vying with the West in the scope and quality of its archaeological work. It is no accident that the youngest and one of the smallest nations, Israel, outstrips the rest of the world in the intensity of its interest in archaeology.

Ninety years ago a German amateur scholar, Heinrich Schliemann, discovered that Hissarlik, which he correctly identified with Troy, is a stratified mound whose successive layers reflect corresponding periods of settlement. Twenty years later (1890) the English amateur Flinders Petrie proved that a high mound in southern Palestine also consists of superimposed layers of occupation, each characterized by its own pottery culture or by a phase of a given culture shared by two or more adjacent levels. Twelve years later Petrie went still farther by introducing sequence dating, through which pottery groups can be dated typologically, even where there is no stratigraphic succession. The discovery by Petrie that pottery could be used by the archaeologist just as the fossil remains of plants and animals are employed by geologists, established his place as the greatest archaeological genius of history.

The next great step forward in method came with George Andrew Reisner, an American who introduced the practice of full recording of everything found by the excavator, from architecture to pottery. For the first time the best surveying, photographic and draughting techniques were used to locate, level and record the results of excavation, while the foremost specialists were associated with the description and interpretation of the results. The Reisner-Fisher method dominated archaeological field work during the twenties and thirties of this century. Then came another notable advance: the Wheeler reintroduction of the use of trenches, which had been largely discarded by the Reisner school. The use of trenches by Sir Mortimer Wheeler and Dr. Kathleen Kenyon has little in common with the practice of trenching in the nineteenth century (and later). As employed by these scholars in Britain, India and Palestine, trenches are used to guide the excavator by thorough analysis of the occupation profiles which they disclose. The walls of all trenches are studied minutely and vertical sections are drawn to scale, indicating all remains of construction, floor levels, deposits of any material, etc., as accurately as possible.

The latest advance in field archaeology consists in the systematic application of geological, botanical, and especially of physicochemical methods of dating to ancient remains. Of all these new methods, radiocarbon is easily the most important; details are given at the end of the volume. First worked out by Willard F. Libby (who has received the Nobel Prize for his achievement) and applied to archaeology by him in 1948, the method now makes it possible to date carbon samples back about 40,000 years. By using the "enriched" sampling introduced by the late H. de Vries, it is possible to push radiocarbon dating some 30,000 years farther back. With the aid of ancient sea- or lake-bottom cores, Cesare Emiliani has apparently succeeded in extrapolating these dates and in reducing the chronology of early man in Pleistocene deposits to about half the generally accepted dating (that is, cutting the duration of the Ice Age from half a million to a quarter of a million years).

It is true that not all experts in radiocarbon dating agree. Carelessly recorded samples, or samples found out of context, have created much confusion. Not all counts have been correctly made, and the margin of error may be higher than sometimes stated. But with scores of radiocarbon installations in many countries and with thousands of published counts, it is now quite certain that the end of the last Ice Age in the Northern Hemisphere may be set about 11,000 years ago (9,000 B.C.). It is also certain that villages were in existence soon afterwards (perhaps even earlier), and that walled towns were springing up in different parts of the Near and Middle East during the seventh millennium B.C.

There is scarcely an area of geography and anthropology which is not being enriched by archaeology. The history of human culture depends to such an extent on environment that geography and archaeology have become interdependent. Not only has man been profoundly affected by his geographical environment, he has also often transformed that environment by cultivation, irrigation, drainage and introduction of new fauna and flora. Neither the history of climate nor that of soils can be fully understood without the help of archaeological data. What is true of geography and related subjects is even more true of the sciences of man. Without careful analysis of archaeological evidence few of the many views held by cultural and social anthropologists can be adequately tested. Linguistic science is equally dependent on data brought to light through excavation before it can safely study the evolution of language. The surprising fact has, for example, been established that there were more radically different linguistic stocks in the Near and Middle East five thousand years ago than there are there today.

In our day archaeology has become the indispensable handmaiden of the world historian and philosopher of history. This is obvious in the case of an historian with the tremendous sweep of an Arnold Toynbee. Many lesser men forget that history deals with entire cultures, just as the time of Herodotus, not simply with a succession of events or institutions. The efforts of some thinkers to set up a barrier between the fundamental methodology of the historian and the natural scientist disregard the fact that archaeology and most ancillary historical studies are thoroughly scientific in their operational logic. If we remember that only the physical sciences operate on the basis of reciprocal validation of controlled experiment and mathematical theory, the fundamental identity of all systematic observation and reasoning becomes clear. Nor should we be worried by the appearance of value judgments in history, as long as the historian understands their nature and limits them to history as an art. As an art, history is like medicine, agriculture or economics, in all of which value judgments are equally necessary for practical application and instruction.

None of the humanities has been as much enriched by archaeological discovery as art itself. Museums and private collections all over the world burst with specimens of ancient and exotic arts whose very existence was unknown a few decades ago. Recent architecture, painting and especially sculpture have been profoundly influenced by the rediscovered arts of the Middle East and Central America. Much abstract and geometrical art has been directly affected by pre-Hellenic or modern primitive forms. The vogue of classicism in art and architecture was directly stimulated by the recovery of classical models in the fifteenth to eighteenth centuries. The decline of the classical tradition and the rapid development of mechanical methods of representation in the nineteenth century coincided with the rise of world archaeology, which provided many of the sources and inspirations for the formation of modern art.

We have yet to mention a vast field of profound human significance to which archaeology is making tremendous contributions — the scholarly study of religion. It is only by reconstructing the evolution of cultic symbolism through the ages that we can understand the nature of religious symbols. Only by comparing early Egyptian, Sumerian, Canaanite and Hittite religious literatures — all of which we owe to the archaeologist — with the religious literature and cult practices of India and the Far East, as well as with the anthropological record of modern primitives, can we form an adequate idea of the relation between myth and ritual. And, above all, it is only through the fullest utilization of archaeological discoveries that we can reconstruct the background of the Bible and follow the early development of the Judaeo-Christian faith around which so much of Western civilization revolves.

With these remarks on the meaning of archaeology for a deeper understanding of modern life, we invite the reader to forget the pressures and frustrations of our day while he loses himself in the romance of a freshly discovered past.

WILLIAM FOXWELL ALBRIGHT

CHAPTER TWO

THE UNITED KINGDOM—I

THE total amount of archaeological activity in Great Britain since the war is enormous and its patrons are innumerable. Universities and institutes, learned societies, schools, even local authorities and, most steadily active of all, the Ancient Monuments Inspectorate of the Ministry of Works—all have been at work, excavating, exploring, recording, conserving every facet of our country's past. To give a single example alone, the Excavations Section of the Ministry of Works Inspectorate of Ancient Monuments reported for a single season— that of 1957–8—no less than forty-four "rescue digs", excavations that is at sites threatened with destruction. And this last phrase gives the reason for this furious tempo. So much of the face of the country has been and is being destroyed— using that word in the sense of the permanent obliteration of the evidence of the past—by enemy action, by the spread of buildings, by the driving of new roads, the building of new industries and not least by the deeper ploughing of intensified cultivation, that it must have seemed to many that the past was disappearing for ever before the bulldozer and under the concrete mixer; and that there was no time to waste.

The result has been a wealth of information and an intensive course of instruction for excavators. No single book could hope to record it all; and since a great deal of it, passionately interesting though it is to its discoverers, is much of a muchness and more suited to the abstracts of a learned publication than a book designed for the general reader, this chapter will be confined to those works which have thrown a new or a vivid or a surprising light on our past.

Undoubtedly the discovery which most stirred public interest in archaeology in the United Kingdom was the discovery of a Temple of Mithras in the heart of the City of London in September, 1954. But although this was a surprise, it was not an accident, but rather the culmination of a whole series of activities and a rich reward for patient investigation and collection of information. The devastation of much of the City, by fire and bombing, by its laying bare the basements of great blocks of valuable property and its bringing about the necessity for the digging of new foundations on the widest possible scale had given the archaeologists the chance to look at levels of London they could never possibly have seen by any other means; and the Roman and Mediaeval London Excavation Council came into being to take advantage of this opportunity and to examine and record every piece of information which came to light in this way and, wherever possible, when time and money were available and the goodwill of contractors and property developers existed, to make excavations on such sites. The Director of these excavations was Dr W. F. Grimes, then of the London Museum and now of the Institute of Archaeology; and much work was also done by Mr Norman Cook of the Guildhall Museum.

Many interesting objects were found; and one particular timber-lined well produced two oddly assorted but well-preserved items: a Roman ladder, made of oak, about 8 ft long and with rungs 20 in apart; and a pair of leather drawers, exiguous "G-string" drawers exactly like those worn by the "Bikini girls" of the Piazza Armerina mosaics found in Sicily. The chief interest of the excavations at this earlier stage lay however in pieces of walls and roads of Roman date which helped to fill in the general plan of Roman London; and the most striking discovery in this respect was the recognition of what came to be known as the Cripplegate Fort. This is at the north-west corner of the City; and discoveries over several years enabled a pretty clear picture to be built up.

It was revealed as a large square auxiliary fort of about eleven acres, and it seems probable that it was built first towards the end of the first century A.D. when the city was recovering after the devastation called by the revolt of Boudicca (or Boadicea) in A.D. 61. It was later to be incorporated as a very large north-western salient of the whole defensive system of the city, when it became a walled city some time after A.D. 140.

Meanwhile interest was being transferred to the area through which the little river Walbrook ran at the time, the area between the Bank of England and the Thames. This had been the scene of considerable discoveries in 1869, when a new road (now Queen Victoria Street) was made. Then a large geometrical mosaic pavement (now known as the Bucklersbury Pavement and preserved in the collection of the Guildhall Museum) was found; and it caused a great stir at the time and during the last three days of the excavations some 33,000 members of the public were admitted to see the remains, a sort of wooden cat-walk being built over the mosaic for the purpose. In the contemporary account reference is also made to traces of a considerable building being noticed on the bank of the Walbrook. But Queen Victoria Street came into being and Bucklersbury was built up; and it seemed likely that this was the last glimpse of this piece of Roman London. Sometime in the last century two pieces of sculpture (now in the London Museum) came to light, supposedly "from twenty feet down, in the middle of the Walbrook"—a fragment of a river god of second century workmanship and a Mithraic relief, a votive offering of Ulpius Silvanus, a veteran of the second Augustan Legion. All these were, so to speak, the known but forgotten clues, in a story which was yet to develop with the help of Hitler's bombs.

Meanwhile, far away in Northumberland at Carrawburgh (Procolitia) on Hadrian's Wall, a simple Temple of Mithras was discovered in 1949 and fully excavated in 1950 by the Excavations Committees of the University of Durham and the Society of Antiquaries of Newcastle-upon-Tyne, under the direction of Professor Ian A. Richmond and Mr J. P. Gillam. Now Mithraism was an ancient mystery-religion which had its origin in Persia, its god being Mithras, the bull-slayer, the god of light and its prophet, Zoroaster. Zoroastrianism forms much of the ancient background of modern Parseeism; but the form of Mithraism which became so firmly established in the Roman Empire in the first centuries of this era was rather different. The shallow and formal "officialism" of the religion of the Olympian Gods, as it was practised at Rome, had left the way open to intense and mystic religions, which not unnaturally swept through the citizens of the expanding Roman Empire like wildfire and in very great variety. Chief among them were Mithraism, Christianity and the worship of Isis; and much against the odds, as it must have seemed to any educated Roman, Christianity, the religion of slaves, triumphed from its very inclusiveness, its all-embracingness, its catholicity. Mithraism was far different: it was extremely exclusive, entirely male and very austere. In practice it became the religion of professional soldiers and merchants. It consisted of small "lodges" and was inculcated by initiation and revelation and was secret. Special and severe tests of courage, endurance and understanding were required of the aspirant, who could, if he were sufficiently devout, brave and constant pass through seven grades, usually known as the Raven, the Bridegroom, the Soldier, the Lion, the Persian, the Sun-courier and the Father.

The Mithraeum discovered at Carrawburgh was a soldiers' chapel and measured some 38 ft long by 15 ft wide at its greatest extent. It seems to have been first built in the early part of the third century, to have been enlarged, to have been destroyed in A.D. 296–7, to have been rebuilt and finally to have been desecrated in the early part of the fourth century, presumably by Christian zealots at the time when Constantine the Great made Christianity the official religion of the Roman Empire and Mithraism became an impolitic cult for a senior officer of the army.

It is in the form of a dark rectangular chapel with a small antechamber, the chapel itself being in the form of a narrow nave between two slightly raised platforms on which the celebrants reclined or stood during the service. In the antechamber was a stone-lined initiation pit, with covers of stone and near by a ritual hearth. With these the aspirant could be put through various tests of extreme heat, cold and partial burial. In the chapel were found two statues and three altars. Of the statues one, rather oddly, was a small statue of a mother-goddess; the other was an intentionally mutilated statue of Cautes. Cautes and Cautopates are two deities attendant on Mithras and the former holds a torch upwards, while Cautopates holds his torch downwards. The three altars all bore dedications by different commandants of the local fort, the two earlier ones being simple altars, the last showing a relief of Mithras with a radiate crown. This radiate crown is pierced right through, so that a light behind the altar would show as a radiance around the god's head.

It is not difficult to imagine the scene—or even to find modern parallels for it. The chapel of a remote frontier post of the Empire; a small chapel of stone and wood, with a wicker partition separating the antechamber from the chapel;

a dark building lit only by torches, or lamps or the fire of the ritual hearth; a small gathering of rather senior officers, with perhaps a visiting officer from an area headquarters, perhaps a travelling merchant who is also a Mithraist. It may be that a young officer is being initiated and the grades of Lion and Raven, in their fantastic animal head-dresses, hold up their torches as the young man is covered over in the chilly initiation pit. In the chapel the visitors and the members of the lodge recline on the platforms and note the altars which have been the donations of former but still remembered commanding officers; and before the niche at the end the Father draws back the veil and reveals the image of Mithras and the light shines through the pierced crown of the bull-slaying hero-god—and sensations of loyalty, solidarity, resolution and ambition pass through the minds of this little group of professional men, who know that on their will, courage and determination depend the security of the Empire and the fulfilment of their own careers.

This then was the background to the finding of the London Mithraeum. During 1954 a large site was being cleared in the City between Queen Victoria Street and Cannon Street, adjacent to Walbrook, in preparation for the erection of a very large fourteen-storey block of offices, and the team of excavators of the Roman and Mediaeval London Excavation Council, directed by Dr W. F. Grimes, were working on the remains of a good sized building and nearing the end of the time allotted to them by the building contractors, when on 18 September their efforts were rewarded with the discovery of a noble stone carved head, life size, whose Phrygian cap securely identified it with the Mithraic cult. The building too had been revealed as a temple about 60 ft long by 20 ft wide—a central chamber with aisles on either side, a triple-apsed west end and a raised platform which probably originally carried an altar. This discovery, somewhat surprisingly, aroused the greatest popular interest and press publicity. The contractors agreed to hold up their work for about a fortnight in order that further excavation might be carried out and as more and more pieces of fine sculpture continued to be found, the Walbrook Mithraeum went on attracting the sort of headline attention which is usually reserved for a particularly grisly murder. Great crowds continued to gather around the block in which the excavation was taking place and from 20 September, the actual excavation was open to the public each evening between 5.30 and 6.30, and on the last two days 25–26 September between 2.30 and 6.30 p.m. Huge queues formed all round the block and on the first day some 10,000 persons visited the site; on the second day this rose to 15,000 and some 3,000 were turned away as dusk fell; and so it went on. It was generally agreed that it was a remarkable discovery and there was a great deal of public concern that it should have to be destroyed when the new building on the site was constructed. It was suggested that the plans should be altered or that the remains should be preserved intact in the basement of the new building. Both those plans however would have been immensely costly and probably impracticable; and there was great relief when early in October, the owners of the site, the Legenland Property Company and their Chairman,

Mr A. V. Bridgeman, announced their intention of dismantling the remains and re-erecting them in the forecourt of the eventual Bucklersbury House at their own expense; and the lifting operation was completed by the middle of October, 1954 (Plates 3 and 4).

Of what did this temple consist? What was its date and site? And what were the objects found in it.

It was the same sort of building as the Carrawburgh Mithraeum, but as be-fitting a metropolitan temple, larger and of much more finished architecture, but it was not so complete, the antechamber at the eastern end not having survived. It was built of stone, principally Kentish ragstone, with bonding courses of tile and the nave was separated from the two aisles by two rows of seven circular stone pillars. The west end was apsidal and here, presumably, would stand the relief of Mithras slaying the bull. In front of this was a plat-form, approached by steps and carrying the altar, which it seems likely was covered by a pillared tabernacle. The aisles were higher than the nave and would serve as benches on which the worshippers reclined or stood. In one corner of the nave was a timber-lined well whose waters would doubtless be used in rites of lustration. This is the basic and first form of the temple which was built shortly after A.D. 150, as was shown by a coin of Hadrian found among the foundations. During the years it underwent a number of changes, in the course of which the floor level of the nave rose about three feet. In the last alteration a stone block had been inserted to carry the latest altar and among timbers supporting this there was found a bronze coin of Constantine the Great (A.D. 307–337) which had been minted in Rome. By this time however the building had been considerably modified; the rows of pillars had been removed; the floor of the nave was level with the apse; and a number of statues had been buried under the later floors for reasons which are not clear.

The objects which were found during the excavations were numerous and interesting. There was the life-size head of Mithras already mentioned and a fragment of its neck and chest was also found, suggesting that this was originally a complete and free-standing statue. Another life-size head was found, a grey marble Athene, originally crowned with a diadem—a beautiful piece of work; part of a plaque in relief, showing an attendant with a lowered torch, Cauto-pates; and part of a circular plaque showing horsemen and dogs. Part of a large stone laver bowl was found and a smaller sandstone bowl. A number of small pieces of statuary came to light: part of the torso of a male figure, whose total complete height would be about twenty inches, flattened at the back and so presumably designed for a niche; a small marble statuette, showing a seated male figure, identified as Mercury from the stumps of wings on his head, the purse in his hand and the ram and tortoise seated before him—Mercury was the patron of sharp-practitioners, as the purse signifies and he was also the inventor of the lyre which he made from the carapace of a tortoise; a small group, showing Dionysus reaching up to a vine, Silenus on a donkey with a tree trunk on one side of him, and, on the other, a satyr and a maenad carrying a wine-jar with a leopard at her feet; two fragments of inscriptions; and a colossal hand, closed round a rod or spout and part of a statue which must have been two-and-a-half times life size; and a most splendid large marble head of Serapis. This last was in excellent condition and, as a work of art, the finest piece found. The head is Jovian in character, with a full curly beard and long curling hair; the lips are slightly parted; and on top of the head is what looks at first sight like a flower-pot but is, in fact, the *modius* or corn measure, an emblem of fertility, and on the sides of it, in relief, are representations of olive-trees. The back of the head is unfinished and it was clearly intended to stand in a niche. It is almost identical, except in size, with a colossal head of Serapis which is now in the Vatican and which it is assumed was a copy from a famous statue, the work of the great Greek sculptor Bryaxis, which stood in the Serapeum of Alexandria.

Serapis is Egyptian in origin and an aspect of Osiris. He was first independently worshipped, as a god of the lower world, in the Egypt of the Ptolemies, and his worship, which gradually included aspects of Pluto, Jupiter and Asclepius the god of healing, spread widely, particularly during the time of the Emperor Hadrian. Dream-oracles were often attached to his temples.

Serapis, Athene, Dionysus, Mercury—these seem odd deities to find in a Temple of Mithras, especially when we recall the nature of the Mithraic cult. Possibly in its later stages the temple became a sort of Pantheon or temple of all the gods; or perhaps in the rising tide of Christianity, the temple patronized by senior officers of the army and the richest merchants of the city seemed like a stronghold for the non-Christian religionists of London—a stronghold which was not to fall until Constantine the Great declared for Christianity.

The last and one of the most beautiful objects to come to light has also a glancing light to throw on this religious struggle. It is a silver casket, round, about 2¾ in high and a little over 3 in in diameter. Inside it is a circular filter, pierced all over with holes in a roughly rosette pattern; and it would seem that the vessel contained liquids used ritually during the service. The whole of the hinged lid and the sides are covered with interlocking reliefs. These are almost all of combat: fighting between men, between men and animals, and between animals. But as well as these scenes there are also some representations of eagle-headed winged griffons with large boxes or crates. Now, it will be recalled, in one of the Piazza Armerina mosaics, a winged griffon is shown with a crate which is in fact a cage in which can be seen a captive man; and concerning this it has been speculated that it may perhaps be a piece of secret Christian symbolism—the sort of thing that a crypto-Christian craftsman inserted into a work commissioned by a powerful non-Christian patron—a sort of artist's "writing on the wall".

It is interesting, in view of the private and secret nature of Mithraism, that this rich metropolitan temple stood alone on the east bank of this little stream, the Walbrook, among scrubby birch and alder, but not far from a road running down from the Forum to the Thames.

But although the east bank of the Walbrook was relatively deserted, the west bank was intensively industrialized, as was also revealed during the contractors' excavations of the same Bucklersbury site as that in which the Mithraeum was found. Here, about forty feet below the present ground level a deep belt of silt was found, sealed in by many feet of Roman deposits. This belt can be securely dated, by a considerable number of coins, to the first hundred years of the Roman occupation. More than eighty coins are known to have been found in it and none is later than A.D. 150. They include coins of Claudius and Nero, great quantities of Vespasian, Titus and Domitian and many of Trajan. Hadrian is also represented and the series comes to an end with Antoninus Pius. But what else was found in this layer and on this site was astonishingly and immediately interesting. Coins, however beautiful, however interesting, are impersonal things—unless they happen also to be currency—and ancient and dead religions are remote from our daily feelings. What was found here was an extraordinarily wide range of tools of a number of crafts and what can only be described as components for a variety of trades. It is characteristic of these tools that they are rather specialized tools—warehousemen's, plasterers', skinners' and furriers', locksmiths' and carpenters'—and that they are amazingly like the tools used by those tradesmen today. It is as though the right design for the job had been found over 2,000 years ago and there had never been any need to alter it since. Indeed it has been said that if a Roman craftsman of this era had been set down in a shop of the same trade (say, in the last century, before the introduction of power tools) he would have found himself perfectly at home there.

These objects merit a closer description. In the group of warehouse tools are double and single hooks, a shackle, two different types of two pronged forks, one straight, one hooked, for fitting on shafts, and still used for handling bales and carcases, a double hand hook of a type still used for seizing bales and a long bale-stitching needle with a bone handle. A great number of keys and locks and latch-lifters were found, together with lock bolts with different kinds of ward-elements. Among carpenters' tools were a claw-bar, a draw-knife, awls or scriving tools, folding brass foot-rules, hammers, punches, different types of chisel and a gouge or drill. Other tradesmen's tools included a stonemason's dividers, curly-bladed skinners' knives, a metal-worker's hammer, a plasterer's spatula of a kind still used, a heavy chopping knife, quantities of writing *styli*, usually with flattened ends for erasing, a small guillotine blade, with at one end a swivel hook and at the other a holder for a wooden handle, a bricklayer's trowel, a small pick suitable for working in an enclosed space, and an entrenching tool identical in general design with those used in the 1914–18 war. Then there were besides a great number of small tools, mostly of brass, either surgical or cosmetic: probes and ear-picks, tweezers, needles of different forms, specialized spoons, and one set of spoon, pick and tweezers mounted together for all the world like a modern "smoker's trinity". In addition a great variety of small brass goods was found: tacks and drawing-pins, hooks for dress-makers (very like the modern hook-and-eye), glass plates, small metal trims and ornaments

for cabinet-making, small brass buckles and brooches, metal pins, little ornaments in the shape of fishes or birds, a horse-brass, and cheap jewellery, one of
these being a little brass ring with a bearded head on it and inside the ring the
word "Amica"—sweetheart, as it were, or "girl-friend" (literally).

They amount, it almost seems, to the contents of several quite small, quite
ordinary hardware shops in a busy industrial district. The state of preservation
is extraordinarily good. One of the rebating chisels found was sharpened by the
workman who found it and immediately put to use. This is not the sort of thing
that an archaeologist would do, but he is usually delighted if someone else has
done it before he could be stopped. In this case the chisel was in excellent
temper and the writer had the privilege of trying it (successfully) on a piece of
wood. But sound though the objects were, they were none of them "outstanding examples" or "works of art"; the point of them is their magnificent
ordinariness and the vividness with which they evoke the day-by-day, run-of-the-
mill life of the lower-middle-class Londoner—the craftsman and the shopkeeper
—and those who worked for and alongside him, nearly two thousand years ago.

The destruction of war, in particular the savage "Baedeker" raids of 1942,
likewise brought an otherwise impossible opportunity to explore parts of the
ancient city of Canterbury; and an exploration of the areas laid bare, more
especially in the southern and eastern parts of the walled city was inaugurated
by the Canterbury Excavation Committee with the blessing of the Ministry of
Works and under the direction of Mr S. Sheppard Frere. These excavations
revealed a great deal which was unknown or obscure about the site's early
history. It seems to have existed as a pre-Belgic settlement in about the third
century B.C.; and subsequently to have become a large village of the Belgic
peoples in the earliest years of this era. In Roman times it developed steadily
but slowly at first; and naturally became systematized with a grid-iron street
pattern. Its great development is in the second century A.D., when it became
wealthy and highly Romanized. The most striking and the most astonishing
discovery of this period was the vast footings of a large continental-style theatre,
with vaulted substructure, a semicircular building with a diameter of 250 ft.
This is a building quite unique for Great Britain; and must have been enlarged
to this size, in Mr Frere's phrase, in "a fit of megalomania" on the part of those
responsible for it. It was quite out of proportion to Roman Canterbury, Dur-
overnum Cantiacorum. The walling of the city took place a little after the
building of the theatre; and the interesting discovery was made that the
mediaeval walls follow the line of the Roman walls and in one place Roman
walling surviving to 7 ft high was found immediately below its mediaeval successor. An interesting fact which emerged was that Canterbury continued to be
a centre of the wine trade throughout the Dark Ages.

After Canterbury Mr Sheppard Frere moved to Verulamium, Roman St
Albans; and directed there several seasons of very interesting excavations. In
the summer of 1956, during the excavation of several houses below the Forum
and alongside Bluehouse Hill, large quantities of painted plaster were found,

considerable sections of which have been patiently reassembled by the Institute of Archaeology and have been recently on exhibition at the British Museum. The technique of this plaster is rather interesting. The walls were made of clay on a basis of flint and mortar. While the clay was still wet, a roller had been passed over it leaving a continuous chevron pattern, which was intended to serve as a "key" for the plaster. In some places the whole of this plaster had fallen forward on the floor, its underside being uppermost and showing the same chevron pattern which it had taken from the clay wall. By the same token, the painted side, falling face downwards, had been reasonably preserved.

On one of the walls there are red panels with thin yellow standards dividing them and with looped swags here and there. On another there are panels of purple with woodpigeons in frames of thin yellow leafage. On another fragment of a rich yellow there are green vine scrolls and here and there among the vines are pheasant-like birds and leopard's heads, not unlike Cheshire cats. Some of the paintings had doodles on them: in one place someone had drawn a bird and an egg, in another someone else had written "equus" (horse).

During the same summer, beneath the northern rampart, broken coin moulds of a pre-Roman Belgic mint were found. These are of clay and simply consist of rows of standard holes into which the molten metal would be poured to form blanks (or flans) for stamping. In consequence they provide no evidence of lettering or design; but it seems likely that they would belong to the mint of the Belgic king, Tasciovanus (20 B.C.–A.D. 10), as under his son, Cunobelin, the mint and the seat of power were transferred to Camulodunum (Colchester).

In the summer of 1959 two important finds were made: a bronze statuette, probably representing Ceres; and a fine polychrome mosaic floor. This was in a good state of preservation and of a simple and impressive design and quality. All round is a wide guilloche border; and in the centre, on a plain ground, a lion, its jaws realistically dripping with blood, savaging the head of a stag.

Links with pre-Roman St Albans were found in 1957 at Bagendon, a few miles from Cirencester in Gloucestershire, by Mrs E. M. Clifford. Roman Cirencester, Corinium Dobunnorum, was one of the largest towns of Roman Britain, its walled area being second only to that of London. Its name refers to a Belgic tribe, the Dobunni, whose tribal capital had not been found. It was thought originally that the Roman town had grown up on top of the earlier, but excavation has now shown that Corinium was built in Roman times on a virgin site. At Bagendon, however, three miles north of Corinium, a site was found in which a series of long earthworks and ditches linked with certain natural barriers to form an enclosed area; and it was in this area that Mrs Clifford made her excavations. They revealed strangely enough that this quiet and secluded valley was the scene of intense industrial activity around and shortly before the beginning of the Christian era. A large and massive stone platform was found and on and around it were discovered the remains of metal-working in various forms and—sure identification of a capital site—the existence of a mint. The principal metal worked was iron and an analysis of the slags shows that these were highly skilled ironmasters while some of the metal they produced is so fine as almost to qualify for the name of steel. They also worked in copper, remains being found of metallic copper, copper slag and examples of copper smelted on to iron. They also de-silverized lead. The iron ore they worked would most probably come from the Forest of Dean, but the copper, lead, silver and gold must have come from farther afield.

As regards the mint, the principal evidence lies in the quantities of pottery coin moulds found, like those found under the Verulamium rampart. These were for making coin-flans which would be later struck with the die. A number of small silver coins of the Dobunni were found on the site, showing on one side a pattern derived originally from a prancing horse, on the other a face, probably female and maybe intended to represent a Celtic goddess. About a third of the coins found were of copper, plated with silver; but whether these were forgeries or represent an official debasing of the coinage, it is not possible to tell. Among the coins, however, is a stranger: a silver coin of Epaticcus, the brother of Cunobelin, who moved his capital from Verulamium (St Albans) to Camulodunum (Colchester). This coin is in Romanized style and the inscription records that Epaticcus was the son of Tasciovanus—whose coin moulds it seems were those recently found at Verulamium. Incidentally this is the farthest west that a coin of Epaticcus has been found.

Probably the most interesting Roman discoveries to be made in a single site are those concerning the successive phases of the Roman Villa at Lullingstone in Kent. A considerable number of its features are quite outstanding: the two adjoining mosaic rooms, the one with its large and curious "carpet" of mosaic and its central panel of Bellerophon mounted on Pegasus, with female heads representing the seasons surrounding it, and the smaller lunette mosaic with its Europa and the Bull and its mosaic inscription giving a witty Latin couplet; and of course the quite unique room devoted to Christian worship, with its wall paintings of praying figures and especially the Chi-Rho monogram inside a wreath with two pecking birds below. All these things, however, and the fascinating "detective stories" which led to the identification of the site and to the uncovering of the successive stages in the house's history, have been fully told in a fascinating book by the excavator himself, Colonel G. W. Meates, F.S.A. (*Lullingstone Roman Villa*, Heinemann, 1955).

A remarkable discovery, made as the result of two accidents three years apart in Norfolk, is of especial interest in view of its close parallels with the hoard of parade armour found at Straubing in south Germany and with the splendid Syrian silver masked helmet which is believed to have been found near Ems. In August of 1947, during dredging operations in the River Wensum near Worthing in Norfolk, a splendid Roman parade helmet, without front part or visor, was thrown up. With it were found some fetters and a padlock. It had a feather-patterned crest which ends over the brow in an eagle's head, and on either side of this was a dragon-like monster in *repoussé*. It was of parade weight and would have been no use in action and it was made of a yellowish metal, probably "gilding metal" a compound of copper, tin and zinc; and it appeared to have been gilded. More than three years later, in November 1950, by an extraordinarily fortunate chance, the front part of the same helmet was found. This is in the form of an outer visor, with a T-shaped aperture; and it seems likely that this aperture was originally filled with an inner visor modelled with human features. One of the cheek pieces of the outer visor shows Mars with a shield, the other Victory with a wreath and palm, while over the chin is a Medusa-head, with snaky locks ending in eagle beaks. This outer visor also bears traces of gilding; and this extremely interesting object is now in the Norwich Castle Museum.

Two other especially interesting Roman objects came to light in 1954, during the excavation of Holborough Knob, a Roman burial tumulus on a spur of the North Downs near Snodland on the west bank of the Medway. This mound was shortly to be destroyed in the quarrying operations of the Associated Portland Cement Manufacturers, Ltd, and this firm provided the funds and equipment for a complete excavation under the direction of Mr Ronald F. Jessup. It was found, when levelled, to contain two burials, a primary cremation burial and a secondary inhumation burial and to date most probably from the first part of the second century A.D. Around the primary burial, which is in the centre of the mound, were a group of post-holes and it would look as though a temporary structure was erected for the final ceremonies; and, also around the burial, were three pits to receive ritual offerings. One of these, oddly enough, contained a folding wrought-iron chair, somewhat after the fashion of a campstool, of the type which is sometimes shown on Roman Imperial coins as used by commanders in the field. The secondary burial was in the form of a lead sarcophagus resting on a wooden bier and containing the skeleton of a very young child, most probably a girl. The lid of this was ripped up by the bulldozer during the excavation—no burial was thought to exist in this outer part of the mound—but fortunately it was very satisfactorily straightened again by a local plumber who showed the greatest interest in the work and pride in his craft. The sides and top of the sarcophagus were decorated with scallop-shells in relief, but on the top, in addition, were three bead-and-reel rods in the form of a Y, and in between the two arms the forms of a naked satyr accompanied by an infant satyr—symbols of the Dionysiac mysteries. This is normally an Eastern Mediterranean concept, but whether it was made by a Kentish craftsman working from an Eastern pattern book or by an Eastern craftsman, no one can say. The Roman Army, after all, was an extraordinarily cosmopolitan affair and must have done much to spread a very wide selection of cultural fashions and customs over the far-flung provinces of the Roman Empire, in very much the same way that the British Army and administrators did throughout the world in the last century.

Also in 1954 and also in Kent, but on the other side of the county, at Lyminge near Folkestone, an extensive Jutish cemetery was found and about forty inhumation burials were excavated with a quantity of rich finds of objects. There was no previous knowledge of this cemetery's existence but Lyminge was a place of some importance in Jutish times. In A.D. 633 the sister of King Eadbald retired there to found a nunnery after the death of her husband, Edwin of Northumbria; and later in the same century it was a prosperous iron mining centre.

The objects found have much in common with those from the Frankish cemetery at Rhenen in the Netherlands; and it is clear that there were both political as well as cultural and commercial links with the Merovingian Franks on the other side of the Channel. About A.D. 570 King Ethelbert of Kent married a Frankish wife and it is possible that there was some Frankish settlement in Kent at this date or earlier. Two of the most outstanding objects found are certainly of Frankish origin. One of these is a glass beaker, about $7\frac{1}{4}$ in high, of amber glass of the snouted or claw-beaker type, with two rows of those curious elephant-trunk protuberances on the lower part of the body—which is very like one found at Rhenen. The other is a complete and undamaged cylindrical bottle $6\frac{1}{2}$ in high, of a generally carafe-like shape—and this is the only complete example of this kind and period ever to be found in this country. These were probably made about the middle of the fifth century A.D. and the bottle seems to be a descendant of a Roman tradition which had survived in the Rhineland. A considerable number of objects of jewellery of bronze and gilt bronze also have a Frankish look, being usually *cloisonné* with garnet and coloured glass mounted in *cloisons* with a backing of gold leaf. These include brooches, belt buckles and a purse mount in the same general style as the famous Mildenhall purse mount. Two of the finest brooches in the same style and forming a pair, but made of silver gilt *cloisonné* with garnets, were found in the richest tomb, which was that of a woman. She was the only person to be buried in a coffin. She wore the two brooches mentioned, which were square-ended, at her waist, a head-dress interwoven with gold braid and two circular jewelled brooches, also of silver gilt. From her waist hung a silver-gilt spoon. This was $6\frac{1}{2}$ in long with a circular bowl and a straight shaft ending in a loop. The shaft was ornamented with *niello* and its junction with the bowl was decorated with a series of bird-heads, the eyes being represented with small garnets. In the centre of the bowl are nine circular perforations in the form of a right-angled cross. Immediately beside this spoon was a ball of rock-crystal (with a diameter of $1\frac{3}{4}$ in) in a silver sling and a cylindrical mount and ring. Spoons and crystal balls have previously been found, usually together, in Jutish burials—usually burials of rich women—and presumably they have some religious significance. What this significance is, however, is still puzzling.

CHAPTER THREE

THE UNITED KINGDOM—II

THE greatest of English ancient monuments is, of course, Stonehenge; and from 1951 onwards it has been the subject of selective excavation to clear up some of the problems of its constructional sequence; and a full scale field and photographic survey has been undertaken under the auspices of the Department of Prehistoric Archaeology of the University of Edinburgh, directed by Professor Stuart Piggott, Mr R. J. C. Atkinson and Dr J. F. S. Stone, assisted by Mr R. S. Newall and with the consent and co-operation of the Ancient Monuments Department of the Ministry of Works. The principal findings resulting from these researches have been most admirably (and entertainingly) described by Mr Atkinson in his book *Stonehenge* (Hamish Hamilton, 1956); but it is proper that some of the principal points should be summarized here.

Excavations beside the Heel Stone (which lies to the east, apart from the circles) have shown that it belongs to the first phase of Stonehenge, for which a radio-carbon date of 1848 B.C., plus or minus 275 years has been established. Some re-excavation of the "Y" and "Z" holes (which surround the outer sarsen circle) has resulted in their being dated somewhat earlier than was previously thought —they belong it seems to the Bronze Age of the Middle Second Millennium B.C. Any connexion of Stonehenge with the first centuries B.C. and A.D.—and so with the Druids—has now been completely disproved. In fact the Druids have as little to do with the building of Stonehenge as Charles I has with the Druids.

Curiously enough, some of the most interesting recent discoveries in this great monument have been made with the camera and a 30-ft high self-supporting ladder. The photographic survey by Mr Atkinson has brought to light for the first time ancient carvings of Bronze Age tools and weapons on the big sarsen stones. These carvings are quite shallow and need favourable light conditions to be seen, but once seen they are perfectly distinct and are also accurate portrayals. It should be mentioned at this point that the sarsen stone is incredibly hard and turns all normal modern metal tools. The most frequent representation is of the bronze axe-blade of the type current at the end of the British Early Bronze Age, about 1500 B.C., faithfully reproduced at natural size. All these axe-blades are shown with the cutting edge uppermost and without their hafts. But the most remarkable and significant carving is of a full-size hilted dagger, about a foot long, with a tapering blade with accentuated shoulders and a large pommel. Since the axes are so accurately portrayed, we may assume that the dagger is likewise an accurate portrait and we are confronted with the fact that it resembles no known Western European type of Bronze Age weapon, but that it does resemble daggers known from the Aegean, in connexion with the Mycenaean shaft-graves of about 1600–1500 B.C. There is evidence of trade connexions between Bronze Age Wessex and the Mycenaean world; and all these points together support a date of about 1500 B.C. for the building of the main monument of Stonehenge when the great sarsens were erected. The use of the self-supporting ladder enabled a number of very revealing photographs of the upper parts of the sarsens to be taken; and the thing that they principally reveal is the extraordinary engineering skill and patient mason's work of the sarsen builders. How the builders, for example, lifted the lintel stones on top of the trilithons is still a mystery—though Mr Atkinson has suggested a method— but these lintel stones were prepared with deep sockets on their under-sides which fitted over large upstanding tenons carved on the top of the trilithon stones. Furthermore these lintel stones were tooled into a curve, presumably by means of stone malls, and also splayed upwards and outwards in such a way as to counteract perspective and so not detract from their massive majesty.

An interesting pair of experiments was also carried out, with the co-operation of the B.B.C., in support of the now almost universally accepted theory that the bluestones were brought to Stonehenge from Prescelly in Pembrokeshire. One of the objections to this belief has been—how, with the means available, could such large stones be brought such great distances by land and water? Well, an imitation bluestone was cast in reinforced concrete; and the experiment was made to see if such a mass could be manhandled across rough land and water with the appropriate means. The boys of Canford School took the part of the land team and successfully pulled the imitation bluestone by sledge and ropes; and boys from Bryanston School equally successfully mounted the stone on logs laid across three simple punts and poled it along by water.

In February 1958 the Minister of Works (Mr Maudling) announced in the House of Commons the intention of the Ministry of Works to re-erect five fallen stones at Stonehenge. This caused a certain amount of to-do: on the grounds of expenditure of public money—which will be dealt with later; and on the grounds of what might very roughly indeed be called "sacrilege", i.e. tidying up a ruin, destroying the romance and beauty which the passage of time had wrought, and/or imposing a sort of phony reconstruction on a defenceless public. This last objection was fairly speedily dealt with. The re-erection had the approval and indeed recommendation of the archaeologists who had most recently been working on the monument; and indeed the agreement of most people who gave the matter any thought. Furthermore the fallen stones concerned were only those which were known to have fallen in historic times. These were: stones 57, 58 and 158, the two standards and the lintel of a trilithon in the inner horseshoe, which were known to have fallen in January, 1797; and stones 22 and 122, a standard and a broken lintel, which originally linked stone 22 with stone 21 (which was still standing) in the outer sarsen circle. It was moreover proposed to repair the broken lintel stone 122, before placing it in position.

The operation began in March 1958. At no time was the monument closed to the public, but the northern quadrant (in which all the stones concerned lay) was fenced off and a metal mat was laid to prevent the destruction of the surface and to carry the crane and other necessary equipment. The task was carried through steadily and the last major operation, the lifting into place of the lintel stone (158) of the re-erected trilithon, took place on July 9, 1958. One of the stones of this trilithon (58) was found to have a crack; and before lifting it a canister of radioactive sodium (provided by Harwell) was placed underneath to see if this would provide information on the nature and extent of the crack. It did provide some information—and the lifting was proceeded with—but not quite enough and after the lifting had taken place it was thought that weathering might enlarge this crack and accordingly the stone was drilled and a few non-corrosive rods were inserted to reinforce it.

After the stones were in place and securely anchored in their former positions, the site was tidied up and the level of the soil was reduced a few inches to bring it to something like the original ground-level.

The cost of this work was estimated at £8,500; and to those who objected to this expenditure it was pointed out that Stonehenge is the only uninhabited monument in the care of the Ministry of Works which shows an annual profit. As it turned out the expenditure can be even more impressively justified. Stonehenge's income derives from paid admittances (at 6d a person) and the sale of postcards and guides. The attendance figures over a period of years are known and although the figures for the sale of publications are not so neatly available they are obviously related to the number of attendances. For the five-year period beginning 1954, the attendance figures are as follows:—

1954	184,700
1955	184,300
1956	215,100
1957	229,900
1958	325,000

In other words in the year that the stones were re-erected the figures rose by 95,100, or in terms of money £4,755—a very promising first year's return on a capital expenditure of £8,500. And this does not take into account the increased sale of postcards and guides. If all public expenditure were as profitable as this, Ministers of the Crown would be the world's best businessmen.

Some of the most interesting post-war archaeological discoveries to be made in the United Kingdom have been made in the Shetland Islands, or, more particularly, in the southern part of that long principal island of the group, Mainland: at Jarlshof, at Clickhimin and on St Ninian's Isle. These are sites where it is more than ordinarily easy to revisualize the past. In England and in southern and industrial Scotland the evidences of so many generations, so much history, so many revolutions, industrial, social and agricultural overlie the past like a vast and thick overburden; in Shetland it is different and the Picts and Vikings seem unobscured to the view. True, you may most likely approach the island by air, but it is more like a voyage of exploration, a trip into another dimension, than a routine run between one standardized airport and another. You leave Aberdeen and are soon over the northern seas, not very high up, so that the expanse of water seems infinite. It is a lumpy sea, dark blue with patches of murky amethyst—and you wonder if that is what Homer meant by the "wine-dark" sea—and in it lies a small geographical relief model, which is Fair Isle. The first landfall is Sumburgh Head, the tremendous promontory which is the southernmost tip of Shetland. Behind it the contours fall away almost immediately to a narrow neck of green, grassy land, a foot or two above sea-level and about a half a mile, it seems, between the eastern and the western sea; and this, you learn so rapidly that you haven't time to be apprehensive about it, is the airstrip.

The shape of Shetland is a curious mixture of the savagely jagged and the blandly streamlined, the product of sea and wind. The coasts are deeply indented with wicks and voes, the cliffs and rocks are fierce, theatrical and black, the land is laid over deep blankets of peat imposed on the rock skeleton and has something of the shape of snowdrifts and it is either dark in colour or brilliant green; the sands are white; and the sea is a vivid blue. There are no trees to be seen; there are few houses, stone-built, scattered, strategically sited to avoid the wind; a single road winds up the narrow length of the island northwards; and the simple airport building looks like a sparsely maintained outpost. Two or three hundred yards away are the green mounds of Jarlshof, a quietly prosperous settlement in Bronze Age, Iron Age and Viking times. A few miles away up the western coast is St Ninian's Isle, joined to Mainland by a spit of sand, where Christianity gained a foothold in Shetland; and about twenty miles up the east coast, just behind Lerwick, the only considerable town in the islands, is Clickhimin Loch with the broch tower on its island.

The excavations at Jarlshof and Clickhimin have all been conducted by the Ministry of Works under the direction of Mr J. R. C. Hamilton, then an Inspector of Ancient Monuments for Scotland. The first operations in 1949–50 were concerned with the Viking settlement at Jarlshof; the second with the Bronze and Iron Age settlement also at Jarlshof, during 1951 and 1952; and from 1953 in the Bronze Age and Iron Age site at Clickhimin. All these operations were to a large degree complementary, but since the Vikings were the latest comers historically it is perhaps better to discuss that excavation last.

The Jarlshof site was entirely covered with drifted sand—which has helped in its preservation—and it lies beside a sheltered bay under the lee of the great headland of Sumburgh. Part of the settlement has been eaten away by the encroaching sea and part lies under the ruins of a mediaeval building. Near by is a considerable stretch of level and fertile ground—of which the modern airstrip is part. Furthermore the headland was the site of a beacon and so, in addition to its other advantages, Jarlshof must have had some strategic value—although, except for one period its history for many centuries seems to have been peaceful and undisturbed. Most settlements in Shetland seem to originate with late Stone Age colonists who arrived about 2000–1800 B.C., but their life and dwellings are far better represented at Clickhimin. These peoples were succeeded by late Iron Age colonists from the continent; and somewhat before the beginning of the Christian era, these newcomers, like their relations in the mainland of Scotland and farther south, appear to have been apprehensive of some great threat, piracy, slave trading or the like and at that time to have started building massive fortifications. In Scotland, north of the Great Glen, in Orkney and Shetland, these fortifications took the form of broch-towers, the remains of hundreds of which still remain, especially in Shetland. On the island of Mousa, not far from Jarlshof, a broch tower still stands to the height of 38 ft. These brochs were circular towers, narrowing somewhat as they ascend, not at all unlike the *nuraghi* of Sardinia and to a modern eye, very similar in shape to the cooling towers which are such a feature at electric power stations. The circular walls were hollow and contained a stair; and it seems probable, from evidence found at Clickhimin, that the hollow centre was divided by wooden platforms which served as living floors.

Such a broch had been built at Jarlshof and it was probably somewhere about forty feet high. In the centre of the floor a well had been sunk to a depth of 13 ft, the lower sections being cut through the living rock. With the broch was a considerable courtyard and this would most likely contain subsidiary dwellings.

The threat which brought the broch into being either did not materialize or was of short duration, and the courtyard soon began to fill up with other types of dwelling, for which the broch indeed served as a stone-quarry. The first type of dwelling was large and almost circular and at first it had a pent roof around a central hearth. It was later modified in an ingenious way. Large radial piers to support an outward sloping roof were built round the central hearth, dividing the interior into a series of "aisled" compartments facing on that central hearth but communicating one with another through doorways in the piers beside the outer main wall. The floors of these compartments were paved with stones and in the rear wall a series of cupboards or recesses was contrived. The people who dwelt in this house grew corn which they ground on saddle-shaped querns; they kept oxen, sheep, pigs, ponies and a few dogs; they ate fish, seals and wild birds; they used large high-shouldered cooking pots and used slate and whalebone to make various tools.

They were succeeded by newcomers about the first or second century A.D. who built wheelhouses in which the dividing piers were attached to the outer wall of the circular building. These newcomers brought a new type of pottery, hard, well-fired ware with sharply everted rims; the rotary quern; and the odd habit of painting patterns on pebbles with natural dyes. They continued for three or four centuries, the courtyard becoming gradually filled with similar wheelhouses. In time the broch was falling more and more into ruin; and rather surprisingly the well was covered over and water had to be brought some distance from springs.

The site was beginning to mound up with wind-blown sand and in these later years, probably not long before the arrival of the Vikings in the ninth century A.D., another type of dwelling makes its appearance, the so-called "passage house" made in this mounded sand and entered from the surface by a stone stairway. The pottery found in these dwellings is poor thin stuff; and it may well be that these were the people whom the Vikings found on their arrival and took as their serfs—the people of whom the mediaeval chronicler wrote as "Picts who did marvels in the morning and in the evening, in building walled towns, but at midday they entirely lost their strength and lurked, through fear, in little underground houses." And, indeed, as one walks along the close-cropped grass paths and looks down into the stone-walled wheelhouses, with their cramped compartments, their central hearths, their stony cupboards, and their middens filled with limpet-shells—a muscular diet—one can understand a Viking newcomer thinking that he had come among the trolls.

The Clickhimin site is a much more immediately impressive affair and its earlier history is much better represented, but it has no Viking history and it seems to have been abandoned before the beginning of the ninth century A.D. It likewise was excavated and to some extent restored by the Ministry of Works under the direction of Mr J. R. C. Hamilton, work beginning there in 1953.

Clickhimin Loch is a small, roughly circular loch, lying just south of Lerwick. It was in antiquity a sea loch, but later became land-locked and separated from the sea by a narrow strip of land, along which the road now runs. In the loch stands what was once an island but which is now connected with the shore by a narrow peninsula. On this island the broch tower still stands to a height of over 17 ft. Its original height would be about 50 ft and its probable appearance in about the first century A.D. is shown in the reconstruction drawing of Plate 4.

The first inhabitants of the site seem to have been those peoples who came to the islands in about 2000–1800 B.C. and to have brought with them, perhaps originally from the Eastern Mediterranean, a custom of building megalithic tombs. These people established a farmstead on the island and from their culture and from Bronze Age times there survives a solidly built oval house (behind the tower on the drawing) with sleeping cubicles round a large circular hearth. Byres were added, alterations made and after the Iron Age was begun, there came aggressive immigrants who built a massive fortification wall all round the island and a massive stone blockhouse inside and opposite the entrance to this wall. These fortifications were improved gradually, until drastic action was called for by the development of a storm spit across the mouth of the loch which caused the waters to rise several feet. The inhabitants thereupon made a massive breakwater of large boulders at the foot of the ringwall, raised the level of the entrance and added a landing stage with a quay for small boats. After this they began to build an inner defence wall, presumably against the elements—when there came that threat of human enemies which was the cause of broch building all along the northern Scottish, Orkney and Shetland coasts; and the men of Clickhimin (perhaps newcomers) began to build their broch tower.

Hundreds of tons of stone must have been ferried across to the island and the tower began to rise, between the blockhouse and the site of the oval Bronze Age dwelling and partly based on the incomplete inner defence wall. The broch is of the usual type, hollow, circular and with an inner and outer wall with a stair between, but in this case there is evidence that the interior was provided with wooden galleries which were probably used as sleeping floors above the central hearth and paved surround. As was the case at Jarlshof the dangers which caused the building to come into being receded, and a wheelhouse was built inside the broch; and subsidiary buildings were added outside as the island was occupied for many generations. As years passed the strait between the islet and the mainland silted up and in about the sixth or seventh century A.D. a causeway was built connecting the islet with the mainland. No Viking remains have been found and it would seem as though the site ceased to be inhabited.

Such was not the case however at Jarlshof, where excavations on the Viking site were begun in 1934 by Dr A. O. Curle and continued by Dr J. S. Richardson, broken off by the war, resumed and concluded in 1949 by J. R. C. Hamilton; and these excavations have revealed a remarkably large Viking settlement, which probably reached its greatest extent about the eleventh century A.D. Some nine long rectangular Viking houses were uncovered, buildings of stone and turf with wooden roof timbers and roofed with turf shingles anchored with ropes and large stone weights in a style which was continued in Shetland crofts of comparatively recent date. The shape of some of these long perished roof timbers has been preserved to this day by the masses of peat soot which had formed against them around the hole in the roof over the central hearth. These long houses were usually built down a slope, as the lower half was often used as a byre and the slope made drainage easy. In their later years, as fresh long houses were built, the older dwellings were converted into byres or storehouses. One of the houses was destroyed by fire and this may have been the result of the punitive raid which Harald Fairhair, King of Norway, is supposed to have made on Shetland around A.D. 870. Otherwise the scene is one of uneventful peace over very many years. There are no weapons among the finds, practically all the artefacts are local and there is hardly any evidence of objects brought in as the result of raiding or trade. The people of Jarlshof were engaged in agriculture—cattle, sheep, pigs, ponies and the cultivation of bere (a form of barley)—fishing and weaving (line-sinkers and loom-weights are among the commonest objects found); and they seem to have beguiled the long winter nights with gaming pieces and counters. They had a small smithy where crucibles used in making bronze were found. They made objects from bone—pins and hog-backed combs —and bowls and lamps from the steatite or soapstone which they quarried at near-by Cunningsburgh, where it is still possible to see how they carved their bowls in the quarry itself. Among the objects made in soapstone was a miniature quern, which must have been a child's toy, as the material is too soft for the real grinding of corn. Another toy is a carved bone, which must have been used in the same way as a modern "snoriben", that is a bone which is spun on a double strand of wool. Another interesting object, which still survives in use on Shetland, is the tethering "swill" of which several were found. These are flat oval stones, pierced with three holes. The central hole takes the tethering rope, while from the outer holes run separate ropes, each to a single sheep. These are now made of wood and called "wolga", but their purpose then as now, was to tether a pair of sheep, without their ropes twisting, and so to keep them on the narrow strips of pasture between the "rigs" of cultivated ground. This strip cultivation was common among the Vikings and is still not uncommon in Shetland.

A few miles north of Jarlshof and also on the west coast of Mainland lies St Ninian's Isle, a small, beautiful and deserted island, linked to the coast by a sandy spit, which is sometimes broken by winter storms. It was known to have had a mediaeval church and was in fact just the sort of place to attract a Celtic hermit. From 1955 excavations were conducted there by a group of students under the direction of Professor Andrew C. O'Dell of Aberdeen University. A church was indeed uncovered, some 50 ft long by 23 ft wide and with an apsidal east end; and trial pits revealed that it overlay an Iron Age complex. The site appeared to have been used as a burial ground for some 2,000 years. The foundation level of the church is about 8 ft below the modern ground level, thus making further excavation difficult; but with the assistance of Messrs Tawse, and with equipment lent by the County Road Surveyor, excavations were continued for a farther 6 ft downwards. This led to the most remarkable discovery, for at about 5 ft below the church, a schoolboy helper uncovered with his trowel a thin slab of stone lightly engraved with a cross; below this, fragments of rotting wood; and among this the bright green gleam of weathered copper.

This hoard was carefully unearthed and was found to consist of twenty-five metal objects and a porpoise bone which had probably been used as a reliquary. The objects were fragile and in some cases stuck together with corrosion, but they consisted of a number of shallow bowls, twelve penannular brooches, a hanging lamp, two curious horseshoe-shaped objects, three "thimbles" and one or two other items. Most of the objects were covered with Celtic ornament, *repoussé* or punched and encrusted with stones or glass; and were obviously of such great interest that they were flown immediately to the British Museum for treatment in the laboratory there.

Here Dr Plenderleith's team, led by Mr R. M. Organ, were presented with a most ticklish task, since it was discovered that some of the elements of the metal were still in an unstable condition and indeed some of the objects needed as many as eighteen separate operations—but the reward was remarkable. None of the objects was bronze and all were silver, many of them being silver-gilt. But it was a base silver, containing a heavy proportion of copper and it was the copper which had produced the bright green corrosion. The inlays were found to be of brown or blue glass and, in one case, red enamel.

Some of the objects are unique and all are of very great interest; and although they have affinities with objects made in England and Ireland, it seems fairly clear that they are all of Scottish origin, of Celtic design and probably dating from the eighth century A.D. There are twelve brooches, all of the same general shape—penannular, that is almost ring-shaped—with a long straight pin. One of them was much larger than the rest, being over 4¼ in. in diameter, but the remaining eleven were about half this size and although none were identical they were all remarkably alike in general appearance and quietly elaborate in decoration. All were covered with various forms of rope or interlace ornament; and in every case the open ends of the ring were elaborated into larger ornament made up of cellular elements filled with filigree interlaces or sometimes inlaid with coloured glass, some of which had been lost in antiquity. There were seven shallow bowls, in varying degrees of preservation and rather less than 6 in. in diameter. These were decorated with punched and *repoussé* designs, one of the best showing a typically Celtic beast, whose tail, tongue and ears all develop to become part of the general running interlace design, while another has an interior central plaque, roughly shield-shaped and inlaid with red enamel. The hanging lamp, which is unique in this material, is likewise a shallow bowl, with a central ornament, both inside and out, and with three elaborately *repoussé* escutcheons on the outside which held the suspension rings. These last are curious. They are very awkwardly placed and if the lamp had indeed been used in suspension from them, they would quite clearly have led to a distortion or even a breakage; and it would look as though the lamp was never used in the hanging position. What had originally been thought to be parts of the lamp were discovered on cleaning to be a "pricker", a sort of tooth-pick with a curved head; and a most delightful spoon. The shaft of this spoon has a loop at one end, but the other is a tiny dog's head, the dog being engaged in licking the contents of the spoon. The three silver "thimbles" are covered with interlaced Celtic ornament and are pierced through with a horizontal hole. It is suggested that they may have been belt ornaments, the whole being used for purposes of attachment. There is also a somewhat squatter object in the same style, which may have covered the pommel of a sword or dagger.

The last two objects are perhaps the most beautiful. They are horseshoe-shaped and the inner curve is open as if to allow of them being fitted on to an end of a leather strap or piece of fabric; and they may indeed have served as belt-ends or something of that nature. In both cases the horseshoe ends in animal heads, one of them being rather dragonish, the other like a melancholy long-snouted dog; and all four animal heads have inlaid glass eyes. In both the body of the horseshoe is chased with complex designs, each side being different from the other. One of them—the one with the melancholy dogs—bears a Latin inscription on either side. The letters are quite reasonably clear, but the abbreviation is so drastic as to make the interpretation rather speculative. One side is fairly straightforward: IN NOMINE D(EI)S(UMMI) or "In the name of God the Highest; but the other can be read either as: RES ADKILIS P(RES) B(YTERI)S S(AN)C(TI)O or "The property of Adkil the holy priest"; or as RESAD FILI SP(IRIT)US S(AN)C(TI)O or "— of the Son and Holy Spirit", the final "o" being considered as an ornamental filler. But, as must be pretty clear, the field is open to other interpretations, especially on the basis that remote Celtic Latin was probably not very good Latin.

In 1949 and 1950 excavations were carried out by the Prehistoric Society under the direction of Dr Grahame Clark with a party of Cambridge students, at Star Carr, Seamer, near Scarborough which have thrown a great deal of light on the Yorkshire of nearly 10,000 years ago. To call it Yorkshire is perhaps a little parochial as at this time Great Britain was still part of the continent. The North Sea did not come into being until the early Post Glacial period, whereas the Star Carr site dates from the Pre-Boreal, which may be dated tentatively to 8000–7000 B.C. At this period land, mostly fen-land, stretched continuously from Yorkshire to Esthonia; and it was peopled by Mesolithic hunter-fishers, living usually on the edges of the lakes and known now as Maglemosians or "people of the great bog". Many traces of these people have been found in England, but a good site was needed for their closer study. Thanks to the researches of Mr John W. Moore such a site was located at Star Carr and during the course of excavation it proved to be not only a very rich site, but also considerably earlier than the classic continental Maglemosian sites.

The excavation began in the summer of 1949, providentially a very dry summer, as the site is full of water. The conditions for the preservation of such organic materials as horn, wood and bark were however excellent and a very clear picture of the site and its inhabitants began to emerge.

It lies on the north bank of the lake which is now the Vale of Pickering, and it appears to have been occupied seasonally, but possibly over a number of years, by a small group, perhaps a single family. To make the site they threw down tree-trunks and antlers on the reeds at the edge of the lake and consolidated it with stones and lumps of stiff clay; and it is on this platform that great quantities of their artefacts have been found. Their principal materials were the antlers of the red deer and flints, separately and in combination. The flints comprise: small pointed flakes for barbing and tipping arrow-heads, scrapers for preparing skins, burins for shaping and preparing weapons and tools from antler and bone; and small axe and adze blades. From the antler horn, most beautiful spear and harpoon heads were made, with multiple barbs on one side only. Antler was also used to provide handles for flint axes, and also as hammering tools. In one case the base of an antler with some of the bone still attached had been fashioned and ground and bored to take a shaft and so to form a mattock. The efficiency of some of these tools is shown by the fact that some of the birch trunks which form the platform had clearly been felled—and this is the earliest example of tree-felling yet observed. One of the oddest uses to which deer-material was turned is illustrated in several examples. In these the frontlet of the red deer is used, with the antlers still attached, but the tines are somewhat shortened—perhaps to lighten the object. Holes had been made in the parietal bones; and it is quite clear that this prepared frontlet was worn on occasions by the men of Star Carr. Whether it served for some cult purpose—like the animal masks which are seen in some Magdalenian cave paintings—or whether it was used in hunting for decoy purposes, can hardly be conclusively decided.

Birch bark rolls were found on the site and it is natural to believe that this was used as material in some form or other. Stone beads also were found. A single dog's leg bone was found, but otherwise these hunters seem to have had no domestic animals. They principally hunted the red deer and the roe deer, but the bones have also been identified of elk, wild ox, wild pig, beaver, fox, marten, badger and hare. A great number of birds were also represented; and these include red-throated diver, greater and lesser grebe, merganser, stork and crane. The climate apparently restricted the trees to birch, willow and pine and was too cold for hazel. Radiocarbon tests from some of the birch brushwood give the dates 7888–7188 B.C.

CHAPTER FOUR

FRANCE

ARCHAEOLOGICAL discovery in France since the war has tended to be over-shadowed in the public estimation by the accidental war-time find of the Lascaux Caves with their magnificent wall-paintings and their subsequent development as a tourist centre. Yet splendid though this Magdalenian menagerie is, it would be unfortunate if it were to cause the neglect of, for example, four discoveries of the greatest interest in Vienne, the Côte d'Or, Yonne and Corsica, ranging in time from about 150,000 B.C. to 500 B.C. and including the earliest of "museums", the earliest known naturalistic representation of the human form in sculpture, and the largest known and one of the finest Greek bronze *craters* in existence, a huge vessel in which the thick wine of antiquity was mixed with water when serving.

At Vix, near Chatillon-sur-Seine, in the Côte d'Or, there stands a Celtic township of the Late Hallstatt era, about 500 B.C., which was found in 1930 and has since been systematically dug, with very rich discoveries of pottery, weapons, jewellery and the like. In 1953, however, M. René Joffroy, the Curator of the Vix Museum found the cemetery of this township and in particular the remains of a very large tumulus, about forty-four yards across, which had been levelled to the ground in Gallo-Roman times as a quarry for road-metal. The tomb which this mound covered however had not been touched by the road engineers of 2,000 years ago and it was discovered intact by M. Joffroy some nine feet below ground level. It consisted of a chamber about ten feet square and it contained the burial of a Celtic Princess or Queen, some thirty years old, and obviously of very great wealth and power. She had been buried in her chariot—such chariot burials are not uncommon in this time in history, eight being known in France and recently discovered examples in Hungary, Siberia and China are described elsewhere in this book—and the four iron-shod wheels, each with ten spokes radiating from a central bronze-covered hub, were standing against the side of the tomb. Round the skull of the princess still rested a massive gold diadem, weighing over a pound. This is a three-quarter circlet, the two ends of the frontal opening being lion's paws which clasp large orbs, and linking the orbs and the circlet itself are two small winged horses. A quantity of other jewellery, anklets and a torque of bronze, brooches of iron and bronze, and a number of necklaces were also found with the skeleton; and it appeared that the wooden framework of the chariot had been covered with leather, ornamented with bronze studs.

Rich though these finds were—and the diadem is unique as well as beautiful —they pale before the other furnishings of the grave. These included two Greek cups, two bronze bowls in a large bronze basin, a bronze Etruscan wine jug with a trefoil spout and palmetted handle, a silver *patera* with a gold boss; and an enormous bronze *crater* of singular beauty and magnificence. This colossal Greek wine-vessel has a lid and the lid is crowned with a statue. The whole thing stands 5 ft 4⅝ in high—the height of a smallish woman; is over a yard across at the opening; and weighs over a fifth of a ton (4 cwt 11 lb). It is richly, even magnificently, decorated and yet contrives to give an impression of the most noble dignity.

Its general shape is well shown in the illustration (Plate 5). The two handles are of some complexity. Between the two ram's-horn scrolls with their beaded edge is, in each case, a typically Greek Gorgon-headed figure with staring eyes and protruding tongue—the face that appears on so many Greek coins. A pair of serpents are entwined with the arms of this figure; and the legs are in the form of a pair of serpents. Between the arc of the handle and the neck of the *crater* are simple scrolls on each of which stands a lion looking backwards over his shoulder. Round the neck of the *crater* itself is a frieze of figures in high relief which is a miracle of art, craft and intrinsic interest.

This consists of eight four-horse chariots, each with a charioteer. Between the chariots are seven helmeted *hoplites*—heavy-armed foot-soldiers, heavy-armed, that is, in the strange Greek tradition, wearing greaves, breastplate, helmet and shield, but otherwise stark naked. These, it is suggested, are the seven champions who appear in Aeschylus' "Seven Against Thebes", the eighth chariot being that of Adrastus, who did not take part in the attack. These repeated groups of figures, though at first sight alike, are in fact subtly differentiated and the groups of horses in particular, their separate identities brilliantly distinct in what is after all a very small depth of metal, amount to an extraordinary feat on the part of the craftsman. The lid of the *crater* is pierced with holes in a rose pattern and was presumably used as some form of strainer. It is crowned with a statue— 7½ in high—of a hooded goddess, who is probably Hera of Argos. This is a work of singular beauty and purity of line, but in a completely different style from the reliefs of the frieze, being much more what one thinks of as archaic or Etruscan.

By any standards, this is an astonishing piece of work; and when one reflects that it was buried with the body of a Celtic Princess in Burgundy, before the time of Pericles and the Elgin Marbles, when Themistocles was defending Athens against Xerxes and Horatius keeping the bridge against Lars Porsena, it is impossible not to marvel.

By what route it reached Burgundy is open to argument; it is certainly Greek workmanship, but again whether from Sparta itself or from Laconian colonies in Southern Italy, is also open to argument. The reason why ever it was sent to Vix seems clearer. It was a pawn in the tin trade. Vix lies at what was then the highest navigable point of the Seine. The rich trade in tin from

Britain would come so far by water; whoever controlled the beginning of its next stage on the way to the Mediterranean was obviously a person of very great strategic power, precisely the person most likely to receive sumptuous presents, such as this glorious *crater*, from the astute merchants who handled the transport of a metal vital to the bronze industry.

In the Department of Vienne, near the small town of Angles, there is a huge block of limestone, Le Roc aux Sorciers, traditionally a meeting-place for witches, fallen from a cliff beside the river Anglin. Between the block and the cliff is a prehistoric rock shelter used from the Early Magdalenian times of some 12,000 years ago. This site, which had been sporadically investigated before the last war, has been, since 1948, the subject of systematic investigations by Miss Dorothy Garrod, then Professor of Archaeology in the University of Cambridge, and Mlle Suzanne de St-Mathurin. First working at what was later found to be the upstream end of the shelter, they found themselves confronted with a mass of limestone fragments, which, it seemed, had resulted from the fall of the wall and roof of the shelter in ancient times. Among these fragments they found remains of what had obviously been a frieze of sculptures carved in relief on the rock surface. Despite the fragmentary nature of the material there were found figures or parts of figures of horses, bison, ibexes, chamois and at least one human head—a man's face in relief in which the features had been brought up with the aid of applied colour.

Rewarding though this was and probable though it seemed that there were other pieces of sculpture to be found in the pile, nevertheless the task of seeking them was appalling and, in Miss Garrod's own words, "the discovery presented us with the alarming prospect of trying to put together a huge jig-saw, of which the pieces varied from bits about the size of a match-box to blocks weighing several tons."

Accordingly, they moved to the downstream end of the shelter; and this they found had been abandoned in Late Magdalenian times as the result of its filling up with the debris of day-to-day living, and that there had been no collapse here of the roof or walls. When they removed, therefore, the rubbish of some 12,000 years ago, they were confronted with walls covered with sculptured reliefs of the Early Magdalenian period, extremely well preserved considering their antiquity except for the upper parts, where the humic acid in the higher levels of the soil had eaten away some of the surface of the rock.

Among the most remarkable of these reliefs were two horses, a scene showing several ibexes together, and a quite unique group of three naked female figures. All these sculptures are in a fairly, but not consistently, low relief and all are completely naturalistic, reflecting not only a high degree of skill but a disinterested observation and an interest in the intrinsic beauty and nature of the objects portrayed. They represent in fact an artist's love and not a magician's scheming.

Of the two horses, one is a rather plump mare with slim legs, bending her head back in a characteristic attitude either to look backwards or to nuzzle her shoulders. The other horse, not so well preserved, is seen in a grazing posture, with the head down and the lips turned back from the teeth to crop the grass.

The ibexes form a unified composition and a vivid scene of action: a small flock had been disturbed and two young males aggressively confront the disturber, while a female with a young animal and an old male make off in the direction of safety. The old male is shown stumbling; and the scene is obviously one that the sculptor of so long ago has often seen and here vividly recalled for an unthinkably remote posterity.

These reliefs are without question outstanding but not utterly surprising once one has accepted the now fairly general view that the Magdalenian cave artists worked because they enjoyed their work: but the relief of the three female figures is unique and unparalleled.

It shows three life-size female figures in shallow relief, side by side in what was later to become the classic "Three Graces" grouping; two are full-face on, one is shown in three-quarter face. From the setting of the figures close to the roof of the cave, it is clear that there was never any intention to include the heads and, similarly the legs dwindle away without attempting the feet, but the rest of the figures are portrayed fully, gracefully and naturalistically and, broken though they are and difficult to see except with cunning lighting, they nevertheless revise our ideas of what sort of man our Magdalenian ancestor was; and suggest in him a degree of sensitivity and even sophistication which are hard to visualize even many thousands of years nearer to our own times.

On the other side of France, near Avallon in the Department of Yonne, some 118 miles south-east of Paris, lies the prehistoric site of Arcy-sur-Cure, which extends the history of France back from the Magdalenian times of Angles far into the pre-Mousterian eras of some 150,000 years ago. Here very extensive researches have been carried out under the auspices of the *Direction des Monuments Historiques* and the *Centre National de la Récherche Scientifique*, directed by Professor André Leroi-Gourhan. This is a very remarkable site for a number of reasons, first on account of its northerly location, but principally because two caves, the Cave of the Hyena and the Cave of the Reindeer, which lie about eleven yards apart, cover together a span of about 140,000 years of continuous occupation, or rather occupation interrupted only by natural disasters such as flooding, collapse, and the like. The Cave of the Hyenas starts with the end of the Acheulian Period and became filled nearly to roof level, in the Post-Mousterian Age, with successive occupation layers, flood deposits and the like; and the nearby Cave of the Reindeer began to be occupied before the Cave of the Hyena was abandoned, in the Late Mousterian Age and continued to be used through Post-Mousterian, Chatelperronian, Aurignacian, and Magdalenian periods.

Here, perhaps, we should pause. It is easy to speak of an occupation of a site continuing through 140,000 years and lasting from the end of the Acheulian era to the Magdalenian; and it is easy to accept this without realizing very sharply what it means. The mind makes the same sort of resistance to the idea of "light-years". If however we push back the beginnings of recorded history to the date of 2000 years B.C., when the scribes of Sumer began to record the glories of their country's past, we perceive that the total of human recorded history amounts to little more than 4,000 years—and yet how distant these Mesopotamian scribes seem, and how many generations separate us from them. The length of occupation of the Caves of the Hyena and the Reindeer is *thirty-five times as long* as the total of recorded history.

The two caves together provide a unique document, a history book showing how *Homo sapiens* takes over from Neanderthal man, reforming his habits and superseding his skills, but taking over from him and improving many of his characteristic tools.

Outstanding or exceptionally interesting "incidents" in this age-long "local history" are the upper and lower jaws of a Neanderthal man (among the ten most ancient human remains yet discovered) which were found in the Early Mousterian layer in the Cave of the Hyena and which fit together sufficiently well to show precisely the profile of Neanderthal man; mammoth femurs (huge fossil bones) which were evidently used as cutting-out tables in Early Magdalenian times and which still show the scratches made by flint points used in cutting out animal skins; and in a Late Mousterian level (in the Cave of the Hyena) the remains of what must be the world's oldest "museum", a small collection of curios, nodules of iron pyrites, fossil shells and fossil madrepores, collected at distances far from Arcy and brought back to the home cave there by what must have been Neanderthal men—a strange light on creatures generally thought of as sub-human brutes.

It was in 1955 and 1956 that M. Roger Grosjean made a series of discoveries in the valley of the Taravo in Corsica which threw an entirely new light on the prehistory of that island and showed it to be probably the centre and *locus classicus* of a culture of which the previous traces had been found in southern France and northern Italy and also—if a recent discovery is taken into account —Malta: the civilization of the statue-menhirs. The statue-menhir is a development of the menhir, the classic standing stone, on which have been carved, or engraved, anthropomorphic attributes, either as originally carved for that purpose or as additions transforming an ordinary menhir.

That is the formal description of statue-menhirs. In effect they are rough shafts of stone, some 7, 8 or 9 ft high, with heads and shoulders more or less roughly shaped, with craggy and enigmatic features, sometimes bearing sexual attributes, sometimes without; occasionally weapons appear on the shaft; often shoulder-blades and sometimes the back-bone appear; they are not unlike primitive but larger versions of the classic Greek Herms, but their expression is brooding and daunting.

It had long been known that Corsica had some statue-menhirs—indeed Prosper Merimée, the French novelist, noted the existence of two of them more than 100 years ago; but when in 1931 Commandant Octobon published his important work on the subject, mention was made of five statue-menhirs in Corsica, of secondary interest only. As the result of certain accidental discoveries, followed by the systematic work of M. Grosjean, Corsica now has no fewer than thirty-eight and is probably the most important area of all for this sort of megalithic art.

The principal site in the valley of the Taravo is Filitosa, where the remains were discovered of what had been a ceremonial centre with several statue-menhirs grouped about a central altar thick with the black ash of animal remains. (Another similar altar, associated with a statue-menhir, was later found not far away). This "high place" at Filitosa had been overturned by a different civilization (perhaps that of the *nuraghe*-builders of Sardinia) in about 1600 B.C. and these new peoples used the statue-menhirs or fragments of them as a quarry in their megalithic wall building.

A number of the statues have now been re-erected; and the massive brooding features are most impressive, suggesting a parallel—which can not be sustained —with the statues of Easter Island. Nearly all of them have carved on the shaft swords or daggers which suggest a link with those recently found on some of the Stonehenge sarsens (as described in another chapter); and it would appear that this cryptic and relatively short-lived civilization, as manifested in Corsica, is a link in the chain of cultures moving during the Bronze Age from the Eastern Mediterranean towards our own islands, in the dawn of British history.

CHAPTER FIVE

NORTHERN EUROPE

GEOGRAPHICAL and political divisions are usually arbitrary—and especially so in archaeology, where migrations and successive cultures and influences produce an effect like an ancient oil painting, many times repainted, scraped, varnished, cleaned, revarnished, recleaned, restored and so on. The mixture is human, moral, artistic, intellectual, even climatic, in infinitely varying proportions. No neat chemical formula will suffice.

However, for the purposes of this chapter it is proposed to lump together Sweden, Denmark, the Netherlands and North Germany, where, very generally speaking, classical influences were late or indirect or both and where underlying all art forms is that odd "Celtic", "Gothic", "Scythian" strain, which in its odd, obsessive, romantic quality seems so remote from any Mediterranean civilization. Its various names are intentionally put inside quotation marks in the last sentence, because these are names given for local manifestations of the same thing or very similar things; and in its first origins it now seems to derive from Siberia. Classical art is concerned with portraying the single thing or person in its naturalistic ideal, the thing-as-it-is at its best or (later) truest; African art starting from the object aims to extract its significance or its essential meaning; but this "Siberian" art sees everything in a nightmare flux, nothing is static, everything is melting into something else. The antlers of a stag are endlessly prolonged and end in flowers, flowers produce faces, branches become guilloches and in later times letters become trees and plants, flowers sprout human faces; it is the parent perhaps of both romantic poetry and *art nouveau*.

Perhaps the most important development in archaeology in Sweden has been the acquisition by the Central Office of National Antiquities of the whole of the Old Uppsala site. This was the great burial ground of the early Swedish kings —of the fifth and sixth centuries A.D.; and, most unfortunately, in the seventeenth and eighteenth centuries the Swedish Crown disposed of it and as a result buildings grew up on it and even gravel pits began to encroach thereon. Since 1928 the Crown and Royal Academy of Letters, History and Antiquities have been gradually acquiring the land; and by 1955 the whole site was secured and the Central Office could proceed systematically to clear and reinstate this most important of Sweden's archaeological sites.

Meanwhile valuable information on the times of these early Swedish kings was coming from a series of excavations at Ekero in Lake Malar showing in particular the wide and distant contacts of the Scandinavians of those times. Among the objects found was a bronze scoop of Egyptian origin, probably made in the Alexandria of the sixth century A.D.; a bishop's staff of the eighth century, from Ireland, set with stones and encrusted with enamels; and most remarkable of all, a small bronze statue of the Buddha, seated on a lotus flower and with a gold caste mark on the brow, North Indian work, most probably of the eighth century A.D. This last, incidentally, was found in the neighbourhood of a workshop or smithy, where great quantities of domestic utensils of bronze and iron, finished and half finished, were found, together with a surprising number of keys, locks and amulets and slag and unworked metal.

A most unusual technique was employed in the exploration in 1951 of a gravefield at Hogom, near Sundsvall. Here one of four large burial mounds was opened, but the actual excavation was done back at Stockholm, in the laboratories of the Conservation Department, the actual sepulchral chamber being entirely encased in plaster on the site, lifted in this manner and transported to the museum for examination at leisure. Here X-ray photographs were taken before the chamber was opened and the position of all the objects noted. Among these objects were a sword, a bit, daggers and a set of elaborate silvered buttons and a pair of glass "no heeltaps" tumblers, drinking vessels, that is, with a rounded base which prevents their being set down unless empty and turned upside down—a roistering feature not uncommon in the Dark Ages (Plate 57*b*).

A very rich burial site came to light in 1954 at Tuna in Badelunda. Here excavations had been made for the foundations of a house and in the spoil heap therefrom were found grave goods from what must have been one of the richest prehistoric graves in Sweden, as far as gold was concerned. They included no fewer than four gold rings, a gold pin and fragments of Roman vessels of bronze and glass beakers, all datable to the fourth century A.D. An investigation was organized and it was discovered that this burial chamber was part of a considerable necropolis. Some eighty single cremation graves, from the fourth century to the late Viking Age were found; and also eight very remarkable boat graves. One of these was outstanding: the boat was made from a hollowed log, skilfully carved to resemble the desired shape, fitted with a keel of pine and with stem-posts and ribs of juniper, these being fastened to the keel with treenails driven through the bottom. There was also a board on either side, sewn with osiers to the hollowed log. It dates to the middle of the ninth century. By a very considerable technical achievement it was possible to raise these fragile remains intact, though in sections, and restore and reassemble them in the Research Laboratory of the Museum of National Antiquities in Stockholm.

A somewhat similar technical skill, deployed on a huge scale has been recently seen in the project for raising the seventeenth century warship *Vasa* (which sank in Stockholm harbour on its maiden voyage on 10 August, 1628)—but this hardly comes within the scope of this book.

A number of interesting archaeological discoveries have been made in Denmark; and Danish archaeologists are besides outstanding in their work in two fields: palaeobotany and especially pollen analysis—whereby it is possible to establish what were the common plants at any given level and so perhaps to establish, for example, what were the economic plants of the time, what was the vegetable diet of the people concerned and, to some extent, what was the climate; and in the treatment of objects and bodies preserved in peat. Peat, as will appear later, has in some circumstances fantastic preservative qualities. It was after all a Danish gravedigger who said a tanner's body will last nine years in the earth. Hamlet asked: "Why he more than another?" to receive the reply—"Why, Sir, his hide is so tanned with his trade, that he will keep out water a great while; and your water is a sore decayer of your whoreson dead body"; and it is indeed the tannic acid in peat which is the preservative factor.

Inland from the east coast of Jutland lies what is now the Illerup valley. This was formerly—say, at the beginning of the Christian era—a lake which gradually filled up with vegetable detritus until, comparatively recently, it became a peat-hag. At the beginning of this century, it was cleared, the pools were filled in, the river channel was deepened and the land became water-meadow. In 1950 further drainage systems were begun with a view to making the valley into cornland and in May of that year workmen making a 4-ft-deep ditch struck a quantity of old iron. This turned out to be a collection of swords and spearheads and a report was made to the local museum. As a result, on the initiative of Professor Glob of the Aarhus Museum, Inspector Harald Andersen began a regular excavation. In several seasons of digging which followed, the mine detectors of the Danish Army were used with considerable success, not primarily to locate the buried objects but to register their depths and so to show the level to which spades could be used with safety.

What was discovered was the arms and equipment of about sixty warriors of about A.D. 450: fifty-six long Germanic cut-and-thrust swords; forty-five shield-bosses (which look rather like small steel-helmets of modern type); forty-five daggers; over 100 spear and lance heads; and nearly 200 arrow-heads—all of iron. In addition there were a number of belt buckles and scabbard mounts and other small items of equipment. All of these weapons had been rendered unusable, the swords bent and twisted, lance- and spear-heads had been blunted and their barbs were hacked off, while the shield-bosses had been savagely battered. Many of these weapons showed the action of fire; and it was quite clear what had taken place. There had been a battle near-by and the weapons of the defeated army had been gathered together, put in a pyre and burnt. Then the weapons were systematically made unusable, taken down to the lakeside and there thrown out into the waters of the lake. It was the aftermath no doubt of a battle between Danes and Jutes at the time when the Danes were moving in and the Jutes, under pressure, were beginning their migration westward to Britain. Perhaps they took this custom of battle with them and perhaps it is the origin of that legend of King Arthur in which the dying king orders his sword Excalibur to be thrown far out into "the shining levels of the lake". Whether the Jutes offering up the weapons of the vanquished to their god of battles, likewise thought that arms "clothed in white samite, mystic, wonderful" were stretched out from the misty waters to receive them we cannot tell. But it is not hard to recreate such a scene.

Also in Jutland, on the north side of the Limfjord (which makes the northern extremity of Jutland an island) is Lindholm, where since 1953 excavations directed by Dr Thorkild Ramskou of the National Museum of Denmark have uncovered a very large Viking cemetery, the largest known in fact except that of Birka in Sweden. It covers nearly sixteen acres, contains over 500 known graves and stretches in time from about A.D. 600 to A.D. 1100. The earliest and the latest graves are inhumation burials but the very great majority are cremations. The procedure in these Viking burials seems to have been somewhat like this. The dead man was wrapped in his clothes and burnt, together with varying amounts of grave goods; and sometimes a horse, a sheep or a dog was burnt with him. After the flames had died down, the remains were gathered together and placed in the cemetery, sometimes with a pot on top of them. Over this a layer of soil was placed, some four or five inches thick; and round it large stones were set up. In the earlier graves these stone enclosures were circular, square or triangular, but as the Viking Age proper approaches the enclosure is more and more frequently ship-shaped. As the ship was essential to the Viking way of life, so perhaps it appeared that it was necessary for the after-life. True ship burials are of course well-known; but ships must have been costly objects, only to be sacrificed in the case of wealthy chieftains and families capable of indulging in "conspicuous waste". And the ship-shaped stone enclosure must have been a reasonable substitute in families where the ship itself was still necessary as capital plant. Many of the enclosures were robbed of their stones to make later enclosures; and in some cases "ghosts" of the original enclosures survive, where sand blew into the original stone holes and has remained to form a pattern of lighter coloured patches.

Grave goods are not commonly found. There are of course a number of bronze brooches and the like; in one grave there was an amulet of amber, in the form of a hammer—the hammer of Thor—showing that Christianity was still far away in the ninth century; and in a grave of the tenth century was a handful of Kufic silver coins, one made in A.D. 900 in Tashkent—striking evidence of the far-reaching trade of the Vikings.

After the conversion to Christianity of the Danes in the eleventh century the cemetery fell into disuse and was covered with sand, but in the latter part of that century a small settlement grew up on top of it. From this short-lived settlement comes a remarkably fine silver brooch in the shape known as the "Anglian beast"—a highly formalized dragon-like creature whose tail is prolonged into a complex pattern, for all the world like those flourishes with which Victorian writing masters used to adorn their signatures. This was found with a coin of the German Emperor, Henry IV, struck between 1039 and 1045. Among other coins found on the site there were: one of Canute (struck in England) one of Hardicanute (struck in near-by Alborg), two of William the Conqueror and seven from the reigns of the Danish kings, Sven, Estridsson, Harald Hen and Canute the Saint.

Returning to that grim remark of Hamlet's Gravedigger on the durability of corpses, we come to the successive discoveries of the Tollund man, the Grauballe man and, over the border in German Schleswig-Holstein, of the executed 14-year-old girl.

In May 1950 peat-cutters in the course of their work at Tollund in central Jutland uncovered a male body so perfectly preserved that, as well as Professor Glob of the Aarhus Museum, the local police were notified as there appeared to be a presumption of murder. Murder—or at all events violent death—was proved; but it had taken place about 2,000 years previously. The man was lying on his side with his knees bent and his eyes closed as though asleep, naked except for a leather cap, a belt and a cord of twisted leather thongs about his neck. Except for the dark bronzy colour, the result of the tannic acid in the peat, the body was perfectly preserved, even in detail. The hair of the head, the eyebrows and lashes, the stubble on the chin were as if the man had died the day before. He was a handsome man of strong personality; and he had died by hanging.

Why? Now, in all, about 100 bodies are known to have been found in the peat like this over the years; and they have nearly all been naked or very scantily dressed. Many of them had nooses round their necks, others had crushed heads, broken limbs or mortal wounds and others were tied hand and foot. In the days of the Scandinavian gods hanging was not thought of as a dishonourable death; the peat hags were evidently the scenes of some mystical cult or other; and the suggestion has been made that these were ritual killings—in which one person died for the fertility of the country or the tribe. The Tollund man, incidentally, was in a state of erection and this provides a striking parallel with the neolithic cave drawings found near Palermo in Sicily and discussed elsewhere in this book. Furthermore the contents of Tollund man's stomach were examined; and it was found that he had eaten no animal food for some time before death and that his food had consisted of a porridge of vegetables and seeds containing barley, linseed and persicaria together with a few wild plants such as sheep's sorrel, white goosefoot, brassica, corn spurrey and the like—which suggests perhaps a diet of preparation before a sacrifice.

An attempt was made to preserve this body as an exhibit in Aarhus Museum, but without success; but it was thought that the lessons then learnt might lead to greater success when applied to another male body which was likewise found in the peat at Grauballe in the Kedelmose in 1952. This body was likewise in an excellent state of preservation—for example, it was possible to take the man's fingerprints—and he too had suffered a violent death. His throat had been cut; and it is believed that he had been a sacrifice to the fertility goddess, Nerthsu.

The discovery of bodies in peat then is not uncommon over a number of years; and considerable scientific interest had been aroused by these discoveries. Consequently when such a discovery was made by peat-cutters in Schleswig-Holstein in 1953 it was immediately reported and action was taken on behalf of the Schleswig-Holstein Museum at Gottorp Museum by Dr Karl Schlabow; and the body was lifted in a single huge block of peat and transported to the Museum in a modern motor hearse—probably the first time that such a vehicle was used to carry a 2,000-year-old corpse. When the layers of peat were removed, a most pathetic sight was revealed: the naked body, almost perfectly preserved, of a 14-year-old girl. She was lying on her right side, but with her shoulders thrown back, her right arm raised defensively, her left arm limp on the ground. Round her neck was a leather collar, tied round her eyes a cord-like bandage, still completely preserved; and the left side of her scalp had been shaved—about three days before her death. Under her back was a large stone; and the cause of her death—or, as it seems, execution—was almost certainly forcible drowning. Not far away there was found, but not so well preserved, the body of an adult male, who had been strangled with a hazel rod. Both bodies are dated by pollen-analysis of the layers of peat to about the beginning of the Christian Era; and two passages in the *Germania* of Tacitus seem to fill out the rest of this grim story. In one the punishment of an adulteress is described: "After the cutting off of her hair, the husband drove her forth from his home naked in the presence of the neighbours." And in the other, cowards, runaways and unclean persons are described as being drowned in bogs under a cover of interlaced branches.

In 1951 a most interesting large-scale excavation was made in Holland at Rhenen, on the Rhine between Utrecht and Nijmegen—resulting in finds with interesting parallels in Kent, Germany and Sweden. The site is a Merovingian Frankish cemetery containing about 900 graves mostly of the sixth century A.D. and the excavation was conducted by the Netherlands State Service for Archaeological Investigation under the direction of Dr P. Glazema. The nature of the soil is such that neither wood nor bone is preserved; and each grave survives only as a dark patch recording the size and shape of the coffin and the result of the decay of the wood. Inside this dark shape lie the grave goods but sometimes these, notably such things as shields and spears, protrude beyond this shape and so indicate that they were laid on or beside the coffin.

Of these grave goods many were weapons such as swords, axes, daggers and arrows; but the greatest interest probably lies in the glass and jewellery. Nearly all the graves have a drinking vessel of some kind; and the commonest form of this is a glass beaker, either with a very small foot or else with a rounded base of the single-draught variety mentioned earlier as having been found in Sweden. In the poorest graves this type of tumbler is found in pottery. In a very rich grave, however, a splendid example of the lobed beaker was found, the first of its kind to be found in Holland. This is a slightly waisted glass beaker on a tiny foot; and about a third of the way up the side, just before the waist, there are applied about half a dozen pendent lobes of hollow glass, somewhat in the shape of elephants' trunks—a curious but oddly beautiful effect, which must have called for considerable skill in the glassblower. A very similar lobed beaker was found in Kent in 1954. Other glass objects were shallow bowls of considerable simple beauty, one being lightly fluted, another having a whorled design in green and white glass. And this brings us to the glass beads. The Frankish women appear to have worn quantities of jewellery, especially in the form of necklaces and bracelets of beads, and although some of these are of amber and rock crystal the majority are of glass or glass paste of many colours, whorls of green and white being frequent. These beads look to be Oriental and may well be the result of trade; but the glass objects and industry seem to derive from Roman times and it may well be that Syrian craftsmen had settled in Western Europe, as Syrian merchants were everywhere very active in the later Roman Empire. The metal jewellery, however, mainly of bronze, shows no Roman influences and is of the characteristic North European style earlier referred to with elaborate interlacing and highly schematized animal designs, birds of prey providing the principal motifs. Round brooches, with cellular ornament set with flat garnets were evidently very popular; and under the garnets the jeweller would put a piece of gold foil with a chequered pattern, so that the gold would shimmer through the garnet. A particularly splendid piece is a silver-gilt hair-pin of a baluster design, rather like the head of a drum-major's staff. This likewise seems to have been a popular design, as a copy in bronze was also found.

One of the objects found, which serves as a link to the next excavation described, was a wooden bucket, whose shape and design was completely preserved by its bronze and iron ornament. Round the lower part were three simple iron rings; round the middle and the rim were elaborately ornamented bands of bronze and two mounts to carry a hinged handle, semicircular in form and decorated all over with a pattern of incised concentric circles.

Some eighty miles south-east in the brown-coal area, which lies to the west of Cologne, very extensive opencast mining operations have led to the destruction of many historic and prehistoric monuments; and the Rheinisches Landesmuseum, the Rhineland Preservation Society, and the brown-coal industry have co-operated to examine and record, before their destruction, the monuments which have come to light. One of the most interesting discoveries made concerns the valley of the Erft, the village of Morken and a mound known as the Husterknupp, which was traditionally the seat of a famous Rhineland noble family, the Counts of Hochstaden. The village of Morken lies about a kilometre from the mound and the church of St Martin in the village had been built on a spur jutting out into the valley. There was reason to suppose that this church had been built on an earlier Frankish burial-ground after the Franks were converted to Christianity; and as both church and village were doomed to demolition, an excellent opportunity for confirming this arose. Several Frankish graves of the sixth and seventh centuries, with the usual grave goods were discovered in the spring of 1955; and then, below the church of St Martin an exceptionally large grave chamber with a very rich range of objects was found. It was quite clear that this had been an important Frankish prince of about A.D. 600. The Franks were usually buried in a simple oak coffin. In this case a chamber over 6 ft wide and 9 ft long had been built and lined and roofed with oak boards, and in this the coffin had been placed with a wide variety of grave goods beside it. In the coffin beside the body lay a long two-edged sword, with fragments of a wooden scabbard and a curious button which must have adorned the sword-frog. It is made of meerschaum with an ornament of bronze, with a cellular decoration of inlaid garnets. By the prince's right arm lay two daggers and a tinder-iron; round his waist was a belt ending in a splendid buckle. This was iron inlaid with silver, brass and garnets; one end of it is in the form of a human mask below two very stylized animal heads; while the tongue, of silver, also consists of a human head inlaid with garnet and set between two birds' heads with hooked beaks. The symbolism of this would seem to be security despite threats from all sides. In the mouth of the dead man—as Charon's obol—was a gold coin of the Byzantine Emperor, Tiberius Constantinus (A.D. 578–82).

Against the coffin the prince's shield had been propped. This was a round buckler of which the large iron central boss and the hand grip had survived. The grip was enriched with bronze ornament and ended in bronze animal heads which seem to show that it was the work of a sixth century Scandinavian armourer.

In the open part of the chamber, beside the coffin, lay a number of objects, of which the most splendid was the prince's helmet. This was of a domed type ending in a boss designed to carry a plume. The framework consists of six bronze plates, between which are six other oval bronze plates, gilded and decorated with embossed patterns. Riveted to the under side of these are iron plates, for the helmet, although a magnificent object, was also practical armour as several sword dints show. On the frieze which is the lower rim of the helmet appear groups of human masks between monster heads (as on the belt buckle) and between these are vines with grapes on them and little birds. It was probably made in a North Italian workshop. Other objects included: a round-bottomed green glass beaker; a very shallow bronze basin with small feet and handles, in which were some textile fragments, some of them of silk; a battle-axe, scissors, an earthenware pot, a large whet-stone, some horse harness and a large wooden bucket. In one corner were the tips of three spears and a pair of scissors; beside the great helmet bones of beef, pork and chicken.

At the time that this great noble was buried the Frankish Empire was riven by the feud between the two Queens, Brunhilde and Fredegunde—the historical origin of the Niebelunglied; from the place of his burial it seems possible that he was among the first Frankish Christians (he was buried facing east) and that he may be among the forebears of the great house of Hochstaden, one of whose most famous members was Konrad of Hochstaden, Archbishop of Cologne, whose name is connected with the building of the great Cathedral; and so from a rich Frankish grave both the Christian and what we may call the "Wagnerian" strains of German history seem to stem.

CHAPTER SIX

FROM SAAR TO BALKANS

As WE move southwards from the Saarland through Southern Germany to Austria and on to Yugoslavia and Bulgaria we encounter different civilizations in contact and reaction, Celtic, Roman, Hellenic and Byzantine.

In February 1954, in what was then the separate political entity of the Saarland, at a place called Reinheim in the valley of the Blies, the richly furnished grave of a Celtic princess of the fifth century B.C. was found by accident during the digging of building sand. The excavation was then taken over and directed by the Landeskonservator, Dr Josef Keller. The burial had taken place in an oak-lined grave-chamber and it was marked by the very great richness of the personal jewellery of the dead princess. Furthermore, unlike the Celtic princess buried at Vix and discovered by Dr Joffroy, this noblewoman was surrounded by objects of almost exclusively Celtic manufacture and design.

The two finest pieces are a torque and a bracelet of a pure bright yellow gold. The torque has a twisted section, the bracelet is round; and the ends of both are elaborately decorated in a generally similar fashion. Each end of the torque has two bosses at the foot of each of which there is a lion mask. Below each of these pairs of bosses is a human face with a prominent and pointed nose and round staring eyes. Bands frame this face and end in tassels below the chin. The head-dress is the head of a bird of prey with a long hooked beak, whose spread wings frame the temples. The bracelet is similar but richer. There are the same pairs of bosses, the same lion masks, the same bird of prey head-dress, but the human figure is treated more fully and has arms folded on the breasts and scaly shoulders from which wings arise. The bird head-dresses recall the sculpture of distant Hatra, but otherwise these objects of jewellery are unique.

The dead woman was wearing another gold bracelet, a less elaborate affair, with a scroll and palmette ornament; a bracelet of clear glass and another of a slatey stone; two gold rings with an embossed looped design in two registers; an elaborately embossed gold pectoral plaque; and two bronze brooches of great beauty. One of these last showed a cockerel with a flowing tail and it was inlaid with pink coral, while the other, which probably originally had a large coral inlay, ended in linked human and animal heads. Beside the princess was a bronze mirror with an anthropomorphic handle and great quantities of beads of amber and multicoloured glass, the remains of a fine iron chain, two bronze pendants in human form and a number of amulets. Also in the grave were two gold bands with pierced ornament which may perhaps have adorned

43

a sceptre; three small round dishes of gold, a round gold plaque, two bronze bowls and a truly magnificent Celtic bronze wine-pourer. This last is about eighteen inches high and is rather like a richly-bellied coffee jug with a handle of great interest, a straight tubular spout and a lid crowned with a curious figure. This last has the body and legs of a horse—rather gone at the knees; the ears are roughly equine but the head is human, rather large in proportion to the beast, but wearing moustaches and a trimly pointed beard. The handle which joins this lid to the wine-pourer body contains two human heads, one above the other, similarly moustached, similarly bearded, each wearing a head-dress which seems to be a highly stylized version of the bird head-dress which is such a feature of the torque and principal bracelet. The lower head moreover has ram's horns developing from the temples.

Now although all these heads are here used as ornaments, and although they are schematized and elaborately treated, they are nevertheless strongly individual and unlike anything else of this period; and it is not difficult to imagine that they typify or even perhaps portray those Celts who around this period—the fifth century B.C.—and from pretty much this area—the Saarland—experienced a great military, political and artistic resurgence and began to expand, into England, Spain and Northern Italy. In about 388 B.C. they swept down into Italy and captured the city of Rome. In the next century they moved down the Danube into the Balkans and invaded Greece, plundering Delphi in 279 B.C.; while one branch of the race swept in to Asia Minor and founded the kingdom of Galatia and so incidentally provided a new type of figure—the Barbarian—for the later, Pergamene, Greek sculpture. In this Reinheim tomb we may see therefore the culture of a people at the beginning of this great expansion.

Gold features in a number of discoveries made in Germany; and before passing on to the Straubing hoard mention should be made of the "Nuremberg Gold Helmet". This last was found by a workman stubbing out tree trunks near the Franconian village of Etzeldorf. As found, this amounted to a large quantity of thin gold sheet elaborately embossed, which has subsequently been assembled in the German National Museum at Nuremberg and discovered to form a tall conical head-dress which is believed to date from about 1500 B.C. and to be of religious significance.

The Straubing Hoard was likewise found by accident. During building operations at Straubing, workmen hit upon a quantity of iron tools and below that a large bronze cauldron face downwards over the most astonishing collection of Roman parade armour ever found. The find was reported and Herr Joseph Keim of the Straubing Museum and Dr Hundt were able fully to investigate and to recover some 116 items, perhaps the whole of the material which had been buried there, probably about the middle of the third century A.D.

The great majority of these items seem to have come from the "sports store" of a Roman cavalry formation and consist of extremely elaborate human and horse armour of very thin bronze silvered and gilded; and it was obviously never intended for battle use but for the elaborate sham fights, tournaments and ceremonial displays which were part of the life of the cavalry of the Imperial Roman army. There was in fact at Straubing (Sorviodurum in Roman times) a permanent frontier post on the Danube, garrisoned by a cohort with cavalry auxiliaries, originally recruited in Syria.

Seven vizor masks were found, these being metal masks in the form of a human face, which hinge on to the helmet and entirely cover the face of the wearer, with pierced holes for the eyes, nostrils and mouth. All are of thin bronze, gilded. Four of them show idealized youthful features of classical type, with short, thickly wavy hair; but the other three are quite different, with features of a more barbaric type and incorporating a "Phrygian cap". The suggestion (made by Professor Gerhard Bersu) is that these were made in a local workshop on the Lower Danube, while the others come from a central military workshop. On the other hand the "Phrygian cap" suggests the Mithraic cult which was general in the Roman armies and one of the grades of this cult was "the Persian". Only one helmet proper was found to which such vizors would be fitted and as it happens it fits none of the seven vizors found. It is of beaten iron in the form of a curly head of hair with two simulated fillets and it is decorated besides with silvered and gilded bronze mounts. Like most of the pieces it carries three different names in a punched inscription, each name being followed by a T (for *turma* or squadron) and these presumably indicate the successive owners.

Five greaves were found. These also were of thin bronze, with embossed ornament, the ground being silvered while the ornament which is in shallow relief is gilded. It takes the form of panels, dividing up the area of the shin and filled with animals, such as dolphins, eagles and panthers with fish tails and with mythological or human subjects—such as Hercules, Mars standing on a giant and human heads-and-shoulders, some of them wearing "Phrygian caps". In addition six knee-caps were found, of a type to hinge on above the greaves. These are also gilded and silvered and usually moulded in the form of female heads, Minerva wearing a Corinthian helmet, Bellona goddess of battle and the like.

Even richer than these, however, were the seven chamfrons found. These are pieces of armour to cover a horse's face and all consist of three panels: a central panel, with most elaborate reliefs and two side panels with pierced holes to go over the horses's eyes. All, incidentally, must have been made for rather small-headed horses. The seven fall into two types. Five of them have long panels, covering the horse from above the eyes to just short of the nostrils; while the other two are much smaller, being more like ornamental spectacles with a central panel to act as an anchor. The ornament is too rich to describe quite fully, but it will perhaps give some idea of their splendour if one of each type is described. All of them are of thin bronze, gilded and silvered and in general the relief is much higher than in the human armour. In one long chamfron the central panel shows the naked Mars, with sword belt, helmet, shield in left hand and spear in right, standing on a giant whose legs end in snakes. Above him is an eagle holding a wreath. The side panels are symmetrical and almost identical. The huge eye-bosses are pierced in a lace pattern and encircled with two large snakes; and above them are winged victories bearing wreaths, while below are Castor, on one panel, Pollux on the other, leading horses. The background is covered with punched geometrical designs. Other chamfrons of this type show Minerva, Mars in armour, Gorgon heads, heads of Persians and dragons. The only perfect short-type chamfron has for its small central panel a large head of Ganymede in a "Phrygian cap", above and round which appears the eagle which is carrying him off to Jupiter. Above this design is a small basket between two human heads in profile. The roughly pear-shaped side panels have larger versions of this same head and eagle, with winged Victories above, but both these Ganymede heads are quite ruthlessly and crudely punched with holes to admit light to the eyes of the horse. The other short chamfron has a long central panel but it appears to be a botched-up job, the result of a not uncommon Army habit of "cannibalization".

The other objects of art are seven small bronze statuettes on pedestals (and four empty pedestals). These are male and female deities, including an infant Mars, a Mercury, a dancing Lar and the like; and they look as though they might have been the ornaments of a household shrine in a villa.

The rest of the hoard consists of tools and odds and ends of equipment, including seven iron hipposandals, a primitive form of horseshoe supposedly used for sick horses, a bit, a length of chain, keys, saws and the like; and this odd mixture has led Professor Bersu to suggest an origin for the hoard. About the middle of the third century A.D. this part of the Roman frontier was over-run by Germanic tribes; and this collection of heterogeneous material was perhaps gathered together by looters and hidden. Then perhaps the tide of warfare ran the other way and the looters were killed or otherwise prevented from collecting their booty; and the hoard had to wait 1700 years to be discovered and to throw a brilliant light on at once the ceremonial and the routine life of a Roman cavalry squadron of Syrian origin stationed on the outskirts of the Empire beside the Danube.

In August 1950, accident again—the digging of foundations—led to a remarkable discovery at Niederemmel, not far from Trier. Here a very fine Roman sarcophagus of the fourth century A.D. was found and when opened was discovered to contain a truly astonishing glass goblet. This is a basically bag-shaped vessel $7\frac{1}{8}$ in high with a greatest diameter of $5\frac{7}{8}$ in; but it is carved from a single block of glass and consists of a plain smooth central container, entirely surrounded with a filigree network also of glass joined at a few points by thin columns of glass to the main body. This network pattern consists of circles of thin glass, each circle touching each of its four neighbours at one point and at each point of contact there is a small glass rosette, somewhat in the form of a St Andrew's cross. This is not only a remarkable and very rare example of Roman glass, it is also a triumph of refined craftsmanship and an object of surprisingly simple beauty. Craftsmanship of this order often leads the craftsman into displays of bravura—as will shortly be seen in some gold vessels found in Bulgaria—but in this glass goblet, brilliant skill has been controlled by the most refined taste.

This was of course, during the fourth century, a district of great importance and wealth, an Imperial centre from which began the rise to power of Constantine the Great; and examples of wealth, taste and courtly style may be expected to come to light. And indeed that greater accident which is the destructiveness of war led to a number of discoveries in Trier, the Roman *Augusta Treverorum*. In the winter of 1944–5, during the battle of the Ardennes, Trier was bombed by the United States Air Force; and this, like the German bombing of the City of London, led to a number of discoveries which would never otherwise have been made. In the course of clearing up and reconstruction between the end of the war and 1951, a number of excavations were conducted under the direction of Drs Kempf and Eiden. The great basilica had been gutted by fire and it was found that during the fourth century it had been used as the throne-room of Constantine the Great and his successors. The Cloister of St Irmina was found to overly a very extensive Roman granary and storehouse; and below the Cornmarket, 13 ft underground, a fine and large mosaic floor was found, in very good condition. It had been made, quite obviously, about the time that the Roman Empire became officially Christian on the orders of Constantine the Great; and it is a curious mixture of pagan and Christian iconography. One can easily imagine the designer suddenly confronted with a complete shift in Imperial fashion and determined, at whatever cost of consistency, to incorporate motifs which have suddenly become modish. Quite apart from this light on the trials of interior decorators 1,600 years ago, the mosaic is one of great intrinsic interest. One of the subjects is the triplet birth of Castor, Pollux and Helen from the egg laid by Leda. The principal characters in this scene are named and there is a curious mistake in the mythology. The husband of Leda—and the suppositious father of the triplets—is called Agamemnon, instead of Tyndareus. The great majority of the subjects of this floor, however, are individual servants shown at their various tasks and each servant is named. It provides an odd parallel to the mosaic at Torre de Palma in Portugal where it is the master's favourite horses which are portrayed and named.

Magdalensberg, a 3,000-ft peak in the Carinthian mountains near Klagenfurt in Austria, with a Gothic church on the summit, has for a very long time indeed been known as an important archaeological site. As long ago as A.D. 1502 a splendid Greek bronze of the fifth century B.C. was discovered there. This is a major work of art and it originally was intended as simply a naked *ephebus*, a young man, that is. About the first century B.C. however it received certain additions, a helmet, and an axe and a shield and was thus transformed into a Celtic deity, Mars Latobius—a "promotion" which was recorded in an inscription on the upper thigh.

Some serious excavation was carried out before the First World War—in 1907–8—but this was broken off and not resumed until 1948 when the large-scale excavations (which are still continuing) were begun by the Austrian Institute of Archaeology with the help of a subsidy by the Provincial Government and under the direction of Professors Praschniker and Egger.

These have proved to be very rewarding excavations and fully established that there had been a large Celtic *oppidum* on the site before the Roman settlement which came into existence in the first century A.D. It seems fairly certain—though it has not yet been proved beyond a doubt—that this site was Noria, the capital of the prosperous Celtic kingdom of Noricum, which peaceably became a part of the Roman Empire around 15 B.C. The buildings of the Roman settlement have been found to be rich, luxurious and prosperous. Outstanding among them is a large temple with twin *cellas*, which it seemed likely had been dedicated to Dea Roma and the Emperor; a large hall with an apse; and a hall of archives with thirteen niches. It seems possible that these thirteen niches may correspond with the thirteen *civitates* of the kingdom of Noricum to which Pliny refers.

In addition, palaces, extensive and luxurious bath-houses, central heating systems and family vaults all attest a high standard of civilization which had been continued by the Romans from an existing condition rather than initiated by them. Imperial Roman provincial capitals are well enough known, it is their non-Roman origins which are most interesting and so it is with Magdalensberg. One of the oddest pre-Roman finds on the site is an extraordinary clay statuette which has been tentatively associated with the worship of that already mentioned Celtic god, Mars Latobius. This is the crude and lumpish figure of a man, seated apparently in a shallow bath—for all the world like one of those baffled middle-aged men who inhabit the world of James Thurber.

In 1959, however, Professor Rudolf Egger, announced what is quite easily the most important discovery to have been made on this site—namely the existence of a pre-Celtic alphabet. Apparently letters have been found, engraved on vases, cups and tablets, which form part of an alphabet written from right to left, as in various Oriental alphabets. It is hoped that these will make it possible to establish what language was spoken in Noricum before the Celtic period.

The importance of this discovery has been affirmed by Professor John Evans on the following grounds. Apart from the Roman and Greek alphabets, some other alphabets, such as the Etruscan and the Iberian, have been known to exist in Mediterranean Europe; but it had always been assumed that the peoples of temperate Europe had remained illiterate until the Roman Empire was extended north of the Alps. This discovery seems completely to overrule this assumption; and Magdalensberg may yet prove the fountain-head of a quite new knowledge of pre-Roman Central Europe.

Only a brief summary of Hungarian archaeological activity can be attempted; but some indication can be given of sites which have been worked. One of the most interesting and indeed curious of them is a burial ground at

Szentes-Vekerzug. This has been dated to about 550 B.C. and it is thought that it is linked with the first wave of Scythians to reach Hungary. In one part of this necropolis—which is assumed to be an outer part—some twelve horse tombs have been found. In three of these the horses were buried in pairs; and with one pair were found the rims of four wheels together with the iron parts of the axle-tree, sufficient to allow of a reconstruction of the whole cart. A quantity of harness was found together with harness ornaments, some of which was of gilt bronze. Again it has been possible to discover what was the Scythian manner of harnessing their horses. With these horse burials there was no trace of any human remains.

An odd parallel was discovered near Alsonemedi, about fourteen miles from Budapest, where a cemetery of the "Baden people", who may be dated to the end of the Bronze Age, was found. Here two elaborate tombs were found, presumably of chieftains of the people; and in one of them, beside the human skeleton and facing each other were the skeletons of two oxen.

Other activities have been pursued at Istallosko (an Aurignacian cave site); at Lovas, near Lake Balaton, where very ancient workings of red lead have been discovered; at an Early Bronze Age site at Polgar-Basatanya; a "Baden culture" site at Budakalaszi; and at two Roman sites, a proconsular palace at Roman Aquincum and a frontier fortress near the modern steel town of Sztalin-varos.

Since the end of the war Bulgarian archaeologists have been particularly active; and for the summary of their activities on which these notes are based I am greatly indebted to Mr Velizar Velkov of the Archaeological Institute, Sofia.

A number of palaeolithic sites in the Vrachanski district and near Lovech have been investigated by Mr N. Djambazov and considerable flint industries of the late Palaeolithic (40,000–12,000 B.C.) found; for the first time, that is, south of the Danube. Of the Neolithic, Eneolithic and Bronze Ages, a considerable number of village burial mounds (particularly of period 3000–2000 B.C.) have been explored; and one in particular near Karanovo in the Novo Zagora district has proved to be of especial interest. This is a huge mound, 775 ft long, 496 ft wide and 40 ft high and in the course of excavations by Messrs Vassil Michov and G. Georgiev between 1946 and 1957 a complete sector was dug. Much pottery, personal ornaments and cult figures were found and the foundations of a number of dwellings, together with the remains of an early neolithic burial—the oldest burial place yet found in the East Balkans. Five periods of cultures were defined and a number of points of Bulgarian chronology between 3000 and 2000 B.C. were solved. Much light also has been thrown on the relations between the peoples then living in Bulgaria with those in Asia Minor, Troy and the Aegean and for that matter with those living north of the Danube. Karanovo promises to be a key site in Bulgarian archaeology and has already earned for itself the name of the "Bulgarian Troy".

The Iron Age in Bulgaria was marked by striking and rapid development;

and the discoveries match the age. In the tenth century the Thracians settled in the land and developed their powerful state. A number of Greek colonies came into being on the western Black Sea coast; and in the third century the Celts passed through the country, some of them remaining in Southern Bulgaria and setting up a Celtic kingdom which survived for some decades. Excavations were carried on at a number of Greek colonies: Apollonia (modern Sozopol) by I. Venedikov; Mesemvia (modern Neceber) by Venedikov and I. Galabov; Bizone (modern Karvarna) by M. Milchev and others; and Odessos (modern Varna). Of these perhaps the most rewarding were those at Mesemvia, where more than 100 graves of the fourth to third century were excavated, one of which was distinguished by the richness of its gold jewellery. The excavations also uncovered a Thracian town older than the Greek settlement; and perhaps most interesting of all an inscription in the form of a treaty between Mesemvia and a Thracian ruler called Sadala. This refers to the tribute paid to Sadala and his ancestors (who are named) and mention is made of the colony's theatre and of the festivities held in honour of Dionysos. The date of the treaty is the end of the fourth and the beginning of the third century B.C.

Several Thracian cemeteries have been found and excavated, including one at Ravna which dates from the first half of the tenth century B.C. and is therefore the earliest Thracian necropolis in Bulgaris. The most remarkable burial mound discovered is that which is now known as the Kazanlushka Grobnitza. This is a fourth century mound, domed, which was found, in excellent condition, in 1944 by D. Tzonchev at Filipovo near Plovdiv. The interior walls of this are covered with mural drawings and inscriptions which in their complicated composition, originality and method of execution make this burial mound a unique monument of antique art. The central room is distinguished by what is called the "funeral oration"; while many other drawings depict chariots at speed and groups of foot-soldiers and cavalry.

Among the most important major excavations has been the uncovering of a whole Thracian town called Seftopolis by Professor D. P. Dimitrov, now at the bottom of the newly-built Georgi Dimitrov Dam. A very large area of land was uncovered and three periods of ancient settlement were established: a Thracian settlement from the time of Philip II; a considerable town centre from the time of Sevt III, which was destroyed and burnt; and finally a settlement dating from the end of the third century B.C. It had clearly been a well-planned town with a fortress wall some six feet thick. Among the very numerous objects found were pottery, jewellery and money and evidence of a number of handicrafts— among which may be mentioned the baking of bricks—a craft which appeared in the second half of the fourth century simultaneously in Greece and Thrace. Among the pottery were a number of imports from Greece and there were also some seals from the isle of Thasos, which seems to establish the fact that there were trading relationships between Seftopolis and the Aegean world. Fragments of monumental sculptures and many terracottas were also discovered. One of the most interesting objects found was a tablet inscribed in Greek characters and running to thirty-seven lines. It mentions the name of a town, Kobile, and gives a topographical description of it. It also throws some light on the Thracian law and religion of the time.

Two extremely rich treasures which have been found in Bulgaria throw a vivid light on the extreme wealth and lavishness of the Thracians of the fourth and third centuries B.C.: the silver treasure of Lukovet; and the gold treasure of Panagurishte.

The silver treasure which was found near the town of Lukovet is considered to be a collection and Dimitrov suggests that it was the property of a rich Thracian and that it was intentionally buried—perhaps as Mr Pepys buried his plate—as no trace of settlement or buildings have been discovered near it. It consists of several hundred items: thirteen silver dishes, three iron bits for horses, about 200 chain links of different kinds and a number of items which were parts and ornaments of horse harness. It is of Thracian manufacture and a splendid product of Thracian art.

The gold treasure is astounding, by any standards: for its richness, for it totals 16 lb 5 oz Troy in gold; for its magnificent state of preservation; for its brilliant workmanship; and for its barbaric oddity in violently combining classical themes, with Persian and even "Scythian" motifs. The treasure was found in December 1949 in a valley in southern central Bulgaria by three brothers who were digging clay and it was found about $7\frac{1}{2}$ ft down without any covering or container. It had presumably been buried for security during a time of danger. It consists of nine pieces, all of gold—six of which are illustrated on Plate 6—and all of them presumably a banquet service of simply regal splendour. It is quite clear that they were made by a Greek craftsman, perhaps of Northern Asia Minor, presumably to the order (and to the taste) of an extremely rich Thracian prince. Tsonchev dates them stylistically to the end of the fourth century B.C.; but Venedikov suggests the first quarter of the third century and believes that they were almost new when they were buried. They consist of two stag's head *rhyta* and one ram's head *rhyton*; a rhyton in the form of a running goat; three *oinochoe* (wine jugs) in the form of women's heads; a most elaborate two-handled rhyton-amphora; and a *patera* or dish.

To describe the last first. This dish is circular and nearly ten inches in diameter. In the centre is a plain recess; the remainder is entirely covered with three concentric circles of negroheads in relief—to the number of seventy-two—and an inner circle of acorns. Separating these reliefs are lotus and palmette designs. These negroes are presumably the "just Ethiopians" of Greek tradition; nevertheless they seem extremely exotic in ancient Thrace. The two stag's head *rhyta* and the ram's head *rhyton* are basically alike and are wine pouring vessels. Very roughly they may be said to be shaped like a half-boot, with the animal's head as the boot itself, the wine being poured into the leg of the boot and emerging through an orifice in the animal's lower lip; and while the animal's head is brilliantly naturalistic in treatment, the leg of the boot as it were is simply used as the ground for a series of reliefs in Classical themes. All three have handles, the upper part of which is in the form of a lion with its forepaws on the rim, the lower end terminating in a woman's head. In the ram's head *rhyton*, which is the smallest of the three (about 4¼ in high) the reliefs show a seated Dionysus with three maenads, one of whom is identified with the inscription "Eriope". The two stag's heads have branched and palmated antlers: the reliefs on one showing the Judgement of Paris; on the other, Heracles killing the Corinthian stag on one side and Theseus killing the Bull of Marathon on the other.

The goat *rhyton* is more in the form of a drink horn, about 5½ in high, with the lower part in the shape of the forequarters of a horned and bearded goat, running and somewhat in the Achaemenian Persian style, the orifice being a short spout between the beast's legs. On the upper part appear in high relief the deities Hera, Apollo, Artemis and Nike. This *rhyton* has no handle.

The other three *rhyta* are in the form of women's heads with classical features. Two of them, a pair, are 7¼ in high, while the third is a very little smaller. Each of these heads is crowned with an arbitrary jug mouth, which is also linked with back of the head by means of a handle, the upper part of which is in the form of a highly humanized female sphinx. The two which are a pair have elaborate but similar "hair-do's" and at the base of the neck (which is also the base of the vessel) a formalized necklace, with a lion-mask pendant in the centre. This lion-mask also serves as the orifice for the liquor. The third of this group is more elaborate than the other two, the head being crowned with two winged griffins. It has no necklace at the throat but only a lion's head to serve as the orifice.

We come finally to the largest and most remarkable object, the gold *amphora-rhyton*. It is over 11 in high and weighs nearly 60 oz Av. It is in the general form of a two-handled *amphora*, but its rounded base shows a relief in the form of a rosette and beside this are two negroheads, the mouths of which serve as orifices for the wine. The two handles are in the form of centaurs, whose equine forelegs are poised on the rim of the vessel, while their human arms are raised as though about to grapple in a wrestling match. The main body of the vessel is entirely covered with classical reliefs. On one side is a guard and seven armed figures, on the other the infant Hercules (perhaps) strangling two snakes, with kneeling satyrs playing on double flutes. A trumpeter also appears; and it has been suggested that the whole shows a scene from an unknown Greek play, perhaps on the discovery of Achilles in the isle of Skyros.

An interesting feature, not previously mentioned, is that the negrohead *patera* bears an inscription of its original weight—196 drachmae and ¼ obol—or, in modern weights, about 846.9 gr. It now weighs 845.7 gr. This almost exact correspondence supports the view that the objects were new when buried; and the presence of the inscription also suggests that the goldsmith was working strictly to order and had to account in detail for all the precious metal supplied to him to work in.

The period of Roman rule left a profound mark on Bulgaria and a considerable number of Roman sites have been the subject of excavation since the war, notably at Serdica (Sofia), Eskus (Digen), Ratsiaria (Archar), Martsianopol (Rekar Devnya) Phillipopol (Plovdiv), Augusta Triana (Stara Zagora) Nikopolis ad Istrum (Nikyup). Of these probably the most interesting are those at Eskus, where T. Ivanov has laid bare the layout of a town, with drainage system, Temple of Fortuna, shops and various public buildings. In one of these a floor mosaic was found showing a scene from an unknown play by the Greek writer of comedies, Menander. This mosaic dates from the end of the second or the beginning of the third century A.D.

Very extensive excavations of mediaeval sites have also been carried out but these are somewhat out of our purview; and enough has been said to show both the intense activity of Bulgarian archaeologists and the rich field which lies at their doors.

The Yugoslavs likewise are fully conscious of the richness of the central part of the Balkan peninsula as a little-worked source of archaeological information of the first importance especially as regards their own origins, whether from the Thracians, Illyrians and Dacians of the Iron Age or from the later incursions of the Slavs. This point of view was very forcibly put by Djurdje Boskovic in an address at the tenth anniversary of the Archaeological Institute of the Serbian Academy of Science in 1957 when he discussed the archaeological problems which faced the Institute. Many of these were organizational and even ideological and relating to the need of producing trained men and specialists and of regularizing and co-ordinating all sorts of work done—and they need not perhaps concern us. The aim of the Institute was stated to be the study of the past at all those epochs at which it appeared that other historical sources were missing. This is of course a fair enough description of archaeology but it is a little daunting to learn that the Institute felt compelled to fix an arbitrary forward date for their researches at A.D. 1815. Browning's "Oh, that a man's reach should exceed his grasp" is all very well, but it is difficult not to think that a young organization, conscious of its lack of specialists, would do well to concentrate on a small number of limited objectives instead of taking nearly all human civilized history as its field.

However, the first lines of attack, as laid down, were not quite so extensive and indeed they promise to provide interesting information. Working forward from the earliest times, they may be summarized as follows. The exploration and study of palaeolithic caves of Gradac and Risovaca; and the study of the Morava-Vardar line of communication which was so important in Neolithic and the early metal ages. This leads to the study of race movements and the arrival of the Illyro-Thracians and their trading and agricultural activity. Next follows the Greek and Roman penetration into the Balkans; and to study this systematic excavations were planned at Demir-Kapija, at Margua, at Nish and at Gamzigrad. The next stage concerns the Byzantine culture and its early contact with the Slavs; leading to the establishment of the Slavs, especially in Serbia, in the Middle Ages.

It should of course be mentioned that much has been done in Yugoslavia in connexion with the preservation and conservation of what are among the chief glories of the country—its splendid Byzantine frescoes and mosaics—and indeed what has been done amounts, as a result of cleaning, revelation and restoration, to the discovery of unsuspected masterpieces.

PLATE 1. The self-deified King of Commagene, Antiochus I (*c.* 69–34 B.C.): a colossal head from a row of huge seated gods on the summit of Nemrud Dagh, in eastern Turkey.

PLATE 2. The secret temple and meeting-place of senior officers and rich merchants of Roman London, *c.* A.D. 150: the temple of Mithras on the bank of the Walbrook—in a reconstruction drawing by Alan Sorrell.

PLATE 3. The broch tower and island stronghold in Clickhimin Loch, near Lerwick, Shetland—as it was in the 1st century A.D., in a reconstruction drawing by Alan Sorrell.

PLATE 4. The fascination of archaeology. The site of the Mithraeum found in the City of London, with an endless queue of sightseers winding round the entire block.

PLATE 5. The great bronze crater, found in the tomb of a Celtic princess of about 500 B.C. at Vix, in Burgundy. Its height, including a lid which is not shown, is 5 ft 4⅝ in, its weight about the fifth of a ton.

PLATE 6. Part of the gold treasure of Panagurishte, Bulgaria. Greek work, 4th–3rd century B.C. (*a*) *Rhyton* in the shape of a woman's head; (*b*) ram's head *rhyton*; (*c*) large *amphora-rhyton*, with centaur handles; (*d*) another woman's head *rhyton*; (*e*) a goat *rhyton*; and (*f*) a dish with seventy-two negro-head reliefs.

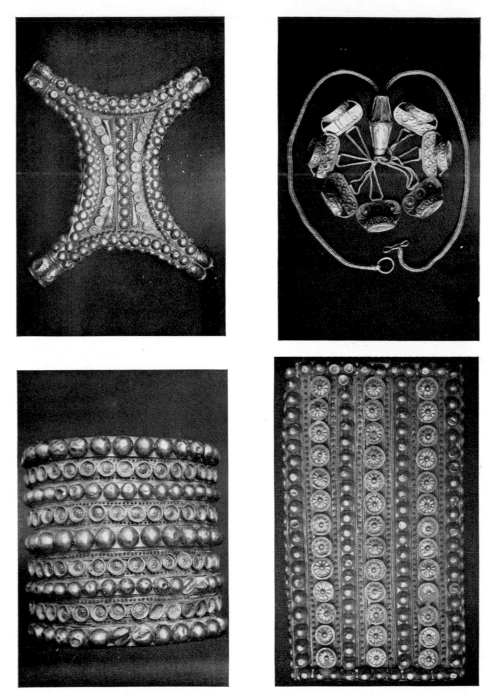

PLATE 7. Part of the "Treasure of Argantonius" (7th–6th century B.C.) found near Seville, Spain. (*a*) A breastplate; (*b*) necklace and group of pendent seals; (*c*) bracelet; and (*d*) typical plaque—all gold.

PLATE 8. A Falstaff of Magna Graecia: Silenus, in a terracotta antefix from Gela, southern Sicily.

PLATE 9. Mosaics from the Imperial villa at Piazza Armerina, Sicily. (*a*) The griffin and the caged man; (*b*) the owner, perhaps the Emperor Maximinian, and his bodyguard—both from the "Big Game" mosaic; and (*c*) one of the "Bikini girls".

PLATE 10. The dancers of Monte Pellegrini, near Palermo. Masked figures surround a pair of acrobats or self-stranglers, in a palaeolithic cave drawing of
unique beauty and naturalism.

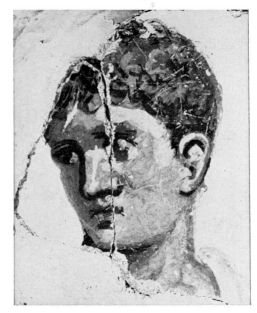

PLATE 11. Fragments of Roman wall-painting from Stabiae—impressionism of 1900 years ago. (a) A child playing the Pan-pipes; (b) a winged head; (c) a mourning woman; and (d) a young woman.

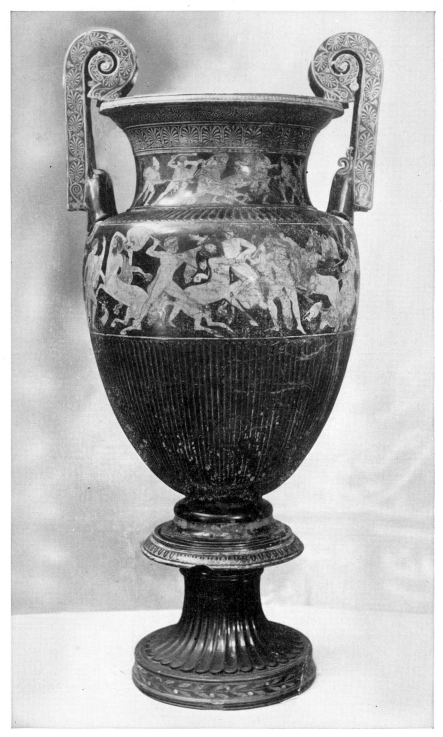

PLATE 12. One of the finest of the Attic vases recovered from the necropolis of Spina, 3 ft 7¼ in high, with separate and intact base. In the upper register, Heracles and the wild boar and (on the other side) a dance of maenads; lower register, the deaths of Priam and Cassandra and (other side) the battle of the centaurs and the Lapithae.

PLATE 13. Spina. (*a*) Treasure from the mud—splendid Attic vases appearing as the liquid mud is washed away from Tomb 113. (*b*) A pleasant fish dish, showing sardines, a squid and two John Dories. (*c*) A convivial scene on a drinking vessel —Silenus, in the role of Apollo, plays on the lyre to Dionysus and Hermes.

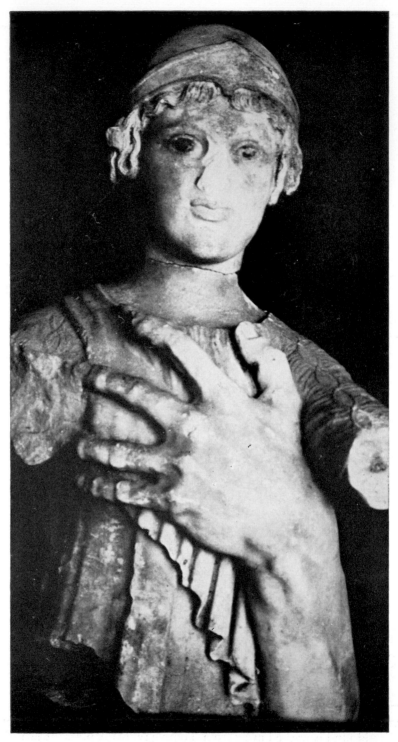

PLATE 14. From the "mine of statuary" discovered in the Grotto
of Tiberius, at Sperlonga, Italy. A hand, in Hellenistic style,
clutching a small statue of a goddess, in Archaic style.

CHAPTER SEVEN

PORTUGAL AND SPAIN

FROM an archaeological point of view, it is Roman Portugal—the province of Lusitania—which is best known and post-war discoveries have continued to enrich this aspect. The three principal cities of the old province, which was somewhat larger than modern Portugal, were Olisipo (modern Lisbon), Emerita Augusta (which now lies in Spain and is called Merida) and Conimbriga (modern Condeixa a Velha) which lies south of Coimbra and should not be confused with it. Coimbra's ancient name was Aeminium. Conimbriga was considerably excavated before the war. After the war, however, a road was being made to enable tourists to approach and visit the very interesting ruins. During the engineering excavations for the stage of the road nearest to the main gate of the ancient city, a splendid palace was discovered just outside the walls; and this has now been properly excavated. It has been revealed as a perfect example of a city dwelling in the grand manner of the later Imperial Roman times. It follows the usual classical plan of such buildings, but not slavishly and it is especially interesting to note that the architect has taken full advantage of the site and also of the plentiful water supply which was available. The building has many courtyards and the principal feature of these is found in the pools and open-air tanks of water, some of them ornamental, others more utilitarian, being designed to provide water for the gardens which adorn these courts and which are usually edged with very fine mosaic pavements.

Perhaps the finest Roman mosaics yet to be found in Portugal, however, were those which were accidentally discovered in 1947 at Torre de Palma, a rich farm in High Alentejo. The accidental revelation of some significant stones by a labourer led to an extensive excavation by Dr Manuel Heleno of Lisbon University and the discovery of four splendid mosaic floors which have been offered to the Lisbon Archaeological Museum by the present owner of Torre de Palma, Senhor Joao da Costa Falcao. What was discovered was a prosperous agricultural settlement centred on a rich and luxurious villa. A huge cylindrical mill-stone for an olive press and a range of storage tanks and jars indicate that it was, as it is today, a rich oil producing district; and the presence of bath-houses, provided with hypocaust, and allied buildings and a small forum and especially the mosaics of the great house confirm that it was a prosperous centre. The date seems to be about the third century A.D. The mosaics are of very fine quality and of several different types. One huge floor, in almost perfect condition, is like an enormous Oriental carpet, with an all-over geometrical design of

interlocking jagged units, surrounded with a guilloche border. The finest is the
frieze of the Nine Muses, which is worked with extremely small stones and has
backgrounds finished in fan-like patterns of a kind found in the Palace of the
Byzantine Emperors at Istanbul. This shows the Nine Muses in a row, in somewhat statuesque poses; and a number of panels of mythological scenes, which
include items from the Labours of Hercules, Theseus and the Minotaur, and a
triumph of Bacchus. Another pavement shows interlocking patterns of flowers,
and is of great beauty and charm, but unfortunately is the least well preserved.
The most interesting of these mosiacs is however the pavement of the horses.
These seem to form a Lusitanian equivalent of the eighteenth century gentleman's sporting gallery—as it were his paintings by Stubbs or Marshall. It
shows the portraits of five horses, all named (Hiberus, Pelops, Inacus, Leneus
and Lenobatis). Each is shown separately in a guilloche border and each bears
a palm on his head—one, Hiberus, two palms—to show, presumably, that he
was a winner, champion or favourite of his owner. All are standing in profile,
with the forequarters turned slightly to face the viewer, except one, Lenobatis
(the "grape-treader") which is shown full face with a great number of trophies
strung about his neck. These horses provide a number of links with the present.
This district of Portugal is famous to this day for its breed of horses; and the
fact that the horse which wears two palms is called Hiberus ("the Iberian")
suggests that it was local-bred; while the horse Leneus (which is one of the
epithets of Bacchus) bears a palm-tree brand on the near hindquarter—and the
palm-tree is still the crest of the great house and the origin of its name, Torre de
Palma.

About 150 miles south-east, at Seville in Spain, an extraordinarily rich treasure of gold was found, also by accident, and the site was immediately excavated
under the direction of Professor Juan de M. Carriazo of the University of
Seville. This site is on the top of a hill called El Carambolo, about two miles
from the city, in the grounds of the Royal Seville Pigeon Shooting Society. This
society was enlarging its premises in readiness for an international meeting in
1959 and in September 1958, during the construction of a small formal garden,
workmen found just below the surface a massive gold bracelet; and then,
near-by and a little deeper, in a pottery vessel, the remainder of the gold
treasure, another bracelet, a necklace, two breastplates and sixteen rectangular
plaques. On excavation the site proved to be the foundations of a building with
a very thick layer of ashes containing lumps of clay bearing impressions of bark
and wood. There were quantities of animal bones, but none human, and very
large numbers of broken pottery fragments; two arrowheads of bronze or
copper and lumps of the same metal and a mass of what appears to be iron;
a small baked pottery ladle of Neolithic type and some fragments of ostrich
eggs (Plate 7).

The gold treasure is extremely well preserved, of 24-carat gold and of a total
weight of 94.8 oz Troy. All the pieces are of virtually the same design and must
have constituted a "set". The basis of the decoration is alternating parallel

lines of bosses and recessed pans usually containing rosettes and these parallel lines are separated by lines of tiny bosses. The two bracelets—which are both extremely massive and nearly five inches wide—and eight of the plaques (which are simple rectangles, four of them $4\frac{3}{8} \times 2\frac{3}{8}$ in, the other four $4\frac{3}{8} \times 1\frac{3}{4}$ in) exactly follow this pattern. Eight other plaques, $3\frac{1}{2} \times 2$ in, are slightly simpler, the bosses being recessed, the pans being plain without any rosettes. The two breastplates are like rectangles with the corners pulled out—not unlike the shape of an animal skin rug, without head or tail—and here the same principle of decoration is simply adapted to fill in this rather odd shape. The necklace, a chain carrying a group of seven pendant seals—there was originally an eighth—is slightly more sophisticated. The seals are somewhat after the style of fob seals and the decoration of the setting varies, there are three pairs and an odd man out, which was doubtless matched by the missing one. It is suggested that they formed the regal panoply of a single person: the necklace and its pendents with the eight seals of office hung round the neck, a massive bracelet was on each upper arm, a breastplate on either side of the breast and the sixteen plaques probably adorned a belt—a magnificent and barbaric spectacle. Who would the wearer be? A king of Tartessos, it is suggested, of the seventh or early sixth century B.C.

What was Tartessos? And who were the Tartessians? Little is known about them and their country,, except for literary sources. They were known to the Greeks, their country is the Tarshish of the Bible, they are mentioned in various itineraries, notably that of Rufius Festus Avienus. They lived around the lower Guadalquivir (which was itself called Tartessos); they were rich in agricultural assets and their abundant mineral resources included gold, silver, copper and tin; they were organized as a powerful kingdom and the names of some of their kings are known, the most famous being Argantonius, who lived for 120 years, ruled over Tartessos for eighty years and died about 550 B.C. It is tempting to think that this is perhaps the panoply of such a legendary patriarch—the "Treasure of Argantonius" has a romantic ring; but the Phoenicians were established not far away, having set up Gades (Cadiz) as a trading centre about 1100 B.C.; and a further study of the materials and the site will be necessary before the identification with Tartessos is complete.

In 1952 and 1953, not far from Santander in northern Spain, the Rev Dr Jesus Carvallo found two more caves with Aurignacian drawings on the walls in the celebrated Monte Castillo at Puento Viesgo. This is a conical hill beside the River Pas and early this century it was found to be riddled with caves containing drawings of Aurignacian, Solutrean and Magdalenian date, that is to say from about 20,000 to 15,000 years ago, flint tools, especially of the Magdalenian period and considerable remains of cave bear, including a complete skeleton —a remarkable discovery inasmuch the cave bear was not previously thought to have lived in Spain, or at all events to have been contemporary with *homo sapiens* there. In general the drawings in the Monte Castillo are not equal to those of near-by Altamira, being usually earlier and plainer in style, but the caves themselves are more spectacular and those that were known had been made accessible and lit with electric light. Until the 1952 discovery seven large caves were known, of which two contained drawings, the Castillo and the Pasiega caves. Engineers, under Dr Garcia Lorenzo, were however continuing the search for other caves, which Dr Carvallo believed would be found lower in the mass of the hill; and in April 1952 an eighth cave was found which was called Las Monedas. This is a fantastic and complex cavern, more than 175 yards long, with several forks, a petrified waterfall, a hall with stalagmites like organ pipes of alabaster and a low vaulted chamber with some twenty-eight drawings all made with charcoal points and in outline only. The majority are Aurignacian (c 20,000 years ago) but some may be a little later, of the period called Solutrean. The quantities of animals represented are as follows: horses, 13; goats, 4; bison, 3; deer, 2; bulls, 2; bears, 1. The drawing of the bear is especially interesting in as much as it is only the second one known in Spain, the other being at Cortezuli, Vizcaya. There is one tiny human figure, of Neolithic age. The drawings of horses are the most interesting from the artistic point of view: one, headless, being like a rapid calligraphic Chinese drawing, while another, which is probably among the later drawings, is full of warmth and character, an individual pony, standing slightly depressed by the weather, seen by an artist and captured by his hand. Quantities of cave bear bones, but no complete skeleton, were found.

In September 1953, Dr Lorenzo found another cave which Dr Carvallo promptly explored. This was extremely difficult of access, even after some blasting, but after an entry had been made it was found that some of the stalactites had been coloured red and it was evident that prehistoric man had been there; and it was assumed that there was another entrance. This was found and it led to a gallery some eighty-two yards long, like a forest of white columns, extremely beautiful but containing neither carvings nor drawings. But it was found to lead to a semicircular chamber or hall with a low ceiling and smooth walls and about 97 × 91 ft. This contained both drawings and engraved pictures. It is Dr Carvallo's theory that the men who made these drawings made them as prayers for success in the chase and that such prayers were made in the greatest seclusion possible and that therefore the drawings are normally to be found in the remotest parts of such systems of caves. The chamber of drawings in this particular cave—which has been named the Chimneys cave— is a case in point; and Dr Carvallo considers that it can perhaps be thought of as a holy place, a "palaeolithic oratory" in the network of caves which make Monte Castillo a positive troglodyte city.

The drawings in this particular cave included some of the enigmatic quadrilateral designs, often cross-hatched, which are not infrequent in such caves, but they are mainly animal drawings and mostly, like those of Las Monedas, charcoal outline drawings. The subjects include: two small bulls in combat, a bull, a deer, a goat, a stag, a fine complete drawing of a she-goat and a heifer; the hindquarters of an elephant, a beautiful horse's head, goats and deer and three very clear stags with large horns which may perhaps be identified with *Cervus megaceros*. In addition there were several engraved pictures, which had been originally made in clayey, chalky rock, some with the finger, others with flint or wood points. These last included bulls, a deer and a goat. Another long gallery was found, about $65\frac{1}{2}$ yds long, and in this there were traces of red drawings, but traces only, which it was impossible to distinguish.

CHAPTER EIGHT

SICILY, LIPARI, SARDINIA

ARCHAEOLOGICAL activity in Sicily since the war has been directed with energy and with purpose—and with the blessing and assistance of the Italian Government who have rightly regarded the exploration and revelation of Sicily's extremely rich past as a constructive way of helping a poverty-stricken island to reap a rich harvest from the tourist; and, perhaps most important of all, this activity has been blessed with amazing luck and has brought rich rewards.

Luck played an especial part in two discoveries in the early '50's which both throw unique light on Sicily's remotest past, while one is unique anywhere in the world: the cave drawings in the island of Levanzo; and those on Monte Pellegrino near Palermo.

Levanzo is a rocky desolate islet to the west of Trapani at the north-west extremity of Sicily, inhabited by fishermen and riddled with caves. In 1949 a young Italian artist, Signorina Franca Minellono, while visiting the island, entered a cave by chance and saw on the walls of it a number of stylized human figures painted in black; sketched some copies of these and later showed them to Professor Paolo Graziosi in Florence. He recognized them as the rather stick-shaped men and "violin" women of the eneolithic period, which are well-known in Spanish caves but rare in Italian; and accordingly went to Levanzo himself to study and record them and found excellent examples of these types in association with similarly stylized paintings of mammals, fish and dagger-like objects; and in the floor of this grotto, which he partly excavated, he found examples of eneolithic and also the earlier Gravettian industry, together with the remains of various pleistocene animals, oxen, stags and horses such as *Bos primigenius, Cervus elephas* and *Equus hydruntinus*. But, far more important, he found a narrow passage leading to an inner chamber of the grotto, on whose walls were more examples of the Neolithic paintings—and a series of splendid much older naturalistic engravings of the animals whose remains he had found in the outer cave. Outstanding among these are a young stag, looking over its shoulder, a fully grown stag, bulls and cows and an early type of horse. These were at the time the first completely naturalistic drawings of the palae-olithic period to be found in Italy and are comparable with the Franco-Cantabrian animal drawings of the period. Furthermore the presence of the drawings and the remains of the animals concerned suggest that the islet, now 11 miles off shore, was then linked with the mainland of Sicily by broad fertile plains.

Meanwhile remains of the same animals had been found by Signora Iole Bovio Marconi and Professor Bernabo Brea in caves in the slopes of Monte Pellegrino near Palermo. One of these caves (Addaura II) had been used during the war to store some shells and in 1945 these munitions were demolished in the cave by some unit of the Allied Forces. The force of the explosion violently shook down the stalagmites and various concretions on the wall and revealed the bare surface, but at the same time covered it with thick dust. By 1952 however wind and dripping water partly cleared the walls and a sportsman, taking shelter, noticed engravings on the surface; and this information was reported to Signora Bovio Marconi, who is the Superintendent of north-west Sicily; and she was able to discover about thirty engraved figures, all palaeolithic and all rather small (between 5 and 15 in high)—and all well preserved, since they had been covered with limey deposits for thousands of years until the explosion of the shells brought them to light again.

These engravings are of the greatest interest: first because the animal figures are primitive and stylized while the human figures are detailed and naturalistic —which is an exact reversal of what is usual in palaeolithic cave art; and secondly because the human figures, which are full of movement and beauty, are for the most part integrated into an extraordinarily vivid scene of a very grim nature.

These human figures are naked, with two possible exceptions, and are drawn in outline and shown as having a graceful and elegant physique. There is no attempt to portray the extremities of the arms and legs—which calls to mind the "Three Graces" of Angles-sur-l'Anglin—the heads have masses of long hair, but the faces are either highly schematized or masked, probably the latter, since some, at any rate are clearly seen to be wearing strongly beaked bird masks.

The scene referred to is composed with considerable art and is concerned only with male figures—although female figures appear elsewhere on the wall— and of these there are seven standing in a rough circle about what appear to be two "acrobats" performing evolutions on the ground in the centre. Four of the standing figures are simply watching the evolutions; two, both wearing bird masks, appear to be dancing, with their arms raised above their heads; the seventh, also masked and a powerful and imposing figure, stands in a manner strongly suggesting that he is directing the rite. The two "acrobats" are face downwards upon the ground, but violently arched in a bow and are both markedly ithyphallic. It was at first suggested that they were wearing light capes and that this was perhaps some initiation ceremony; but a later suggestion is that the lines (which were thought to indicate capes) are in fact cords, tightly drawn from the neck to the ankles, thus causing the violent arching of the body and, in time, the inevitable self-strangulation of the "acrobats"—a theory supported by the condition of erection (Plate 10).

However this may be, the scene is unique, extremely vivid and the individual figures are of great beauty; and to quote the Abbé Breuil, the doyen of palaeolithic cave drawings and engravings—"This is a new capital fact in palaeolithic art". All, moreover, revealed by the routine demolition of a few defective artillery shells.

It was however in its Greek period that Sicily reached its highest glories and greatest prosperity: a period which began with the arrival of Greek colonists at many points on the coasts of the island from the eighth century B.C.; reached its zenith in the fifth when Syracuse was the rival of Athens; and entered on its decline in the third, when the Sicilian Greeks, for the most part, backed the wrong horse in the wars between Rome and Carthage and were broken in the victory of Rome—though naturally Hellenic influences survived for long after Magna Graecia was in decline.

Work illuminating this period has been going on principally at three sites since the war: Gela; Serra Orlando, now identified with Morgantina; and Selinunte.

Gela, which lies on the south coast of the island, was the subject of considerable excavations early in the century. During the early 50's it has undergone a fresh archaeological survey under the direction of Dr Dino Adamesteanu, with especial reference to the spread of the Greek colonists into the interior.

The founders of Greek Gela were settlers from Rhodes and Crete who arrived about the beginning of the seventh century B.C.; and it now appears that they had made considerable advances inland very soon afterwards at a number of points, notably at Butera, which they made a stronghold to dominate their road into the hinterland, and where a monumental burial vault has been found. These excavations and the accident of building operations in Gela itself have revealed a number of characteristically delightful Gelan terracotta works. The hill of Gela had no stone and its artists as a result developed an especial skill in terracotta, particularly in the production of antefixes in the form of Silenus and Gorgon heads. The most striking discovery, however, in recent years is a great fortification wall of dressed stone, topped with mud-brick. This has been remarkably well-preserved as the result of being buried in sand-dunes; and it now presents a truly outstanding and in some respects unique example of Greek military architecture (Plate 8).

As implied above, most of the Greek sites in Sicily are coastal, at least in the beginnings; the Serra Orlando site, which has now been revealed as Morgantina, lies well inland from the east coast of Sicily, in the province of Enna. It was indeed for this reason that it was chosen by the expedition sponsored by Princeton University and jointly directed by Professors Erik Sjoqvist and Richard Stilwell which began work there in 1955. The idea was to find out how soon the Greek colonists established themselves in the interior. The site which occupies a two-mile-long ridge about 1,600 ft above sea level has revealed prehistoric layers dating from about the twelfth century B.C. and these huts continue until at least the eighth and possibly later centuries. By the middle of the sixth century however large rectangular houses of mud-brick on stone foundations are found in many parts of the acropolis and it is quite clear that there was an inland Greek city established by this date by pioneers from the east coast of the island—a discovery which revises previous opinions about the status of the Greeks and the native Siculians at this time in history. Decorative terra-cotta reliefs have been found dating from this period and a quantity of fragments of imported Attic pottery. A rock-cut tomb of this period, a family tomb, was built in the Siculian manner, but contained an extraordinarily wide range of pottery—good quality imported Attic black-figure ware, local Siculian pots, pots made locally by the Greek colonists in imitation of the Attic ware and imported Corinthian ware—all of which strongly suggests a rich settlement (which could afford to import) an established place (which could set up its own manufactures) and a place on reasonable relations with the indigenous inhabitants, in as much as it was using their burial habits and their local pottery in ceremonial circumstances.

Much the same combination of pottery—local ware with imports of Corinthian, Ionic and Attic black figure pottery was found in 1953 in archaic tombs at Megara Hyblaea, a Chalcidicean Greek colony on the east coast a little north of Syracuse during excavations conducted by the French School at Rome and the Supervisory Body of Syracusan Antiquities. In addition these tombs yielded a splendid red-figure Attic *crater*, used as a cinerary urn and dating from about 470 B.C.; and a quite unique piece of sculpture of the sixth century—a limestone seated figure of a nursing mother, suckling twins. This lacks the head, but when complete must have been about three feet high; and it is a powerful and realistic work quite unlike the classical Greek ideal.

However, to return to Morgantina: this settlement came to an abrupt end about the middle of the fifth century B.C. when the native Siculians are reported to have conquered and destroyed the town; and it was not until the mid-fourth century that Morgantina prospered again. Its prosperity then was great and its agora was laid out on a truly monumental scale towards the end of the century and it seems likely that it was promoted under the patronage of Agathocles, King of Syracuse. Great flights of steps, 180 ft wide, surround it on three sides and although the project was never finished, being interrupted by the First Punic War (264–261 B.C.), it remains, as it has been laid bare by the excavators, a truly impressive sight and one of the finest and best-preserved Hellenistic agoras outside Asia Minor. After the Second Punic War, the victorious Romans gave the city to the Spaniard Moericus and his mercenaries for their services during the campaign; and even in the second century, the coinage of the city, in the general style of the beautiful Syracusan coins, bore the Latin inscription HISPANORUM. During this period a number of pleasant residential buildings were erected, some with attractive mosaics and a new and smaller market-place was built. The city was in decline and by the time of Augustus Strabo could say that "Morgantina used to be a town, but now it does not exist".

Towards the western end of the south coast of Sicily stand the ruins of another Greek colony, Selinunte, and this during recent years has been the scene of intense activity under the direction of Signora Iole Bovio Marconi,

Superintendent of Antiquities of North-west Sicily. These ruins include the remains of three temples; and one of them, the second largest and the most classically beautiful, is being re-erected, using only the surviving material from the great tumbled mound of column drums and other architectural members, except where occasionally a little new stone is needed for reasons of support. It is a large temple, some 220 ft long by 83 ft wide, with six columns on the short sides and fifteen on the long; and it is a Doric temple of great purity, probably though not certainly dedicated to Hera. By 1958 practically all the columns had been re-erected and most of the capitals are in position—a quite considerable feat of precision engineering as is clear when one realizes that each capital weighs about 20 tons. The replacement of the cross-members and the restoration of the architraves and triglyph remained to be done; but enough had been done by this date—in a possibly unique feat of reconstruction—to bring back the splendours of that magnificent building which the citizens of Selinunte raised between 470 and 460 B.C.—and which probably fell into disuse after that period of disaster for the Greeks in Sicily, the Second Punic War of the mid-third century B.C.

It is however to the period when Sicily had become a mere, though delightful, appanage of Rome and indeed a period when Rome itself was in decadence and the centre of power was shifting to that Byzantium which was soon to become Constantinople, that the most splendid post-war discoveries in Sicily are to be dated. These are without question the mosaics of the fourth century A.D. imperial villa at Piazza Armerina.

This magnificent villa stands some 5 km from Piazza Armerina, near the ancient main road which crossed the interior of the island from Catania to Agrigentum, not far from Enna, the flowery landscape where Pluto carried off the lovely Proserpine to be his queen in Hell. The site was identified early in the last century and was the scene of some excavations as early as 1889. Serious excavation was begun in 1929 and a large and splendid mosaic of a massacre of giants by Hercules was discovered. These and others were restored and covered and the work suspended owing to the war, and the extraordinary nature of the discoveries was not made known until 1949. In 1950 the task of continuing the excavations on a worthy scale and with adequate financial support was entrusted to the Antiquities Department of Eastern Sicily under the direction of Professor Gino Vinicio Gentili. It soon became clear that this was a truly magnificent villa and that the mosaics were the largest and finest Roman mosaics known. It was clear too that this was so rich and luxurious an establishment that it could only have been maintained by an Emperor or a nobleman, in Dr Johnson's phrase "rich beyond the dreams of avarice"; and that perhaps the most astonishing thing was that there appeared to be no reference to it in literature or history. To be brief on this point, it is now generally believed that it was indeed an Imperial villa; and that the Emperor in question was Herculius Maximinianus, a common soldier from Pannonia, who was elevated to the purple by his friend the Emperor Diocletian in A.D. 283 and who abdicated (albeit reluctantly) with Diocletian in 304, reassumed the purple the same year, fled from his son Maxentius, and after unsuccessfully attempting the murder of his son-in-law, Constantine (who had married Maximinian's daughter Faustina) committed suicide in A.D. 310 at the age of 60. Gibbon briskly says of him: "Ignorant of letters, careless of laws, the rusticity of his appearance and manners still betrayed in the most elevated fortune the mean-ness of his extraction. War was the only art which he professed."

Nothing of this, it seems safe to say, appears in the splendid mosaics which appear to reflect, in the most elaborate way, to be sure, the tastes and humours of a scholar and a gentleman, combined with a passionate love of animals and the chase. But perhaps Emperors were as frequently surprised by the achieve-ments of their stewards as modern governments are by the activities of the Arts Council (Plate 9).

The best-known of the mosaics—which is also the latest and the least satis-factory from an artistic point of view—is the group of "Bikini girls". Its fame derives from the oddity of its subject and the strange topicality of its style at the time when it became generally known, towards the end of 1951. It shows a group of girls, skimpily attired in tiny G-strings and narrow bras, almost ex-actly resembling the then fashionable two-piece bathing costumes called "Bikinis" from their presumably atomic effect on the bystanders. It was hazarded at the time by scholars that the mosaic represented a water-spectacle and indeed that it threw light on the gymnastic activities of women in the later Roman Empire. This may be so: one indeed is wielding dumb-bells, another the discus, another running; but another confines her activities to twirling a para-sol, and in the centre stands one, crowned with a garland of flowers and holding a branch of palm. It seems safe to assume, in the words of the once popular song, that "her bathing suit never got wet"; and that the scene is as topical as the costume and is in fact nothing more or less than a Bathing Beauty Contest.

The other mosaics are much more varied and of much greater art and higher craftsmanship. Besides the Labours of Hercules already mentioned there are many scenes from classical mythology: Eros and Pan; a Dionysus myth includ-ing the death of Lycurgus, the destroyer of the vines; scenes from marine myths, including Arion and the dolphin; Homeric subjects, such as Odysseus and Polyphemus; theatrical scenes; fanciful subjects such as Cupids fishing and gathering grapes and miniature circus scenes with children driving chariots drawn by birds; allegorical subjects such as a group of the Seasons; a chariot race and an unfortunately fragmentary torchlight race; and, richest of all, the two great hunting mosaics.

These two scenes are quite distinct in subject, though similar in manner, each consisting of a number of incidents linked in a wide and diversified landscape; and they can conveniently be distinguished under the titles "The Chase" and "The Big Game Hunt".

The Chase is concerned with hunting for the pot and for sport and involves the use of horses and dogs. Among its incidents are: the morning start; the pursuit of deer on horseback towards prepared nets; the capture of a wild boar; dogs chasing a wolf into a cave; hunting birds with birdlime and with hawks; hunting the hare on horseback with a spear—a vivid and rather pathetic scene, this; a sacrifice to Diana, goddess of the chase; and a delightful picnic, under an awning stretched across the branches of a tree, with the horses tethered near-by and the huntsmen reclining at their ease around a fat roasted bird.

The Big Game Hunt however is concerned with the capture of wild beasts, presumably for the amphitheatre; and it shows a variety of fights between animals, lions and panthers leaping on stags, huntsmen capturing lions and boars, a mounted huntsman galloping away from a tigress with a tiger-cub in his arms; a panther being beguiled into an open cage in which a kid is tethered, while huntsmen hide near by behind their broad shields; captured animals being carried into captivity, in carts, pulled along on ropes, carried in crates on poles between two huntsmen; a man carrying an ostrich in his arms up a gang plank into a waiting ship—these are the elements of this great picture; and in it is perhaps a portrait of Maximinian, a richly robed patrician, with two armed bodyguards watching the hunt; and finally, like a sudden change of key in a piece of music, an enigma, a winged griffin holding in his talons a cage in which crouches a man, signifying—what? The hunter hunted or the biter bit? Or the vanity of human pleasures?—and so perhaps a solitary secret Christian comment in an establishment otherwise completely pagan.

Light on the various (and obscure) movements of peoples and cultures which create the history and influence the development of Sicily and indeed the Western Mediterranean, has been shed by excavations in the near-by Aeolian Islands; and also, to some extent, by discoveries in Sardinia.

The Aeolian Islands lie some fifty miles to the north of the eastern end of Sicily's north coast; and excavations have been conducted there in the islands of Lipari and Panarea by Dr Bernabo Brea, Superintendent of the Antiquities of Eastern Sicily (at the expense of the Ministry of Instruction and the Sicilian Regional Council). At the Lipari site an extremely rich sequence of cultures was found: from a Neolithic contemporary with the oldest known in Sicily (that at Stentinello) through Late Neolithic, Early, Middle and Late Bronze Ages, to the Iron Age and the Greek, Roman and Mediaeval cities which followed each other on the site. Some of the characteristic Middle Bronze Age oval dwellings were found at Lipari; and a complete village of the same type on the promontory of Milazzese, a natural fortress on the island of Panarea. There are three successive types of Neolithic pottery, associated with a very prosperous stone industry, almost exclusively in obsidian; and it is to this valuable, in those days, volcanic glass that the growth of an export industry is due; and this perhaps accounts for the fact that in the Early Bronze Age layers have been found fragments of Minoan pottery (Late Minoan I.A., dating from about 1550 to 1450 B.C.) proving that the Minoans were already trading in the Western

Mediterranean as early as this. In the fourteenth century, as appears from pottery found in Panarea, the Mycenaeans followed in this trade; and evidently left a considerable mark in these islands, since fragments of locally made pottery have been found bearing signs (potters' marks, presumably) which closely resemble the Mycenaean linear script.

This is the period of Homeric legend; and one story, which Diodorus Siculus tells, concerns Liparus, son of Auson, king of the Ausonians of Latium and Campania, colonizing the islands and giving his name to the largest of them. This is confirmed in a general way by the appearance in the Late Bronze Age of a new type of pottery—characterized by cup and bowl handles in the form of animal heads and horns—which is closely related to the later "Apennine" culture of mainland Italy. This Ausonian type of pottery continues, mixed with Sicilian imports, but it would seem that the islands were in decline, and when Greeks from Cnidos arrived there in 580 B.C. they found only 500 inhabitants, the "descendants of King Aeolus", who invited them to stay and protect them; and from this point the Aeolian Islands are part of Magna Graecia.

The oval hut village of Panarea finds a visual parallel in the tightly packed township which has been revealed round the *nuraghe* of Barumini in the Cagliari province of Sardinia.

Nuraghi are towers in the form of truncated cones, constructed of huge stones, usually with hollow walls. They bear a strong physical resemblance to the broch towers, which are common in north-west Scotland and especially in the Shetland Islands, but some authorities claim that the resemblance is purely coincidental and that the *nuraghi* are confined to Sardinia. Be that as it may, there are literally hundreds of *nuraghi* in various stages of development and preservation in Sardinia; and the thousand years of Sardinia's history before the coming of the Carthaginians and the Romans is called the Nuraghic Age and is divided into various periods, Archaic, Primary, Middle Nuraghic and so on.

A very large *nuraghe*, with a complex township around it, at Barumini in southern central Sardinia, has been excavated during 1951 to 1956 by the Archaeological Service of Sardinia under the direction of Professor Giovanni Lilliu. Previously this monument was entirely covered with earth, ruins and scrub and resembled a small isolated hill. After clearing, the central tower, the *nuraghe* proper, stands over 45 ft high and the sequence of construction seems fairly clear. This central tower, built of megalithic basalt, cannot be later than 1070 B.C. and is probably earlier. It had three storeys and a spiral stair in the thickness of the wall. In the next phase, four subsidiary towers were added and linked with a curtain wall, in the courtyard behind which a well was sunk. In the third phase, the Upper Nuraghic Primary, the stronghold was much strengthened; the ground level entrance was closed and the only entry was by ladders, some 21 ft above ground; an outer wall was built and a watchtower, from which the commander called out his commands through conch-shells (some of which have been found). This period seems to have lasted from the eighth century to the end of the sixth, when the fort was dismantled after a long siege by the Carthaginians.

As regards the village which surrounded the stronghold. This may not have existed in the first phase, at all events no trace survives. During the second phase there were a number of oval huts of stone set in a clay mortar, very similar to Bronze Age dwellings in Sicily and Cyprus and those recently uncovered at Panarea. In one hut, which is however rectangular, there are pits cut in the stone pavement containing small votive offerings. In the third phase, which reflects the full Nuraghic civilization, there was a considerable population grouped round the stronghold and some sixty huts survive, including a large circular building with seating all round the interior and containing a betyle, a sacred stone representing a *nuraghe*, and a stone basin. A number of domestic objects and some bronze votives throw light on the daily life of the inhabitants; and some of them, especially bronze brooches, tell of contact with the Carthaginian and Italian mainland civilizations. After the Carthaginian massacres at the end of the sixth century B.C. Barumini entered on a slow decline. The inhabitants who survived returned to the site and a modest agricultural prosperity came into being, but its character became progressively modified under the periods of Carthaginian and Roman domination; and it appears to have dwindled out of existence about the time of Augustus.

Sardinia is of course remarkably little-known considering its position in the Mediterranean and its size; and a collection of the strange bronze statuettes which are characteristic of its Nuraghic civilization, which toured several European capitals and was shown by the Arts Council in London during November and December 1954 had positively the impact of a new and startling discovery.

CHAPTER NINE

ITALY

THE ancient history of Italy is so well documented and so many of those documents have become part of the treasury of the world's literature and, with Greece, have been the richest single inspiration and source material for that literature; and the soil of Italy has so long been a quarry from which the world's palaces and museums have been furnished—that it would seem unlikely that there was anything left to find. But that has not been the case: so bountiful is that soil and so rich, powerful and creative the civilizations which have possessed it that new, strange and beautiful things have continued to be revealed in it to a degree difficult to parallel anywhere else in the world.

Several things have contributed to this. Not least the enlightened attitude of the Government, who realizing that Italy's past is one of her greatest present assets—both spiritually and touristically—have made funds available to the Superintendencies of Antiquities for continued activity, as for example, at Pompeii, Stabiae and Baiae. Land reform has led to intensive cultivation in districts which were formerly wildernesses, with a consequent revelation of the hidden face of the past, as in Etruria. Land reclamation, as around Lake Comacchio, has led to the discovery of the great Etruscan city of Spina in the mud which has emerged from the waters. Modern methods of cultivation, in which the tractor-drawn plough digs a deeper furrow than ever before, have revealed long-hidden buildings, as at Paestum. Aerial photography has peered through the veil of the soil, as in the Etruscan cemetery-cities north of Rome; and such new techniques as the use of electrical resistivity methods and the ingenious "periscope photography" apparatus pioneered by the Fondazione Ing. Carlo M. Lerici (and described elsewhere in this book) have enormously speeded up the reconnaissance and preliminary stages of excavation, with a consequent great saving of time, labour and expense.

These last have been most spectacularly demonstrated in the great Etrurian necropolis sites, north of Rome, where there are literally thousands of burial mounds in immense cities of the dead. Many treasures from these tombs have of course been found in the past—and there is an especially rich collection of them in the Vatican Museum—and many of the tombs have been robbed at different times from antiquity onwards. They consist of rock-cut, or rock-built, chambers covered with a tall mound of earth; and, as a rule, these mounds have been ploughed flat with the result that the tomb chambers were lost to sight—but not to aerial photography. In the aerial photograph, taken at the appropriate seasons of the year, parch-marks or crop-marks, reveal as it were an X-ray view of the landscape. Mr John Bradford of Oxford University first examined Etruria from the air during the war while serving in Italy; and in subsequent years began compiling maps from aerial photographs of many of the Etruscan necropolises. At Tarquinia, he mapped over 800 levelled tumuli and at Cerveteri at least 400; at Monte Abbatone he was able to locate about 600 tombs; and at a smaller cemetery, at Colle Pantano, he found forty hitherto unmapped tombs. It is perhaps worth recording here that aerial photography proved so accurate and so revealing that not only was the outline of each tomb (invisible on the surface) clearly seen but the actual entrance to the tomb could be distinctly seen in very many cases.

In this district, with the support of the Superintendent of Antiquities of Southern Etruria, Professor Renato Bartoccini, the Lerici Foundation of the Milan Polytechnic, headed by Ing. Carlo M. Lerici, began to deploy the technical devices developed by this institution and, as described elsewhere, first exactly defined the area of selected tombs by means of electrical resistivity soundings; then, after locating by this means the centre of the tomb, drilled a hole through the roof of the tomb chamber; and inserted a metal tube, containing a source of light and a tiny Minox camera. By rotating the tube a series of, usually twelve, exposures was made; and this film, when developed and printed, would reveal the contents of the tomb before ever a spade was inserted. Later, this apparatus, called usually the "photographic recorder" and the technique, generally known as "periscope photography" were further developed with the use of the Nistri periscope, by means of which the observer can see inside the tomb, before deciding whether photography, with its consequent delays and expense, is necessary.

Among the most interesting discoveries made by this means was a painted tomb (the first to be discovered since 1892 in this district) found in March 1958 at Tarquinia. In view of the forthcoming Olympic Games in Rome, the subject had a poetic appropriateness, as it showed a group of athletes running, leaping, dancing and throwing the discus. At Vulci, a large five-chambered tomb was found—evidently a family tomb used over a period of years—containing inscriptions in Etruscan and Latin (though not a bilingual inscription) and an elaborately carved sarcophagus with scenes in high relief showing a massacre of maidens watched by the winged figures of two deities, the male and bearded Charun and the female Vanth (Plate 56f and g).

Meanwhile, in much the same district, the British School at Rome, under its Director Mr J. B. Ward Perkins, is engaged on a surface survey of as many as possible of the antiquities in the area to the north and west of Rome, between the Tiber and the sea, the heart-land in fact of ancient Etruria. This is a very considerable task and one which it is impossible to summarize adequately here; and it is perhaps sufficient to mention briefly a few things which have emerged. First, a system of Etruscan roads which will bear comparison with anything the Romans achieved in the same area a few centuries later—roads designed for heavy traffic and furnished with surface drainage, cuttings and tunnels; second, a system of *cuniculi* with which the Veii district is honeycombed. These are underground tunnels with regular vertical shafts, which strongly resemble the well-known Persian *qanats*, but the *qanats* were built as aqueducts, whereas the *cuniculi* are drains, which have in fact saved this district from the erosion which is elsewhere common in the Etruscan landscape. Third is an early Roman road, the Via Amerina, which has been surveyed and found to contain, between Nepi and Falerii Novi what is most probably the oldest surviving Roman bridge. This was almost certainly built about 240 B.C. and is thus about twenty years older than the previous claimant to the title, the Ponte Milvio, in Rome.

In the summer of 1954, an even more spectacular discovery in the field of Etruscan archaeology was made just south of the Po delta, in the area of Lake Comacchio. This large area of water and swamp, it is known, came into existence in the Middle Ages as a result of a shifting of the earth's surface; and indeed the whole delta of the Po has moved northwards since antiquity. In this district stood the mixed Etruscan-Greek city of Spina and the news that the Italian government proposed to reclaim about 8,000 acres of marshland on the southern side of Lake Comacchio beside the River Pega was of great interest to archaeologists—and also to clandestine diggers, who, unlike the archaeologists, were prepared to work in some 16 in of water. However regular archaeological work, under the direction of Professor Paolo Enrico Arias of Catania University, was put in train, with astonishing success. The level areas of mud and sand emerging beside the drainage channels concealed an immense necropolis of the fifth century B.C. The tombs were found by probing with an iron rod; and digging was begun whenever the probe struck a solid object. The site was of course waterlogged, with the water-table about three feet down; and probably only workmen accustomed to working in these marshlands could have coped with it. In general the practice was to surround each excavation with a light caisson of hinged wood, to keep back the liquid mud. In these conditions it was often possible to "excavate" with a jet of water; and, as a result, innumerable beautiful fifth century Attic vases were discovered in almost perfect condition. Between 21 July and 30 September of this first year more than 180 tombs were excavated by these methods—which gives some idea of the richness of the site and the simplicity of this improvised technique. Most of the burials were inhumations, but the poorer ones were cremations, the ashes being placed in simple pots covered with a lid. The inhumations however were rich in grave goods, from the children's tombs—in which were found terracotta dolls with articulated limbs, seashells, and various toys among which may be mentioned a rattle in the form of a distended sun fish with a part-human face—to those rich tombs where the dead man had taken on his last journey large and splendid Attic vases of all types and of the greatest beauty, a number of gold objects, principally jewellery, and bronze candelabra decorated with miniature statuary of athletes and personages of Classical mythology (Plates 12 and 13).

One of the most splendid of the vases came from a tomb which contained two candelabra and eleven bronze vases. It is of the first half of the fourth century, in a style closely allied to that of Meidias and it stands 3 ft 7¼ in high with a separate and intact fluted base. It has two handles arching up to above the top rim and elaborately painted with palmettes and flowers. The subjects on the body of the vase fall into two groups: the upper register, on the neck between the handles shows a dance of Maenads on one side and on the other Heracles struggling with the wild boar of Calydon; while the lower register, below the handles, and on the vase's greatest circumference, shows on one side the murder of Priam and Cassandra and, on the other, the battle between the Centaurs and the Lapithae. Another two-handled vase, of austerer shape and earlier date (*c* 440 B.C.) shows Hephaistos returning to Olympus on horseback, accompanied by satyrs. On a drinking vessel a Silenus, disguised as Apollo, plays the harp to an audience of Hermes and Dionysus—a delightful scene in which the characters might well be the forbears of Feste, Sir Andrew Aguecheek and Sir Toby Belch. A type which is frequent and presumably popular—which would not be surprising in a maritime city—is a plate decorated with designs of fish, among which squids, John Dories and sardines are easily identifiable.

Among objects discovered later, and of especial interest, are a number of perfume bottles in fanciful shapes, such as a swimming duck, whose tail is the mouth of the bottle, stags, sphinxes, dogs and seated cattle; and a magnificent kylix or drinking cup of great size, nearly two feet across and with two handles, a ceremonial loving cup as it were, poised on a very small base and stem. Unfortunately it was found in fragments and its restoration posed a number of problems. Nevertheless it must rank as a masterpiece of Greek vase painting and is almost certainly by the master of the Penthesilea Cup (now at Munich) and dates from about 460 B.C. The central interior subject is two young men, one on horseback, lowering their spear points before an altar. Around them runs a frieze of the Labours of Theseus; and on the exterior, interspersed with palmettes, are two Homeric subjects—Odysseus and Ajax quarrelling over the arms of Achilleus in the presence of Agamemnon, and on the other side Achilleus and Memnon struggling before the goddess of the dawn, Eos.

Meanwhile aerial photography of this rich marshy area was revealing much of the plan of the city, as well as its necropolis; and it would seem that Spina, as indeed Spina it certainly is, was a town something like Venice, built on piles in a nexus of canals. Its area seemed from these photographs to cover about 850 acres.

Articulated terracotta dolls of the same kind as those discovered in the children's tombs of Spina, mentioned above, were found in some quantity in a cemetery just south of Paestum, which was discovered as the result of a bulldozer falling through into a tomb. This cemetery was accordingly excavated under the direction of Dr P. Claudio Sestieri, Superintendent of Antiquities for the Provinces of Salerno and Potenza. It was found to be a Greek cemetery of the fifth century B.C. re-used by their conquerors, the Lucanians, in the fourth century. The children's tombs alone contain terracotta figurines; and these figurines are peculiarly touching emblems of sympathy. A boy's grave contains a miniature bronze breastplate and figurines of dogs and other animals; a girl's on the other hand will have a miniature bronze mirror and neat terracotta dolls, whose jointed limbs are made so that the doll can sit or stand or be fitted with clothes; a baby's tomb will hold a rattle, a hollow ball of terracotta with a loose pebble inside; and many contain the comforting figurine of a goddess, who seems to combine the motherliness of Hera, mother of the gods, with the nature of Persephone, queen of the underworld.

This Hera-Persephone combination, a not unnatural one for a goddess of fecundity and fertility, is connected with what is undoubtedly the most remarkable discovery of all those made at Paestum, to say the least of it—the finding of the untouched underground shrine.

The excavations of the first site were extremely rewarding. The remains of eleven temples were found in addition to those already known and justly famous and among the quantities of votives found there was sufficient material to identify the deities concerned, so that the conventional names of Basilica, Temple of Neptune and Temple of Ceres can now be abandoned. The first two buildings are temples of Hera, while the third is a temple of Athene. In addition terracotta statues were found, ancient ivories, marble sculpture and quantities of fine vases, Attic, Corinthian and local.

The second site was at first disappointing, with Roman remains overlying poorly preserved Greek remains; but presently there came into view an enclo·sure wall for a temple, made of large blocks of squared limestone; and inside this precinct but below its ancient ground level there appeared the tiled roof of a small rectangular building, 13 ft long by $9\frac{3}{4}$ ft wide, and when the walls were cleared on three sides—the fourth side being built into the native rock—the building was found to have a total height of $7\frac{1}{4}$ ft—and to be in fact about the same size and pretty much the same shape as the average suburban gardener's greenhouse. It had however no entrance whatsoever and appeared never to have had one. One of the tiles was broken and this was removed; and the tiles were found to be supported by limestone slabs. One of these was broken and it was found possible to remove part and so make an aperture into the interior. A hand mirror was used to direct some light into the interior and all, director, workers, bystanders peered into the darkness and speculated on the contents. It appeared to be a tomb—but burials were forbidden inside the city; perhaps it was the tomb of the founder of Poseidonia; at all events it was clear that it had been untouched for some 2,500 years; and it was with very strong emotions that Professor Sestieri lowered himself by means of a ladder into the darkness of a sanctuary, which, it became clear, had been purposely designed to be concealed from all human eyes, a sanctuary without door or windows and whose roof was some $3\frac{1}{2}$ in below ground level. Along the north and south walls were ranged eight bronze vases of exquisite workmanship, six hydrias and two amphoras filled with pure honey; and in the north-east corner a large Attic amphora, intact and in the best period of the black-figure style.

In the centre beside a bench made of two pairs of blocks of stone were what had appeared at first to be bones but which were in fact iron rods, to which were attached the remains of pieces of wood and some metal network—in other words the remains of a bed. The walls were covered with a thin white plaster except for the middle blocks of the small east side and the ceiling also was plastered; and it is clear that an entrance had been left in the east end until the last minute, when all the offerings had been placed in position and that this entrance was eventually sealed from the outside. This was in fact a tomb; but a tomb without a body, not the tomb of anyone who had died in the ordinary sense of that word, but the tomb of a deity. From the richness of the offerings, no minor demigod or nymph, but a major divinity; from the nature of the offerings, vessels associated with water, and the contents, honey, a goddess not a god. But the deities of Olympus are immortal—except for one, Persephone, who is born each spring when she returns from the underworld and dies each winter when she returns to Hades. On fragments of pottery in the precinct appears the letter M, which could stand for *Mētēr* (mother); and it may well be that this strange shrine is the ceremonial tomb of Hera-Persephone, mother-goddess, fertility goddess, year-spirit; and that here is the centre of one of those mystery-cults which underlie the bland surface of Olympian religion and of which we know so little.

The nine vessels in the shrine are of the greatest interest and beauty. The amphora, which dates from the second half of the sixth century B.C. is a noble, simple and dignified vessel with two unadorned handles. On its side, below a frieze of double palmettes are two vivacious scenes in black-figure: a bacchic dance of satyrs and maenads; and the apotheosis of Heracles, borne to Olympus in Athene's chariot. The eight bronze vessels—a unique collection for Southern Italy—recall the splendid crater of Vix (described in the chapter on France) but no single one is so richly elaborate. Five are hydrias of the same general shape, with two horizontal handles and one vertical handle; and it is on these vertical handles that the artist's skill and fancy seem to have been lavished. One is a lion standing on its hind legs, resting its forepaws on the rim and seeming to look into the vessel; in another the lion's head remains, but the body is stylized-away and joins the curve of the vase between two female heads; in three others, the handle joins the rim between two small *couchant* lions, while the lower end becomes a superbly modelled woman's head—full of character though only an inch high—with hair in four plaits, between two *couchant regardant* rams. The sixth vase is a small amphora with the handles in the form of two clenched fists; and a second amphora and a final hydria have similar ornaments and seem to have come from the same workshop.

Even so the riches of Paestum were not exhausted; and with the development of agricultural reform and continued deep cultivation in the plain of Sele, the discoveries in the Greek and later Lucanian cemetery to which we have already referred in connexion with the children's tombs, continued with close co-operation between the tractor-drivers and the archaeologists; and a number of untouched tombs were uncovered. Many of the tombs are painted and these are Lucanian tombs mostly of the fourth century. The style is mostly that of the earlier Greek and it is possible that Greek painters were working for their Lucanian conquerors: but on the whole the paintings are less accomplished and the figures are often rather chubby. They are however vigorous and lively and can perhaps be considered as supplying an interesting link between Greek and Roman painting. In general the short sides of the tombs show scenes relating to the life of the occupant, while the long sides show funeral customs, including gladiatorial games and dancing. One long wall, for instance shows a race for two-horse chariots; another, gladiators laying on with a will, all bleeding from at least one wound. A short wall shows a seated matron spinning wool while her maidservant brings in some more wool; another shows a warrior returning in triumph on a rather hairy-maned horse to be greeted by his wife holding out a cup of wine. He is wearing a plumed helmet and a breastplate, which is made up of three circles of metal.

Precisely such a bronze breastplate was found in a tomb in the Fuscillo district, where a warrior was discovered in a complete set of parade armour. This comprised the bronze trefoil already mentioned, which had been attached to a leather doublet; a bronze sword-belt whose ornament included birds, a griffin and a gazelle; a lightweight bronze helmet mounted on thin leather with two wings and cheek pieces and between the wings a socket for a plume. By his side lay a lance, a dagger and a second sword-belt. By his feet were wine craters. All the tombs were liberally furnished with pottery and vases, mostly of Greek origin; and it is noteworthy that the Lucanians put far more pots in their tombs than did their predecessors the Greeks.

Not far from Paestum the ancient and wealthy Greek colony of Velia (to give it its Roman name) or Elea, to give it the Greek fourth century name, has been very largely excavated, also under the direction of Dr Sestieri; and much of its fine architecture, set in one of the most beautiful parts of southern Italy, has been revealed.

A little farther north, in the Superintendency of Antiquities of Campania, under the famous Professor Amedeo Maiuri, work of the greatest interest has been going forward. In 1951 an ambitious programme of excavations at Pompeii was begun, with a grant of funds from the Italian Government. So familiar a tourist spectacle has Pompeii been for so many years, that it was something of a shock to realize that at that date two-fifths of the site remained to be uncovered. At the other end of the Bay of Naples and in the same year Professor Maiuri resumed excavations at Baia, ancient Baiae, the world's first fashionable spa and Imperial Rome's most luxurious holiday resort—and, incidentally, the scene of Nero's killing of his mother in A.D. 59. Here on the cliff slope, where such of Baiae, as is not under water, is now to be found, have been uncovered a series of terraces, together with a nymphaeum pool which was probably designed for aquatic spectacles; and it is no difficult feat of the imagination to repeople these terraces with the rich, the luxurious, the beautiful, the dissolute and the infirm of Nero's time in the sort of scene that perennially fascinates and disgusts the satirist.

Much of Baiae, however, is now under water as a result of relatively modern earth movements; and the plan of the ancient town is clearly visible from the air. Here skin divers, led by Signor Raimondo Bucher, have been exploring the remains.

At Stabiae, now Castellamare di Stabia, which was overwhelmed in the same eruption of Vesuvius as that which buried Pompeii and Herculaneum in A.D. 79 Professor Libero d'Orsi, under the higher direction of Professor Maiuri, began excavations on a small scale in 1950 which were however crowned with considerable success. Two villas of considerable luxury were uncovered, one at Fondo de Martino, the other at Fondo dello Ioio, of great architectural interest. But undoubtedly the finds of the greatest interest and peculiar value were the fragments of Roman painting, mostly figure painting and portraits; and although some of these are excellent examples of what one might expect, a number of others, which it is tempting to think are by the same hand, are extraordinarily modern and impressionistic. They are painted in a rapid confident manner, catching in each case a moment of time and a moment of emotion, in a way which recalls Gertrude Stein's pregnant phrase "verb pictures" as opposed to "noun pictures" (Plate 11).

In Rome itself on the Aventine Hill, an interesting excavation was begun by the Augustinian Fathers, but later with the permission of Professor Pietro Romanelli, carried on by the Dutchmen Drs M. J. Vermaseren and C. C. van Essen. This underground excavation was at first thought to be in the premises of that Prisca who was baptised by St Paul; but this proved incorrect and a new interest developed from the fact that Mithraic ceremonies had taken place in the underground rooms next door in about A.D. 195. The premises, which are relatively large in view of the enclosed nature of Mithraism, had been wrecked in antiquity, presumably by Christians, and all the finds are fragmentary. Nevertheless paintings can still be discerned showing a procession of the grades through which the Mithraist passed, a sacrifice of a ram, a boar and a bull by members of the grade of "Lion", other "Lions" carrying offerings and watching Mithras and Sol partaking of a sacrificial meal; and inscriptions of the opening lines of Mithraic hymns. Fragments of marble and plaster sculpture were found, with certain striking resemblances to those found in the London Mithraeum. In particular there is a plaster Serapis head, obviously derived from the same Bryaxis original as the marble Serapis found in London, but in the Rome Mithraeum this formed part of a reclining figure, which incorporated a lead pipe carrying water to a purification vessel below. A marble torso of an ephebe, identified as Dionysus, was found which is very like the marble torso found in London. Other statuary includes a head of Venus (perhaps the planet rather than the goddess) a Mithras head with cast-up eyes, an initiate's head with a rapt expression and a statuette of a standing full-length Serapis. This excavation, while of the greatest interest intrinsically, gains an additional interest from the fact that it was taking place at exactly the same time as the dramatic discovery of the Mithraeum in the City of London.

At near-by Tivoli, since 1950, extensive excavations have been conducted in that part of Hadrian's Villa known as Canopus, under the direction of Professor Pietro Romanelli, and an extraordinary wealth of statues in the Greek style and copies of Greek originals has come to light, presumably executed for that great lover of art and all things Greek, the Emperor Hadrian. Notable among these are four 10-ft high marble caryatids which closely resemble the famous caryatids of the Erechtheum on the Acropolis at Athens (one of which is in the British Museum). All the Erechtheum caryatids have lost their hands. The Tivoli caryatids however have theirs and all have approximately the same pose—one hand holds a circular cake while the other lightly lifts the hem of the *peplos*. Other statues found included two reclining river gods, Tiber and Nile, colossal statues of Mars and Mercury, and, strangest of all, a huge Silenus acting as a pillar in the manner of a caryatid. The original canal of the Canopus feature has been excavated and restored and many of the newly-found statues have been erected on its brink to form a delightful and evocative *mise-en-scène*.

More recently, a great number of ancient statues have been found in the area of Professor Giulio Jacopi, Superintendent of Antiquities, Rome I. Among these may be briefly mentioned a marble Sylvanus with a dog, found near the Appian Way, a delightful small marble statue of an actor in the role of the Angry Old Man, found in the underwater remains of a villa near Anzio, and a rare, full-length statue of the Emperor Antonius Pius which admirably captures the mild, benevolent and philosophic temperament with which history credits him.

Professor Jacopi's most astonishing discovery, however, is the great mob of statues, still, at the time of writing, emerging from the Grotto of Tiberius on the sea coast at Sperlonga, not far from Terracina (Plates 14 and 15).

This is a cave opening on the seashore between Gaeta and Terracina, into which the sea-water flows in certain conditions of stormy weather. Its name derives from a tradition that it was here that Sejanus saved the life of the Emperor Tiberius from a fall of rock. At all events in the summer of 1957 fragments of first-rate Greek sculpture in marble began to be discovered there and in the excavations directed by Professor Jacopi these rapidly increased in splendour and number. Among the chief first pieces to be found were some anguished heads and torsos and what seemed to be the body of a huge snake or monster—and an inscription reading: "Athanodoros (son) of Agesander, Age(sa)nder (son) of (Pha)nia and (Poli)doros (son) of (Polid)oros." Now these are the names given by Pliny to three sculptors of Rhodes who executed the statue of Laocoon for the House of Titus. Furthermore it was in the remains of the House of Titus that the world-famous Laocoon group which is now in the Vatican was discovered in the time of Michelangelo. These things being so it was at once assumed that here in the Sperlonga grotto was the original of the Laocoon; and it was perhaps this assumption that insured such world-wide publicity for the discovery.

It would now appear that this was a false assumption—though so great is the quantity of fragments that there may still be a version of the Laocoon story to be assembled from this gigantic three-dimensional jigsaw. Laocoon or no Lao-coon, the discoveries and the potential are far more exciting. It is surely far better to find an unknown masterpiece than a copy of a known one; and it seems strange to assume that a team of sculptors capable of the Laocoon group were capable of nothing else.

Another inscription was found which is fragmentary but which can never-theless be deciphered as an epigram in Latin verse by Faustinus, a rich dilet-tante and a friend of the poet Martial, who claims to have adorned the cave with sculpture and in the verse refers to the *crudelitas Scyllae*, "the cruelty of Scylla", the legendary female monster who, with the whirlpool Charybdis, made the Straits of Messina such a hazard for sailors, among whom were Odysseus and his men. A number of the fragments—the anguished heads and bodies already mentioned, the monstrous serpent fragments and a large piece showing a bearded sailor clutching a rudder—could perhaps be parts of a group showing the struggle between Odysseus and his crew with Scylla. One fragment shows a hand in the Hellenistic style clutching a small statuette of a goddess with staring eyes and in the archaic style. It was at first suggested that this was part of a group showing Odysseus and Diomedes carrying off the Palladium at the sack of Troy; but Professor Jacopi, following a scholiast's note to Aristophanes' *Acharnians*, points out that many ships carried a Pallad-ium-like statue as a tutelary deity; and that what we have here may be another part of Scylla group, a sailor holding aloft the image of the goddess in an attempt to avert Scylla's attack.

Among other interesting fragments found are a colossal leg and hand, which are in scale with a statue nearly twenty feet high; a beautiful marble head of Athene wearing a Corinthian helmet; a cheerful bearded Silenus head crowned with ivy leaves and berries; and a colossal Ganymede carried off by the eagle. This last, which was found near the entrance of the cave is of a bluish marble except for the head of Ganymede, which is white; and this may be a marble version of a bronze group, referred to by Pliny but no longer surviving, by the fourth century master Leochares. This was perhaps the most striking single piece found before winter compelled the breaking off of the excavations. Structurally these excavations had revealed that there appeared to be two artificial pools in the cave—a circular one near the mouth, with a four-sided one farther in—and these may have been used for aquatic entertainments. At all events it proved impossible to keep them pumped clear of seawater during the winter; but since by then over 1,000 fragments of sculpture had been found, there was perhaps enough work to be getting on with without further excavation for the time being.

CHAPTER TEN

GREECE—I

UNDOUBTEDLY the most important archaeological activity in metropolitan Greece since the war has been the continued excavation of the Agora of Athens, the civic and commercial centre of the city in ancient times over many centuries. This excavation has been the work of the American School of Classical Studies in Athens and it was begun in 1931 and carried on steadily until 1940 with the generous support of Mr John D. Rockefeller and the Rockefeller Foundation. It was of course interrupted by the war, but neither the excavations nor the finds suffered any serious damage during the war, nor during the civil war of 1944, when the area was a sort of no man's land between the opposing sides. Work was resumed on a small scale in 1946, and on a greater scale in the following year, under the field direction of Professor Homer A. Thompson; and it was under his aegis that the work went forward steadily to the completion of its major tasks in 1956, when the rebuilt Stoa of Attalos was opened by the King of the Hellenes as a museum to house the finds made and to illustrate the history of this area—one of the great germinal areas of nearly all succeeding civilizations.

What was the Agora? Literally, the market-place—in effect, far more than this, the heart and brain of Athens from about the beginning of the sixth century B.C. (from which the earliest civic buildings date) to A.D. 267 when it was savagely sacked by the Herulians, barbarians from the north, and never recovered from the disaster. This was, in fact, the period during which Greek art, architecture, drama, philosophy, science and political thought grew, developed and reached their full maturity; the period when under the impetus of Alexander the Great's conquests Greek culture spread throughout the Levant, to Persia, Mesopotamia, Egypt and India, when the known world was Hellenized; the period when Semitic Christianity, with the already Hellenized St Paul, met Greek philosophy and, to say the very least, fused and interacted to form that ethical foundation which has been the basis of all pre-Marxian Western Civilization; and the period, moreover, when Roman dynamism and capacity for organization were most receptive of Greek thought and influence and so developed to form a world power whose benefits, especially in the rule of law and what may perhaps be called the *common sense* of civilization, are with us today—if we care to preserve them. And all these things had their germ in the Agora of Athens.

The excavated area comprises some twenty-five acres in the heart of modern (as of ancient) Athens, lying at the north-west foot of the Acropolis; and from this some 360 nineteenth century houses were removed, homes being found in the suburbs for the 5,000 or so displaced inhabitants of the area. The over-burden of the centuries—in some cases forty feet of it and an average of ten—has been stripped off and removed to the outskirts of the city; and the original square reached, together with the remains of the buildings, mostly public, which surrounded it. Its history was found to go back much farther than those civic beginnings in the sixth century mentioned previously: Neolithic, Bronze Age and Early Iron Age peoples all inhabited the site—and, to mention a single example, a wonderful collection of cosmetic pots of the Geometric period was found in the grave of a rich woman of the ninth century B.C.

The square was crossed diagonally by the famous Panathenaic Way, the route of the Panathenaic procession to the near-by Propylaea and the ascent to the Acropolis. As the Acropolis, on which stood all the finest manifestations of Greek religion, looked down upon it from the south-east; so from the south looked down the Areopagus, Mars' Hill, where St Paul preached, and brought to the Athenians the new light of revealed Christianity (Plate 16).

The period of its greatest spiritual splendour is naturally debatable and must equally naturally be selected in accordance with the temperament and tastes of the debater; but it can hardly be questioned that the period of the Agora's greatest material splendour was about A.D. 200 when Athens was the world's university and when, while all the magnificent buildings and monuments of classic Athens still stood unaltered, the district had also been enriched with a number of splendid later buildings with which, for example, Attalos, the second century B.C. King of Pergamum and later Caesar, Augustus and Agrippa had acknowledged their debt to Athens.

Before enumerating the principal buildings which have been revealed as standing there at that date, it is perhaps worthwhile to describe the most fre-quent and characteristic type—the stoa. This is in effect a covered colonnade of one or two storeys, usually raised above ground; behind the columns runs a walk; and behind the walk rows of shops—the ideal form of urban planning in a sunny country; and, since there were stoas on all sides of the agora, it is clear that at every time of day and in every condition of weather there was always somewhere convenient and pleasant to walk, talk, transact business, or take the air in that condition of relaxed comfort which is essential for the development of a refined civilization.

On the west side, from the northern corner, where the Panathenaic Way entered the Agora on its way to the Acropolis, there stood in order: the Stoa of Zeus where Socrates used to stroll; the Temple of Apollo Patroos; the Metroon or Temple of the Mother of the Gods, where the archives were kept and the tub of Diogenes stood—there is perhaps a natural connexion between public records and cynicism; in front of it stood the Monument to the Eponymous Heroes, rather legendary characters from whom the tribes of Athens derived their names; next stood the entrance to the Tholos and the Bouleuterion, the administrative centre of ancient Athens—the places where one would expect to see statesmen, or politicians, like Cimon or Pericles, Nikias or Cleon. Farther south, and rather outside the Agora proper, was a large building which is thought to have been the Strategion—the War Office, as it were; and beyond this again a quarter of sculptors' workshops. On the slopes above this western side stood a large Hellenistic building which may have been an arsenal and near it that still magnificently preserved and beautiful building which used to be called the Theseion, but which is now identified as a Temple of Hephaistos. From the entrance to the Tholos and right across the whole southern side of the Agora ran the huge Middle Stoa and behind it lay several other stoas to form an especially commercial and legal district—what Aristotle would have called an Agora of the Merchants. In front of the Middle Stoa and jutting right out into the centre of the Agora was the huge Odeion of Agrippa, a two-storeyed colossal building with a façade of giant statues, a sort of Athenian Festival Hall.

All down the eastern side is the huge stoa which Attalos, the second century B.C. King of Pergamum in Asia Minor, built—and to this we will return in due course. Behind it lay the Market of Caesar and Augustus and the Library of Pantainos.

Along the northern side, from east to west, ran a group of smaller stoas: the north-eastern stoa; the Stoa Poikile, or Painted Stoa, which has given its name to the Stoic philosophy since it was in this shade that its founder, Zeno, propounded its tenets; and the Stoa of the Herms, in front of which stood, on the farther side of the Panathenaic Way, the Altar of the Twelve Gods and beyond that the Temple of Ares, which was erected on that site at about the same time as the Odeion.

This completes the circuit of the Agora. Its open space however, crossed diagonally by the Panathenaic Way, was dotted with shade trees—a pleasant feature which is being repeated in the present lay-out of the area—and diversified with a number of monuments of various kinds. These included a Quadriga in front of the Stoa of Attalos; and the near-by Bema or Speakers' platform; the statues of the Tyrannicides, Harmodius and Aristogeiton—who became as it were the ideal heroes of the French Revolution; and a number of altars and statues. While on either side of the Panathenaic Way, as it left the Agora at the south-east corner, were a pleasant apsidal Nymphaeion, a fountain house, the Mint and the Eleusinion.

As can be readily imagined the discoveries made over this great period of years on a site of such richness and one exploited on such a scale are so many and so important that it is impossible to do them justice in the space available here; and I shall mention only three things more, one because it is essential, one because it is a sort of detective story, and one, which although so slight, is so evocative as almost to make audible a bellow of laughter of 2,375 years ago. To take the last first. Among the objects found in the Agora soon after the war was the broken base of a drinking cup, on one side of which, not inappropriately as it turned out, was a goose flapping its wings; on the other were scratched the words HYPERBOLOS ANTIPHANOS—Hyperbolos the son of Antiphanes—a relic not only of the ancient Athenian custom of ostracism, but also of the last occasion on which it was used. This custom, which was especially though not solely Athenian, was regarded as one of the great safeguards of democracy and was designed to curb the power of individuals. If it was resorted to, the citizens would each scratch on a potsherd (or *ostrakon*) the name of the person considered most dangerous to the community. If the same name appeared on a sufficient number of sherds, about 6,000, that man was "ostracized" and was bound to go into exile from Athens, for ten years. In 417 B.C. two men, Nicias and Alcibiades, were both considered a danger to the state. Accordingly on the motion of one Hyperbolos the son of Antiphanes, ostracism was resorted to. Alcibiades, however, that brilliant and unreliable charmer, had suggested a little arrangement to Nicias; and as the followers of both united for the occasion and did what they were told, the vast majority of potsherds, like this historic example, all bore the two words HYPERBOLOS ANTIPHANOS—and Hyperbolos the son of Antiphanos ("an insignificant person" the historians describe him in their chilly manner, a sort of fifth century Widmerpool) indignantly left Athens for ten years; and the once excellent custom of ostracism expired in a shout of laughter and was never used again.

The feat of detection concerns the Temple of Hephaistos formerly known as the Theseion. This is a beautiful and very well-preserved marble temple; and the triangular pediment of the east gable is empty of sculpture. Some 200 years ago the English architect, James Stuart, noticed that in the footing, the base ledge, of this triangle, there were the bedding marks of the elements of a group of sculpture. Since this temple slightly preceded the Parthenon, it was obviously of great interest to know something about this missing sculpture, although it seemed unlikely that it would be possible to do so. However during the excavations around the temple, a number of fine fragments of sculpture of the right period (*c* 440 B.C.) were discovered, in which the fronts were slightly weathered while the back surfaces were still fresh—which was compatible with their standing in a pediment—and these comprised: a draped female torso, with drilled holes in the breast which obviously supported the bronze shield and Gorgon's head, and so was readily identifiable with Athene; a fine male torso, similar to one in the frieze, and so identifiable with Heracles; a reclining male figure, suitable for the south corner of the pediment; and a raised horse's hoof. All these are a little under life size and would match very suitably with the bedding marks of the pediment and would be right for size for the appropriate places in the space available. Since the central bedding mark is very large and clearly indicates a throned figure; and since the two supporting standing figures are now seen to have been Athene and Heracles; this enthroned figure could have been no one than Zeus himself. The whole composition therefore sorts itself out: Zeus enthroned, with Athene on his right and Heracles on his left; on either side of them, an equestrian feature, most probably from the shape of the bedding, a four-horsed chariot; and in the extreme corners reclining figures, one certainly male, the other perhaps female. (See Plates 18 and 19.)

Finally, the Stoa of Attalos. After the Temple of Hephaistos, this was the best preserved of all the buildings surviving on the Agora site. Parts of the walls still stood to their original height; and sufficient architectural elements survived to reveal exactly what it had been like. It had closed the east side of the Agora and was about 380 ft long and 65 ft deep. It was a continuous portico, supported by two rows of columns, behind which stood twenty-one single-roomed shops, each with a wide doorway looking out through the columns on to the Agora. A second storey repeated the design. This building was erected by Attalos II, King of Pergamum (159–138 B.C.), who had studied at Athens as a young man.

Since it had been decided that a museum must be built to house all the finds made in the Agora; and since it had also been decided that the best way of achieving this was to rebuild one of the Agora's original buildings; it soon became clear that the obvious building to rebuild was the Stoa of Attalos. The task of rebuilding was included by the Greek Government in the programme of rehabilitation of museums and archaeological sites and received considerable financial support under the Marshall Plan; and was carried out by the American School of Classical Studies on behalf of the Greek Government. Work began in April 1949; and among the first tasks to be put in hand was the carving of the pillars by the skilled marble workers of modern Athens, in accordance with the design and measurements of the surviving fragments—and it is of interest that each of these newly-made pillars now incorporates a fragment of marble from one of the original columns. The task was completed in 1956 and the rebuilt Stoa was dedicated in its new use by the King of the Hellenes in September of that year (Plate 17).

It was built in the first place, therefore, by a foreigner acknowledging his debt to Athens; it was rebuilt, 2,100 years later, through the agency of strangers from the other side of the world, likewise acknowledging their indebtedness to the Mother-city of civilization.

The two other great continuing excavations in Greece have been at two famous sites, both associated with Homeric heroes, Agamemnon's Mycenae and Nestor's Pylos. At each Greek archaeologists have shared the site with foreign workers. At Mycenae Dr J. Papadimitriou, Ephor of Antiquities for Attica and the Argolid was working on part of the site with the British School at Athens under the late Professor A. J. B. Wace on another; while at Pylos in the western Peloponnese the work was shared between Professor Carl W. Blegen of Cincinnati University, and Professor Sp. Marinatos, Head of the Antiquities Department of the Greek Ministry of Education.

The most remarkable discovery made at Mycenae by Dr Papadimitriou was a grave circle of royal tombs of about 1600 B.C. lying outside the citadel and containing an extremely rich and varied collection of grave goods.

When that famous traveller of antiquity, Pausanias, visited Mycenae in A.D. 150 or thereabouts, he found a poor and insignificant village whose inhabitants however showed him the glories of their past, the walls, the Lion Gate, the tholos (or beehive) tombs and the rest and they linked them with the most famous names of ancient Mycenae—Atreus, Agamemnon, Clytemnestra, Aegisthus. The beehive tombs they called the treasuries of Atreus and his family; and one grave circle within the walls they said contained the tombs of Agamemnon and his comrades, murdered on their return from Troy; and another grave circle, outside the walls, they identified with Aegisthus and Clytemnestra, who were not considered fit to be buried inside the citadel. Of these two circles, the former is that which Schliemann excavated some eighty years ago; the latter was discovered and excavated by Dr Papadimitriou during 1952 and 1953. Both circles are of course much older than the epoch of the Trojan War; here indeed *vixere heroes ante Agamemnona*, and here were buried, round about 1600 B.C. the members of the kingly families of those first Greeks, who entering Greece from the north about 2000 B.C. established themselves in the Peloponnese and came to dominate the peoples likewise of Crete and the islands.

Dr Papadimitriou's circle was surprisingly fortunate in its history. It is a circle of nearly thirty yards diameter enclosed with a massive wall of roughly hewn blocks of limestone, a little more than five feet thick. This circle was intersected twice in its history; first in the fourteenth century B.C. when the outer wall of the beehive tomb of Clytemnestra cut an arc into it, but without touching any of the tombs it enclosed; and then in modern times by a road and aqueduct, which destroyed one minor tomb and passed over, without damage, a major one. The circular wall, in antiquity, would not conceal from the passer-by the tombs themselves, which would appear as small mounds, each crowned with a *stele*, an erect stone slab set in a base of *poros* stone. In excavation each of the tombs was found to contain a large number of animal bones and it is clear that each funeral ceremony was concluded with a funeral banquet after the style of that given by Achilles for Patroclus and described by Homer in the *Iliad*.

The tombs, both large and small, are shaft tombs, cut down into the conglomerate rock to a depth of between 9–12 ft. The floor is laid with pebbles; and various arrangements were made for fitting wooden beams to roof in the tomb before filling in. Some contain a single burial, some several and these have apparently been used like family tombs, over a period of years, but the sexes are kept distinct in death—there are male tombs and there are female tombs. Among them are found the remains of dwelling-houses of much the same period which were destroyed at the time when the grave circle was first consecrated. To distinguish the graves from those of Schliemann's circle (which were given Roman letters) these have been given Greek letters to identify them; and they comprise—Alpha, Beta, Gamma, Delta, Epsilon, Zeta, Eta, Theta, Iota, Kappa, Lambda, Mu, Nu, Xi, Omicron, and Pi.

It is obviously impossible (and inappropriate) to describe all of them here;

and brief descriptions will be attempted only of three: a male tomb, Delta; a female tomb, Omicron, the "Crystal tomb"; and an infant's tomb, Xi.

Delta was a rich grave, containing three burials; and among the grave goods were two bronze swords, other weapons of bronze, a number of pots and seventeen arrowheads of red stone, which had been buried in a leather bag, traces of which remained. One of the bronze swords was a magnificent work of art. The blade was engraved with a series of griffins, while the hilt had a large pommel of ivory and was itself covered with gold over the hand-grip and shoulders. The gold of the grip was embossed with an all-over scroll pattern, while the shoulders end in four animal heads, two of them bulls, the other two lions.

Omicron was the grave under the modern road and its excavation was a ticklish job; but its richness amply justified all the labour. It contained two burials, one of them packed at one end without offerings; the other, obviously a princess from the richness of the grave goods about her, was buried at full length in the centre. By her side were three pottery vases and—an absolutely unique piece—a bowl of rock crystal in the form of a duck. The bird's head is gracefully bent back and forms the handle, while the tail forms the spout; and the whole thing is exquisitely carved from a single large block of rock crystal, the longest measurement being nearly six inches. The funeral adornments of this princess were of the greatest richness; there were three bronze pins with crystal heads and a silver pin with a gold head; there were two necklaces of amethysts and carnelians and one of amber and another necklace made of beads of gold filigree in the shape of birds and spirals; there were two gold bracelets of repeated spirals; two diadems of embossed gold sheet and a pin, presumably for the hair, with a head of gold sheet in the form of a water-lily.

The principal occupant of the grave Xi was a little girl no more than two years old, who had been buried with a diadem of gold leaves, gold ear-rings, two gold rings to hold the hair together at the temples, a gold finger ring, a tiny gold rattle, a necklace of precious stones, with a faience amulet in the middle and a number of small pottery vases. This does indeed present a touching and pathetic picture of an infant princess cut off untimely; but the presence of another child's skeleton, bundled in alongside without offerings, and of a third child, buried in a flexed position nearby but outside the grave, with four small pottery vases, suggests that these were the playmates of the two-year-old princess and while it is no doubt possible that all three died perhaps of the same pestilence, it is difficult to suppress another, and a grimmer, thought.

The operations of the British School at Athens under the late Professor Alan J. B. Wace at Mycenae re-opened after the war in the summer of 1950; and the first season was occupied with a number of interesting projects, some in close co-operation with the Greek authorities. These included the restoration of two cyclopean blocks in the Lion Gate, the exploration of the Epano Phournos tomb, the repair of the entrance to the beehive tomb, traditionally called the Tomb of Clytemnestra, and the re-examination of what has been known since

1886 as Tsountas' House. However it was another discovery made this season which was to engage the British School's attention continuously until Professor Wace's death in Athens in 1957.

We have referred previously to a modern road which cuts across one side of the Grave Circle which Professor Papadimitriou excavated. Beside it, about 120 yds south of the Grave Circle, a massive cyclopean wall supports a terrace and on this terrace were found the ruined remains of a large building which had been destroyed by fire. In one gallery of this building were found a number of large stirrup jars which had evidently been used for oil. Many were overturned, some had their spouts knocked off and others the stoppers pulled out. Many were distorted and partly vitrified by the great heat of the fire and it seems clear that the building was deliberately set on fire as an act of destruction. The method of stoppering these jars is interesting. The spout was plugged with a clay stopper shaped like a champagne cork, through which were threaded strings which were wound round the spout; and these presumably served both to secure the stopper and to draw it out when needed. Next a cap of damp clay was pressed over both plug and spout, after the fashion of the cover of a vacuum flask. In some cases this still preserves the finger-prints of the servant who fixed it; and finally a seal was pressed into the damp clay several times. This building was given the name of the House of the Oil Merchant.

As was later discovered, the House of the Oil Merchant was the middle one of three houses side by side, the others being the House of the Sphinxes to the south and the House of the Shields to the north, the names being derived from the distinctive finds made in each.

In the House of the Oil Merchant, besides the oil vessels already mentioned, and in spite of the severity of the fire in these premises, a number of clay documents in the Linear B script were found and a few fragments of fresco from wall paintings which seem to have shown human beings and perhaps bulls.

In the House of Shields, which is thought not to have been a private house, a large number of ivory models of figure-of-eight shields were found. All have dowel holes at the back and the supposition that they were decorative units was proved by the discovery of casket fragments with the shields so attached as a decoration in relief; and there is also an ivory plaque with a similar shield carved in relief. A number of ivory inlay motifs—dolphins, "sacral ivy", leaves and the like—were found; and also a small ivory head of a Mycenaean warrior wearing the boar's tooth helmet of the kind mentioned in Homer. Other ivories included tiny pillars and other architectural units—exquisite examples of the cabinet maker's skill—which look like toys but were probably for the decoration of caskets. In this house a number of very fine stone vases were found, in which the drill marks in the interior can still be seen. These are of various types of stone, such as limestone, steatite, serpentine and pudding-stone. One especially fine vase however is of green porphyry, the Lapis Lacedaemonius which is found only at Krokeai, half way between Sparta and the sea. On the Acropolis a partly worked block of the same stone was found, showing

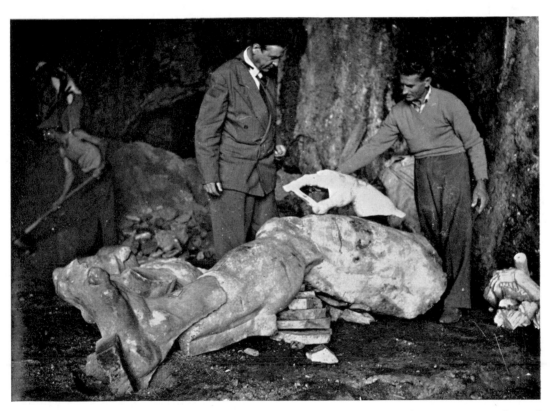

PLATE 15. Also from the Sperlonga Grotto. (*a*) A male figure, perhaps a companion of Ulysses; (*b*) a large statue of Ganymede, carried off by an eagle; and (*c*) an enormous leg and hand—on the left is Professor Jacopi.

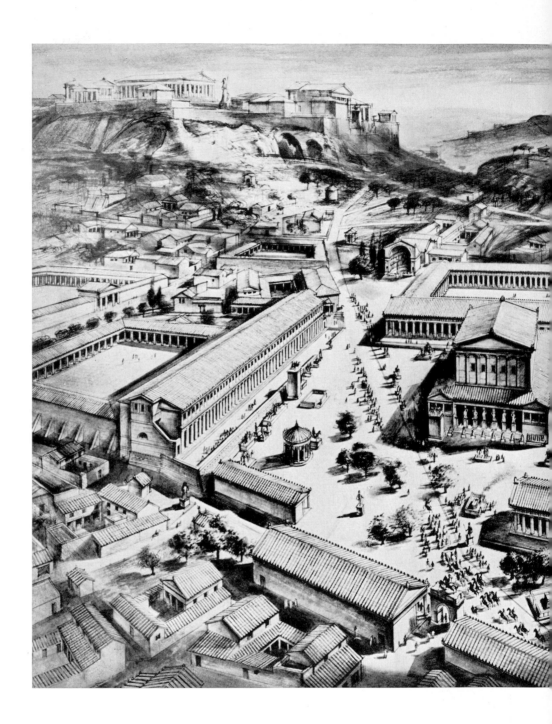

PLATE 16. The heart of Athens at about 200 A.D., the time of its greatest material splendour. In the left background is the Acropolis, while in the foreground the Panathenaic Way crosses the Agora diagonally, with the "Theseion" on the right and the Stoa of Attalos on the left. A reconstruction drawing by Alan Sorrell.

PLATE 17. The rebuilt Stoa of Attalos, overlooking the now excavated Agora of Athens. (*a*) The exterior, with the Acropolis in the background; and (*b*) in the lower colonnade of the stoa, which is used as a museum.

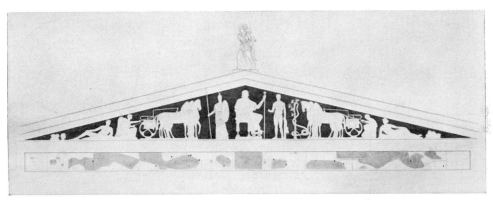

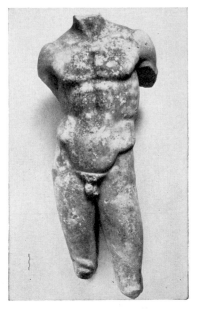

PLATE 18. The elements of a detective story (*a, c, d, e,* and *a* in Plate 19).
19a shows the footings of the pediment of the "Theseion", beside the Agora
of Athens. These marks, plotted at the foot of 18c, gave some idea of the
nature of the missing statuary. The reclining torso (18a), the Heracles torso
(18e) and the Athene with holes in the breast for the Aegis (18d) exactly
fit the requirements and so enable the excavators to suggest (18c) what the
whole group was like. 18b, found at Knossos in Crete, shows two elements
of a fine and, when complete, large ivory statuette.

PLATE 19. For 19a see the description of Plate 18. 19b shows both faces of an *ostrakon* or potsherd with the scratched name of Antiphanes, an echo of the tragico-farcical incident of Alcibiades' time. 19c is an ivory found at Knossos and shows a Minoan house façade with its raised front door, probably a precaution against floods.

PLATE 20. Evidence of the domestic civilization and art of Mycenae—from the late Professor Wace's excavations. In *a, b, c* and *d* are examples of functional design for the kitchen: a funnel to catch any overflow, a tripod pot for cooking in ashes or charcoal, dippers which are also strainers and ladles with bases adapted to stand without spilling. In *e* is the famous double sphinx ivory.

PLATE 21. The splendid and almost perfect beehive tomb (c) near the Palace of Pylos. Although this had been robbed a number of small jewels remained, including this engaging owl (b) in repoussé gold leaf (one of six); and (a) this splendid cushion-shaped gold seal with its curly-tailed seated griffin.

PLATE 22. From the beehive tombs at Myrsinochorion near Pylos, excavated by Professor Marinatos: (a) and (d) two bronze daggers inlaid with
gold, silver and *niello*, (a) showing stalking leopards in a rocky landscape,
(d) nautiluses and submarine rocks. The hilt of (a) is covered with gold
sheet and the three studs of (d) are also gold. (b) and (c) A solid gold
bead-seal from the same tomb, showing a bull with a broken spear in its
back, the reverse being cloisonné with a blue paste in a scale or feather
pattern.

PLATE 23. Pylos and Corinth. (*a*) The *diolkos* or paved causeway across the isthmus over which ships were hauled from the Gulf of Corinth to the Saronic Gulf. (*b*) The bathroom in the Palace of Nestor at Pylos. (*c*) The Palace of Nestor, from the storerooms, looking over the throne-room with the large circular hearth, towards the entrance. The archive rooms are in the right background.

PLATE 24. Corinth—a starting gate for the runners in the Isthmian Games. In (*b*) is shown the pavement with postholes and narrow slots running back to the starter's pit; while in (*a*) is a modern reconstruction of how the system must have worked.

PLATE 25. A classic "Aphrodite" some 2,000 years before her time. A singularly beautiful little terracotta statuette from the Neolithic levels at Lerna, not far from Argos.

PLATE 26. One of the finest Proto-Attic vases ever found—from Eleusis. 4½ ft high, it had been used, secondarily, for the burial of a child and its pictures tell stories which are still told to children—(below) Perseus and the Gorgons and (above) Odysseus blinding Polyphemus.

PLATE 27. (a) A huge crater or wine-mixing vessel from a "butler's cupboard" in the Palace of Phaistos, with large free-standing lilies, the upper groups of which were originally linked with
white pottery chains. (b) A very large "fruit stand" with dentel-
lated edge, painted with a complex design of interlacing spirals.

PLATE 28. Rich and interesting pottery from the Minoan Palace at Phaistos (*a, b, c* and *d*).
(*b*) A shallow one-handled dish with, painted on it, a stylized snake-goddess and two dancing
women; (*c*) an *oinochoe* in a checkered design *en suite* with the huge crater of Plate 27; and
(*d*) a tall three-handled wine-jug with scallop shells in relief.

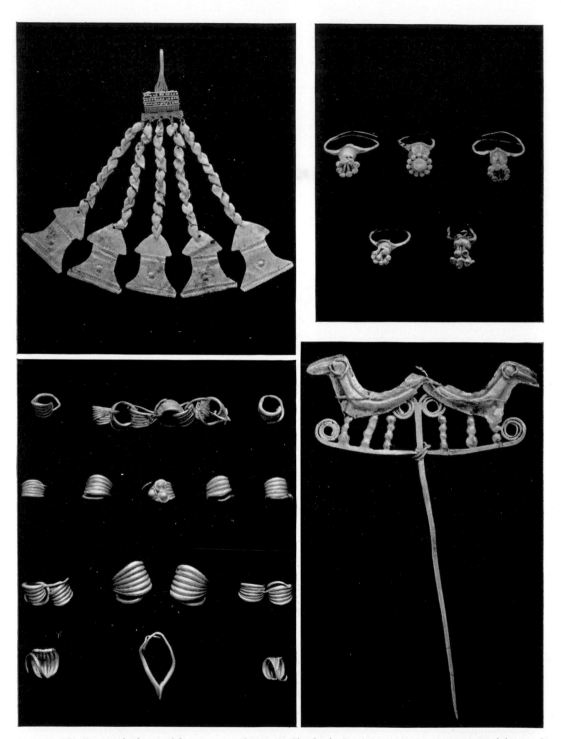

PLATE 29. Part of the gold treasure from Poliochni, Lemnos, contemporary with, and second only to, the gold treasure which Schliemann found at Troy. Ear-rings of various types: (*a*) compound, (*b*) floret and (*c*) shell and wish-bone; and (*d*) a large pin with a pair of bird-figures.

that the material was locally worked. Blocks of the same stone were found by Sir Arthur Evans at Knossos in the Lapidary's Workshop; and this would seem to show that there was a close cultural relationship between Mycenae and the Palace Period of Knossos, which was already Greek at that date, about the fifteenth century B.C. Also in this house a number of vases of faience were found, probably of Syrian and Phoenician origin.

The most remarkable discovery in the House of the Sphinxes was an ivory plaque about 3¼ in high by 2¼ in wide, well-preserved in all the essential parts. It is carved with great strength and delicacy. It shows two sphinxes, with outspread wings, standing breast to breast in the posture of the lions of the Lion Gate and with the fore-paws resting on the capital of a fluted pillar. On either side of this are three sets of "horns of consecration". The sphinxes wear "lily crowns" and their hair streams out behind. The column is in a style which oddly anticipates the Hellenistic Pergamene style; and there is one very similar to it among the ivory architectural units in miniature which were found in this house as well as in the House of the Shields (Plate 20).

Quantities of domestic pottery of many types were found in what was probably a store room of the House of Sphinxes; and what is most remarkable about them is the variety of specialized and functional design, such as dippers which are also strainers, ladles which have flattened bases and turned down handles, so that they stand steady when put down, and funnels with a device for catching any overflow of liquid.

In all the houses were found clay documents in the Minoan Linear B script, which the late Michael Ventris showed (to the satisfaction of nearly everybody) to be Greek and legible as such on a syllabary-basis. Nearly all these documents have been read as lists and inventories. An especially interesting series gives a list of plants or seeds, including celery, fennel, sesame, coriander, cummin, mint and so on, while another tablet lists such foods as figs and olives on one side and vases on the other. Nearby a number of carbonized seeds were found, but it was too much to expect an exact parallel and these turned out to be vetches, chick peas and lentils.

An odd architectural fact emerged in the excavation of the House of Sphinxes. The walls of the basement were made of stone and on the top of this was laid a cross-beam of wood. This cross-beam not only supported the floor-joists but acted as a basis for perpendicular wooden members which strengthened the main "cladding" of mud-brick—which would seem to indicate that a Mycenaean house was not unlike an English black-and-white house—a rather unexpected conclusion.

In general these houses combine to throw a general as well as a detailed light on Mycenae from the fifteenth to the thirteenth century. They show that there was a rich and established community outside the walls of the Acropolis—nobles, merchants, bourgeoisie and the like—who had commercial links with Crete, the Levant and probably Egypt, who read and wrote and kept commercial records and who lived well and even elaborately; and whose prosperity came to an end about the end of the thirteenth century, when their houses were destroyed, although the Acropolis was to hold out for a century or so more. The Mycenaean summer was ending and the peoples of the Proto-Geometric Age—whoever they were—were moving in.

On the west coast of the Peloponnese, in that district known anciently as Messenia, there lies a bay almost closed by a long island. Both were famous places: the bay, the Bay of Navarino, was the scene of the famous naval victory of A.D. 1827 when the allied fleets of Great Britain, France, and Russia, under Sir Edward Codrington defeated the navies of Turkey and Egypt; and the island, the island of Sphacteria, was the site of a great Athenian victory in 425 B.C. when Cleon's general, Demosthenes, resoundingly defeated the Spartans, as Thucydides relates. It was only in 1939 and with the resumption of excavations in 1952 that it became apparent that this quiet neighbourhood had a much earlier and greater claim to fame and that it had been the site of a Mycenaean palace, contemporary with and perhaps as important as Mycenae itself. Although there is no documentary evidence, there can be no doubt that this was ancient Pylos, the capital of the great family the Neleids, whose most famous king was Nestor, all things considered the noblest and most likeable of the Homeric heroes and one whose material contribution to the siege of Troy was second only to Agamemnon's.

The excavations at Pylos have been a joint Hellenic and American affair: the American section being directed by Professor Carl Blegen of the University of Cincinnati, the Greek by Professor Sp. Marinatos, Head of the Antiquities Department of the Greek Ministry of Education. The Americans have been concerned with the palace itself, the Greeks with a number of beehive tombs (tholoi) in the district; and since, in some measure, the palace sets the scene and also, somewhat unexpectedly reveals the tragic story, we will reverse the order followed in describing the work at Mycenae and tell the American story first.

The palace, whose site was first discovered in 1939, lies in an elevated and commanding position at a place called Epano Englianos (or Englianos), a little over three miles to the north of the Bay of Navarino and about the same distance from the Ionian Sea, which lies in the west. It is a singularly beautiful wooded site with mountains rising near by, streams and cultivated slopes all around and the sea near enough to give a tonic vitality to the atmosphere; a a palace beautiful at all events in design; a dynasty, outstanding for nobility and wisdom; the setting of the Second Book of the Odyssey, in which Telemachus, son of Odysseus, seeks help and advice in his search for his lost father and receives both in good measure, in circumstances of generous hospitality and urbane good manners—an idyllic place. The real Arcadia was not far away, the idealized Arcadia of the poets was there. It was a great country mansion with, as far as yet seen, no works of fortification, abounding in its security and its prosperity. It was utterly destroyed about 1200 B.C. and never reoccupied.

By 1956 a great deal of the ground plan had been recovered and the rooms excavated. It consisted basically of two long rectangles, one very much bigger than the other but both with their long axes running north-west–south-east. The smaller rectangle may be earlier and was perhaps a prototype of the great palace. The larger is at least 60 yds long by about 40 yds wide. The entrance gateway lies at the south-east end, a simply pillared propylon, between two sets of rooms which may have risen to towers. It leads into a large courtyard mainly open to the sky, but with a portico on the right and immediately in front, probably supporting galleries. In the centre of the portico facing is a doorway and at one side of a small platform, which was probably the station of a porter or a sentry. This doorway led into a vestibule, about 45 ft wide and 12 ft deep. On either side doorways led off to staircases leading to an upper floor; but facing and in the centre of the long side was another doorway with another porter's platform; and this doorway led direct into the throne room. This was a room 42 ft long by 37 feet wide, in the centre of it was a raised circular hearth over 13 ft in diameter, with four bases for fluted columns standing in a square round it and supporting, presumably, a clerestory above it. On the right-hand wall, as we enter, and about level with the hearth is the base for the throne, and beside it, to the king's right hand, a recessed drain in the floor, designed no doubt for the convenience of the king's libations. The floor was of stucco, which had been renewed several times, marked out in squares, and decorated in several colours of paint. The stucco of the hearth had been renewed at least five times and painted with a design of flames. Numerous fragments of fine plaster show that the walls too had been painted with gay patterns.

All these features which have been described lie in a straight line down the long axis of the palace and they are entirely surrounded by smaller rooms, pantries, holding hundreds of domestic pots, mostly unused, mostly unpainted, magazines and storehouses, and three other rooms of especial interest, a bathroom and two archive rooms (Plates 23*b* and *c*).

The bathroom lies between the large courtyard immediately inside the entrance gate and another courtyard away to the right. In one corner of the bathroom was a stuccoed stand for two large storage jars either to hold water for the bath or wine for the bather, this latter cheerful thought being indeed the more probable since several wine cups were found alongside. Farther along the same wall was the bath, a large terracotta vessel of modern bath shape, fixed in a large oblong block, with a built-in step to help the bather get into the bath, which incidentally was painted in spiral patterns of light paint on a dark ground. Inside it lay a broken wine-cup. The bath has no plug-hole and the water was presumably baled out on to the ground where it would run away to a drain in the floor. Here, says Homer (in Pope's translation)—

> 'The last fair branch of the Nestorean line,
> Fair Polycaste, took the pleasing toil
> To bathe the prince, and pour the fragrant oil.
> O'er his fair limbs a flowery vest he threw,

And issued, like a god, to mortal view.
His former seat beside the king he found
(His people's father with his peers around);
All placed at ease the holy banquet join,
And in the dazzling goblet laughs the wine.'

The two archive rooms, one found in 1939, the other in the early 'fifties lie side by side on the left side of the entrance gate. In these two rooms were found lying on the floor or on clay shelves round the walls between 900 and 1,000 inscribed clay tablets. All these bore writing in the Minoan linear B script. It was fairly clear even before this script yielded up its secrets to the late Michael Ventris and Mr John Chadwick that these tablets were lists. Lists indeed they are—of men, foodstuffs, weapons; and it is difficult not to see in them the administrative documents of a full-scale attempt to meet the threat of a great emergency, the disaster which came and put an end to this happy, prosperous and civilized kingdom.

Less than a hundred yards from the palace, a large *tholos* or beehive tomb was found standing on a small eminence in a vineyard and this was excavated during 1953 under the supervision of Lord William Taylour. The beehive tomb is the characteristic royal or princely mausoleum of the later stages of the Mycenaean Age and it is, as its name implies, a large hive-shaped domed building, the majority of which is underground. It is built of stone and approached by a descending entrance passage and entered through a stone-built doorway, which was presumably walled up again after each interment. It usually contains several burials and these may be in different styles: pits or shafts are sometimes sunk in the floor of the tomb; a stone cist may be built on the floor; and sometimes the body is simply laid on the floor of the tomb.

Most of the splendid tombs of antiquity were robbed in antiquity; and those built towards the end of a civilization would seem to be even more liable to plunder than most.

The great tholos by the palace was no exception. It was found to be splendidly built of limestone blocks; to have a floor-level diameter of 30 ft $8\frac{1}{8}$ in and with its walls still standing to over 15 ft of an original 24 or 25 ft; and to have been thoroughly plundered in antiquity. The burials were all disturbed; and the robbers had ransacked a deep curving pit at one side and a cist at the other. However the robbers were careless or hasty or perhaps sated with the wealth they had already found. At all events they left behind a quantity of small but rich and beautiful objects. These included quantities of fragments of gold leaf, hundreds of amber beads, 248 amethyst beads, and many others of gold, faience and paste, and a number of fragments of ivory. There were two amethyst seals, one showing a cow and a calf, the other a combat between a man and a lion; a small gold figure-of-eight shield, about $1\frac{1}{2}$ in high, precisely like the ivory shields found by Professor Wace at Mycenae; and six engaging little owls made in *repoussé* from gold sheet. These last may well be the owls of Athene, which would be charmingly appropriate since this goddess visited Pylos disguised as a human, Mentor, the companion and adviser of Telmachus. There was also a gold signet ring, the bezel being an oval showing a wild-goat, a shrine with the double axe or horns of consecration above, a god ascending and a worshipper with hands upraised; and finally a magnificent large gold seal, in the form of a cylinder flattened to something like a cushion shape. One side of this bears a raised net pattern with bosses at the junctions; the other shows a seated griffin, with wings upraised and spread and head turned back, the tail being erect and curly. The feet and legs are those of a lion, the head that of a hawk, topped with an aigrette-like crest, from which ribbons hang down. At the foot is an elaborate border of Mycenaean-style decoration. Much of the detail is done with a pitted technique, which would give the imprint a granular effect (Plate 21).

If these were the trifles the robbers could not pause to collect, what were their spoils like? It is a great temptation to think that this is the tomb of Nestor himself; but it is not always the greatest kings who have the greatest tombs.

Three years later and about three miles east of the palace, above the village of Myrsinochorion, Professor Marinatos, the director of the Greek excavations in the region of Pylos found and excavated two smaller *tholoi* of the greatest interest, one of which proved to have been absolutely untouched. These were smaller and simpler tombs than the tomb by the palace; their diameters were about 16 or 17 ft and their approaches were not lined with stone; each was the tomb of a prince rather than a king—or, in the language of the Pylos tablets, of a *Pasireu* or a *Lavageta* and not a *Vanax*.

The first of these tombs was fairly well preserved and it had been thoroughly robbed in antiquity. In the approach were two burials of the second century A.D. which are like a vivid incident from some unknown story: one is of a child of between 4 and 6, the other is of a man, who had been wounded in the head and then beheaded, buried with hands folded across his breast and with the skull replaced—back to front. When this burial took place, the dome of the tholos would still be standing above ground, some fourteen centuries after it was built.

There had been many intruders in the tomb, some as late as the fifteenth century A.D. and no burial was found *in situ*. There were however two groups of pots, a few gold-plated beads, a bronze pin and some stone arrowheads. There was also a well-preserved bronze frying-pan with the remains of a joint of meat, either lamb or kid, the funeral meal of the dead man.

The other tomb was in bad condition and must have collapsed within about sixty years of its construction—a figure arrived at from the fact that it contained a number of burials and that no robbers had been at work except for a little plundering between interments. A wine jar by the entrance is of about 1500 B.C. The last burial was of a man who had been laid out on the floor; there was a shaft which contained a single burial, a princess of about 15 years old; and another shaft in which five persons had been buried one on top of another.

The burial on the floor was of a man in the prime of life, with a magnificent set of teeth. On one side of him lay a curved two-pronged fork of bronze, a fire-hook presumably—one of those basic and functionally designed tools which can still be bought at the ironmonger's; and on the other side a rich collection of personal property—ten swords and daggers, some of them gold-studded, a large spearhead, a bronze mirror with an ivory handle carved with a trefoil of rosettes, two cylinder seals, a dozen vases and the same quantity of gems such as sardonyx, carnelian, agate and lapis lazuli.

Buried with the princess was only a very large necklace of finely glazed polychrome beads and a prismatic glass bead-seal, which was on the right arm.

In the other shaft, however, there were great riches. The uppermost burial was still *in situ*; and beside the left hand lay a truly beautiful inlaid dagger. The handle is lacking, but the blade itself is over nine inches long. At the hilt end are three round gold bosses and the whole of the central panel of the blade, which follows the shape of the blade, is inlaid in gold, silver and that black paste which is called *niello*, in a design of five nautiluses swimming among sea creatures and elements of a marine landscape, the line of nautiluses, which diminish in size towards the point, being alternately gold and silver. The other side of the blade is the same; and beside the dagger lay thirteen spirally engraved gold buttons, which no doubt decorated a leather belt. In the right armpit of the dead man lay another inlaid dagger, even more splendid. Here the hilt survives and is entirely of gold sheet, covering the pommel, the handle and the shoulders of the blade and coming down to a point on either side of the blade in a sort of widow's peak. It has an all-over pattern of small studs, to give a good grip, one supposes, and on the head of the blade incorporates a triple stud pattern like that on the other dagger. The blade has inlaid panels like the other dagger and of the same shape and materials, gold, silver and *niello*. The design is of three leopards in different stalking postures separated by rather stylized rocks and tree trunks. There is nothing stylized about the leopards however and they are portrayed with a magnificent lithe naturalness (Plate 22).

Round the neck of this dead man lay huge necklaces of amber—like the man buried on the floor of the tomb—and at his side also lay a small mirror; and there was another dagger with gold rivets and a gold ring to the hilt.

The other finds lower down in the shaft were much confused and not so numerous, but they included a number of gems and gem-seals, pottery ranging in style from about 1500 to 1425 B.C., a silver goblet and some leaves of gold. The gem seals and gold bead seals found in this tomb were of the greatest beauty; and among the subjects they show may be mentioned: bulls seated, a bull captured in a net, a wounded bull, a winged griffin very like the one found in the Palace *tholos*, a woman offering lilies at an altar, waterfowl in flight (in the very popular modern manner), lions dying or leaping on antelopes and two lions with a pair of gods.

Two interesting discoveries throw light on the burial ceremonies. From certain grooves in the floor of the entries of the Pylos tombs, it appears that the bodies were brought into the tomb for burial on chariots; and from the fact that in all the tombs larger or smaller quantities of flint or obsidian arrowheads are found, usually near the door and usually (when found undisturbed) pointing towards the interior of the tomb, it would certainly seem that the burial ceremony concluded with a salvo of arrows—which suggests that the military funeral of today has a longer ancestry than perhaps was realized.

CHAPTER ELEVEN

GREECE—II

So rich is the soil of Greece and so intensive the archaeological activity which has taken place there since the war that it is impossible to give an adequate account of every important excavation; and some of these must wait for fuller description in a possible later volume. Among those should be mentioned the excavations of the French School at Argos, Dr Papadimitriou's excavations of what appears to be an Iphigeneia cult temple in Euboea, and the German School's excavations under Dr Kuntze at Olympia. These last, incidentally, were initiated, somewhat reluctantly, at the insistence of none other than Adolf Hitler.

A very remarkable and rewarding series of excavations was conducted annually from 1952 to 1956 by the American School at Athens under Dr John L. Caskey, the Director of the School, at Lerna. Lerna, which was the marshy haunt of that monster the Hydra, the slaying of which was one of the labours of Heracles, lies about six miles south of Argos where Mt Pontinos reaches almost to the sea and is the cause of a clear cold spring which creates the marshes of the legend. It was an inhabited site from early Neolithic times to the Classical era and a considerable mound of debris has accumulated. Much of this has been lost by erosion and cultivation—orchards overlie a great deal of the site and the last war added a tank ditch and gun emplacements to its features (nice subjects for the archaeologists of the distant future)—but the older strata were untouched and fairly near the surface.

There seem to have been two Neolithic phases. The first, a long period, for which no remains of houses have been found, is characterized by simple mottled pottery, of the so-called Variegated or Rainbow Ware and skilfully fashioned tools of flint and obsidian. The second Neolithic phase, nearly as long as the first, is one of houses with rectangular rooms of mud-brick on stone foundations, thin-walled pottery with red slip or with a reddish or blackish lustrous glaze, sometimes with panels of linear decoration, and stone or bone tools—and a quite astonishing terracotta statuette. This is a female figure which was probably originally 8 or 9 in high and is now, through the loss of the head and neck and (perhaps) the feet $7\frac{1}{4}$ in high. Of this little naked "Aphrodite", Dr Caskey rightly says, "It is a figure of youthful maturity, full without heaviness, gracefully natural in its pose. The shoulders are rounded, the arms cross lightly over the body below the breasts; waist and hips and, most particularly the planes and curves and transitions of the lower back are rendered with skill and sensitivity.

The legs, in contrast, are schematized as solid tapering pedestals without articulation. One wonders how much attention the sculptor paid to the head and the features of the face. Whoever he may have been, he seems somehow to have anticipated the naturalistic elements of Greek art by more than 2,000 years and his little statue stands closer in some respects to Aphrodite of the classical period than to the primitive idols and fetishes of his own era" (Plate 25).

Perhaps art and artists are always oscillating between the naturalistic and the abstract; and it is simply that in the vast expanses of prehistory we simply have not enough material accurately to plot all the oscillations; but perhaps, and more probably, it is not a question of art at all. These and images like them in many centuries are objects of religion and utility; and if the usual gross "mother-figures" and the mean striped female cult figures which turn up at Lerna a thousand years later "work" better than this lovely little "Aphrodite", they *are* better than her; and since they embody the symbol, they are preferred by the hierarchy (who create the symbol) to the work of the artist (who creates the beauty). And yet, at unexpected points in time, like philosophy with Dr Johnson's friend, the artist "keeps breaking in" and as at Altamira, at the cave-shelter of Angles-sur-l'Anglin and the initiation rite of Palermo, and at Lerna, some maker with a eupeptic love of life, some prehistoric Rubens or Neolithic Renoir, bursts the bonds of utility and convention and portrays with life and love the living thing he knows and delights in. And perhaps—in parenthesis—the great ages of art are those when the great mass of his fellows are in accord with him.

After this Neolithic culture at Lerna, Early, Middle and Bronze Age (or Helladic) cultures follow each other in gradual transition—a rather surprising feature since most other sites in the north-east Peloponnese show unmistakable signs of widespread devastation at the end of the Early Bronze Age. The characteristic activity of these new settlers seems to have been the construction of large buildings, the most remarkable of which has been called the House of Tiles from the quantities of rectangular terracotta roofing tiles found among the ruins. The house of tiles is a large building, about 83 ft long and nearly 40 ft wide; and, like the Palace of Nestor at Pylos though on a smaller scale, it consists of a large hall approached through an antechamber and surrounded by other smaller rooms, a staircase giving access to an upper storey.

Whether this was a temple or a palace, it was regarded with awe and reverence and when it was destroyed by fire (by accident, not intention, it would appear) the ruins were carefully covered over with a low circular mound (accurately centred on the building's centre) which was dressed with gravel and bordered with a circle of rounded stones. And for some generations the site remained untouched, as though hallowed or, perhaps, accursed.

Other outstanding discoveries were two great shaft graves in the style of the Mycenaean grave circles and dating from the earliest phase of the Mycenaean period, *c* 1600 B.C. Both however had been ransacked in antiquity and even the skeletons were removed, only quantities of broken pottery remaining.

Bulldozers, deep ploughs, power-dredgers and mechanical excavating gear generally have all done their quota of accidental reconnaissance for the archaeologist since the war; and it was in fact a bulldozer operating near the Greek Military Engineers' School at Poseidonia in the Isthmus of Corinth which first put Mr Nicholas Verdelis (Ephor of Antiquities of Corinthia and the Argolid) on the trail of a most interesting engineering feat of some 2,550 years ago. There are various references in literature, including Thucydides and Aristophanes, to the Diolkos, a device for transporting ships across the Isthmus of Corinth from the Gulf of Corinth to the Saronic Gulf, thus serving the same purpose as the modern Corinth Canal and cutting out the need for the long and dangerous voyage round the Peloponnese. In modern times the late Harold N. Fowler discovered a stone pavement on the south side of the western end of the modern canal and identified this as the western end of the Diolkos; and from this and the stone paving uncovered by the bulldozer Mr Verdelis, in the course of two years' excavations in 1956 and 1957, financed by the Greek Ministry of National Education, has been able to plot its course for nearly a mile and to uncover the causeway at several points, notably one well-preserved stretch of about 170 yds long (Plate 23a).

To begin with the Diolkos is not straight but proceeds in long smooth curves designed to achieve the gentlest gradient possible, and it consists of a roadway paved with massive limestone slabs. Its width varies between $11\frac{1}{2}$ and $16\frac{1}{2}$ ft and generally its surface is marked by two deep parallel grooves 4 ft 11 in apart. At certain points however these grooves disappear and are replaced by low parallel walls, the same distance apart. At their beginnings these walls are only an inch or two high but rise gradually to somewhat over a foot. The inner faces of the walls are slightly concave and signs of wheel marks occur between them. They are found where the gradient or the curve increases; and it is clear that empty ships were mounted on wheeled trolleys with a wheel base of 4 ft 11 in and hauled, presumably by slaves, along the grooves of this causeway, the low walls giving greater security where there was danger of the trolley leaving the track. Near these low walls there are carved certain letters in the local Corinthian alphabet; and it is possible that these were road signs, as who should say "Gradient increases: more slaves" or "Curve and down gradient: dead slow". The character of these letters enable the causeway to be dated to the time of Periander (625–585 B.C.) the tyrant of Corinth and one of the legendary Seven Wise Men of Ancient Greece who, it is said, was the first man to conceive of the plan of digging a canal through the Isthmus.

In the same district, an expedition of the University of Chicago, under the auspices of the American School of Classical Studies and directed by Professor Oscar Broneer identified and began to excavate the site of the Temple of the Isthmian Poseidon. This was in antiquity a great Panhellenic centre and the site of the Isthmian Games, to which contestants came from all over Greece and which had the good fortune to achieve immortality in eight of the extant odes of Pindar. The identification was made in 1952 and an extensive campaign was mounted in 1954.

The temple itself seems to have been built some time before 600 B.C. and to have been destroyed in a very fierce fire in the early years of the fifth century B.C. Most of the metal objects had been fused into shapeless lumps; but among the pottery was a fragment of a red-figure mug bearing a dedication to Poseidon and so providing a written identification for the temple. An interesting discovery was a deposit of 135 silver coins mostly from early Corinthian and Aeginetan mints, varying in date and evidently contributions by worshippers at the temple. What makes this temple-collection so vividly interesting is that it contains several counterfeits, coins of base metal with a thin covering of silver.

About 460 B.C. another temple, in the Doric order, was erected, about 177½ ft long by 82 ft wide, of *poros* stone covered with a thin stucco of marble dust, but with roof tiles of white marble. This temple too was destroyed in a great fire, in 394 B.C. But about fifty years after, it was rebuilt, a good deal of the fifth century material being re-used; and in later years it was considerably altered and modified and the walls and floors faced with thin marble slabs in Roman times, but its general appearance probably remained much the same. In the second century A.D. it must have been crowded with statues as Pausanias who visited it mentions no fewer than fifteen statues and one chariot group. In the reign of Justinian I (A.D. 527–565), a military engineer called Victorinus (presumably a Christian) was charged with rebuilding fortifications in the Isthmus and demolished the temple completely to provide himself with building material.

The excavations, after some exploratory work in 1955, were resumed in 1956, with two principal objectives: to continue exploration of the temple precinct, and to try and find the Temple of Palaimon. This last was the second most important building of the Isthmian Games and was traditionally supposed to contain in its crypt the body of the youth Melikertes-Palaimon, whose drowned body was brought ashore by a dolphin and in whose honour King Sisyphus instituted the Isthmian Games. In the event a Palaimonion of Roman times was discovered built over an earlier stadium; but the most interesting discoveries were those connected with the Isthmian Games themselves. These included fragments of two Panathenaic amphoras, one bearing the additional inscription "Damon dedicated it", it presumably being the prize won by Damon at Athens and brought back by him to his home city for dedication to Poseidon; a stone jumping weight; a number of round lamps, which have no handles and which were presumably cult lamps connected with the games; and what was presumably a starting-gate for foot races in the earlier stadium. Part of this is now covered by the Roman Palaimonion, but the full design is quite clear. It consists of a stone pavement, marked out in grooves and in the form of a very shallow isosceles triangle. The long base is the starting line for sixteen runners. In the middle of the short perpendicular to the apex—in the heart of the triangle that is—is a pit about 3 ft deep, in which the starter stood. From either side of the pit run eight grooves which join the base line of the triangle—the runners' starting line. Where each groove joins that line there is a post-hole and a bronze staple. Similar staples are found at the pit-end of the grooves. It seems quite clear that each post-hole held a post carrying a hinged bar (*balbis*) which could be raised or lowered by a string which ran through the staple at the base, along the groove in the pavement, through the staple at the pit end, to the hand of the starter in the pit; and so he would be able to release any or all of the runners at will (Plate 24).

Although all remains of the sanctuary area of Eleusis, the site of the Eleusinian Mysteries and one of the greatest and most interesting religious centres of the pagan world had been uncovered in a long series of excavations which began in 1882, the cemetery area of the town had remained untouched; and in 1952 a systematic investigation of it was begun as a joint project of the Greek Archaeological Society and of Washington University, St Louis, Missouri under Professor George E. Mylonas of Washington and Mr John Travlos.

It is a huge cemetery, about a mile long and in use from about 1800 to 1100 B.C. and later from about the fifth century to the beginning of the Christian era; and historic and prehistoric graves are mixed together in a rich confusion.

The most interesting discovery made therein is the "Story of the Tombs of 'The Seven Against Thebes' "—a sort of detective story with twists and surprises in the best manner of Wilkie Collins. It begins, in a sort of a way, in the second century A.D. when that traveller and gossip Pausanias, described the Sacred Way and the outer temples of Eleusis, refrained from describing the rest—"My dream forbade me to describe what is within the sanctuary" and proceeding to the roads leading from Eleusis to Thebes and to Megara, said that beside the latter he saw "the graves of the men who marched against Thebes". These are the seven champions who took part in the fratricidal war which followed the death of Oedipus. Of his twin sons Eteocles became King of Thebes, while Polyneices sought the aid of Adrastos, King of Argos, to drive out Eteocles. Adrastos gave Polyneices his daughter in marriage and a great army was collected led by Adrastos, Polyneices, Capaneus, Hippomedon, Parthenopaeus, Amphiaraos and the savage Tydeus. These are the Seven Against Thebes, who provided both Aeschylus and Euripides with themes for tragedy; and all perished in the savage battles at the seven gates of Thebes except only Adrastos, Polyneices and Eteocles the twin brothers perishing simultaneously in savage hand-to-hand combat. Euripides, Plutarch and Pausanias all say the heroes were buried near Eleusis, and Pausanias even said he had seen their tombs.

Towards the end of the first season the excavators came upon a large tomb, surrounded by a ring of large stones. The covering stones had gone but the walls were intact. Nearby other large tombs were revealed, until it was seen that here were six prehistoric tombs in the same level and all six were separated off from the rest of the cemetery by a low wall. True, among the six were two other smaller tombs of earlier date and lower level, but there were no later tombs and it certainly seemed as if this area had been set aside in the Historic period. Were these the tombs of the Heroes?

The excavation of the tombs was disappointing, but baffling. All had been investigated in the past. But not it seemed by tomb-robbers. In four the skeletal remains were disturbed as little as possible and the shafts through which they were investigated were re-sealed by pouring in small stones. The other two had been similarly treated but had been disturbed again at a later date. Among the stones poured in in these operations were fragments of pottery of the Classical period (450–325 B.C.). It seems clear therefore that these tombs were found in the Classical Era, investigated, resealed, walled off, and set aside as untouchable. The classical Eleusinians therefore must have been convinced that they had indeed found the tombs of the six heroes; and it must have been these which were pointed out to Pausanias.

Has modern excavation confirmed their belief? Alas, no. Although their furnishings were removed in antiquity, sufficient evidence remains to show that more than six persons were buried here, sufficient pottery has been discovered to show that the graves are not contemporary one with another and that they are indeed sometimes separated by entire centuries.

For the rest, the Eleusis cemetery proved unusually rich in children's tombs and it seems possible that the section excavated may have been one reserved for children's burials. These burials are usually richly provided with toys, miniature images and tiny pots, and are of many kinds, some being in terracotta coffins, stone sarcophagi, trenches covered with tiles, ancient graves emptied for the purpose and, most frequently, inside pots of great variety. Many of these pots are discarded wine vessels, one was an archaic amphora beautifully painted with animals, and one was one of the finest Proto-Attic vases yet discovered. It is a very large vase—over $4\frac{1}{2}$ ft high—three handled and painted by an unknown master of about 650 B.C. Although cruelly broken by ploughing, it has been restored with great success and its vivid paintings show scenes from Homer and Hesiod: Odysseus and his companions plunging the burning spar into the single eye of Polyphemus; and what is believed to be the earliest pictorial representation of the Gorgons, the scene shown being Perseus escaping with the decapitated head of Medusa, while Athene holds up the pursuit of her infuriated sister Gorgons, Stheno and Euryale. And the centuries are indeed bridged when we think that a child of 2,600 years ago was buried in a vase telling stories which are still told to the children of today (Plate 26).

Far removed from this, in northern Greece beside the Salonika-Edessa road, during building operations and the excavation of a basement, two column drums were found in May of 1957; and later excavations conducted by Dr Photios Petsas, Ephor of the Twelfth Archaeological District, Salonika, revealed that this was the site of Pella, the capital built by King Archelaos about 400 B.C., developed by Philip II of Macedon, and for a while, under Alexander the Great, the capital of the known world. The site is very large and very promising and very little is known about it, but great kings ruled here, Aristotle taught here and Euripides died here and this is the centre from which the great civilizing influence of Hellenism spread throughout the world in the three last centuries before Christ. Preliminary excavations have revealed a very large building with fine pebble mosaic floors showing such subjects as Dionysus riding on a panther, a lion hunt and a griffin attacking a stag; but these are just scratches of the surface and it is obvious that much remains to be discovered.

CHAPTER TWELVE

THE ISLES OF GREECE

SAMOTHRACE, a large, mountainous and infertile island at the northern end of the Aegean, not far from the Gallipoli peninsula, is perhaps best known to most people as the place of origin of one of the most famous and beautiful statues of antiquity, the Winged Victory of Samothrace, which is now in Louvre at Paris and was found in 1863 by Champoiseau when visiting the island. In antiquity Samothrace was famous as a cult centre for the mysteries of the Cabeiri, the unspecified "Great Gods"; and it was to make an exhaustive survey of their sanctuary that the Archaeological Research Fund of New York University (under the auspices of the American School at Athens) began operations in Samothrace in 1938. These excavations were interrupted by the war and were resumed in 1948 under the direction of Karl Lehmann.

The sanctuary lies in a valley at the foot of a 5,000-ft mountain and commands a view over the blue waters of the Aegean. Among the buildings which have been investigated or discovered are: a simple hall of about 500 B.C. used for the first degree of initiation and a small sacristy for records; the rotunda dedicated by Queen Arsinoe of Egypt in the early third century B.C., and, beneath this, sacrificial precincts dating from the seventh century; and the temple of the "Great Gods", a building of the third and second centuries B.C., which has a façade of Doric columns, an interior chamber between aisles and an apsidal end. Buried beside a corner of this building was a sister statue to the famous Victory, somewhat later in time (about the middle of the second century B.C.) and although graceful, quite lacking in the robust vigour of the Winged Victory. This state comes from the roof of the building, a position in which she would be able to look across to the magnificent hillside site on which the Winged Victory originally stood.

This hillside site was investigated with a view of discovering the original setting of the Winged Victory and also of settling the disputed date of the statue by studying datable pottery fragments around the foundations of the monument; and these points were settled. The statue can be dated to the years round 200 B.C. and it also appears that the statue, which it will be recalled is standing in the prow of a ship, stood behind and above a basin filled with water and framed partly by marble steps, partly by large natural rocks. Also, and most unexpectedly, in a water channel connected with this basin, another fragment of the statue was found, a right hand of marble, broken off at the wrist and with fingers and thumb missing. Even so, there was more luck to come, for when

Dr Lehmann and his associates visited Vienna to study some fragments found by an Austrian expedition to Samothrace in the 'seventies of the last century they found among them a thumb and part of the ring finger which exactly fitted the breaks on the newly discovered hand. To add to the value of these discoveries, these fragments make it possible to say that the right hand was empty and open, thrown up in a bold gesture of hailing and leadership, a fitting pose for so vigorous a statue.

The other principal discovery was part of a marble frieze (about 6 ft) long from an Ionic propylaea to the sanctuary. This shows a string of dancing maidens with a harp player and dates from about 330 to 310 B.C., but is in an archaistic manner and is perhaps the oldest major Greek work in this particular style.

In the neighbouring island of Lemnos, the excavations of the Italian Archaeological School of Athens conducted between 1930 and 1936 by Allessandro della Seta were resumed in 1951 under the direction of Professor Luigi Bernabo Brea. These excavations have revealed on the hill of Poliochni on the east coast of the island a vast inhabited area of the First Bronze Age, closely connected with Troy and indeed less than 40 miles distant from it as the crow flies. It began as a hut village considerably earlier than the rise of Troy I and very quickly became an urban settlement with solid city walls. It must have been one of the most important places in the Aegean during the period of Troy I and Troy II; and indeed at that time it was more than double the size of Troy itself. It was violently destroyed, almost certainly as the result of an earthquake about the same time as the burnt-out stratum in Troy which Schliemann called the "burnt city" and which was possibly some time about 2300 B.C. This destruction marked the end of Poliochni's prosperity, although life did continue on the site, in a very much reduced way, until about half way through the second Millennium B.C.

Quite easily the most outstanding discovery made was the finding of a treasury of gold jewellery. This discovery was made, by accident, at a point where digging had ceased in 1953. When digging was resumed there in 1956, it was necessary first to clear away suckers of plants which had grown up there; and as these suckers were pulled up their roots brought small gold objects with them. When collected and assembled this gold treasure was found, for quantity, variety and artistic interest to be second only to the gold treasure which Schliemann found at Troy and which he at first called "Priam's Treasure". The Poliochni treasure is indeed closely related to the Great Treasure of Troy and like it testifies to the high artistic and technical level reached by the Anatolian craftsmen of this age (Plate 29).

Perhaps the most interesting single piece is a large gold pin. This is a pin nearly 4 in long ending in two spirals and crossed with a bar likewise ending in spirals. The four spirals support two animal figures (probably birds) looking outwards and formed of thin layers of gold turned over and joined together along the edges. Next in interest and of more complex construction are two pairs of ear-rings. These are most elaborate and rich. The hook springs from a basket-like construction of filigree work of differing designs but of the same principle. From this basket, in each case, hang down five fine gold chains, to which are attached, all down the length, a number of petal-like gold leaves and each chain ends in a rather bollard-shaped pendant which, it is suggested, is a stylized idol. The effect of these ear-rings, when worn, would be one of great richness. A considerable number of small gold ear-rings, made of gold wire, in the form of shells or, more accurately, in the form of those "shells" of butter made by drawing a special instrument along a block of butter, were found and these are very like examples found at Troy. Five similar, but not identical, ear-rings resemble flowers from which the petals have been removed but the stamens left standing; two slender gold torques and sixteen gold buttons with embossed centres were found; and several thousand gold beads and necklace elements of varying sizes, shapes and degrees of complexity, some of which are of solid gold, while others are of gold sheet which have had a nucleus which has now perished. The shell ear-rings, it is worth noting, are of different qualities of gold, some being almost pure, while others are of a pale electrum.

All the major pieces are broken and the ear-rings are usually odd ones; and Professor Brea suggests that this hoard was not a jewel casket, but rather some wealthy family's gold reserve.

From 1952 to 1955, the British School of Archaeology at Athens under the direction of Mr M. S. F. Hood conducted a series of excavations at a coastal site in southern Chios. Chios, one of the largest islands of the Aegean, lies quite near the Turkish coast at the same latitude as Smyrna (modern Ismir) and was until 1912 under Turkish rule. Archaeologically speaking it is almost unknown although it was an important centre in antiquity and is one of the places credited with being the birthplace of Homer. It was a member of the Ionian League and like other members of that league eventually came under the rule of Athens.

The scene of the excavations is now known as Emporio and its ancient name is unknown, although it is possible that the archaic city may have been Leukonion ("white town") a city founded by families exiled from the chief city of the island because they had killed the king in a brawl at a wedding feast. It is a singularly beautiful site and consists of an almost circular harbour, looking towards the Turkish coast, protected on the south by a curving isthmus which rises to a rocky promontory; and sheltered on the north by the steep slopes of Mt Prophetes Elias. Here were found remains covering some 3,000 years: on the isthmus and the slopes of the promontory, an Early Bronze Age settlement, going back to the third millennium B.C.; on the promontory a Roman fortress which seems to have been destroyed in the mid-seventh century A.D.; a little inland, a Christian basilica which perished about the same time; near the harbour, a series of sanctuaries which may end at the beginning of the fifth century B.C. when the Persians took a savage revenge on the island for its part in the Ionian Revolt; and, overlooking the harbour, on a shoulder of the mountain and its slopes, an archaic acropolis and town of about the seventh century B.C., which was abandoned at about the end of that century, perhaps as the result of an earthquake.

It is this archaic site which is perhaps the most interesting. The acropolis consists of about five acres on the summit of a spur and it was surrounded by stone walls, 6 ft thick. Within this enclosure were two buildings: the *megaron* of the king, a long single-roomed house with a columned porch; and a temple, a very plain rectangular building built round an earlier altar, and with another altar in the open air. It seems to have been dedicated to Athene. Outside the walls were the houses of the little city, simple one roomed dwellings, smaller versions of the king's megaron, clinging to the slope and with steep roads winding in and out among them. A scene which it is easy to think approximated to that in Keats' mind when he wrote:

'Who are these coming to the sacrifice?
  To what green altar, O mysterious priest,
Lead'st thou that heifer lowing at the skies,
  And all her silken flanks with garlands drest?
What little town by river or sea-shore,
  Or mountain-built with peaceful citadel,
Is emptied of its folk, this pious morn?
And, little town, thy streets for evermore
  Will silent be; and not a soul to tell
    Why thou art desolate, can e'er return.'

In the sanctuaries beside the sea-shore, two interesting features were discovered. One was a pilaster base in the form of a lion's paw, made of blue-grey marble and about $1\frac{1}{2}$ ft high. This was found in the Christian basilica but it had been reused there and came from a fifth century B.C. temple. This is a motif common enough in furniture and tripods, but in architecture it seems to be confined to Chios. The second interesting point is that the temple from which this came was apsidal with a façade of four Ionic columns. It dates from the early fifth century and apsidal temples were rare as late as this. It seems to have succeeded a building which was also apsidal, or even possibly circular in form; and it is perhaps worth mentioning that the island sanctuary of the "Great Gods" in Samothrace was also apsidal.

The greatest of all the isles of Greece is of course Crete; and it was in Crete, of course, that at the beginning of the century Sir Arthur Evans discovered a great and indeed unsuspected civilization, the Minoan, much as Sir John Marshall at Harappa and Mohenjo-daro revealed the Indus Valley civilization. Since the war archaeological activity in Crete has been twofold: at Knossos, interrupted and dispersed, by the British School; and at Phaistos, continuous and concentrated, by the Italian Archaeological School at Athens.

The Italian excavations, which began in 1950, have been directed by Professor Doro Levi and they have been concentrated mainly on the south-eastern edge of the imposing western courtyard of the Palace; and their results have been threefold. They have shown that four palaces were built one on top of the other; they have brought to light an extraordinary wealth of beautiful, unusual and extremely striking pottery; and they have cast a new and revolutionary light on the dating of the earlier phases of the Minoan civilization.

The task of uncovering the four palaces has been slow and laborious, but rewarding. The walls in each of the excavated palaces were made in the usual Minoan way of small stones bound together with clay and frequently reinforced in all directions with wooden beams, probably as a precaution against earthquakes; and they were then covered with a plaster containing a lot of straw and then usually painted by way of decoration. When one palace was superseded, the rooms of it were levelled off and filled with a concrete of lime and potsherds (sometimes whole pots); and this concrete, which had set as hard as stone and perfectly capable of blunting the workmen's steel picks, has both made the work extremely difficult and slow and has also played its part in preserving certain aspects and recesses of the earlier palaces.

It is in such recesses, particularly recessed wall cupboards and, in one case, an underground repository, that the great wealth of pottery has been found. This is in a great variety of shapes and designs: beautiful polychrome and Kamares ware, eggshell ware of almost metallic thinness, ware decorated *à la barbotine* (i.e. with relief knobs in a sort of bramble pattern) and a number of curious and specialized shapes. Among these last may be mentioned examples of the "firebox", the "birdcage" and those curious horned vessels, which Sir Arthur Evans thought might have been used for keeping thread in—the sort of thing that we can imagine Ariadne using and possibly lending to Theseus to "thread his way" into the heart of the Labyrinth. One vessel is a sort of shallow sauceboat with a roughened knob in the centre—extremely like the modern lemon-squeezer. Found together, *in situ*, was an incense-burner consisting of three units, an elaborate stand in polychrome and relief, a pierced egg-shaped vessel which stood on the stand and probably contained the burning incense, and a large two-handled, footed vessel with a pierced base which seems to have fitted on top and served to diffuse the smoke of the incense.

But the most extraordinary group of pottery was one found altogether by a wall cupboard: the dining-room vessels of a rich and sumptuous civilization. Chief among them is a huge *crater*, like a vast wine goblet. The foot is moulded in alternate ridges and depressions rather like the edge of a pie, the rim is folded over. It is richly painted in several colours in a chequerboard pattern with bands of a coral design. Attached to the stem are four free-standing large white lily flowers; and on the body, just below the rim, there are two groups of two similar lilies. On the rim itself are four rings and from these rings hung a looped chain of white pottery links. Associated with this crater was an *oinochoe*, a spouted wine-pouring vessel, painted in the same manner; and it is clear that the two were a set used in banquets, some 1,500 years before this became the practice in Greece. With these were two tall three-handled spouted jugs, one of which was painted in alternate bands of dark and light, with a running white spiral on the dark band, and groups of scallop shells in relief on the light band; while the second had a painted decoration in polychrome of spirals interspersed with rosettes and rather fern-like patterns. The same sort of decoration, but much elaborated and developed, is found on a very large "fruit dish"—a shallow dish on a thickish foot—and here the rim is not only turned over but is cut into a great number of reflexed daisy-like petals. Still in this same "Royal butler's pantry" was a basket-like vessel of severely beautiful shape, very highly burnished and bearing an all-over wave decoration of red on yellow; a huge cylindrical vase with a built-in strainer; a "pilgrim flask" and two *rhytons*. These last are those drinking vessels which have a fine hole in the base and which one can not help thinking must have been rather messy utensils towards the end of the banquet. They are however of great refinement and beauty. One, which is a reversed pear-shape, is of white, prickly all over with barbotine decoration except for three bands of violet; and the other, which is spherical, is black with a pattern of parallel bare branches in white (Plates 27 and 28).

Among the interesting motifs painted on pottery and found by Professor Doro Levi may be mentioned: fragments showing Minoan women, rather schematized in form, dancing; a shallow dish showing two women dancing on either side of a highly stylized snake goddess; and a diminutive amphora showing two naked men with upraised arms, crudely drawn, walking among crocuses. This last is very rare indeed and possibly unique.

In the earliest layers of these palaces a few seal imprints were found, some carrying motifs derived from Egyptian symbols, but some showing linear letters; and in substructures in another excavation (near the Central Court) several thousand seal imprints were found together with about two dozen written tablets. These tablets principally carry hieroglyphic script but some of the inscriptions show signs of development to the shapes of the Linear Script A. Under the level where these were found, a deep Neolithic layer was excavated; and these discoveries, together with a weight of other small indications seem to indicate that linear writing began to emerge about 2000 B.C. when the first Palaces were being built; that the neolithic in Crete came forward to very nearly the same date; and that the Early Minoan phase was not in fact a long period, but a very short one of rapid transition; and that the Minoan civilization developed to its maturity with an amazing speed.

Of the British School's excavations in Crete the most recent is that initiated in 1957 under Mr M. S. F. Hood, the Director of the School; and the chief discoveries made were a group of ivories and an early tholos (or beehive) tomb. The ivories were discovered on the south side of the Royal Road leading from the Palace of Knossos to the Little Palace; and here inside an area of about 30 by 15 ft quantities of pottery dating from about 1900 B.C. to the destruction of the Palace about 1400 B.C. Among the rubbish and fragments of pottery of this latest phase the ivories were found. Many of them seem to belong to a box or casket but they also included parts of two ivory statuettes, outstanding not only on account of their beauty and craftsmanship but also because of their size—as the complete figures must have been larger than anything of the sort yet found in Greece (Plates 18*b* and 19*c*).

The casket fragments are mostly strips and mouldings of ivory with slots and dowel-holes on the back for attachment to a wooden foundation and much resemble those found by the late Professor Wace at Mycenae; but one very well preserved piece gives a vivid picture of a Minoan house façade. It is a grim façade of ashlar masonry with five slit-like windows, one on either side of the door and three smaller ones above in an upper storey. The door itself is apparently panelled with two cross-bars and is placed two courses of stone work above ground level, possibly as a flood precaution against water rushing down the steep slopes after heavy rains. The two ivory figures are human and when the larger was complete it must have stood some 16 in high and was of course made up from a number of separate pieces of ivory joined together. There are two surviving pieces of this: the right back of the trunk, from the shoulder to the waist; and the right arm. This arm was held out at right angles to the body and bent, again at right angles, at the elbow, while the fist was clenched—the whole approximating to a Communist salute. The work is one of complete naturalism, accomplished with great technical skill, the veins and muscles of the hand and arm being shown in subtle but distinct relief, with an almost Baroque insistence.

The other statuette, smaller in about the ratio of 7 : 9, also consists of two pieces: again a right arm, outstretched with thumb and fingers spread, and the right hip, clothed in apparently a close kilt. On the back of the right fore-arm is a slot which suggests that perhaps the complete figure had an open cape or draping of some sort. This has the same delicate and meticulous workmanship as the other; and both must have been either by the same artist or at any rate from the same workshop.

The tomb was found on the slopes of the hill called Gypsades not far from Hogarth's Houses. It is a small tomb (about 12 ft in diameter) and appears to have been used as a family tomb from about 1900 B.C. until at least some date later than 1600 B.C., when the floor was raised. Alongside the circular *tholos* was a rectangular ossuary to which the bones from the *tholos* were removed whenever a new burial was made. This perhaps a development of sensibility. In most continuously used ancient tombs, the bones of previous burials are usually indifferently shovelled to one side whenever a fresh interment takes place. As regards contents, the tomb was very poor, but its great interest lies in its date. Most of the Cretan *tholoi* are thought to have been built about 2000 B.C. At first they were thought to have been the inspiration of the mainland beehive tombs; but then this idea was abandoned on account of the great gap in time between them. This latest discovery, however—a *tholos* which was standing and in use when the first beehive tombs were being built in mainland Greece—once more revives and strengthens the theory that the idea came from Crete.

The other interesting excavation by the British School in the neighbourhood of Knossos took place some years earlier, in 1951. During the levelling of a site for a new hospital, several Minoan graves were discovered and since these lay in what may be called the British area of Knossos, Dr Platon, the Ephor of Antiquities asked Mr Piet de Jong to investigate them on behalf of the British School. They comprised four or possibly five graves, but since the doubtful one had in any case been ransacked in antiquity, there were for all practical purposes four graves: three chamber graves, one shaft grave. They stood by themselves and there were only a few burials in each grave; and they would seem to be the small private burial ground of a leading family. A leading family, because they were very rich burials, securely dated by the pottery to the last period of the Palace of Knossos, say 1450–1400 B.C.

The most important single piece was a helmet, bell-shaped with a hole for the plume on top and with cheek pieces, made of thin bronze sheet, a unique piece in fact although the shape is well-known from contemporary frescoes and the like. The pottery also was interesting; but the outstanding feature of the grave-goods was the wealth of formidable weapons, possibly the most formidable weapons found for the Near East of 3,500 years ago. These included: a long bronze sword with a gold covered hilt, the sword blade being nearly 20 in long; a large spearhead with a butterfly engraved across the spine of the blade; other large spearheads; a smaller spearhead, perhaps for a hunting spear; a business-like dagger with three gold bosses near the hilt; and a number of bronze arrowheads. The spearheads in particular are beautifully made weapons; and the find as a whole illustrates what Evans called the "military and indeed militaristic" aspect of the last phase of the empire of Knossos.

CHAPTER THIRTEEN

CYPRUS AND SYRIA

CYPRUS forms here, as it has done in history and prehistory, a convenient bridge between the Hellenic cultures and the Semitic and so Mesopotamian and Egyptian cultures. There is also the additional link in that the distinguished French excavator, Dr Claude F. A. Schaeffer after working at Enkomi (near Famagusta in Cyprus) which he identified with the ancient Alasia transferred, in 1951, to Ras Shamra in Syria, the famous site of ancient Ugarit.

Between the end of the war and the development of the unhappy political situation, Cyprus was the scene of considerable archaeological activity: at Curium and Kouklia in the south-west; at Pigadhes in the north-west of the central plain; and at Enkomi-Alasia in the east, near Famagusta.

The excavations at Curium were conducted by an expedition of the Pennsylvania University Museum, under the direction of Mr George H. McFadden; and were the continuation of those undertaken between 1934 and the outbreak of war. Ancient Curium lies about twelve miles west of Limassol in pleasant woodland behind the imposing white cliffs of Episkopi Bay. From one of these cliffs, writes Strabo in the time of Augustus, those who touched the altar of the god were flung into the sea. The god in question was Apollo Hylates (Apollo of the woodlands) and the temple and the sanctuary are his. The remains which are mostly of the early Imperial Roman times, although the sanctuary is much earlier in origin, consist of a large enclosure with two entrances, the Paphos Gate on the west and the Curium Gate on the east. Inside this enclosure are the temple and a number of other buildings of which the principal ones are the North-West building, a long rectangular building approached by steps and divided internally into two long naves by a central wall; the South building, which is a range of five deep U-shaped chambers side-by-side; and the South-East building, which may perhaps be identified as the *prytaneum* or senate-house. These two last buildings were excavated in 1951 and 1952. The south building consists of five rectangular chambers, side-by-side, opening off a common portico. They are identical in shape and only separated by narrow corridors. Each has a U-shaped platform along three walls, with a colonnade of Doric pillars on it; and from an inscription discovered it appears that they were called *exedrae* and that Trajan, during his fourth consulate (A.D. 101) built the two most westerly of them and dedicated them to Apollo Caesar and Apollo Hylates. Previous to this discovery there is no record of an 'Apollo Caesar"; but since the sanctuary was damaged in an earthquake of A.D. 76–77 which did severe damage in Cyprus, it is suggested that in gratitude for imperial grants-in-aid for the rebuilding, the local priesthood decided to establish a cult of Apollo Caesar. The South-East building, which adjoins the row of *exedrae*, and which may perhaps be identified with the *prytaneum*, is built round a circular court with porticoes all round, and a number of pieces of marble sculpture, of the Roman period, were found here. They include two fine female heads, one of which may be an Aphrodite; and a statue of a youth, taking part in a ball-game, which stood in a window niche overlooking the courtyard. This may have been an administration building; but it seems more likely that the court was a *palaestra*, or small gymnasium—there are baths just outside the near-by Curium Gate—with porticoes and small rooms for the leisured discussions of the elders. It is also suggested that the five *exedrae* served as hostels for delegations visiting the sanctuary and were perhaps reserved for citizens of a particular city or members of religious or similar guilds.

Near the actual temple lies an area called the Archaic Precinct and this has been the chief source of a number of interesting *ex-voto* statuettes and the like, in bronze and terracotta. These range in time from the sixth or perhaps seventh century B.C. to the second A.D. and throw an interesting light on a local style and standard of workmanship over a period of nearly a thousand years. They include horsemen, satyrs and animal figures, especially deer.

Not very far away, at Kouklia, the modern name for the site of Old Paphos, a joint expedition of the University of St Andrews and the Liverpool Museums, directed by Mr T. B. Mitford and Mr J. H. Iliffe conducted excavations during 1950–2 which led to a somewhat surprising discovery.

During their first season, which was of an exploratory nature they dug two sites, about fifty yards apart. The first revealed first a late mediaeval building, then a Roman building with a mosaic court of the first or second century A.D. Below these lay successive remains of pottery from Hellenistic through Classical, and Archaic to Geometric, i.e. about 1000 B.C. There was no obvious floor level however and in one point a dump of Archaic figurines and the like was found, discarded offerings no doubt from some near-by temple.

The other site, the mound, proved richer and more enigmatic. In general it appeared to date from the fifth century B.C.; but it contained a quantity of broken statuary, some of it of considerably earlier date, and was marked by signs of very fierce burning which in some places had reduced the marble to the consistency of sugar. Among the more interesting pieces were: a broken stone cone with inscriptions in the Cyprian linear syllabary; part of the marble wings of a sphinx, painted in red, blue and green; and two limestone torsos of youths wearing the old fashioned jerkin and "Cypriote belt" —a curiously modern-looking garment, uncommonly like a jock-strap or swimming trunks. In one case the sculptor has portrayed with exactitude the string knot with which the two halves were drawn together and it can be identified as a reef knot.

In the second season the mound continued to yield fragments of sculpture of very high merit: another youth in a jock-strap; another in the Egyptian style, wearing a kilt; and a bearded head wearing the double crown of Egypt, in the Assyro-Persian style and dating from about 525 B.C.—perhaps a priest-king of Paphos. In some respects however the most interesting thing found was the upper part of a twelve-sided column, in which each of the twelve faces bore a deeply-incised symbol of the linear syllabary, filled with bitumen. Also in the mound were found some courses of an ashlar wall, a ditch and a complex of rock-cut tunnels which had in some places been deliberately blocked; and it became highly probable that this had been a siege-mound dating to the early years of the fifth century.

Other sites in the neighbourhood yielded remains of Classical, Archaic, Geometric, Bronze Age and even Chalcolithic date. This last period, which is of especial interest in Cyprus and Syria, is that late stage of the Neolithic, when copper was already being worked but was still rare and its date is around 3000 B.C. Of especial significance were two untouched tombs of the early Geometric period (about 1050 B.C.) in which among the many contemporary pots were two Mycenaean vessels (at that time 300-year-old heirlooms); and this seems to indicate that here at least the Bronze Age was succeeded by the Iron Age without the general devastation which is believed to have marked the transition generally.

In the third season the nature of the mound and indeed a number of vivid details of its history were revealed. It was indeed a siege mound and it can be ascribed to the Persian attack on Old Paphos in 498 B.C. and it illustrates very vividly the tactics used in the siege of Plataea (429 B.C.) which Thucydides described. The mound lies over the ditch and against the wall of the city; and since at its centre it survives to a height of some 25 ft, this gives some indication of the height of the city wall. This wall consists mainly of a core of Late Bronze Age mud bricks of large size—the typical size being about 15 in long by 5 in wide—faced at various later periods with stone. The buttress which fortifies the gate near the mound is of fine ashlar. Into the mound had been heaped everything the attacker could lay his hands on, earth, stones, building material, statuary and tree-trunks; and in among it can be found the bones of those who perished in the attack, scores of arrowheads and spearheads, and a number of stone balls, flattened on one side and weighing up to 30 lb. It is very tempting to regard these as ballista ammunition; but, as far as is known, there was no "artillery" in the Greek world until at least a century later. Over against the mound the city wall seems to have been strengthened to meet the threat of the mound; but the most interesting counter-measures by the besieged were three or more tunnels cut under the city walls and into the heart of the mound. In these saps were still found niches to carry the miners' lamps (some of which survived *in situ*) and near by were jugs to slake their thirst. At the head of the sap it appears that the tunnel was braced and perhaps lined with timber and then a bronze cauldron, filled perhaps with pitch, was set up. This and, presumably, other combustible materials were then set on fire. This would have something of the effect and heat of a lime kiln; and since, as has been mentioned, the mound contained a quantity of tree-trunks, the purpose of the operation was undoubtedly to cause the mound to collapse.

Whether or not it succeeded in this purpose, it was, in the end, in vain. Old Paphos fell to the Persian besiegers; and a fine ashlar building near by, a little later in date and with certain parallels in style to the buildings of Darius I and Xerxes at Persepolis, may well be the house of the Persian governor after the Persians' conquest of the district.

During this same season nine Bronze Age tombs, at a site called Evreti lying within the perimeter of the walls of the Bronze Age city, were excavated. These tombs had been in use from 1450 to 1150 B.C. but the remains of the earlier periods had been cleared away during their use between 1230 and 1150 B.C. Despite looting and disturbance in antiquity they were still very rich tombs, containing fine pottery, gold jewellery and ivory—with a strong resemblance to corresponding finds from the Enkomi-Alasia cemetery at the other end of the island. The finest ivory is a mirror-handle, the broad part where it joined the actual mirror, being quadrilateral and showing in deep and lively relief a Mycenaean warrior slaying a lion. Other ivories included engraved box-lids, the carved handle of an iron knife, which was studded with stones which may have been seed-pearls, and a spoon in the form of a shovel of which the handle curves over in the shape of a duck's head. The gold includes armlets, rings, fragments of frontlets, ear-rings and the capping of cylinder seals. One of the rings is a signet and the bezel (or vitreous paste) shows two bulls and two letters in Cypro-Minoan script. Other gold rings have *cloisonné* bezels, dots and scrolls of paste being separated by *cloisons* of gold. A number of the ear-rings are of the kind called boat-shaped, that is to say rings of which the pendent half is very much thicker than the part which passes through the lobe of the ear; and there are as well four in which the pendant part is a delightfully executed ox's head.

During 1950 and 1951, at Pigadhes in the north-west corner of the central plain of Cyprus, not far from Myrtou, an expedition jointly sponsored by the Ashmolean Museum, Oxford and Sydney University, New South Wales, and directed by Miss J. Du Plat Taylor of the Institute of Archaeology and an Australian archaeologist, Miss Seton Williams, excavated a sanctuary which had been accidentally discovered in 1949 by villagers in search of stone. It was probably first occupied in the Middle Bronze Age, but the sanctuary in the form in which it was found was probably built about 1300 B.C. and continued in use until the Early Iron Age when it was overthrown by an earthquake. It consisted of a rectangular courtyard with store-rooms on two sides. Slightly off centre was a massive altar of ashlar blocks. Against the east wall it appears that sacred animals were stabled. There are a number of pierced stones and a stone shelf which could have served as a manger. There is little clue to the dedication of the sanctuary, unless this may be sought in a bronze bull figurine of about 1300 B.C. found among the debris of the altar; and two terracotta bulls with snakes entwined in their horns. In the store-rooms were found some bronze tripods, ring-stands and incense burners. The incense burners are not common in Cyprus and these most resemble the type found at Megiddo and other Palestinian sites. Another link with other cultures was an Egyptian heart amulet with a cartouche which is probably that of Ramses III. Perhaps the most striking object found was a *rhyton* of the late fourteenth or early thirteenth century. This is one of those curious drinking vessels, which, in the last analysis, are based on the funnel. This example is especially funnel-like, being in the form of an elongated cone, decorated at either end with bands of paint and, in the central section, with a stylized palm-tree and Mycenaean-style flowers.

Four miles north of Famagusta and north of the River Pediaeos, lies Enkomi, the island's most important Bronze Age site. Its burial ground has long been known and unofficial diggings as well as expeditions in 1898, 1913 and 1930 have uncovered there rich treasures of jewellery, ivories, bronze and pottery which have found their way to the British Museum, the Metropolitan Museum, New York and the Louvre. But the site of the ancient town eluded discovery and it was generally believed to have disappeared under alluvial soils carried down by the Pediaeos. In 1934 Dr Claude F. A. Schaeffer, under the auspices of the Académie des Inscriptions et Belles Lettres of Paris, investigated the site again and did discover an important building of the twelfth century B.C.

These investigations were not then pursued however and later the war intervened. However, after service with the Free French Navy, Dr Schaeffer returned to the island with the support of the Commission des Fouilles, Direction Générale des Relations Culturelles in 1946; and in 1947 he invited the co-operation of the Cyprus Antiquities Service. This was agreed to by the Director, Mr A. H. S. Megaw; and Dr Porphyrios Dikaios, Curator of the Cyprus Museum, directed part of the operations.

The history of the site covers some thousand years, and a number of details of that history emerged during the course of the excavation. It also transpired that Enkomi may be identified with Alasia, the capital of the island, mentioned under that name in the Tell Amarna correspondence (dating from the time of Akhnaten, father of Tutankhamen) and contemporary Babylonian, Hittite and Ugaritic (Syrian) records. The name, Alasia, was also given to the whole island and may well be derived from a Sumerian word for copper, which is interesting when we think that the modern name for the metal is the same as that of the island.

It is, then, perhaps convenient, to give here a rough summary of this history, as revealed, before proceeding to a description of the chief discoveries made.

From the twentieth to the seventeenth centuries B.C. it appears to have been a steadily prosperous copper-producing and trading centre—not unnaturally since it was such a rich source of the vital raw material of the widespread and splendid Bronze Age Civilization. Around the end of the seventeenth and the beginning of the sixteenth centuries there appears to have been a period of general distress, which ended however about 1550 B.C. when another period of general prosperity, lasting nearly 200 years set in. This was a period of close association with Egypt and towards the end of it, a king of Alasia is corresponding with the Pharaoh Akhnaten. During Akhnaten's reign (1370–1360 B.C.) Alasia was destroyed by an earthquake. It was rebuilt however and about 1350 there begins a period of Achaean ascendancy in Cyprus (which may perhaps correspond with that period of Achaean expansion which culminated in the capture of Troy). In this connexion it may be mentioned that modern Cypriote Greek is an archaic dialect, showing affinites with that of Arcadia, the homeland of the Achaeans. This was a prosperous period, but towards its close, say 1225 B.C., the Achaeans seem to have been superseded by other Mycenaean rulers, possibly from Rhodes; and the later stages are marked by the building of massive fortifications. About 1200 B.C. comes the arrival of the Sea People, who perhaps include the Philistines, those conquerors who coincide with the end of the Bronze Age. In Cyprus they consolidated, we may suppose, before that further expansion towards Egypt and that defeat at the hands of Rameses III c.1190 B.C., which turned the tide of their conquering advance. In Cyprus they appear to have settled down without undue disturbance and devastation and to have intermarried and become Cypriotes before very long. It is, after all, perhaps sensible to remember that invasions and conquests usually only change the rulers and governing classes and the general population tends to remain much as it was before. Somewhere about 1150 B.C. Enkomi seems to have suffered in that general change of climate, which brought a wetter and more Atlantic type of weather to Central Europe and the Mediterranean after the warm dry continental climate which had characterized the Late Bronze Age; and Enkomi at this period was the victim of heavy and even disastrous flooding. Indeed this change may have been one of the factors which caused the population to desert this important city about 1050 B.C.

At the start of his excavations Dr Schaeffer discovered wall foundations to the north, south and east of the city and a stone wall of gigantic dimensions, part of those massive fortifications which were built in the later part of the thirteenth century, when all over the Bronze Age world the rulers of that beautiful and rich civilization were preparing for their last stand against the newcomers.

Meanwhile a trial trench sunk by Dr Dikaios had encountered what was part, obviously, of an important building, the walls being built, as to the lower half, of large carefully dressed limestone blocks, with upper parts of *pisé* with a white lime facing. There was evidence of domestic occupation, but two rooms, adjacent to each other, were obviously a private sanctuary of some sort. One room contained the skulls of oxen and deer antlers, the remains of sacrifices to the god; while in the other in a corner, in a pit dug in what was probably the debris of the collapse of an upper floor, was the god himself (Plate 30).

This is an extremely interesting statue. It is in excellent condition, of bronze and about 2 ft high. It shows a youthful male figure, naked except for a fringed and belted loin-cloth, standing firmly on both feet, with the left hand resting on the heart and the right hand outstretched, palm downwards, at waist level. The head is wearing a conical cap, curly, as if made of sheepskin; and it is horned, with bull's horns pointing upwards and forwards. The face wears a slight, private smile, in the Mycenaean fashion, the nose is in the same line as the forehead in the classic "Greek" way, and the ears are rather prominent.

It appears to date from the mid-twelfth century, when the Sea People were established at Enkomi; and it is presumably one of their deities. Dr Schaeffer believes that this is the earliest representation of Apollo, the Apollon Alasiotes mentioned in a Greek-Phoenician inscription, and called in the Phoenician Reshef. Reshef was indeed a deity, a god of fertility; and Apollo may have an Oriental ancestry of this kind. Mr Dikaios, however, is more inclined to think that this is the god Nergal, whose name occurs frequently in the Tell Amarna correspondence between the king of Alasia and the Pharaoh; and in one of the letters, where pestilence in Alasia is mentioned, the phrase "the hand of Nergal is on the land", which could refer to the striking gesture of this statue, if we suppose that the gesture is, as it were, an attribute of the god. On the other hand the Tell Amarna correspondence is of the first half of the four-teenth century, 200 years earlier than the shrine in which the statue was found; and we need to suppose that the worship of Nergal had survived a drastic change of cultures, if we are to accept this god as Nergal. Apollo-Reshef would be the new god, Nergal the old one.

The two most interesting discoveries made in the later years of the excava-tions by Dr Schaeffer were, first, those associated with two tombs; and second, those made in what is called the "Achaean chieftain's house".

In an east-west street of the ancient city, a row of houses was found, Early Iron Age dwellings, superimposed on buildings of the Late Bronze Age. Below the foundations were a number of burial caves cut into the chalk below. Most of these had been found and despoiled by ancient or later tomb robbers, but two were found untouched, within a few feet of each other.

The first of these was apparently the tomb of a priestly family of the four-teenth century B.C. and contained three skeletons, two male and one female. They were lying on benches cut in the chalk in the spacious chamber and were surrounded by rich gifts. The female skeleton was surrounded by a great number of painted Mycenaean vases, golden ear-rings and finger-rings of delicate work-manship in filigree or engraved, two finger-rings with bezels carved with a good luck formula in Egyptian hieroglyphs, and a miniature statue of a child, in silver, used as a pendant. Also found in the tomb were examples of what one can only call the sophisticated bric-a-brac of the toilet table in alabaster, ivory and faience. On the breast of one of the male skeletons however was a pectoral of two large gold plates, laid in the form of a cross. Both bore the em-bossed representation of two winged sphinxes on either side of a tree of life. On his right hand was a gold ring engraved with the same motif. Beside his elbow were two large metal cups. Both were covered with a heavy lumpy green en-crustation and both were assumed to be bronze. They were sent to the Research Laboratory of the British Museum for treatment under Dr Plenderleith. They were discovered to be silver, covered with a corrosion leached out from the copper alloyed with the silver; and the larger was so thin and so corroded that nothing could be done about it. It was also quite plain. Not so the other: here, X-rays revealed a bull's head and flower pattern with startling clarity. It was subjected to a long and complicated treatment, with complete success and emerged in almost its pristine condition and beauty. It is a shallow cup (about 6 in in diameter and 2 in deep) with the typical Cypriote "wish-bone" handle. The legs of the wish-bone are barred with inlays of *niello* (a black metallic compound) and the junction is crowned with a knob ending in a rosette. The interior is plain; the exterior is inlaid in gold and *niello* with a complex but perfectly organized pattern. Round the rim is a border of black *niello* inlaid with equidistant and equal gold spots; while round the base are ten gold rosettes set in *niello* and separated from each other in a running looped design in *niello* and gold. In between these two borders are six bulls' heads with long curving horns, made up of gold and *niello*, all different in detail though similar in size and effect. Separating the bulls' heads are balanced pairs of flowers, in the same two media. This is a work of remarkable beauty and richness, similar in shape and design to the Dendra Cup which was discovered in the Peloponnese between the wars by Professor Perrson and which dates from the same period.

The near-by grave was a very large one, which had been in use from the Late Bronze Age to the Early Iron Age; and it contained some fifty-five burials, more than 370 complete vases, some of faience and multi-coloured glass and many other burial gifts. Its chief interest lay in the fact however that there was a period when it was not in use, after which there was a series of Iron Age burials; and these last deposits were in contact with the earlier ones. It is therefore clear that the Iron Age conquerors, who were thus opening and reusing a tomb of the conquered, nevertheless completely respected these earlier burials, despite the presence of rich grave goods, including diadems in gold and took pains not to damage the fragile glass and faience of their predecessors; and it seems reasonable to think that at Enkomi-Alasia the transition of cultures took place easily and smoothly, without undue destruction or protracted hostility.

The largest and most extensive building found at Enkomi was one in the western part which seems to date back to the period between 1350–1250 B.C., the period of Achaean ascendancy, and it is very well built of large ashlar blocks of stone, some as much as 9 ft long and 4½ ft high. The walls are double-faced and the upper courses are hollow, linked with cross-slabs, in a manner found in Schliemann's grave circle at Mycenae. The blocks were moreover worked to fit together with a tongue-and-groove technique. From its style, size, and Achaean connexions, this has been called "the Achaean chieftain's house". It is palatial in style, with big windows and several entrances, with the main rooms grouped about an inner court. It was briefly occupied by the "Sea People" conquerors, but after destruction by fire was partitioned into small houses and work-shops for casting bronze; and about this time, which may coincide with that climatic change mentioned above, the building was several times flooded and the large doors and windows of the building were walled up and the floor-levels were twice raised. The scale of these floods can be grasped when it is realized that in this part of the town they left behind deposits of sand and gravels nearly 3 ft thick.

In levels associated with the time of the fire, which may well be linked with an earthquake which occurred about 1100 B.C. were found two bronze seated deities and a throne, which, with the Apollo-Reshef-Nergal statuette, provide our sole light on the pantheon of the "Sea People" rulers of Enkomi. To begin with this seated deity is much cruder artistically than the horned deity and is almost schematic in style. It is not large and, as first found, consisted of a throne without arms, made of bronze, the seat being made to represent leather thonging. In the front edge of the seat were two up-standing tenons to hold the seated image in position. The seated image was a man wearing a tightly-skirted dress and holding both hands rigidly in front of him. It was awkwardly made and despite the presence of a tenon under the thighs did not fit the throne and leaned awkwardly back against the back of it. However in a slightly lower level, the original seated image was found, which fitted the up-standing tenons exactly and sat on the throne with some approach to dignity. This second figure has a large-nosed rather genial face and is holding a large cup in the right hand—which may perhaps account for the expression (Plate 31).

The history of this little group is therefore reasonably clear. In the earthquake and/or fire the throne and its original occupant (the cup-bearing figure) were lost. In the days of reconstruction the throne was found again, but not the deity; and a new and somewhat clumsy successor was made to fill the vacancy.

It is however perhaps unkind to speak so disparagingly of this pretender to the throne. Only fifty years separated the earthquake from the final abandonment of the site; and Enkomi-Alasia and its inhabitants were obviously in distress and decline when this clumsy deity was put together. An amateurish propitiation of the gods—confident races need no gods or can spare time, energy and skill to make splendid ones.

In 1953, after the formal excavations had been closed, Mr Dikaios found among sherds which had been used as the foundation for a thirteenth century B.C. hearth a most important inscription in the Cypro-Minoan script. This measures some $4\frac{1}{2} \times 3\frac{3}{4}$ in and is inscribed on both sides, one side containing twenty-two lines, the other sixteen, but these are not so well preserved. It is hard-baked clay of pinkish colour and is obviously a document of major importance, being the only considerable text in this script (Plate 30b and c).

In 1950 Professor Schaeffer transferred his attentions from Enkomi to Ras Shamra on the Syrian coast, the site which he had been excavating annually from the late 'twenties until 1939 and which in 1933 he had definitely identified with the capital of the North Syrian kingdom of Ugarit, previously only known from written records in Egyptian, Babylonian and Hittite documents of the middle of the Second Millennium B.C. From the beginning it had proved an exceedingly rich and indeed sumptuous site, producing treasures of art, striking religious objects connected with Baal and Dagon, documents in a language unknown until the discovery of bilingual tablets; and indeed fully supported the account of its exceptional wealth which Rib-Abdi, Prince of Byblos, had made in a letter which he wrote to his patron, the Pharaoh Amenophis IV and which was preserved in the Tell Amarna Archives.

The resumed excavations were concerned with the palace which Rib-Adbi described; and by the end of 1953 some 12,000 sq yds of this impressive building were uncovered and the southern and eastern limits had not then been reached. Among the features disclosed were sixty-seven rooms and halls, five large courtyards, eleven staircases leading to an upper floor and seven porticoed entrances. In the eastern wing of the palace, under a heap of charred debris was found a quantity of palace furniture, which had been taken from private rooms possibly in an attempt to save it in a crisis.

In this pile of furniture a number of outstanding pieces were found, of which the most notable may be mentioned. First perhaps is a trumpet, about 2 ft long, carved out of a single elephant's tusk and bearing, in relief and engraving, near the mouth piece, a naked goddess guarded by sphinxes with outspread wings. Next may be mentioned the ivory top of a circular table which originally stood on a single columnar leg supported on a base of three lion's feet. The top, with a diameter of rather more than a yard, was covered with three registers of carving, showing griffins, winged lions and winged bulls guarding the Tree of Life. And finally there was the largest single ivory carving to be found in the Near East, a panelled bedfoot of about 1350 B.C. and obviously from its subject matter the bed of no less a person than the king himself. In all it is about 3 ft 4 in wide and about 1 ft 8 in high and it contains sixteen beautifully carved panels in a generally Egyptian style. The individual panels are about 9 in high and vary somewhat in width. The central panel shows a standing goddess, horned and bearing the sun disk on her head, and she is giving suck to two royal striplings who stand in front of her and her expression is one of serene benevolence. On one side of this central panel are others dealing with the king as warrior and hunter of big game, killing lions, overthrowing his enemies and the like; while on the other side are domestic and courtly subjects, such as the young king and queen standing face to face and embracing each other fondly, the queen making offerings, and various court officials. The actual bedstead which these panels would adorn would most probably be like those found in the tomb of Tutankhamen; and the combined richness and elegance of this piece of furniture conjure up a royal ambience of great wealth, refinement and sophistication (Plate 32a and b).

Near the palace were discovered several private houses, spacious dwellings in one of which were found a number of texts, some in Babylonian cuneiform, others in the Ugaritic alphabetic script and one in the Cypro-Minoan Linear B, the first example of this script to be found outside Crete, Greece and Cyprus. A quantity of bronze armour was found in a neighbouring house and among this was a splendid bronze sword blade about 2½ ft long, of obviously European type, but engraved near the hilt with the cartouche of the Egyptian Pharaoh

Mineptah (1219–1210 or 1199–1191 B.C.). This Pharaoh was famous for having defeated the Sea People in a sea and land battle near the Delta; and it would seem as though his name was being used as an inspiration in those wars against the Sea People which marked the end of the Bronze Age.

This sword and the Cypro-Minoan tablet may perhaps be linked with a tablet found among administrative tablets from the Royal Palace which lists thirty families or houses, giving the number of wives, some of noble birth, and their children living under each roof. All these families originated in Alasia in Cyprus; and it seems likely that there was a colony of Cypriote traders living in Ugarit in Mycenaean times.

The tablets as a whole form an immense mass of administrative materials, lists of towns and taxes due, military material, and military levies, including members of an élite corps. Business documents of all kinds are to be found, notes of transactions and letters of credit relating to dealings in such commodities as horses, cattle, wine, oil, vinegar, wool, copper, lead, real estate and military equipment. Interesting and important single documents found are: a manual for treating sick horses; a long-hoped for bilingual text in classical Babylonian and the unknown Hurrian language; and what is probably the world's earliest horn-book, a small tablet giving the thirty signs of the Ugaritic alphabetical cuneiform script in their original order. Since this order is almost the same as the Greek alphabet from which our modern alphabet descends we have here the 3,400-year-old ancestor of our children's spelling-books.

A great number of Royal documents were also found, dated by references to individual kings who were contemporaries of the Pharaohs Tutmosis II, Amenophis III and IV, Tutankhamen, Horemheb and Rameses II. These tablets record Royal rulings and decrees, refer to a postal service with Egypt and the Hittite Empire and in one case grant a merchant the privilege of importing goods from Crete duty-free. There is a king's will with special provisions for the status of his widow; and a tablet listing the trousseau of the Queen Ahat-Milku, whose gold jewellery alone weighed about 33 lb and whose property included fifty-three different kinds of goods from jewellery and clothes to beds, chairs and footstools. These Royal documents are rarely sealed with the seal of the reigning king but rather with a dynastic seal, like an early Third Millennium seal, which refers to an ancestral king, Yaqarum, son of Nikmadu, King of Ugarit—which is as though our present Queen were to use only the Seal of William the Conqueror (Plate 32c, d and e).

Among the tablets recording Royal judgments it is perhaps remarkable that only one recorded the death penalty; and that was for treason. In another case where palace officials had combined to make a forgery of the Royal seal, the guilty parties were only exiled and their properties divided among more reliable subjects of the king.

In 1953 two archive rooms were found of the greatest historical importance since the tablets in them were concerned only with political, diplomatic and economic subjects. Many of them were concerned with relations with Ugarit's powerful northern neighbours, the aggressive Hittite kings from Suppiluliuma to Thudhaliyas IV and also her traditional allies, the Egyptian Pharaohs of the eighteenth and nineteenth dynasties. There is for example a treaty with Suppiluliuma and its covering letter, which refers to a revolt of certain kings against their Hittite overlord; and it is clear that the Hittite king, to prevent Ugarit joining his enemies, offers a formal alliance, which Ugarit accepts under pressure but without enthusiasm—a situation which has familiar parallels in these modern times. To quote Professor Schaeffer's own words, this is history "written by the very actors of the great contest of the fourteenth and thirteenth centuries" and a valuable addition to the Amarna texts found at Tell Amarna some seventy years ago.

Before passing to the excavation at the great eastern Syrian site of Mari, reference may be made to a superb silver and iron helmet which is now one of the treasures of the Damascus Museum. This had been found in clandestine diggings near Homs (ancient Emesa), came into possession of the museum and was brought to London for restoration in the Research Laboratory of the British Museum. This helmet, which dates from about the time of the Crucifixion, is one of those which completely cover the head and the face and the visor is indeed a portrait mask. It was made of iron and, although in the general style of a parade helmet and splendid enough to be one, was sufficiently sturdily made to be of use in battle.

The iron cranium was originally covered with cloth, the pattern of the texture being preserved in the oxidized iron and this cloth was probably a protection against the heat. A narrow silver band runs from back to front, with rosettes at either end. Round the brow, in silver, runs a laurel wreath in relief, and the neckguard, also covered with silver, bears an embossed design of acanthus leaves, birds and a butterfly. Both the wreath and the neckguard are parcel-gilt. The visor is in the nature of a life-mask and lifts up and forward from a single hinge on the brow. It is quite obviously an individual portrait and its owner must have been a member of the Sampsigerami, a dynasty of Hellenized Arabs then ruling at Emesa under Roman patronage. The eye-slits are long and narrow, but under each a trefoil of holes pierces the underlid and this must have had the effect of giving a bifocal vision.

The restoration of this helmet was, incidentally, one of the most striking achievements of the British Museum Research Laboratory. The whole inner shell of the helmet and visor is of iron; and iron when it oxidizes expands. This had done so and it had violently burst and distorted the silver mask; and the silver itself was in a very brittle condition. It was discovered, by testing a tiny flake, that the silver could still be annealed. The now completely inert iron oxide was removed by various delicate operations from inside the mask; and the fragments were put aside; and work began on the silver mask. This consisted of annealing it to restore its "nature", reinforcing the back with silver wire, closing gaps and restoring the original shape and where necessary silver-plating tiny spots and lines by means of the "ragging" process. This was then washed in distilled water, re-washed in acetone to dry it and the iron fragments replaced in their original position.

In the course of these operations the method of the original craftsman became clear. It would seem that he worked from a life-mask of the owner or an equivalent exact replica portrait. Working from this he then hammered out a slightly larger mask in thin wrought iron. With this in front of him, he then produced a mask in silver, slightly larger again, by the *repoussé* method; and fitted the two together, probably adding finishing touches with the engraving tool. The helmet when worn with the visor down would produce an effect of inhuman splendour, yet within human terms of reference, godlike, remote but still uncannily recognizable.

The ancient city of Mari was identified and revealed by Professor André Parrot in 1934 at Tell Hariri near Abu Kemal on the Euphrates not far from Syria-Iraq border and it was the subject of annual excavation by a French expedition directed by Professor Parrot until the outbreak of war. In the winter season of 1951–52, with the encouragement of the Syrian Government, excavations were resumed, again under the direction of Professor Parrot.

Mari is a site of very great antiquity which was continuously occupied by every pre-Christian civilization from 3000 B.C. to the Seleucid rule which followed the conquests of Alexander the Great in the fourth century B.C.; and it is essentially a Mesopotamian rather than a Levantine city, but, standing as it does at the western extreme of Mesopotamia in that "fertile crescent" to the north of the deserts, it is a bridge site and we can imagine it as an outpost and a transmitter of that urban civilization which had its beginnings in the valley of the two great rivers, Euphrates and Tigris.

The principal discovery of the first post-war season was an enormous construction of reddish sun-dried bricks, which was discovered to be the remains of a Third Millennium ziggurat, a "Tower of Babel" that is. A trench through the centre found its base, 29 ft down, and a foundation deposit which dated it to the Early Dynastic period. In its vicinity two sanctuaries were found, with a mass of shattered votive offerings. Among these were large quantities of bone and mother-of-pearl fragments which were the remains of bone and shell mosaic panels; a number of the characteristic Kaunakes, or flounced skirt statuettes; and a small but magnificent carved head of a man. This seems to have been part of a larger piece of sculpture, from the way the brow is carved in a scalloped line as though to slip into a prepared socket. It is of stone with traces of shell and lapis-lazuli, incrusted about the eyes and brows. It is only a small thing, nearly $1\frac{1}{2}$ in high, and it is perhaps dangerous to make too much of it; but it is nevertheless, one of those portraits which emerge from antiquity from time to time which have such a vitality and perhaps, as well, some kind of affinity with modern sympathies that it seems as though one immediately recognizes the individual original and is in tune with him across thousands of years.

In the next two seasons work was continued on the sanctuaries inside the *temenos* or sacred enclosure of the ziggurat; and they were found to number three and to be dedicated to the three deities, Ishtarat, Ninni-Zaza, and the sun-god Shamash. The floors were strewn with broken statues and figures, and patient restoration has brought to light not only a number of interesting works of art, but also, through the means of the inscriptions, the names of personages and what may be called facets of history. Historically the most important is a hitherto unknown king of Mari called Itur-Shamagan, a bearded figure with hands clasped across the breast, which was assembled from forty-five fragments. With him were his elder brother, Salim; his cup-bearer, Nani Suwada; and a character called Mesgirru, who is described as the "overseer" of the country. Another king is revealed obliquely, in the inscription on the back of an engaging seated figure, a female musician called Ur-Nanshe (or Ur-Nina) ("the Great Singer") who has dedicated her life for the King, Iblul-Il. Two goddesses were also found, a seated enthroned figure which is probably Ishtarat, the goddess of love, and a head which may be identified with Ninhursag. Still further quantities of elements of shell, bone and ivory mosaics were found. Among them are an engaging pair, male and female banqueters, the man pondering a cup of wine, the woman with arms clasped across her breast. There are recesses in both these—where the beard would be in the man, on the head and tumbling tresses of the woman—and it seems reasonable to suppose that these recesses were filled with some coloured inlay. They are a pleasant pair in any case but have the accidental additional value of appearing to have been drawn by Mr James Thurber and to be in fact characters in that perpetual "War between the Men and the Women" which he has revealed.

In the eighth season (1953) still more of these mosaic-elements were found, including some, especially, showing the sacrifice of a ram, the animal being thrown upon its back, while a man kneels by the head and holds together the two forefeet. More broken statues were found: a huge battered head of a king; the torso of a woman who had dedicated her statue to the goddess Ninni-Zaza; and a fine head of an elderly woman, who might perhaps have been Ur-Nanshe in age, although there was unfortunately no inscription surviving to prove it. There was also a fine standing figure of a worshipper with clasped hands and wearing the flounced skirt.

In the courtyard of the shrine of the goddess, Ninni-Zaza, was a grey basalt standing stone, a conical betyle, like one of those stones set up in high places and worshipped by the Canaanites and Phoenicians, and common enough among them, as the Bible witnesses. It is however the most easterly found and shows that Semitic types of worship had reached the Euphrates valley as early as the middle of the Third Millennium B.C. It had evidently been worshipped in the courtyard, as strips of bitumen were laid out on the ground around it, as if they were carpets or tracks for the priests circling about it.

Another interesting and indeed cryptic religious feature came to light, during the same season. In the temple of the sun-god Shamash, in the foundations of the early Second Millennium B.C. structure were found nine foundation deposits. These nine were identical terracotta slabs bearing an inscription 157 lines long.

This inscription is in the form of a dedication to Shamash by the King, Iahdun-Lim and bears witness to the king's gratitude to Shamash, especially for the victories granted to his arms against various enemies and most particularly for the fact that the victorious troops of Mari had actually reached the shores of the Mediterranean.

Beneath and symmetrically surrounded by the deposits of Iahdun-Lim was a large pit, which had been filled in antiquity with earth and gravel, which was very easy to remove. Beneath the gravel were only a few potsherds. Two suggestions have been made: either that this was a royal sepulchre, violated thousands of years ago but still venerated; or that it was a *gigunu* or ritual marriage bower set in the heart of the temple. There seems little prospect of solving this puzzle.

Towards the end of this season a large building of brick, with a regularly recessed façade, rather like the early *mastabas* of Sakkara, was found and called for convenience "the Redans Monument". On fuller excavation it proved to be smaller than was expected; and was thought to be the private house of an official. In one of the rooms were found the three first pre-Sargonid tablets ever found in Mari. In the doorway near an alley was found a large and indeed unique piece of pottery for Mesopotamia—a clay model of a house. This consists of a roughly circular outer wall, pierced by single entrance; and within are nine partitions, eight rooms, that is, arranged round a central courtyard; and the walls of the courtyard are higher than the rest and make a sort of stubby tower. When found it was surrounded with bricks, and all the compartments, rooms and courtyard, which are all open at the top were filled with small pots of the same period—the first half of the Third Millennium B.C. Its significance is mysterious: there is no burial near by; there is nothing to suggest that it represents a temple; and it was found virtually in a street; and another example was found during the same season. For the two of them there is no Mesopotamian parallel; and although, of course, they are of the greatest interest in their own right, as showing what a house of the period looked like above ground, they continue to tease the imagination.

Beneath an Assyrian and Seleucid necropolis were found houses of the First Dynastic Period of Babylon (beginning of the Second Millennium B.C.) with later buildings on the same plan. In these were two hoards of bronze objects, including bowls, a goblet, pruning knives, a tray and hoe. On the bowls and goblet were found inscriptions mentioning the names of two of the daughters of Naram-Sin, King of Akkad. These inscriptions are of great importance as they fill a gap in the city's history. They reveal in fact that Mari, which was destroyed at the end of the Early Dynastic Period (about the middle of the Third Millennium B.C.) was rapidly raised from the ruins, rebuilt and indeed honoured by the Kings of Akkad. Naram-Sin built a palace at Tell Brak (discovered by Professor M. E. L. Mallowan) and since it lies on the same route as Mari he must have been interested in the security of Mari; and Professor Parrot suggests that he may well have installed two of his daughters there, perhaps as high priestesses in the shrines of Mari, as his representatives.

Not all archaeology is on this high and speculative plane; it sometimes speaks directly to the heart. In this necropolis which we have mentioned as overlying this last quarter were many burials of the third and second centuries B.C. Among them was a pottery sarcophagus, of that type which is rather like a cardboard Easter egg. When the upper half was lifted there was disclosed the burial of a woman, with a straw basket laid upon her breast and remains of a bunch of flowers—not the mere representative grave goods typical of the period, but an individual token of love to a lost wife or mother.

CHAPTER FOURTEEN

JORDAN

DESPITE its small area and its tense and troubled history, the Hashemite Kingdom of Jordan has been since the war the scene of considerable activity by the archaeologists; and two of the discoveries made have been of such outstanding importance, each bringing controversy in its train, that other finds have not unnaturally been overlooked; and although Qumran and Jericho dominate the picture they are not the only elements of it; and it is perhaps advisable to discuss those other elements first.

Like most new or recreated kingdoms of the Near and Middle East, Jordan set up a Department of Antiquities, directed and trained by an Englishman, Mr G. Lankester Harding, who remained in charge of it until the political convulsion which saw the departure of Sir John Glubb and the rejection of British assistance and tutelage in 1956.

Cairns in the desert are not uncommon and to this day the Bedouin still erect them over prominent people who have been killed; but the cairns erected by the Safaites, a nomadic people who wandered during the first to seventh centuries of this era about the lava belt which extends between the frontiers of Jordan, Syria and Iraq, have an especial interest. The Safaites seem to have had a passion for writing; and their cairns are always full of almost gossipy inscriptions scratched on stones and sometimes illustrated with pictures. Their language is pre-Islamic Arabic with some Aramaic influence and the script is one of the South Semitic group all of which are extinct except Ethiopian. In 1950 and 1951 Mr Harding and Hassan Awad investigated a very large Safaite cairn near the road to Baghdad; and found in it no fewer than 107 stones with inscribed texts.

The tomb was that of a young and powerful holy man, bearded and equipped with staff, leather bag and wooden begging bowl, one Hania, son of Aqrab, son of Hania, son of Hayar. In the outskirts of the cairn an elderly woman had been buried somewhat later; and this may well have been the holy man's mother, rejoining in death her distinguished son. It would seem that Hania had been killed by an arrow in the back.

The actual inscriptions are interesting and in their simplicity very vivid. That which records the name of the deceased adds: "By Zawar, son of Haras; and he built for his paternal uncle." One carrying a crude picture of a piper and a dancer states: "By Aqriban, son of Kasat, son of Saad. The beautiful woman plays the reed pipe." Another showing a horseman spearing a lion, also records that it is the work of Aqriban and adds: "Oh, Allat, what a horseman!" Allat and Dushares were the chief deities of the Safaites. Another text reads: "By Umaiyat, son of Akul, of the tribe of Hulay. And he grieved deeply for his dog which had strayed. So, O Allat, grant that he may return."

One of the most interesting drawings solves definitely the problem of the "desert kites". These are large constructions of stone walls, often found in the desert, in the general shape of a child's kite; and they have been the subject of considerable speculation, both as to their purpose and date. One of the stones in Hania's cairn shows one of these kites, with a number of goats at the closed end and three men driving other goats to join them beside a palisade; and the inscription reads: "By Menat and he built for Hania and he drew the enclosure and the animals pasturing by themselves." And from this it is quite clear that the "desert kites" were animal compounds for times of danger and that they date from at least the seventh century A.D.

In 1949 four small pieces of statuary came into the possession of the Antiquities Department. They had been found by a man excavating the courtyard of his house in Amman and any other evidence bearing on them was destroyed at the time, if it existed. They perhaps date to about the ninth century B.C. One is the very battered torso of a composite statue of a man, almost life-size; the second is the head of a small limestone figure, a bearded man, who probably originally had eyes of shell or metal; and the other two are reasonably intact statuettes of men. The smaller is 47 cm high and shows a standing king or priest, bearded and with a fillet tied round the hair. The left hand, holding a lotus, is held against the breast, while the right hangs straight down. The robe, which appears to be pleated hangs straight to the feet, and two tassels, with X crosses, hang down in front. The upper part of the robe is draped, like a baldrick from the left shoulder to the right hip. The eyes, which are missing, were evidently inlaid. The head is large, out of proportion to the body and the whole effect is squat but impressive, the workmanship being detailed but rough. This statuette is of a soft limestone. The other, which is nearly twice as big, being nearly 80 cm high, is of a hard grey stone and is basically the same in dress and posture. The feet, however are side by side and the body leans somewhat backward. The eyes are carved, not inlaid; and the figure wears a pseudo-Egyptian crown. The smaller figure has an inscription on the base which eluded translation; and the roughness together with the combination of Mesopotamian effect with Egyptian motifs suggest that this was probably local Jordanian work and quite unlike anything hitherto found there (Plate 46*b* and *c*).

"And Abner the son of Ner, and the servants of Ishbosheth the son of Saul, went out from Mahanaim to Gibeon. And Joab the son of Zeruiah, and the servants of David, went out, and met together by the pool of Gibeon: and they sat down, the one on the one side of the pool, and the other on the other side of the pool. And Abner said to Joab, Let the young men now arise, and play before us. And Joab said, Let them arise. Then there arose and went over by number twelve of Benjamin, which pertained to Ish-bosheth the son of Saul, and twelve of the servants of David. And they caught every one his fellow by the head, and thrust his sword in his fellow's side; so they fell down together: wherefore that place was called Helkathhazzurim (i.e. *the field of strong men*) which is in Gibeon. And there was a very sore battle that day; and Abner was beaten, and the men of Israel, before the servants of David." (II Samuel, 2, 12–17.)

The scene of this grisly "play", "a great city . . . one of the royal cities" was identified in 1956 and partly excavated in that and the following year by an American expedition, directed by Dr James B. Pritchard and sponsored by the University Museum of the University of Pennsylvania and the Church Divinity School of the Pacific, with the co-operation of the American School of Oriental Research in Jerusalem. It lies at el-Jib, an Arab village 8 miles north of Jerusalem and very near the border with Israel. Its bloodstained history continues and while the excavators were turning up the slingstones of the time of David and lumps of shrapnel from the campaign of 1918, they could smell the powder from an Israeli-Jordan border incident a few miles away and see the Jordanian anti-aircraft fire bring down an Israeli aircraft. The identification of the site was more than ordinarily satisfactory as in the first season alone three wine jar handles were found with the word "Gibeon" scratched on them in ancient Hebrew characters—an identification unique in Palestinian archaeology.

The area of the ancient city is large, about sixteen acres, and much excavation remains to be done before all is revealed. Small selected sites were rented from local landowners, excavated, filled in, and replanted with figs, grapes and tomatoes. There appear to have been five cities on the hill: the earliest of about 3000 B.C.; another of about 1800 B.C.; next the city of David and Saul, with its heyday in 800–600 B.C.; next a period of occupation in the first century B.C.; and finally a town of Byzantine and Arab times.

A city wall of Biblical times was discovered, of a general width of 10 ft, enlarged at certain points to 26 ft; but the principal discoveries relate to the inhabitants' incessant search for the water-table of the hill and so a secure water supply within the massive walls. The first of these is a 170-ft tunnel system, with well-worn steps cut in the solid rock, leading to the principal spring, and with access within the city walls. In time of siege, the outer entrance to this reservoir could be shut with a stone door like the portcullises inside the Egyptian pyramids. This system was probably cut from the living rock in the eighth century B.C.

The other water supply is the celebrated Pool of Gibeon and in the course of the 1956 and 1957 seasons this was excavated in full. It was revealed as a circular shaft, with a diameter of 36 ft cut from the solid rock to a depth of 33 ft, with a spiral stairway cut into the side and leading to the bottom, with a solid banister, as it were, also carved from the rock. At this point the ancient engineers gave up the open shaft and continued downwards with a spiral stepped tunnel until they struck water 49 ft farther down. At this point, 82 ft below ground level they carved out a large room to collect the water which dripped from the crevices of the rock; and they pierced two shafts upwards to the floor of the circular pool to provide sources of light for the drawers of water, who had to come down 158 stone steps to fill their vessels before trudging up the same 158 stone steps again (Plate 33).

It is not definitely established when this feat of engineering was accomplished; but its filling-in, which was deliberate, dates from about the beginning of the Jewish Exile, early in the sixth century B.C.; and it seems probable that Nebuchadnezzar in either 598 or 587 B.C. captured the city and demolished its water supply.

From the materials used in the filling in has come the evidence of Gibeon's day-by-day life and the sources of its fame and prosperity. This debris seems to have come from the business district of seventh century Gibeon and it is full of fragments of wine jars. Among them were no fewer than fifty-four handles of wine jars which had been inscribed in archaic Hebrew characters with the names of the makers of the wine. The usual formula is the name of the city "Gibeon", followed by a word which is provisionally read as meaning "the walled vineyard" and then usually one of three names, Azariah, Amariah or Hananiah. Other names occur, but these are so frequent as to suggest that these were the three great wine manufacturers, men whose name on a wine was a guarantee of its quality. In addition to these, as it were, brand names, there were some private seals; and some of these were royal. These last showed the winged sun-disk emblem which was common in Egypt and Assyria, and contained the words "For the King" followed by one of four town names, Hebron, Ziph, Socoh and Memshath; and we can only suppose that these added seals are the Biblical equivalent of "Cuvée reservée"; and that Gibeon was in effect the "Bordeaux" of Biblical Palestine.

These discoveries, interesting though they are, are only a foretaste of the riches to be found when the excavations among the houses of Gibeon are put in hand in the future.

Another excavation in Jordan of great Biblical interest is the large-scale American expedition mounted by Drew University and McCormick Theological Seminary together with the American Schools of Oriental Research, and directed by Professor G. Ernest Wright, the object of which was the investigation of Biblical Shechem. This is the modern Tell Balatah, not far from Nablus and it had been partly excavated between 1913 and 1934 by German archaeologists. The Drew-McCormick expedition started work in 1956 and continued in 1957 and further work was planned for 1959 and 1961.

The most striking remains yet revealed are the fortifications of the Middle and Late Bronze Age periods which are complex in organization and cyclopean in construction. Traces of habitation in the middle of the Fourth Millennium B.C. have been found but Shechem seems to have reached its highest prosperity in the Middle Bronze Age and its zenith seems to have been about 1650–1550

B.C. at which point it was thoroughly destroyed, probably by an Egyptian force. In the Late Bronze Age (1500–1225) it was rebuilt, but on a less impressive stage; and from the absence of evidence of physical destruction and from the fact that the Bible makes no reference to Joshua's conquering it, it would seem that Shechem came to a friendly agreement with the invading Israelites. There are indeed plenty of references to Shechem in the Bible, but little evidence of this period has been found on the site; and in fact Shechem seems to have declined considerably when Omri built the new capital for his dynasty at Samaria. Subsequently however the city enjoyed a sort of Indian Summer in Hellenistic times from about the late fourth century B.C. until its capture in 128 B.C. by that ferocious character John Hyrcanus. Future excavations, however, of domestic buildings on the site (and perhaps a necropolis) may throw more light on what life was like in ancient Shechem.

The story of the Dead Sea Scrolls—certainly the most sensational story in archaeology to catch the public fancy since the war—may one day find an adequate annalist. He will need to be a polyglot, an outstanding Hebrew scholar, a jigsaw specialist, a man with a monumental and genial knowledge of the ways of the Near East and the jovial moral detachment of a Rabelais or a Montaigne. He will need the patience—and the elbow room—of a Proust; he should have affinities with both the Burtons, the translator of *The Arabian Nights* and the anatomist of melancholy; it would be pleasant if he could write like a combination of J. J. Morier and Norman Douglas; and it would be an advantage if he were a priest, of some denomination. This would be a delightful book to read. By the time it is written there will be thousands of others—there are already hundreds—in many languages; and "great Argument/About it and about: but evermore/Came out by the same Door as in I went."

A few facts should perhaps be given; but such are the circumstances of the many discoveries and such the miasma of scholarly rancour which has arisen about them, that this is extremely difficult and unlikely to be acceptable when done.

It all began in 1947—and a worse date could hardly have been chosen, with Jews and Arabs at each other's throats in Palestine and the British Labour Government under pressure of advice and abuse from all the world, in and out of the United Nations, deciding that it had had enough of trying to keep the thing on a Queensberry Rules basis—when a young Arab goatherd pursuing a wandering goat on the savage escarpments near the Dead Sea threw a stone into a cave and heard it break a pot.

As a result members of his tribe came into possession of a number of rolled parchments and various pots; and being aware that antiquities sometimes had a value, smuggled these into Bethlehem, where they consulted a Mohammedan elder. He realized that the writing was not Arabic (and therefore not of interest to him) and referred them to a local dealer in antiquities called Kando, a Syrian, who consulted another Syrian who consulted Mar Athanasius, the Archbishop Metropolitan of the small sect of Jacobite Syrian Christians. There followed a complex series of negotiations, rebuffs, misunderstandings, in a Jerusalem which was growing hourly more dangerous and during which fragments of ancient parchment were carried hither and thither rather as travellers' samples; and by July 1947 Mar Athanasius was in possession of five scrolls, purchased as a pure speculation (since he didn't know what they were) for, it is said, £24 or, according to another version, £50. In November the same year (1947) Professor Sukenik of the Hebrew University returned to Jerusalem and was told that a Bethlehem dealer had three ancient scrolls and, being one of the few scholars capable of making such a diagnosis, almost immediately realized that these were Biblical manuscripts of fantastically unprecedented antiquity and in spite of the danger made his way to Bethlehem and purchased the three scrolls which for some reason or other had not been offered to Mar Athanasius.

Meanwhile Mar Athanasius had been seeking opinions on the scrolls that he held, without much success, even taking them with him to Homs to consult his Patriarch about them. A number of people of greater or less competence saw them during the autumn of 1947 but they appear to have been so sceptical or cautious that Mar Athanasius began to believe that he had made a bad bargain. In February 1948 however one of his monks recommended that they should be shown to the American School of Oriental Research and here at last the Acting Director, Dr J. C. Trever, while not so quick to realize the nature of the scrolls as Professor Sukenik, nevertheless perceived that they were of the first importance and got the bishop's agreement to photograph all the scrolls in his possession, except one, which was not yet unrolled.

One of the scrolls, the Americans realized, was of Isaiah, and some prints of parts of it were sent to America to Dr W. F. Albright, who immediately, like Dr Sukenik, realized the immense importance and the unique nature of the discovery.

In the meantime Dr Sukenik had held a press conference and the news had reached the world's headlines. The hunt was up—or rather it would have been, if the British Mandate had not come to an end to be succeeded by war between the Israelis (as they had now become) and the Arabs.

In this state of affairs, after his monastery had suffered war damage and one of his monks (the one who had suggested the American School) had been killed, Mar Athanasius left the country with his scrolls (which the American School had arranged to publish) and by early 1949 reached the United States where he planned to sell the scrolls for the benefit of the Syrian Jacobite community. Unfortunately for him the publication of four out of his five scrolls, and the doubt thrown on the legality of his title to them, in as much as he had removed an antiquity from the country of its discovery without permission, spoilt the market for them. He was even led to advertise them for sale in *The Wall Street Journal* and a sale was eventually made, in February 1955, for $250,000 to an anonymous purchaser, who turned out to be General Yadin (Professor Sukenik's son) acting for the Israeli Government, and the eight scrolls of the original discovery were at last reunited in Israeli Jerusalem.

The nature of these scrolls and what the scholars have made of them is obviously not within the purview of this book. In February 1949 however archaeology entered into it and Mr G. Lankester Harding, Director of Antiquities in Jordan and Father de Vaux of the *Ecole Biblique et Archéologique Français de Jerusalem* visited the cave at which the scrolls were found and conducted a systematic survey of it. They found that it had been visited several times, that another entrance had been made or enlarged, that there were the fragments of some forty pots in the cave and that some visitor had left behind a cigarette holder. Nevertheless, their visit was not in vain; they discovered that the pottery could not be later than the early first century B.C. and by the most careful sifting of the dusty floor of the cave collected about a thousand tiny fragments of crumbled parchment; and they carried out a brief and not very satisfactory examination of an ancient site above the cave and about half a mile distant from it.

However the next year the same pair of archaeologists under the auspices of the Jordan Department of Antiquities, the *Ecole Biblique et Archéologique Français de Jerusalem* and the Palestine Archaeological Museum, reopened excavations on the site, which is called Khirbet Qumran, and continuing these over some four years eventually uncovered a self-contained monastery with potters' quarters, flour mills, ovens, storage bins and an elaborate system of water conservation in twelve large cisterns. A number of coins were found which serve to date the site with some accuracy. It seems to have come into being about 125 B.C., to have been destroyed by earthquake in 31 B.C., rebuilt about 5 B.C. and finally destroyed by the Roman Tenth Legion in A.D. 68. In the ruins of one of the rooms were found masses of broken plaster with a core of mud bricks, which when reassembled, are seen to be long writing desks with attached benches and since ink-pots of pottery and bronze were also found among the debris it seems certain that this room was a *scriptorium*; and it is not difficult to believe that manuscripts were written here which were among those hidden in the caves under the threat of Roman attack in A.D. 68 together with other manuscripts which could be part of the monastery's library and conceivably even earlier in date than its foundation (Plate 34).

Many believe that this was an Essene monastery and since John the Baptist was almost certainly an Essene, he could well have studied here. Some indeed even consider that Christ himself may have studied here likewise in the days of his tutelage.

Other finds of manuscript have been made in the district, in eleven caves, in all, according to some accounts; and one cave, known as Qumran IV, which was found in 1952, has produced far more material than the original discovery, but it is much more fragmentary and has presented a gigantic series of jigsaw puzzles to the scholars working in the Palestine Archaeological Museum. It comprises fragments of every book of the Old Testament except Esther, most of the known Apocrypha and many hitherto unknown and a number of Sectarian documents.

To most people who have had a Biblical upbringing—fewer now perhaps than formerly—Jericho is the city that Joshua took, after marching round it on seven days, the priests blowing on the ram's horn trumpets and all the people shouting and the walls thereupon falling down—a capture followed by whole-sale slaughter, "man and woman, young and old, ox and sheep and ass", with the sole exception of the family of the most famous of Fifth Columnists, Rahab the Harlot. . . . A horrible and instructive story, no doubt, to which the mind puts forth the instinctive gloss that it was far away and long ago.

In a sense, so it was: the fourteenth century B.C., the later Bronze Age 3,400 years ago. But so ancient is Jericho, that the stratum that was the city Joshua destroyed has been nearly all eroded away and yet there remain layers and layers of habitation going back to at least 7000 B.C. Joshua is nearer to us in time than to the first inhabitants of the city he destroyed.

It was in 1935 that the late Professor John Garstang discovered evidence of settled occupation in Jericho going back to at least 5000 B.C. In 1952 the British School of Archaeology in Jerusalem resumed active work there under its direc-tor, Doctor Kathleen M. Kenyon, and various British, American and Jordan-ian institutions were associated in support of the work, which has gone on steadily since then, despite occasional difficulties arising out of the manifold political tensions which have racked the Near East.

It is impossible here to give anything like a complete account of all the discoveries which Miss Kenyon has made, which are many in number, of the first importance and indeed sensational and, in some degree controversial; and it is perhaps preferable only to indicate and briefly describe the highlights, which are: the plastered skull portraits, the curiously well-preserved Bronze Age tombs, and the incredible antiquity of the city walls and *urban organization* of the first Jericho.

Towards the very end of the 1953 season, in a level which was tentatively dated to about 5000 B.C. seven skulls were found lying together, in a tumbled heap. All of these had been covered with plaster modelled with surprising delicacy into the features of the living person, not a standard or stylized human head, but an individual portrait. One of the seven contained the lower jaw-bone, but in the other six the chin and lower jaw were modelled entirely of plaster. The eyes were filled with shell. In six of the heads each eye was made of two triangular pieces of shell, joined in such a way as to make a perpendicular line in the centre of each eye and giving a somewhat animal effect. In the seventh skull, each eye is a cowrie shell, the opening in the shell showing hori-zontally from corner to corner of the eye and giving the impression of human eyes closed in sleep. The tops of the skulls are left uncovered, although one has bands of dark paint, which may perhaps represent a head-dress. On some, traces of pinkish paint survive and it seems clear that the naturalism of the portraits—for such they must be—was enhanced with the use of colour. In the best preserved the features are modelled with great delicacy, especially in such aspects as the mouth, the nostrils, the eyebrows and the folds of the eyelids (Plate 35*b*).

Miss Kenyon herself has written: "These heads are the earliest known examples of naturalistic plastic representation of the human features which can be claimed as the direct ancestors of modern art. The great art of the Palaeolithic period has no direct descendant. But from the art of Neolithic Jericho the tradition descends through ancient Sumer and Egypt to the art of the Greeks and thence to modern Europe."

It is difficult, indeed impossible, to be certain of the purpose of these portraits. They may be venerated ancestors, they may be the heads of enemies preserved as trophies; the loving care would suggest the former, but then hatred can be a source of meticulous work. Perhaps the most astonishing aspect is that they were made by a people who had not yet discovered how to make pottery—a curious reflection on the seniority of an advanced art form over an elementary utilitarian technique.

The ancient cemetery of Jericho was discovered in 1952, by accident, to the north of the city on the slopes which stretch back to the mountains of Judah. This site was occupied by a very large camp of Palestinian refugees and during this particular year it was being converted from a tented camp into a mudbrick village, each family building its own house. For this purpose the refugees were quarrying in the soft limestone in order to make mortar; and one of them brought Miss Kenyon an Egyptian scarab he had found and which had obviously come from an ancient tomb. As a result she began excavations and eventually it became clear that the refugee settlement overlay a very large ancient cemetery, containing burials from about 3500 B.C. to about the tenth century B.C. The richest of these however belonged to the second half of the Middle Bronze Age (say 1800–1560 B.C.). These graves took the form of a vertical shaft cut into the soft rock; and at the bottom of this shaft there would be a small door in one side leading to the underground burial chamber. This chamber, this family vault, would be used over several generations; and while each burial would be carefully and devotedly furnished with the appropriate grave goods, the previous burials in the same chamber would be treated with the scantest respect and the older offerings and bones would be shovelled to one side and piled higgledy-piggledy in a confusion of breakages.

In 1953 however six tombs were found, which were very different. Each contained a number of burials, between ten and six, but the burials had been simultaneous and the tombs had been sealed up and subsequently undisturbed. It would almost seem as if some plague on the scale of the Death of the First-Born had struck Jericho at this time.

At all events here was a group of richly furnished tombs, untouched for something like 3,600 years and in a state of preservation miraculous outside of Egypt. For in all these tombs there was a wealth of well-preserved *wooden* articles, beds, tables, boxes (both carved and inlaid) combs, stools and platters. There were, besides, fragments of textiles, woven baskets (one containing what appeared to be the remains of a wig) and rush mats—of the same weave as those still commonly made in the district. On tables, platters and dishes were whole joints of meat, whole carcases (for the supply of the deceased) and even steaks, which, though desiccated, had preserved their shape. Every tomb held a quantity of drinking vessels and a number of storage jars, with juglet serving vessels in the mouths thereof; and still in those storage jars could be seen the intact skin of the liquid which had evaporated from them.

Despite this profuseness—this positively Victorian mortuary lavishness—there were curious touches of economy and careless cold-heartedness which give a vivid touch of actuality to the scene. One of the storage jars was a patched one, repaired with plaster of paris; one of the serving juglets had a hole in the bottom and was quite useless; and in one tomb, the body had been dumped half on the bed and half on the table alongside, which carried the joints of meat. I am irresistibly reminded of an undertaker who complained to me of relations who ran their hands over the padded bottom of the coffin to see if any tacks had been left behind. "As if the deceased would notice," he used to say. The professional attitude. . . .

At all events these tombs, with their wealth of domestic goods and household furniture, enable us clearly to visualize the appearance of the rooms of a richer Jericho house of the Middle Bronze Age with its stools, tables and beds: stools uncommonly like the sea-grass stools of today; low tables, coffee tables, as it were, of neat and exact joinery, with shaped mouldings to the edges and always three-legged, two legs at one end, one leg at the other, presumably (on the milking-stool principle) to stand more steadily on an uneven floor; and beds strung with thongs. Even the weave of the mats is known.

Why were these perishable things so marvellously preserved? Professor F. E. Zeuner has suggested that carbon dioxide and other gases collected in the tomb chambers and killed the organisms of decay; and that the reason why these gases collected there lies in the fact that the site overlies a band of crushed rock at the edge of the Jordan Rift which has allowed subterranean gases to ascend at that point; and this factor has some bearing in the controversy which has arisen over the dating of the lowest urban levels of Jericho.

Because of course the really extraordinary and revolutionary discovery at Jericho is the fantastically early date of its earlier stages, stages of such extent and elaborateness as to justify the term urban. It has been generally assumed that the beginnings of human civilization lie in the change-over from food-collecting to food-producing and that communities begin with primitive farming villages, the planned growing of wild grain-plants and the domestication of wild animals. For a variety of reasons it has seemed probable that this took place in the foothills at the north of the "fertile crescent" in northern Iraq; and that Jarmo, the site excavated by Professor Robert Braidwood of the Oriental Institute of the University of Chicago, was typical of the earliest type of village farming communities.

Now Jarmo—which will be discussed more fully in the Iraq section—has provided a number of radio-carbon (or Carbon-14) dates. These dates, by the way, are always shown as a central figure, followed by a plus-or-minus figure, which gives the margin of error; and the dates which Jarmo has given are:

6707 ±320, 6606 ±330, 6695 ±360, 5266 ±450, 6650 ±170, 6570 ±165, 9040 ±250, 8830 ±200, 7950 ±200, 11,240 ±300, 11200 ±200. With the exception of the last two figures which Professor Braidwood says, "are simply not conceivable in terms of comparative archaeological stratigraphy as we now understand it", these figures are very consistent; and Professor Braidwood reckons that Jarmo must lie near, but not at, the very beginning of the era of village-farming communities and that this beginning should be dated to about 7000 B.C.

Right. Now for Jericho. Two of the earlier phases there are called "the plastered floor" phase, and the "hog-backed-brick" phase; and these have given the following radio-carbon dates: 8725 ±210, 8805 ±210, 8200 ±200, 7800 ±160 8785 ±100. This series, though shorter, is remarkably consistent, and gives the earliest possible date of 9,015 years ago and the latest possible of 7,640 years ago. Arguing on this basis therefore the levels of Jericho which gave these dates lie between say 7000 and 5600 B.C. What sort of a place was Jericho then and what were its inhabitants like?

In the first place, Neolithic Jericho was large and populous, as large and populous, it seems, as the later Bronze Age settlement, with perhaps some 3,000 inhabitants. The civilization associated with the plastered skulls preceded, as was noted above, the age of pottery; and its other characteristics at Jericho are well-built houses of rectangular rooms, with solid walls built of bricks of a flattened cigar-shape, patterned in a herring-bone design by the makers' thumbs and with the walls and floors covered with a highly polished coating of gypsum plaster. This is the "plastered floor" phase; and it is an interesting fact, (as revealing a trait in common with "do-it-yourself" home decorators) that the plaster sometimes bears the pattern of a woven reed mat, which had evidently been put down when the plaster was not quite hard. There are some twenty successive phases of this culture and it is associated with a massive defensive wall. In front of this wall a ditch had been made into the bedrock on which the wall stood; and this ditch must have been made by battering the rock with heavy stone mauls (which have been found in considerable numbers) (Plate 35a).

On another part of the site, houses of an entirely different type have been found, which seem to have been made by a different group of people. The walls are curved and the rooms usually round; the walls tend to incline inwards as they rise and the houses may have had domed roofs; and they are built of flat oval bricks with a hog-backed profile. This is in fact the "hog-backed-brick" phase; and it is earlier than the "plastered floor" phase and, from its houses, appeared considerably more primitive. However, in 1955, it was discovered that the massive town wall, referred to above, was built against a tower, solidly built of undressed stones, earlier work than the wall and to be associated with the "hog-backed-brick" people. Furthermore, in the centre of this tower, there was a stair leading down into its heart, twenty steps leading down some 19 ft at an inclination of 30 degrees. The steps were made of slabs of stone about a yard across and the oblique roof above the stair was made of even larger slabs.

After this descent, the path levelled into a horizontal passage presumably leading to the town inside the defences. The purpose of the passage and stair possibly was concerned with the manning of the tower; but whatever its purpose it
is obviously a work of considerable architectural skill, it must have called for
considerable organization of labour, it is so well-built that it has stood for
thousands of years in a countryside frequently racked with earthquakes—and
it is of course some thousands of years older than the oldest Egyptian pyramids.

These then it would seem are the achievements of people, contemporary with
or older than the first village farmers of Northern Iraq. They must have been a
large community, an organized community and a community with a reasonably well developed agriculture to support themselves and to prosper on a site
which owes its prosperity to a single though generous supply of water in an
otherwise arid and difficult country. With the evidence as it is, it seems impossible to deny that Jericho is far and away the world's oldest town that we
know of yet; and that its development shows a fantastic precocity.

Thousands of years later, in about 1600 B.C. Jericho was a walled city, with
a steep plastered glacis sloping down from its walls. This was the Hyksos period
and it may have been as a counter to this warlike people and their chariots
that this form of fortification was developed. This was the city which Abraham
may have seen in his wanderings; this was the city the Egyptians destroyed in
1560 B.C.; and of the later city which Joshua destroyed nothing remains but part
of a house, with a small oven and a jug beside it, perhaps left there by some
Canaanite housewife who fled at the sound of Joshua's trumpets.

CHAPTER FIFTEEN

ISRAEL

THE ceaseless driving intensity which characterizes most Jewish communities rises to its maximum vigour and purposefulness in the new state of Israel. There many things are being done at full tilt; and archaeology, it seems, is one of them.

When the Department of Antiquities came into being in July 1948, it started with many disadvantages. The headquarters of the Mandatory Government's Department of Antiquities lay in the Jordan-held part of Jerusalem; and as a result the new Department had no files, no records, no collections, no library and no maps or photographs, and the collections and library of the Hebrew University, being on Mt Scopus, were inaccessible. The Department, in other words, had to start from scratch, materially. It had however skilled personnel, an ancient tradition of scholarship, and great enthusiasm; and rapidly developed an elaborate and efficient organization. The most active, and for our purpose, the most interesting, section was the Division of Archaeological Survey and Excavations.

From the beginning this division thought in terms of long-term projects, but by the nature of the new state was compelled to abandon or postpone most of them. All manner of public works were in hand, road-building, irrigation, reclamation, the building of new settlements. All these things mean shortage of labour and equipment and financial difficulties; and, also, innumerable urgent short term archaeological activities—to cope with accidental discoveries and to undertake "rescue" operations, to examine as quickly as possible some newly-revealed feature before the bulldozer shovels it into limbo.

Such excavations bring with them many benefits: a wealth of unrelated material and information; a spreading of local interest in archaeology which eventually pays large dividends; and the opportunity of training many archaeologists and workers skilled in the actual tactics of excavation; but it provides an arbitrary and fragmentary picture of the past. Four sites, however, though of unequal importance, are outstanding for the vivid light they throw on Jewish, Biblical and Canaanite history; and these are Beth-Shearim, Caesarea, Massada and, last and most important, Hazor.

Beth Shearim lies on the southern slopes of the Galilean highlands about ten miles from Haifa, on the way to Nazareth; and when, after the rebellion in Hadrian's reign, the centre of Jewish political and religious life shifted from Judaea to Galilee, Beth Shearim became a centre of Jewish learning. For a time it was the seat of the Sanhedrin under the famous Patriarch Rabbi Judah I who around A.D. 200 compiled the Mishna (the collection, that is, of Judaism's oral laws). After his death, Beth Shearim became a favourite burial place for Jews. A great necropolis came into being and Jewish notables were brought there for burial from all the neighbouring countries, including Phoenicia, Syria, Mesopotamia, even southern Arabia. Among the inscriptions can be found such descriptions as "Head of the Elders from Antioch", "the Archisynagogus from Berytus", "Aristeas the Sidonian" and "the Banker from Palmyra".

The necropolis is in the form of many catacombs cut into the soft rock; and most of these catacombs take the form of a number of chambers grouped round a courtyard and entered through stone doors, which still swing on their stone hinges, in some cases. The most frequent type of burial is the *arcosolium*, a recess cut into the wall of the chamber. Extensive excavations had been carried out on the site in 1936–40 by Professor B. Mazar (who later became President of the Hebrew University); and these excavations were resumed in 1953 by Dr N. Avigad on behalf of the Israel Exploration Society and the Hebrew University.

During this last excavation two catacombs of exceptional interest were found. One of them had a triple-arched façade (of roughly Roman appearance) built against the rock-face and about 30 ft wide and some 18 ft high. In two of the three arches there were doorways—at one side, a small, low, single door of a single piece of rock which could be opened from outside; in the centre arch an impressively framed double-door, which was locked from within. This double-door consisted of two large pieces of rock, swinging on rock hinges and with the front faces carved to simulate panels, a door-knocker, and a number of large round studs. In this tomb were inscriptions referring to Rabbi Shimeon and Rabbi Gamaliel. These may well be the sons of Rabbi Judah I—the names are right—and it is possible that the Patriarch himself may have been buried in this family vault.

Not far away, in August 1955, Dr Avigad discovered a huge catacomb containing at least 100 enormous sarcophagi. About 15 ft below the surface the excavators came on the lintel of a blocked doorway and crawled through a small hole into a cave, in which it seemed that enormous wet blocks of stone were tumbled in every direction. After more work a clearer picture emerged. The catacomb, as a whole, had an ashlar façade built against the rock wall and, though somewhat bigger than that of the two Rabbis mentioned above, was of the same style, being of three Roman round-headed arches, each with entrances leading into the interior. This interior, which was all artificially cut out of the soft rock, consisted of a series of vaulted halls and burial chambers of enormous size. The central hall is blocked by a great fall of rock (perhaps the result of an earthquake) but even so is nearly 50 yds long—about half the length of a football field; and another, presumably subsidiary, hall is rather more than 50 yds long. There were niches and *arcosolia* cut in the walls, all of which had been robbed in antiquity; but the chief mode of burial was the sarcophagus of limestone. At least a hundred of these were counted and their average size is 8 ft 2⅜ in long by 4 ft 11 in high. The lids are usually roof-shaped and they weigh between 3 and 5 tons each. These huge blocks of stone would be brought originally from the hills of Carmel and Nazareth; and in many cases their finished width was only an inch or so less than the width of the entrance; and one is left with an awed respect for the engineering skill of the monumental masons and undertakers of Beth Shearim (Plate 36a).

This great funeral vault had been thoroughly looted in early Arabic times, it is assumed. All the *arcosolia* and niches had been forced and emptied of their contents. Wherever possible the lids of the limestone sarcophagi had been forced off and tipped aside; and where they had proved too heavy for this treatment, holes had been broken into the sides. Some of the coffins, it became clear, had been costly imported sarcophagi of marble with sculptures in the classical manner, but these the looters had broken into pieces and sold as raw material. Only splinters of marble and fragments of sculpture remain to hint at past splendours.

Many of the limestone sarcophagi bore carvings of a variety of conventional ornaments, some Roman in character such as garlands hanging from columns, eagles and bull's heads and the *tabula ansata*; others more specifically Jewish, such as lions, rosettes and the *menorah* or seven-branched candlestick. These carvings are, for the most part, rather clumsy and provincial, but have a certain naïve charm—which they share with the carvings which the soldier-farmers of the Roman *limes* in North Africa made and which have been found in such quantity in the desert mausolea near Ghirza. One particularly striking example of this at Beth Shearim is a pair of comic lions facing each other over a pot of water. Another—especially surprising in a catacomb which held the remains of many Rabbis—is a bearded curly-haired male head, a typical country mason's idea of Jupiter or Oceanus.

In this catacomb nearly all the inscriptions are in Hebrew, which is unusual for the rest of the necropolis, where most are in Greek, with others in Hebrew, Aramaic and Palmyrene. Of all the inscriptions in the great catacomb perhaps the most moving is an unofficial one: the remark scratched, perhaps by a mourner, on the wall of one of the corridors, in Greek—"Be comforted, pious fathers, no one is immortal."

The accidental discovery of a huge red porphyry statue during the clearing of a field near Kibbutz Sedot Yam led to several seasons of excavations directed by Dr S. Yeivin of the site of ancient Caesarea. There were two upper layers of the eleventh to thirteenth centuries A.D. and eighth to tenth centuries A.D. of no very great interest, but under these lay a large built up area of the late Byzantine era (fifth to seventh centuries A.D.) of buildings which had evidently fallen into decay owing to a decline in population. Its most interesting building is a long courtyard with troughs on either side.

This courtyard was paved with marble slabs, which had obviously come from some monumental building of an earlier period. The troughs on one side were connected with clay pipes in the wall and were clearly water troughs; while the troughs on the other side had no such arrangement and were intended as mangers. The building it would seem was a central cattle market. At one end is a formalized entrance contrived out of re-used material; and on either side of the opening is a huge statue of a seated male figure, about two and a half times life size.

These are both some centuries earlier than the building in which they stand and were clearly not intended for it. The one on the west stands on a rather small base of local stone and is perhaps a male deity seated on a chair. It is made from a single block of white marble, which had later been cut into two. The figure wears sandals and a well-draped *himation* or cloak, the torso and right shoulder being bare, while the head and right arm are missing. It is dated to about the second to third centuries A.D. The statue on the east, lacks hands, arms and head, which may have been made of different material. What remains however is carved from Imperial porphyry, of Egyptian origin, and this material, together with the fact that the figure is wearing the imperial toga suggests that it represented a Roman Emperor of the third and fourth centuries A.D. It had been set in a grey granite chair, which does not fit the statue, on a block of grey granite.

In a neighbouring room a Greek inscription was found which reads: "Under the Governor Flavius Entolius the mayor Flavius Strategius built out of public funds the wall, the steps and the apse in the tenth indiction. In a good hour." Which conjures up a picture of a mayor, in a Christian community, but with antiquarian leanings, looting pagan buildings with public approval to create, with public funds, a handsome public building, harmonious with his own tastes and redounding to his own credit.

One of the most interesting and intensive of all short term archaeological projects was the fortnight's exploration and survey of the Herodian fortress of Masada carried out by a party of twenty-five under the direction of Dr Avi-Yonah, with Dr Avigad and Dr Aharoni in association, in March 1955.

Masada—the name means "stronghold" in Hebrew—is a huge precipitous rock rising about 1,000 ft from the Dead Sea plain. Its history is brief and bloody. Jonathan, the brother of Judas Maccabeus, built a small fort on the summit between 161 and 143 B.C.; between 37 and 34 B.C. Herod the Great built a palace at one end and elaborately fortified the rest; and after the Fall of Jerusalem in A.D. 70 about 1,000 Zealots held out there for three years against a Roman army of about 15,000 and in the last resort committed a mass suicide rather than fall into Roman hands. The actual fortress on the top of this fantastic rock measures over 2,000 ft from north to south and over 1,000 ft from east to west; and all around its foot is a Roman circumvallation wall, with nine Roman camps or fortifications incorporated or associated with it. The site was in fact well known. It was described in some detail by the historian Josephus in the Seventh Book of his "Jewish War"; and it was visited by a number of explorers between 1838 and 1932, and in 1922 the R.A.F. took a series of excellent aerial photographs. The lack of detailed knowledge about the place lay in the actual physical difficulty of establishing and maintaining an expedition of any size for any length of time in such a fantastic eyrie of rock. Hence the need for a closely planned intensive operation, which owed much of its success to the assistance and close co-operation of the Sappers of the Israeli Army. In this connexion it is perhaps worth noting that the Chief of Staff of the Israeli Army at this time was General Yadin, who in the next few years, after his retirement from the Army, became better known to the world as the excavator of Hazor. But then, it has been said that most officers in the Israeli Army are archaeologists in their spare time.

Access to the summit in ancient times was gained by a zig-zag path on the eastern side, which Josephus called "the Snake". This was repaired by the Sappers, who also installed a winch to deal with the last 100 ft to the summit; and by this means a camp was established on the summit and all supplies, including water, were brought up by this means.

It is a savage and romantic scene, fully in keeping with all we know of Herod's character; and a fit locale for the suicide of the 1,000 Zealots. Most of the summit was bare and was used for cultivation, as Josephus records; and it was entirely surrounded by a casemate wall, with towers, 12 ft thick and 1,400 yds long. A number of buildings still stand with walls up to 12 ft high, some houses including a building for the royal suite and retainers, a barracks and the elaborate store-rooms which Herod stocked with food and weapons to last 1,000 men a siege of a year; and huge rock-cut cisterns which were kept filled with water.

The lack of water is of course the only weakness of this natural fortress; and Herod besides cutting these cisterns on the summit had also carved out a number of large underground cisterns in the north-western cliff. A rock-cut aqueduct with bridge brought such water as was available from the neighbouring *wadis* and presumably whatever infrequent rain fell on the summit was carefully gathered and stored.

All these buildings and works were so to speak functional. To the north of the storehouses and incorporating all the narrow spur which constitutes the northernmost tip of the fortress were Herod's own apartments; and these were more fully examined than the rest. They were cut off from the storehouses by a high plastered wall, at the east end of which is a bench which obviously served for the Palace guard since the plaster behind it is covered with scratched graffiti, which were probably produced in the soldiers' idle moments. Near by was a group of small rooms, paved with mosaics in black and white geometric patterns—the earliest mosaics to be found in Israel at that time—and these rooms were presumably quarters for the guard. Seventy feet below this building was a round tower, with double concentric walls built round an outcrop of rock, hanging like an eagle's eyrie about 1,000 ft above the Dead Sea plain, with breath-taking views in every direction. Thirty feet below this was another terrace built on a series of vaults into a platform about 50 ft square. In the centre of this was an open court with a peristyle of a double row of Corinthian columns, and there was also a balustrade of plaster painted in geometric patterns in several colours. This terrace was used it seems as a royal banqueting hall, a concept outdoing the wildest fancy of a romantic painter. The whole construction was supported on the spur by a retaining wall some 90 ft high and underneath it were some vaulted cellars, which had to remain unexplored. The three levels of these royal apartments were connected by a concealed system of stairs.

The other most striking feature of the whole complex is the siege mound, which still lies against the west face of the rock, which is slightly lower and a trifle easier of approach than the rest. This is an enormous earthwork, sloping up to an eventual height of 300 ft and it was built by thousands of Jewish captives who served as the labour force for the Roman General, Flavius Silva, who commanded the Tenth Legion. It was built, when siege alone had failed to capture the fortress. Its great bulk was crowned with a platform on which a 90 ft tower was built. From this a battering ram was operated against the walls, which were breached within a few days. The defenders put up an inner wooden wall; but one evening the Romans managed to set this on fire and withdrew for the night. On the following morning 2 March, A.D. 73 they returned to the assault, and found seven persons alive in the fortress, two women and five children, the remainder of the garrison, 960 in all, having committed suicide sooner than fall into Roman hands.

Quite easily the largest and most intensive excavation which has been mounted in Israel since the war is the James A. de Rothschild Expedition at Hazor, directed by Dr Yigael Yadin, and operating on behalf of the Hebrew University of Jerusalem, with funds contributed by the P.J.C.A., the Anglo-Israel Exploration Committee and the Government of Israel. The work started in 1955 and has gone on annually since. Dr Yadin is the son of the famous scholar Dr Sukenik—like many citizens of Israel he has taken a Hebrew name—and was previously General Yadin, Chief of Staff of the Israeli Army—a fact which may account for the military precision and efficiency of this series of excavations.

Hazor was always an important city of Palestine in Biblical and pre-Biblical times. It is mentioned in the cuneiform archives of the Syrian city of Mari (c 1700 B.C.), in Egyptian Execration lists of the nineteenth century B.C., in lists of cities conquered by the Pharaohs Thutmose III, Amenhotep II and Seti I; and in the famous El-Amarna letters of the fourteenth century there are complaints to the Pharaoh from the kings of Astaroth and Tyre against Abdi-Tarshi, king of Hazor, and letters from the said Abdi-Tarshi denying the substance of the charges. Hazor is mentioned several times in the Bible: Joshua conquered it and smote the King thereof with the sword, when it was "head of all those kingdoms"; it was the capital of Jabin king of Canaan, whose general, Sisera, was killed by Jael and whose defeat was the subject of the song of Deborah; it was rebuilt by Solomon, together with the Temple, Jerusalem,

Megiddo and Gezer; and it was captured by Tiglath-Pileser III, king of Assyria when Pekah was king of Israel. There is also a reference in Maccabees, as it was the site of a battle between Jonathan the Hashmonean and Demetrius (147 B.C.).

It was suggested by the late Professor Garstang that ancient Hazor might be identified with a large *tell* or mound called Tell el Qedah in northern Galilee, in the Huleh plain, north that is of the Sea of Galilee but south of Lake Huleh. The actual *tell* is described as "bottle-shaped" with the neck pointing west and the broad base to the east, rising about 130 ft and with an area of more than 20 acres; but to the north of the *tell* lies a large rectangular enclosure, with a beaten-earth wall, glacis and moat. Here Professor Garstang made some soundings in 1928, but his discoveries were curiously disappointing and, in view of later discoveries, curiously misleading.

In all, during the first three years, nine sites were excavated: three on the *tell*, referred to as A.B. & G.; and six in the enclosure, C.D.E.F.H. and Point 210. H and A were over 1,000 yds apart. Many cultures were revealed, from the Patriarchal Age or later Middle Bronze, say 1750–1550 B.C. to the Hellenistic or Maccabean period, say 333–63 B.C. The total area of the site is fantastically large; the expedition working there has been large, efficient and energetic, but Dr Yadin has estimated that, working steadily at this pace, it would take 800 years to excavate Hazor completely.

To take the earlier part of the site first: the large rectangular enclosure. As a result of his sounding Professor Garstang had judged that this great area had been used in the fifteenth century B.C. purely as a sort of transit camp with only temporary structures and that by the fourteenth-thirteenth centuries the site's importance as a city had ended—which was very baffling for the scholars who put Joshua's campaigns in the thirteenth century. And these conclusions he based on the complete absence of Mycenaean specimens, the period for Mycenaean pottery in Palestine being after about 1400 B.C. until about 1250 B.C. It was therefore a complete (and pleasing) surprise when the first excavations in Area C revealed about 3 ft below the surface the remains of a well-built city whose floors were littered with Mycenaean pottery and local vessels all dating from the last part of the Late Bronze Age, the thirteenth century B.C. In other words the last city to survive at any rate in this area met its end at about the time most favoured by the scholars for the date of Joshua's conquest. Below this city, another was revealed of the fourteenth century, presumably the city mentioned in the El Amarna letters; and beneath this was yet another layer of the later Middle Bronze Age (late eighteenth to early sixteenth centuries) and this appeared to have been destroyed by fire, perhaps by one of those New Kingdom Pharaohs who recorded that they had destroyed Hazor.

There were a number of interesting finds in this area. In the oldest city large numbers of infant burials in jars, so numerous and apparently contemporary as to suggest a plague or killing epidemic. In the latest city (thirteenth century) were found two Canaanite temples, one on top of the other; and, in a raised central niche, what was presumably the "Holy of Holies". In this were the holy objects, all of basalt: a small seated figure of the god, holding a cup—a figure similar in intention to the enthroned bronze figure Professor Schaeffer found at Enkomi in Cyprus; seven plain *stelae*, and an eighth with carved on it a pair of hands raised in a suppliant gesture to a sun and crescent moon symbol. A little below this row of emblems was a basalt orthostat block with a lion carved in relief on the side and end, seated on the hindquarters but erect on the fore-legs, the mouth open as if roaring. The neighbourhood of this sanctuary contained store rooms full of jars and a potter's workshop. This last contained a perfect potter's wheel made of two blocks of basalt and, lying near by, as if abandoned by the potter when the city fell, a pottery cult mask—a human mask with large eyeholes and arched brows, with rather prominent ears, the whole having an oddly Central American look. Also in the store-rooms and hidden in a jar was what was evidently a cult standard: a bronze plaque with a tang for fastening it to a pole, the surface being plated with silver and bearing in relief the figure of a goddess holding a snake in either hand, with, above her head, a crescent and another snake (Plate 37).

Area C lies at the south-western corner of the great enclosure. Area D lies more than 500 yds away to the north-east, near the eastern edge of the enclosure; and in this area were found five strata, covering much the same period as Area C. Here were found three cisterns for collecting rainwater and these are perhaps the earliest yet found in Palestine; two kilns which may have been used for smelting copper; a rich Hyksos period burial containing amulets and scarabs; and, most important, a fragment of a thirteenth century jar bearing the two letters LT in the Proto-Sinaitic script (the ancestor of the old Hebrew and later Latin alphabets). This was the first time the script has been found in Galilee; and a similar fragment bearing the same letters and meaning "goddess" was found a few years ago at Lachish.

Area E is a small excavation, not far from C and similar to D as also revealing another cistern. A massive wall of many-sided stones was found; and indeed rock was extensively used in the dwellings and the cistern.

In the second season another area on the eastern side of the huge enclosure was opened and eventually became a large excavation. It centred round a large block of stone which as it were outcropped from the surface. When uncovered it proved to be a huge stone altar weighing about 5 tons; and it was clear that in the last stage of the city at this point an attempt had been made to overturn it. If we accept that this was indeed the city Joshua conquered, we can well imagine the victorious Children of Israel when they were putting Hazor to the sword turning to overthrow the altars and high places of the Canaanites. For this area was quite obviously a holy place with offering tables, incense stands, a seated figure and quantities of fine Mycenaean pottery and the ivory stopper of a perfume bottle in the shape of the head of the Egyptian goddess Hathor. Underneath this area was found a complex network of underground tunnels and channels, and for whatever purpose they were made they appear to have been used as reservoirs by the later inhabitants of the site. There was also a rock-cut burial chamber reached by means of a vertical shaft, used apparently over a long period of time (like some of the Bronze Age tombs of Jericho) the bones of earlier burials being shoved unceremoniously to one end whenever a fresh entombment took place. Something like 500 vessels were found in this tomb, including a large number of beautiful Mycenaean pots and a small, but very rare in these circumstances, group of pottery imported from Cyprus, "bilbils" and the as it were fluted Bucchero pots.

At the western side of this same area three very large rock-hewn caves were found, accessible from a deep shaft. The largest of these was over 50 ft long and about 10 ft wide and high. They are notable examples of the engineering skill of the Middle Bronze Age inhabitants of Hazor and they were presumably intended as burial places; but—they were never used as such, indeed they were never used at all and are completely empty except for a few pots which, we may well imagine, carried the workmen's "elevenses". Perhaps they were being built at a transitional period.

By 1957, the excavations in the enclosure had all been made on the outer parts of the area, western eastern and southern; and the time had come to make soundings in the centre and the northern end. The central excavation at Point 210 was in the nature of a trial trench and provided evidence of precisely the same sequence of buildings from the end of the later Middle Bronze Age to the end of the Late Bronze and also at the lowest level showed signs of a number of infant burials and so perhaps of the same epidemic which had been observed in Area C, about 300 yds away. The great enclosure in fact was beginning to appear as a gigantic layer-cake of the same sort of layers and to be in fact a city of about 170 acres with a population which must have been about 40,000, the largest city in Palestine between 1700 and 1200 B.C.

The northernmost excavation—lying nearly half a mile from Area E, the southernmost—was Area H and was one of the most remarkable of all as it revealed a temple with a wealth of temple furniture, a plan very like one of the same period discovered by Sir Leonard Woolley at Alalakh in southern Turkey and constituting an early prototype of Solomon's Temple in Jerusalem. It dates from the thirteenth century B.C. and consists of a porch leading to a main hall, which in its turn (and on the same axis) leads to a Holy of Holies. In the porch are two round pillar bases of basalt—like the Jachin and Boaz of Solomon's Temple. The walls of the main hall and the Holy of Holies are lined, in a manner unique in the country, with orthostat blocks of very finely dressed basalt set on a base of rubble and presumably, from the holes drilled in the upper edge, supporting a wood-beam reinforced brick or mud superstructure. The building had been destroyed by fire and the upper part had fallen in, thereby preserving much of the temple furniture *in situ*. The most striking elements of this were: an incense altar of carved basalt, about $1\frac{1}{2}$ ft square and about 4 ft high. On the top and one side is the emblem of a four-pointed star in a circle in a square, the sign of the Canaanite sun-god, the rest of the sides being carved with quadrangular recesses to give an effect of square pillars. Near by was a large basalt basin, over 2 ft in diameter; and two large earthenware pots with a number of dipper juglets, containers, no doubt, for oil, wine or whatever fluids were used in the ritual. There were several basalt slabs with recesses which probably served as offering tables; and a very fine and large carinated basalt bowl, about 1½ ft in diameter and nearly as tall. Faience beads and cylinder seals were found on the floor; and four quite small bronze figures, all apparently designed to be socketed into wood. One is a fairly naturalistic bull, one is a simplified male deity with a conical helmet and arms stretched forwards; and the other two are highly schematized thin flat female representations. And finally there was a basalt figure of a seated man on a throne. The head had been broken off but was lying near by. This figure is very near the seated figure found in Area F, but does not appear to have been holding a cup and is generally a more accomplished piece of work, but with a considerably less impact. Some idea of the distinction may perhaps be given if we suggest that the sculptor of this image was a much better artist, while the sculptor of the other perhaps had a much more living faith in the power of the deity he was portraying.

Concurrently with these excavations in the great enclosure, three sites were excavated on the summit of the *tell* itself, which it will be recalled has an area of about twenty acres and stands more than twenty feet higher than the level of the enclosure. These three sites are Area A in about the centre; Area B, at the narrow western extremity; and Area G on the slope of the easternmost end.

Area A started from a trench dug in 1928 by Professor Garstang, who found a row of six monolithic pillars there. Another parallel row of pillars was found; and it was discovered that they were originally the pillars of a large public building of the time of Ahab (874–852 B.C.) and that they had been re-used in four subsequent cities, either incorporated in walls, demolished where necessary and finally in the last settlement (a modest affair of the late eighth and early seventh centuries) the tops of the pillars had become part of the floor. There had thus been five successive cities on the site in about 200 years, the pillared public building being used for its original purpose for only the two first occupations; and the next to last of the occupations showed signs of savage destruction and was assumed to be the city of King Pekah which was known (from II Kings 15) to have been captured by Tiglath-Pileser III in 732 B.C. In rather earlier buildings in this neighbourhood, merchants' houses of the time of Jeroboam (786–746 B.C.) there were signs of heavy damage by earthquake, perhaps the same earthquake mentioned by the Prophet Amos. To the east of these buildings and crossing the mound from south to north were discovered the remains of a massive casemate wall, a city wall of the time of Solomon; and at the northern end of this were found the remains of a gateway, with three chambers on either side and square towers flanking the entry on the exterior side. This gateway corresponds precisely in plan and dimensions with the Megiddo gate of the same period; and so not only confirms the statement in the Bible that Solomon rebuilt both Megiddo and Hazor but also strongly suggests that the same architect built both gateways.

Solomon, to shift from Biblical to archaeological terminology, belongs to

Iron Age I; and beside this wall and at a lower level was found pottery of Late Bronze Age II, which suggests that the earlier city of the enclosure which Joshua destroyed extended also over the mound, though it is here covered with a succession of Israelite, Assyrian, Persian and Hellenistic occupations.

This last suggestion was forcibly confirmed in Area G. This excavation was made on the easternmost slope of the mound and showed that the city of Ahab's time extended right to this end of the mound where it terminated in a massive double fortification wall, behind which lay a large rectangular grain silo, the floor of which was covered with a thick layer of ash. Beneath the Israelite fortification walls and in some parts acting as their foundation was an enormous stone-built city wall with a deep fosse at the bottom; and this wall could be dated to the Middle Bronze Age, about 1700 B.C. and is in fact very similar to the contemporary city wall of Jericho.

The other end of the *tell*, Area B, was the most strongly fortified of all, and consisted of a series of citadels, one on top of the other. First, working from the top, was a Hellenistic fort, with beneath it a Persian reconstruction of the Assyrian fort which lay under that. These were removed, to reveal a sequence of impressive Israelite citadels, that of Pekah—which had been savagely destroyed by Tiglath-Pileser III; that of Ahab; and, below this, casemates of the Solomonic city, like those found in Area A.

This very brief summary of intensive but necessarily sporadic excavations of an enormous site has indicated what was the outline of its history; and this may perhaps be even more briefly summarized here. From about 1700 B.C. the whole of the area, mound and square enclosure, about 190 acres in all was occupied by Bronze Age Canaanites and comprised the largest city in Palestine until about 1200 B.C. when it was captured and laid waste by Joshua. Thereafter the 170 acres of the enclosure were unoccupied, but the *tell* continued to be occupied and, since the Bible continues to be the archaeologist's most accurate working handbook for Palestine, presumably contains, still hidden, remains of Jabin's capital, of the time of Deborah. In the time of Solomon, Hazor was rebuilt and fortified on the western half of the *tell*; and in the time of Ahab and his successors, this city grew to include the whole of the 20 acres of the mound's summit. In Pekah's time, 732 B.C., this city was utterly destroyed, though a later modest settlement did develop. The westernmost end of the *tell* however, the citadel, continued to be occupied as a fortified garrison, in Assyrian, Persian, Hellenistic and Maccabean times, after which Hazor becomes "one with Nineveh and Tyre".

CHAPTER SIXTEEN

TURKEY—I

FROM almost the earliest times that land mass which is now Turkey has seen nearly the richest and most varied passage of civilizations of any comparable area in the world; and until the revolution of Ataturk it was one of the most closed to archaeologists. That has all been changed and since the last war especially it has been the scene of intensive and extremely varied activity. A vigorous Turkish antiquities department has come into being; the British School at Ankara, first under Professor Garstang and later under Mr Seton Lloyd, has done much valuable work; in Istanbul American and British groups have been active; at Gordion, Professor Rodney Young's University of Pennsylvania expedition; in the Hittite centres, the German Professor Bossert; at Ephesus, the Austrian School; at Smyrna, the British School at Athens; in Commagene, Miss Goell and Dr Doerner; in the south, at Alalakh, Sir Leonard Woolley; and many others at many sites have revealed innumerable and often surprising facets of the multitudinous pasts of Asia Minor and Turkey-in-Europe.

It is so difficult to know where to start and so impossible with such a varied richness to be systematic that it is simplest to start in the west and to move roughly eastwards and southwards. And with this start, the first discovery is made in the sea, somewhere near Halicarnassus.

In August 1953 Professor G. E. Bean of Istanbul University learnt that Turkish sponge-fishers had brought to a village near Bodrum (which is ancient Halicarnassus) part of a bronze statue; and reaching there a few days later he found on the beach the upper part of a bronze statue of a draped and veiled woman, considerably over life-size, quite obviously a major work of classical Greek art and representing Demeter, the mother of Persephone. It is in what may be described as the same key as the famous marble Demeter of Cnidus, but it is different in pose, feeling and treatment; the head drapery encroaches much more on the face, the head is more downcast, and in short this Demeter is more moving than the British Museum Demeter, whose noble stoicism is somewhat daunting to the would-be sympathizer.

When the fishermen first set it up on the beach, they playfully daubed some red paint on the lips, but this was later shamefacedly removed; and the statue was taken first to Bodrum and later to Smyrna (Plate 38).

It is obviously a beautiful and major fourth-century work of art and outstanding on that account; but it is also a great rarity and a great puzzle. Large Greek bronzes are extremely rare—the metal was too valuable to barbarians to

147

survive disaster—and most of the surviving bronzes have come from the sea, like the fine thunderbolt-throwing Zeus now at Athens. How did this Demeter get into the sea? Presumably from a wreck. But where, when and in what circumstances? The reports of the fishermen are confusing and in dispute: perhaps between Old and New Cnidus, perhaps between the Bozburun peninsula and Rhodes. When? Perhaps in Roman times when the area was a rich source of loot for Roman palaces. But the famous and beautiful statues of ancient Greece were nearly always frequently copied; and no copies of this are known. This last feature suggests that the statue had a very brief life above water; and Professor Bean has put forward the ingenious and attractive suggestion—which must however be pure speculation—that perhaps the statue was ordered by the Cnidians and lost at sea when being brought there; and that—who knows?—the marble Demeter of the British Museum was the replacement ordered in place of the lost bronze.

Not far away lies ancient Ephesus, a city perhaps most famous for its associations with the Apostle Paul but with a long history besides, dating, like Smyrna farther north, from the settlements of Greeks on the coasts of Asia Minor around 1000 B.C. after the fall of Mycenae, refounded by Lysimachus, one of Alexander the Great's successors in the beginning of the third century B.C. and continuing in a state of high prosperity in Roman Imperial times, particularly during the reign of Hadrian (A.D. 117–138).

It has for many years been the subject of excavations by the Austrian Institute of Archaeology; but these diggings, which started in 1896, have been interrupted on a number of occasions by world events and it was not until 1954 that they were again resumed under the direction of Dr Franz Miltner.

It is a very rich site, especially in Hellenistic, Roman and Byzantine remains; and the recent excavations combined to give a full and lively picture of the life of the city. One of the buildings uncovered is a bathing establishment, built in Byzantine times and providing in itself a link between the classical baths and the later Seljuk-Turkish baths and filling in, as it were, the generations between the Roman thermae and the hammams of today. A much larger thermal establishment, however, where a great deal of excavation has gone on, was begun about the time of the Emperor Domitian (A.D. 81–96) and completely restored during that of Theodosius (A.D. 379–395) by a Christian lady called Scholasticia. This was a large, handsome and elaborate establishment, preserved in some parts to the height of 20 ft; and two features of it are very revealing. The basement was used as a public brothel, with elegant public rooms and a mosaic floor with a design of four female heads probably representing the four seasons; while, incorporated in the façade of the building was a temple of the Emperor Hadrian. This is a small but extremely refined classical building with Corinthian columns and a number of marble reliefs, the tympanum over the *cella* door being particularly elegant and interesting. This combination of buildings and functions seems to me particularly revealing of a way of life: in the same nexus, a well-appointed brothel, an elegant bathing establishment (which in Roman times was often a centre for literature, poetry and philosophy) and the temple of the peculiarly official religion, that religion which caters for the almost universal tendency towards loyalty, patriotism and pageantry.

Behind these baths of Scholasticia led a road, flanked with colonnades, statues, shops and mosaic pavements—a rich and attractive shopping centre, a sort of Rue de Rivoli or Burlington Arcade, broken at one point with a nymphaeum or formal fountain dedicated to the Emperor Trajan and surrounded on three sides with tall façades with recesses for statuary. Of the statues which survive the most notable are the Emperor Nerva (A.D. 96–98) and an Aphrodite.

This road leads eventually to the Prytaneium—the equivalent, we may say, of the Town Hall of today. Here was found a large public altar of the Hellenistic period; and a sanctuary of Hestia Boulaia, who was the goddess of the hearth who protected the interest of the *Boulé*, or Town Council, a sort of tutelary goddess of local government. In this sanctuary were made the outstanding discoveries, two superb statues of the goddess on whom the prosperity of Ephesus was founded, Artemis Ephesia, "Diana of the Ephesians", the many-breasted mother of Asia.

Artemis Ephesia has little to do with the Artemis-Diana who was the chaste huntress; and is an Anatolian, Oriental divinity of the moon and of forests and wild beasts and whose "signature", so to speak, is a multiplicity of breasts, arranged symmetrically something like a bunch of grapes. A most unclassical and barbarous symbol in fact, but the best of taste often masks a strong *nostalgie de la boue*; and the Temple of Artemis at Ephesus was one of the Seven Wonders of the World in ancient times and the prosperity of the city derived from the flow of tourists and worshippers and from the sale of reproductions of the image of the goddess. It was, it will be recalled, the threat to the vested interests of the silversmiths which made St Paul so unpopular in Ephesus.

The two statues found, which are the first of Artemis Ephesia to be found in Ephesus, are basically alike. One however is twice life-size and is the less well-preserved. It is a standing figure, the arms of which are lost, with the usual cluster of breasts, a close skirt with a number of panels showing gryphons, sphinxes and bees in high relief, a massive necklace and a tall elaborate crown, of which the upper register shows the pillared façades of temples and the two lower registers, gryphons and sphinxes. The second statue is life-size, extremely well preserved and made of Greek island marble of the early second century A.D.; and, bearing in mind the complexity of the subject, is extremely well organized and effective (Plate 39).

The goddess is shown standing on a pedestal with both feet close together. The elbows are close to the sides and the forearms come forward at right angles, but are broken off about half way down. The features are rounded but firm and dispassionate, the head is erect and the eyes look straight forward and the goddess wears drop ear-rings. The head-dress, as it is now, has the effect of a trim flattened turban and on either side of the head are panels, each with five gryphons in relief. From the waist down the legs are sheathed in a close skirt narrowing to the ankles and made up of three panels in high relief showing rows of lions, gryphons, stags, all seated looking to the front, and a final pair of rosettes. Round the neck is a truly massive necklace of beads and below this several signs of the zodiac in low relief. Below this comes the array of some twenty breasts in three rows. By all the laws of nature, art and decency, these should be horrible and barbaric. But curiously enough, they are not. They do not give the impression of a monstrously deformed woman, they give, rather, the impression of not indeed being flesh at all, they are formal, hieratic, a panoply, something put on to symbolize plenty, generosity, fruitfulness. And when this has been perceived and added to the formalized elaboration of the rest of the apparel and taken into consideration with the powerful tense posture of the being inside the garments, it is clear that the breasts are part of the garment; and that this is, in fact, not a statue of Artemis Ephesia, but a portrait of a priestess wearing the panoply of the goddess—as no doubt on appropriate occasions the appearance of the goddess was staged before the worshippers.

On the pedestal on either side of the statue are three small cloven hooves; and these must have belonged to a pair of stags, with one foot raised—the usual supporters of Artemis. In front of them are two bell-like objects, with an all-over reticulated pattern. In some representations the goddess is shown holding two staves and these may be the ornamental bases of such staves; or alternatively, in Hadrianic coins of the same period, the goddess is shown between a pair of candelabra.

Some 40 miles farther up the coast, over against Chios in fact, lies Smyrna, modern Izmir, and some three or four miles from this lies the site of Old Smyrna, the city of Homer and the war-poet Mimnermus. For four seasons between 1948 and 1951 this site was excavated by a joint expedition of the British School of Athens under its then Director, Mr J. M. Cook and the University of Ankara under the Director of the University's Archaeological Institute, Professor Ekrem Akurgal. Their objective was to find the earliest Greek levels, the first settlements of the Greeks in the Eastern Aegean after the downfall of Mycenae. In this they were successful and discovered that the Greeks had already settled in Asia Minor by about 1000 B.C.; and indeed they uncovered an oval one-roomed house of mud-brick which dates to about 900 B.C. Soon after this rectangular houses with a single large room were built, but in the period from the middle of the eighth to the middle of the seventh, the oval house again became dominant; but immediately after this comes the time of Old Smyrna's greatest prosperity and the appearance of the long house, the *megaron*—a porch with two rooms and women's quarters and a courtyard. Contemporary with these last was a considerable temple with walls of massive polygonal stone and a carefully dressed threshold and a number of column bases. A quantity of small offerings of Greek and Oriental origin were found in the temple, including amulets, scarabs and the like in Egyptian style, which probably came from Phoenicia, and a beautiful small carved ivory lion.

In the sixth century the town was destroyed by the Lydian king Alyattes and

PLATE 30. From Enkomi, Cyprus: (a) Apollo-Reshef-Nergal—a horned bronze deity of about the mid-12th century B.C., when Cyprus was in the hands of the Sea People; and (b) and (c) both faces of the largest document in the still-undeciphered Cypro-Minoan script.

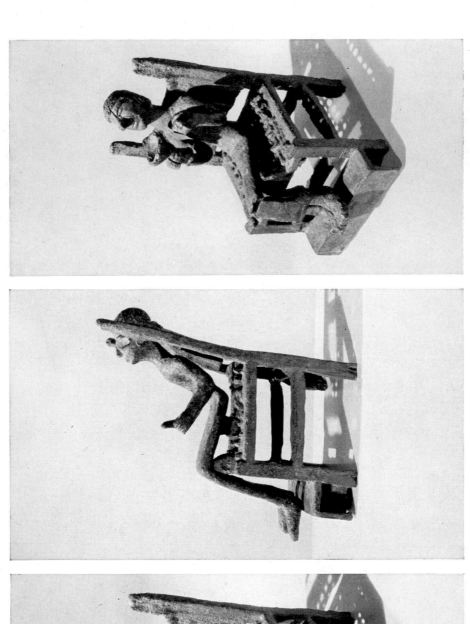

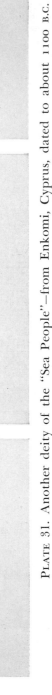

PLATE 31. Another deity of the "Sea People"–from Enkomi, Cyprus, dated to about 1100 B.C. During the excavation the throne (a) was found with the god (b) which quite obviously does not fit it; later in the excavation the god shown in (c) was found, which does fit. Presumably the later god was a rather pitiable makeshift after a disaster in which the first god was lost.

PLATE 32. Ivories and tablets from Ugarit, Ras Shamra, Syria. (*a*) and (*b*) Two of the sixteen ivory panels from the royal bedstead of about 1350 B.C., showing (*a*) a horned goddess suckling two royal children and (*b*) the king and queen fondly embracing. The tablets are: (*c*) a treaty sealed with the great circular seal of the Hittite King Mursil II, fixing the boundaries between Ugarit and the Hittite Empire; (*d*) the world's oldest "horn-book"—the thirty signs of the Ugaritic alphabetical cuneiform script in their correct order; and (*e*) a royal tablet listing the trousseau of the Ugaritic queen, Ahat-Milku.

PLATE 33. The biblical "Pool of Gibeon". This is cut out of the solid rock. Below the foot of the ladder a rock-cut stair goes down a further 49 ft before the water level is reached. The total descent is 158 steps.

PLATE 34. Qumran, beside the Dead Sea, Jordan. In (a) the site of the monastery can be seen, between the tents; and, near the end of the nearer spur, an entrance to one of the caves in which some of the Dead Sea scrolls were found; while (b) is an aerial view of the monastery, probably Essene, in which the scrolls were almost certainly written.

PLATE 35. Jericho. (*a*) Probably the world's oldest piece of advanced military architecture: the circular tower, showing the entrance (upper right centre) to the interior stair—thousands of years older than the pyramids. (*b*) Perhaps the finest of the Jericho plastered skulls, *in situ*. These are presumably portraits, built up in plaster on the skull of the dead man. It probably dates from *c.* 5000 B.C, before the people of Jericho had discovered how to make pottery.

PLATE 36. Beth-Shearim, Israel and Jarmo, Northern Iraq. (*a*) In the central hall of a huge Jewish necropolis, which contained about 100 huge sarcophagi, all of which had been robbed. (*b*) An aerial view of the excavations at Jarmo, one of the world's earliest farming communities, showing the chequerboard of metre-square pits, a technique of exploratory excavation.

PLATE 37. Hazor—where the potter was interrupted at his wheel by the victory of Joshua. Near the sanctuary in Area C, these two still usable basalt elements of a potter's wheel were found with one of the potter's last works, a ritual mask.

PLATE 38. Still with the sea's incrustations on it: the larger than life size bronze Demeter, Greek work of the 4th century B.C., found in the Aegean by Turkish sponge-fishers, somewhere near Bodrum (Halicarnassus).

PLATE 39. Artemis Ephesia, "Diana of the Ephesians", "the many-breasted Mother of Asia"—or a priestess wearing the panoply of the goddess. A life-sized Greek island marble statue of the 2nd century A.D., found at Ephesus.

PLATE 40. A gold bracelet with lion-head ends, from one of the smaller tumuli of the great necropolis of Gordion in Phrygia. Mid-6th century B.C.

PLATE 41. From the greater tumuli of Gordion in Phrygia. (*a*) A siren-headed handle, one of four looking into a large bronze cauldron; (*b*) a black polished vase in the form of a stylized goat, the only decoration suggesting a chain collar; (*c*) two engaging goose vases; and (*d*) a large well-preserved screen of inlaid woods, probably box and yew, found beside the bed of the king. Objects (*a*) and (*d*) are from the largest tumulus, the burial mound of a great king; (*b*) and (*c*) from Tumulus P, the tomb of the four-year-old prince.

PLATE 42. Beycesultan (*a, c,* and *d*) and Harran (*b*). (*a*) Shrines of an unknown Anatolian religion which lasted for about 1,500 years; (centre) an altar of about 2600 B.C. and (on the raised block) an identical shrine of about 2400 B.C. (*c*) The horns of sacrifice: a reconstruction of a Beycesultan shrine of the same type of about 1230 B.C. (*d*) A pair of Bronze Age shrines, side by side and dating from about 1400 B.C. (*b*) The north entrance of the Great Mosque of Harran, with (under the black-and-white measure) a Babylonian *stele* of King Nabonidus (Plate 43 (*b*)) turned face downwards in contumely.

PLATE 43. The northern gateway of Karatepe, with the sculptured and inscribed panels, of about 730 B.C. The importance of the two gateways lies in the fact that the panels on one side were in Hittite hieroglyphic and those on the other in Old Phoenician and that they provide the longest bilingual text of Hittite hieroglyphic. This shows the Old Phoenician inscription.

PLATE 44. Babylonian survivals in the Great Mosque at Harran. (*a*) The upper part of one of the *stelai* which had been set face downwards in the entrance to the mosque, showing a bearded Babylonian figure with the symbols of the deities Sin, Shamash and Ishtar. (*b*) Part of the *stele* found in the north entrance (Plate 42*b*). This gives a new list of Assyrian kings and describes the funeral of the mother of Nabonidus.

never regained its importance, the new city of Smyrna arising on a site some four miles away.

Potentially Istanbul, Constantinople, Byzantium is perhaps the richest of all sites in the world. Whether as Greek colony, capital of the Eastern Empire and a chief city of the Ottoman world, it has been a rich and important place for at least 3,000 years continuously. In particular as the centre of the Byzantine Empire, it was virtually the capital of the civilized world for something like 1,000 years—an absolutely unparalleled record in the history of the world. For some reason or other, perhaps because the title of Gibbon's great book is *The Decline and Fall of the Roman Empire*, we tend to regard the history of the Eastern Empire as a tale of corruption, incompetence, bureaucracy and decay, forgetting perhaps that from Constantine the Great to the Fall of Constantinople is over 1,000 years and that no other empire of anything like the same scale has survived for anything like that length of time. But the continuity which has enriched the city has, at the same time, buried its past. The records are many, the visible remains are few, though noble. Santa Sophia, parts of the great walls, the remains of the Golden Gate still stand as witnesses of the splendour which was Constantinople of the Empire, but the excavations have been few and sporadic.

The most notable modern excavations have been those conducted on behalf of the Walker Trust of St Andrews University, before the war under the direction of Professor Baxter and since the war under that of Professor D. Talbot Rice of Edinburgh University. The scene of these excavations has been in one of the buildings which went to make up the Great Palace of the Byzantine Emperors. The Great Palace was not a single building but was a conglomeration of buildings, courts and gardens not at all unlike the Kremlin, as Professor Talbot Rice has pointed out; and it was in one of the courts of this complex that the excavations took place. The most notable discoveries have been of mosaics of the highest standard of technical excellence; and these, after discovery, have been either roofed over *in situ*, or lifted and transferred to a Turkish building near by.

The date of the mosaics has been argued, some authorities placing them as early as the third century A.D. (from the classical character of some of the figures) others as late as the end of the fifth century; but concerning their quality there has been no dispute. Only at Antioch is there anything really comparable with them, and it is possible that the Constantinople mosaics are of even finer workmanship. Some of the finest work is the borders, which are extremely elaborate with scroll patterns of acanthus leaves, in the loops of which are animals, birds, flowers, fruit and human heads, sometimes obviously personifications, but sometimes also what seem to be portraits. The scenes portrayed are usually hunting or pastoral in character, informed sometimes with a Virgilian sentiment or a homely humour. In one landscape birds are flying round a bush, a peasant milks a goat in front of a reed hut, horses graze and one suckles a foal, and the proprietor sits on a rock near by and pleasantly plays upon the lute. In another a dark and muscular man leads a camel on which ride two chubby boys, one of whom carries a bird on his wrist; in another a mule kicks off his rider and scatters the bundles of firewood which he has also been carrying; and his eye rolls back with a lively vice.

When these mosaics were lifted, great vaulted substructures were found beneath them, with massive stonework, of perhaps the age of Constantine, supporting brick vaulting of several later dates. In some cases the vaults of these structures rose over 20 ft from their original ground level; and for the one sounding down to virgin soil a pit 60 ft deep was necessary; and it was impracticable to make a satisfactory exploration of these huge substructures.

Hardly perhaps to be considered as archaeology, the discoveries in the Kahrie Djami (better known perhaps as the Church of the Monastery of the Chora) are so spectacular that they must be mentioned. When the great churches of Constantinople were taken over by the Turks and converted into mosques, their especial glories, their frescoes and wall mosaics were covered over with plaster as offending against that Mohammedan canon which forbids the portrayal of the human figure; and this treatment, while it buried these transcendent works of Byzantine art, nevertheless helped to preserve them.

One consequence of the Turkish revolution has been the secularization of a number of these ancient churches, Santa Sophia being the most notable example, with the result that works of art which had been invisible since the fifteenth century have once again come to light.

Between the wars, the Director of the Byzantine Institute of America, Mr Thomas Whittemore, was particularly associated with the restoration of Santa Sophia; and concurrently with this work made a start on the church of the Chora. Since the war this work has been continued under the direction of Mr Paul Underwood; and a most spectacular group of frescoes and mosaics has been uncovered and restored. The church was built on the site of earlier structures in the eleventh century and rebuilt with additions in the early fourteenth century at the expense of the Logothete Theodoros Metochites, whose portrait appears in one of the mosaics, kneeling and holding a model of the new church. Before he died political fortune ran against him and he ended his days as a penniless monk in the monastery of the church he had so handsomely adorned.

The principal glories of the church are: the frescoes of the dome, a medallion of the virgin with twelve radiating segments each containing an angel; a mosaic cycle of the Life of the Virgin Mary, in mosaic, in the inner narthex; another dome, likewise in the inner narthex, with mosaic segments showing the "thirty-nine ancestors of Christ"; and in the mortuary chapel, an apse with many frescoes of which a superb "Harrowing of Hell" is perhaps the finest.

One of the most interesting, and successful, series of excavations since the war, in Turkey, has been that mounted annually by an expedition of the University of Pennsylvania Museum under the direction of Professor Rodney S. Young, at Yassihoyuk. Yassihoyuk lies some 60 miles south-west of Ankara on the River

Sangarios (now called Sakarya) and since 1900, when it was first excavated, it has been pretty confidently identified with Gordion, the capital of the Phrygians; and it is now generally accepted as such.

Gordion and the Phrygians are words with romantic overtones. The Phrygians were ruled by a dynasty of kings called Gordius and Midas, and both names have added to the world's treasury of metaphor. Midas was so rich that legend credited him with "the golden touch" and all the glories and miseries that arise from that—and added asses' ears in a spirit of counterpoise; while Gordius symbolized the intricacy of power with a knot so complex that no one could untie it—until Alexander the Great came along and severed it with a single stroke of the sword, thus providing a convenient excuse (and technique) for all revolutionaries since.

The Phrygians themselves are, however, little known. Homer makes them the allies of the Trojans, and Priam's queen, Hecuba, was the daughter of a Phrygian king. They are believed to have entered Asia Minor from Thrace; and their expanding power is thought to have been one of the factors leading to the fall of the Hittite Empire in the twelfth century B.C. Their time of greatest strength and prosperity began in the ninth century and throughout the eighth they were the dominant power in Anatolia, expanding so far to the south-east that they came to be a challenge to the Assyrians. Early in the seventh century their power was broken by the Kimmerians and later they came under Persian domination. After Alexander's conquests Gordion became Hellenized but dwindled away under the Galatians, who appear to have abandoned it in the early second century B.C.

The site as a whole consists of a large mound, the city proper, standing beside the river, with two smaller mounds near by, subsidiary or suburban settlements maybe; and on higher ground, the necropolis, with nearly eighty heaped tumulus-graves, the largest of which is about 165 ft high.

In the centre of the city mound a deep sounding reached a "Copper Age" level of about 2500 B.C. or a little later; above this lay a Hittite level of the fourteenth and thirteenth centuries B.C.; above this were two Phrygian levels, succeeded after about the seventh century by Lydian, Persian, Hellenized Galatian levels and finally a small Roman settlement. More widespread excavations revealed a number of large and massive buildings of the Persian Empire, from the middle of the sixth to the middle of the fourth century; and, particularly, an impressive city wall of about 25 ft thick, faced with masonry on both sides up to about 10 ft, filled with a rubble core and reinforced with timbers and with a superstructure of mud brick. The wooden beams in the masonry face served to carry a decoration of tiles, with moulded patterns in relief, usually geometrical, and painted in red and black on a white slip. It appeared, though, that massive as were these Persian fortifications they had been built on top of even more massive Phrygian buildings, which presumably dated from before the time that Cyrus captured the city in 547–546 B.C. Incidentally, dating from the years when the Persians strengthened the fortifications after they had added

Gordion to their possessions, is a piece of stone on which a Persian workman had scratched the gaming board for that game which is still played, in Anatolia under the name of *dokuz taz*, in England as "Nine Men's Morris"—which gives it an ancestry of at least 2,500 years.

The traces of the Phrygian gate, underneath the Persian, appearing so impressive, it was decided to clear away part of the Persian remains and reveal the Phrygian. This was done and it was found to consist of a passageway of about 67 ft running obliquely through the city wall between massively built gate-buildings containing guardrooms and the like. The walls between which it ran were faced with massive dressed stone, at one point still standing to the height of over 26 ft. In the inner section the walls are jogged back about 8 ft and the extra width is taken up with a low platform on either side, designed perhaps for spectators to processions in times of peace, or in time of war for defenders to stand in ambush in case the outer gate were forced. One of the walls had fallen, perhaps as the result of an earthquake, with the stones still in the same order. Another wall, the inner wall at the north side, had been taken down by builders of the later gate, but as the materials were still available it was decided to rebuild it, the task being entrusted to a local mason; and it was interesting to see that this man and his labourers still used the same methods and tools which must have been used when the wall was first erected, nearly 3,000 years before—a primitive hoist, pick, crow-bar, sledge hammer, mason's hammer, levelling string and measuring stick.

In the city itself, the Phrygian buildings, despite these powerful defences, seem to have been destroyed in a great fire early in the seventh century B.C.; and some idea of the fierceness of the blaze can be gathered from the fact that the plaster on the walls had in some places liquefied with the heat and was discovered as a greenish vitrefied substance. Some large buildings of this period were found, containing large rooms with circular central hearths, like the typical *megaron* of the Greek mainland, of which so fine an example has been found at Pylos; and some of these rooms were paved with pebble mosaic floors. Dark blue and dark red pebbles had been used on a white ground to build up a series of geometrical patterns which were scattered haphazard like a patchwork quilt all over the area. Outside one of these buildings ran a stone bench, presumably for the benefit of those who were waiting to see the great man within; and these suitors had whiled away the long hours of waiting by scratching "doodles" on the wall at their back: two pairs of crude boxers, a variety of animals and birds, including the hoopoe which is still common in Anatolia, and two little houses with double-pitched roofs with *acroteria* at the peak of the gable —a most valuable picture of what the Phrygian houses of Gordion looked like. It is a curious but inevitable thing in archaeology that detailed ground plans of buildings are the commonest things but elevations the rarest. Incidentally these particular buildings with their *megaron* plan and their geometric decoration tend to confirm the tradition that the Phrygians came from Thrace and the north and west rather than from the east.

The necropolis has proved to be of the greatest interest. The first tumulus to be excavated (in 1953) was unusually late and dated from the middle of the fourth century B.C. shortly before the conquests of Alexander and 200 years later than the general run of such tombs in antiquity. It had been robbed in fairly recent times, but enough remained to show that it was the tomb of a young girl of wealthy family who had been buried in a wooden coffin; and the robbers had failed to see the elements of a gold necklace, pendants, beads and shield-shaped plaques decorated with delicate rosettes and palmettes in filigree and granular work. Three of the mid-sixth century tumuli contained the remains of cremations and these contained much gold and electrum jewellery, evidently thrown on the ashes after the flames had died down. The finest piece is a beautiful gold bracelet of circular section with lion-headed ends (Plate 40).

As was stated earlier there are a great number of tumuli in the necropolis, some of them of very considerable size. Care had been taken to keep the mounds of soil above the tomb chamber round (or otherwise symmetrical); and the method by which this was done was discovered during excavation. It was clear that early in the construction of the mound lines of small stones were laid down as radii; and as these were buried in the rising soil, the lines of stones were renewed as often as was necessary, though naturally the radii became shorter as the summit of the dome was approached. The mounds therefore are symmetrical domes, but the actual tombs are not centrally placed, presumably in the hope of defeating tomb robbers, as it is impossible to predict where in these vast "haystacks" the "needle" is hidden. The tombs consist, in eighth-century Phrygia, of wooden chambers built in pits dug below ground level, roofed over with wood and then capped with a pile of stones and then finally covered with the great mound of earth. Now in order to economize in the huge task of shifting the soil of the mound, it was obviously desirable to know whereabouts the tomb chamber was and for this purpose Professor Young and his team hit upon a simple method (which is described in the chapter on techniques). A light portable oil-drilling rig was acquired and by means of a series of soundings from the summit of the mound it was found possible to locate quite easily the cap of stones over the tomb without touching or damaging the tomb chamber itself.

The method was tried out, with complete success, on Tumulus P. This was a mound about 40 ft high, oval in shape with its greatest measurements 45 × 56 ft. The drill revealed the shape and location of the stone cap; and when the excavation had been made, the centre of the tomb was found to lie 26 ft to the south-west of the natural peak of the mound. Further it was discovered that a mast had been erected in the tomb chamber to mark its exact position during the building of the mound and to assist the builders of the mound in siting the peak away from the location of the tomb beneath.

The chamber, when uncovered, was $14\frac{1}{2} \times 11\frac{1}{2}$ ft and $4\frac{1}{2}$ ft high, built of large squared timbers mortised together at the corners and floored with planks laid over small stones. The roof had collapsed with the weight of the stones above and some of the contents were, as a result, badly crushed and all were badly jumbled together. The chamber had apparently been hung with fabric draperies and filled with wooden furniture, chairs, tables piled with offerings in a variety of vessels, and a wooden bed on which the body had been laid. All that remained of the body was the teeth and the evidence of a belt of fine bronze sheet mounted on leather or fabric. These two together were sufficient to reveal that this was the tomb of a child of about four; and the richness of the grave goods showed that it must have been a princely child of the house of Midas. The preservation of the wood was astonishing for Anatolia; and the finest of it was the back of a ceremonial chair or throne. This is of a generally trellis design of wood inlaid in a variety of complex formal patterns, swastikas, Greek key and similar designs, in wood of contrasting colours. The various members of this trellis are joined together in several different ways, with tongue-and-socket, with dowels, and with glue. In the central panel is a circular design of open work, with a strangely Gothic (almost "North Oxford") look. The seat is made up of cross slats, which show traces of a purplish-red fibrous substance which could be the remains of a felt cushion. Herodotus refers to the famous throne which King Midas of Phrygia gave to the Oracle at Delphi; and this chair-back perhaps gives us some idea of what it looked like.

A number of other well preserved wooden objects were found in a bronze cauldron on an iron stand: three delightful little carvings which must have pleased the princely four-year-old in his lifetime, a lion, a lion attacking a bull, and a winged horse eating (and using one of its wings to hold the object it is eating); and some boxes, saucers, dippers and spoons, all of wood. Together with a number of shallow bronze bowls was a bowl of clear glass, fluted and with a central boss, about $6\frac{1}{4}$ in in diameter and the earliest vessel of this kind of glass known to exist. There were many bronze vessels and many fine pots, of which four were outstanding.

One of these is a large round-mouthed round-bellied jug, and probably the finest known example of Phrygian painted ware of the eighth century, its sides and neck being divided into panels by bands of formal ornament with each panel showing an animal figure, lions and bulls on the body, deer and antelope on the neck. The second and third are a pair, similar but not identical and in the form of geese. The foot of each vase is formal, the body is like the body of a plump goose, with the tail for handle and the neck and beak for spout and there is an opening in the back from which the vase can be filled. They are buff in colour and covered all over with geometric patterns in dull black which make an admirable though stylized simulation of feathers. These are a really engaging pair. Equally attractive is the fourth pot, though here stylization has gone much further. It is of polished black ware in the form of a tubby goat. The legs have been shortened in to form four stubby feet. The tail and the horns curl over in si milarcurves and join the back, forming handles on either side of the filling-hole in the back; and the muzzle is simplified into a spout. Round the neck is the only ornament, a double ring of small circles, suggesting a chain collar. The masterly skill, simplicity and affectionate good-humour of this piece are such that they make one feel one knows and likes the potter (Plate 41*b* and *c*).

The excavation of the tomb of the princely child, although so rewarding, was in a sense a trial run for the excavation of the great tumulus, which presented a number of major problems but promised an even richer reward. It was tackled in 1957. Its height, as mentioned before, was about 165 ft and it had a diameter of about 800 ft. This huge mound was accordingly probed with the light oil-drill in the manner previously mentioned and these probings revealed that a cap of stones, with a diameter of about 100 ft lay about 130 ft below the peak of the mound and slightly off centre, to the south-west. As it was quite impracticable to sink a vertical shaft 130 ft deep with a diameter of 100 ft, it was decided to approach the tomb from the side. Accordingly an open trench, about 225 ft long was cut into the side of the mound and this was then continued in a tunnel of about the same length. This tunnel presently met a stone wall about 9 ft high, made of roughly dressed limestone, and surrounding the tomb. Inside this wall and separated from it by a 6-ft filling of rubble was another wall of horizontal round logs of juniper, another filling of rubble and finally the actual tomb chamber which was made of well-fitted squared timbers. In none of these three walls had there ever been any entrance. It was clear that the tomb was made for a single burial and that it was filled, both with occupant and grave goods, from above, then roofed over, capped with stones and finally covered with the soil of the mound—in other words, a colossal operation which could only have been undertaken for a great king.

The actual chamber had a double-pitched roof, supported by shallow gables at the end and a middle gable supported on cross beams. It is 20 ft long and 17 ft wide and in a remarkable state of preservation, one of the walls having bulged slightly and the cross beams supporting the central gable having cracked—but these were the only faults: an astonishing state of affairs when we consider that this is an underground timber building of about 2,700 years of age. The floor was of squared timbers laid on a rubble bed; and the timbers of the walls, which are so well made that the joins are very hard to see, seem to have been finished with the adze and later sanded.

Even if the tomb had been empty, it would have been a fascinating piece of work; and it was far from empty. At the northern end—the tomb is orientated north-south—and in the north-west corner, lay the remains of a collapsed wooden four-poster bed, on which lay the skeleton of a man in the 'sixties, about 5 ft 2 in tall. He lay on his back with several covers of linen and wool in several colours. The position of various bronze brooches suggests a sleeved upper garment and there are traces of a leather skirt ornamented with bronze studs. On a table beside the bed was a linen bag containing no fewer than 145 bronze brooches, some with double pins with elaborate safety catches. In all there were nine three-legged tables in the tomb which had been piled with bowls containing food and drink for the deceased, and other offerings; and all had collapsed with the weight. A great number of iron nails had been driven into the walls

and handled bronze vessels hung from them; but the nails had eventually
rusted and the vessels had fallen to the ground. Along the west wall stood three
large bronze cauldrons, on iron stands; and there were beside 137 smaller
bronze vessels. These included 100 shallow bowls, three of which were simple
hemispheres, the remainder being *omphalos* bowls (i.e. with a central boss) in
several different types, plain, ribbed and petalled. There were jugs of differing
shapes and bowls and small cauldrons with ring or bucket-type handles; and
there were two remarkable *situlae*. These last are bucket-handled cups in the
shape of animal heads, the one a ram, the other a snarling lion. Both are of
excellent workmanship with white paste eyes, the pupils being inlaid black
stone. They are Assyrian in style and the lion *situla* can be paralleled in bronze
weights from the Khorsabad of Sargon II (721–705 B.C.); and these two objects
may well have been imports. Of the three large bronze cauldrons mentioned
above, one is probably of entirely local origin. It has two ring handles, each ring
being set behind a bull's head looking outwards. The other two cauldrons each
have four figures on the rim and it has been suggested that these are imported
figures (probably of Assyrian origin) attached to locally made cauldrons. All
the eight figures are in the shape of sirens, human heads with bird bodies, the
tail and wings pressed against the outside of the cauldron, the faces looking into
it with a comically engaging suggestion of wondering what's in the stew. On
one cauldron, all four heads are female; on the other two are female while the
other two have square Assyrian beards. All these heads are different and they
show a high standard of craftsmanship; and they bear a striking resemblance
to the many small ivory heads found by Professor Mallowan in his excavations
of the Assyrian capital, Calah-Nimrud in Iraq (Plate 41*a—d*).

Near these cauldrons were found a number of leather flaps with embossed
bronze ornament, but what purpose they served is unknown.

The best preserved woodwork is found in two screens which were standing
against the east wall. These are large single panels with scrolled feet at the two
lower corners; and with a single leg (with a similar foot) attached to the frame
at the back to enable the screen to stand. Their purpose is not quite clear; they
may be simply portable screens; or they may have been used as throne-backs
for stools. They are most ingeniously constructed. Each is made up of a number
of small pieces of light wood, probably box wood, tongued and grooved together
and held in place with pegs run through from the front. After this had been done
the front was decorated with elaborate inlays of a darker wood, probably yew.
For the most part this decoration is an all-over pattern made up of square units
of a sort of swastika pattern, but in the centre there are some circular units in
different sizes, some of them incorporating variations of the swastika, others
making up a sort of rosette with units rather like the "eye" of the ordinary dress-
maker's "hook-and-eye". This woodwork is quite un-Oriental in character and
when we remember that King Midas' gift to Delphi was an elaborate wooden
throne, we are led to think that fine cabinet-making of this style and quality
was perhaps a peculiarly Phrygian skill, as well as the major joinery and engin-

eering required to build an underground wooden tomb of such excellence as this.

The general effect of this screen is strangely reminiscent of the famous "Midas Monument" at Yazilikaya. This last is an enormous rock-cut façade, the gable-end of an imaginary building, which is carved with an all-over inter-lacing geometric pattern in relief, which is, so to speak, in the same "key" as the all-over inlaid pattern of the wooden screen.

CHAPTER SEVENTEEN

TURKEY—II

IN THE records of the history of the Hittite Empire as revealed by the innumerable tablets in cuneiform discovered at Boghazkoy there are many references to Arzawa, a powerful western neighbour of the Hittites—about whom nothing else was known. Who were the Arzawans? Where was Arzawa, the state or its capital?

In 1954 therefore the British School of Archaeology at Ankara, under the direction of Mr Seton Lloyd began a series of large-scale excavations at Beycesultan. This site consisted of a large city mound of the Second Millennium B.C. near the headwaters of the Meander and consequently of the right period and location to be an Arzawan capital.

It was discovered to be a potentially very rich site, and levels covering about 1,000 years, from the end of the Early Bronze Age to the end of the twelfth century B.C. were identified. During the Middle Bronze Age it appears to have been a large and prosperous city and a very large palace of considerable elaboration was found. It seems to have had some form of sub-pavement heating and to have had walls of painted plaster on a basis of mud-brick and stone rubble. Wood was used a great deal, but there is no cut stonework. Unfortunately the palace seems to have suffered a devastating fire and very few objects were found among the ruins. There was a later period of somewhat reduced prosperity; and a megaron type palace was discovered of about the thirteenth century B.C. The pottery is mostly quite distinct and individual and, surprisingly, there is virtually no Mycenaean material.

The fourth season, that of 1957, however, proved much more interesting. At the end of the 1956 season, there had been discovered in the Early Bronze Age sounding what looked like the remains of a religious shrine; and as this was a subject about which virtually nothing was known, the clue was eagerly followed up in 1957—with remarkable success. Four sets of twin shrines were discovered at different levels, covering the period of about 2700 B.C. to 2300 B.C.; and in their essentials these pairs were alike and represent a continuous tradition; and the description of one pair will suffice for the lot. The two shrines are side by side and each is a room about 10 yds long by 5 yds wide. At one end of this room stand two clay *stelae*, about 5 ft high with a gap between them; just in front of the *stelae* stand the "horns of sacrifice", a clay block with a semicircular recess in the top. In front are two semicircular curbs, one based on the diameter provided by the "horns of sacrifice", the outer and larger one based on the outer extremities of the *stelae*. Behind these *stelae* are receptacles for offerings; and a series of post-holes suggests that there was a woven screen behind, perhaps designed to conceal the movements of the priest. So far the pairs of shrines are alike. In one however, the "male" shrine, a wooden post arose on the line of the outer curb, opposite to the openings between the curbs; in the other, the "female" shrine, there was no such post, but against one wall what has been described as a blood altar, a clay table with channels to carry off the liquids of the sacrifice to a pottery vessel sunk in the ground at the side. Little flat schematic "mother-goddess" figurines were found among the offerings in the "female" shrines. This group of shrines was in the outer part of the settlement and they were orientated outwards against the settlement wall (Plate 42a, c and e).

Meanwhile, near by in the excavation, an exactly similar but later sequence of shrines was found, covering the period from 1900 B.C. to about 1230 B.C. (Middle to Late Bronze Ages) and these later shrines were on exactly the same basic principle as the earlier, although with some interesting developments of the altar complex. In these later shrines, the *stelae* had merged together to become a continuous wall and the gap between them had become a hole in the wall through which the offerings were passed. The block, the "horns of sacrifice", had however grown and become more elaborate, taking the form of two upstanding units of terracotta, with recurved summits and with circular designs all over them. These stood in front of and on either side of the hole in the wall, so that the worshipper would need to stretch forward between them to pass his offerings through to the priest. On one side of the horns was a high curb containing a hearth, with clay "andirons" and projections supporting a large pottery cooking vessel; and under this lay ashes. Behind the wall lay a profusion of offerings and votive objects. In front of the altar of the latest shrine, a necklace was found laid out, consisting of several rows of beads and small shells.

Thus from about 2700–1230 B.C. with a gap of about 400 years (2300–1900 B.C.) which could no doubt be filled by further excavation, we have the shrines of a continuous form of worship lasting about 1,500 years and of a twofold form, "male" and "female" (which it is of course tempting to equate with the Dionysian-Apollonian dichotomy which seems to underlie so many religions) in a people of whom we know very little else. They were a rich, powerful and individual people, who were Western neighbours of the Hittites and they suffered two great disasters one of which, about 1900 B.C. they recovered from, the other, in 1230 B.C., putting an end to their capital. They were almost certainly the Arzawans; perhaps some great discovery in the future will reveal them as brilliantly as the tablets of Boghazkoy revealed the Hittites.

One of the most important discoveries ever made in Hittite archaeology was that made by Professor H. Th. Bossert at Karatepe in 1946–9. Karatepe and Domuztepe are two ancient late Hittite sites on either side of the Ceyhan River (the ancient Pyramos); and of these Karatepe is the larger and more important. In 1946 fragments were discovered with inscriptions, some in Old Phoenician (which can be read) and others in Hittite hieroglyphic (which could not). This suggested that a bilingual inscription might possibly be found and excavation was started at Karatepe in 1947 by Professor Bossert, with the co-operation of Assistant Professors Bahadir Alkim and Halet Cambel. Karatepe was discovered to be a late Hittite fortress, surrounded by a city wall with rectangular towers at intervals around it. There were two main entrances, north and south, both on the same plan. A long corridor, flanked by towers and decorated on either side by inscribed and sculptured panels, leads up to the main entrance gate, which has recesses on either side, again decorated with inscribed and sculptured panels. These were most impressive but the most exciting feature lay in the fact that those on the left were in Old Phoenician, those on the right in Hittite hieroglyphic. This held out the most exciting possibility—which study completely confirmed. The texts were identical; and what had been discovered was a long and elaborate bilingual document—or rather two documents, since there were two gateways and two sets of parallel inscriptions. It was very soon possible to establish that the language of the hieroglyphs was an Indo-European one and also to discover what the inscriptions were about. They state, among other things that the fortress was built by Asitawandas king of the Danuna and named after himself Asitawanda. He claims to be of the dynasty of Mopsos (a family famous in Greek legends) and that his reign was a time of peace and prosperity for the Danuna. His father was probably Awarikus, who is mentioned in Assyrian texts as Uriki; and this places him in time a little before 730 B.C. This being so he was probably the last king before his country became an Assyrian province about 725–715 B.C. and this limits this very important inscription to a very brief bracket in time. Although some Hittite hieroglyphs had been interpreted previous to this, the importance of this discovery lies in the length of the bilingual, which enormously adds to the known vocabulary and grammar and also provides a considerable historical text.

The reliefs themselves, which are in the form of upright panels with portal lions at the end of each series, are of great interest. They are in fairly shallow relief and show a variety of hunting scenes; representations of the God Bes, a woman suckling a child, an eagle-headed spirit with four wings and winged sun-disk above his head; and what must be among the earliest representations of a sea-going vessel. The captain keeps watch in the bows, the rowers pull on the oars and a helmsman sits under the curved stern manipulating a large squarish paddle on the port side. The reliefs are mostly of rather clumsy workmanship and many give the impression of being unfinished, thus suggesting that the work was incomplete when the catastrophe came (Plate 43).

In striking contrast to the evasive, teasing and inconclusive nature of the discoveries made at Beycesultan—which can be compared perhaps to the basic composition of a huge picture by a great artist in which nearly all the features have yet to be filled in—in striking contrast to this is the massive quantity of explicit material turned up by Dr and Mrs Ozguc at Kultepe in the *karum* of Kanesh, where the detail is as crowded and as cut-and-dried as in a Hogarth engraving.

During the last century clay tablets in the Akkadian language used by the Assyrians were regularly coming to light by various devious channels in Anatolia; and it was eventually deduced that the source was a city mound called Karahuyuk near Kultepe in Cappadocia, about half-way between Boghazkoy and Karatepe. This mound was believed, incorrectly as it turned out, to be a Hittite fortress and several expeditions excavated there without finding any trace of such tablets. Indeed it was not until 1925 that the Czech Hrozny discovered that there was a subsidiary site about 100 yds distant and that it was this which was the source of the tablets. The mound had indeed been inhabited by the indigenous inhabitants of the Anatolian plateau of the beginning of the Second Millennium B.C.—about the time that the great palace at Beycesultan was being destroyed by fire, but the subsidiary site was a distinct cantonment inhabited by foreigners, Assyrian merchants, a commercial establishment in fact, called in their own language a *karum*, and that its name was Kanesh.

The Czech excavators broke the ground here, but it was left to the post-war work of the Turkish Historical Society, begun in 1948 under Dr and Mrs Ozguc, to undertake the systematic excavation of the place.

Five levels in all were distinguished and these date from about 2000 to 1700 B.C.; and of these the three middle levels are the most important. Fortunately for posterity all these three periods seem to have ended with fires, fortunately that is, because as a result the contents of the houses are preserved *in situ* among the ash and ruins and present a lively and detailed picture of the *status quo* at the moment of disaster. In all those houses which had escaped the fire nothing had been left behind.

However, in the majority not only were the domestic utensils and installations of these Assyrians colonists preserved, but also thousands of clay tablets containing notes of innumerable commercial transactions and contracts, giving names, quantities, goods, prices and many other details of a substantial trade, conducted in caravans plying between Anatolia and Mesopotamia.

The standard of currency seems to have been silver; and the principal objects of trade to have been lead and textiles from Mesopotamia and copper from Anatolia.

The way of life of the colonists seems to have been completely Anatolian—they had, so to speak "gone native"—their houses and pottery are local in style, they took Anatolian wives and they seem to have lived at peace with their hosts. In fact, if it were not for the documents, the language of the business transactions and the Mesopotamian seals with which the clay envelopes were sealed, it would be difficult to distinguish them from the indigenous inhabitants.

This particular Assyrian cantonment was not unique, it seems. There were several other *karums* in Anatolia, but Kanesh appears to have been the most important and a clearing house for the others. The goods were carried back and forth by caravans of donkeys and there is no reference to wheeled vehicles; and there is no reference, also, at any point to any caravan being lost—a remarkable testimony to the security of the roads in those distant times.

The houses in which the colonists lived were comfortable and commodious, of mud-brick and wood, plastered both inside and out. They were usually of two storeys, the upper storey being the scene of the family's leisure, the ground floor that of their business and domestic activity. In many cases burials were made under the floor of the house, the body being placed in either a terracotta coffin or a stone-lined cist.

The pottery generally is of the "Cappadocian" type and includes a great number of graceful vessels set on what seems a disproportionately small foot. There are many pots in the form of animals—bulls and lions—and beasts and birds appear as decoration. There is one delightful vase in the form of a painted snail; and, found always with the tablets, a vase, painted and in the shape of a high boot with a long and upturned toe, of a style still worn in Anatolia. This is usually explained as having been used for libations—which throws a new light on the custom at gay Edwardian parties. But there is another suggestion. Similar boot vases, it seems, were used in Mesopotamia as token payments in certain business transactions. And on this basis the verse in Amos—"That we may buy the poor for silver and the needy for a pair of shoes"—is not so much a piece of contemptuous brutality as rather a quotation of the current rate of exchange.

In classical times and later, the areas known as Caria and Lycia—the south-western corner of the peninsula of Asia Minor, over against Rhodes—are of great importance; and in the Boghazkoy Hittite records, which are of late Bronze Age date, there are many references to the Lycians. It has however been growing more and more likely that in Bronze Age times Caria and Lycia were uninhabited; and a series of excavations carried out on the Lycian coast in 1952 by F. J. Tritsch of Birmingham University and Ahmet Donmez of Ankara confirmed this by revealing nothing earlier than the Iron Age; and it seems likely that the Lycians had migrated thither from some other place. Mr Tritsch suggests that it is tempting to think of the Lycians as having come from Crete in the Late Bronze Age to Miletus, moved gradually eastwards and finally southwards into what we now call Lycia.

These excavations besides making this discovery—an austerely satisfactory nil report—also identified the site of the Lycian city of Vehinta as being at Phellos and not at Antiphellos as was previously believed; discovered two important Lycian inscriptions, one of them a bilingual with Greek; and found at Patara, somewhat to the west, a very large marble head of Apollo, a very fine work of the Hellenistic period, associated with fine Greek vases of the late fourth and early third centuries B.C. Two rooms of a temple were found and it may well be that this is the site of the famous Oracle, which Herodotus compared in importance with those of Babylon and Thebes.

1947 saw the conclusion of Sir Leonard Woolley's famous excavations of Alalakh at modern Atchana, in southern Turkey, not far from Aleppo. Alalakh was, it seems, built in the Fourth Millennium B.C. by newcomers to the Amk plain who brought with them a fully developed Copper Age culture and wheel-made pottery. An astonishing feature of this pottery is its persistence; this painted ware is found at all levels from the earliest to the Second Millennium, then disappears for a while and then reappears for a short while after a popular rising had put an end to the Hittite dynasty of Yarim-Lim, this last reappearance giving the impression of a rejection of fashions imposed by an alien governing class.

Among the most interesting of the last discoveries on the site was a façade of a royal palace of the early Third Millennium. This was adorned by a row of immense circular mud-brick pillars, still standing to 10 ft and with a diameter of about 4 ft. Nothing parallel to this had previously been discovered in Turkey or Syria; and the closest parallels are to be found in Sumer, at Warka and Kish; and it would seem as if Alalakh at this period had close links with southern Mesopotamia.

A large and complex royal tomb, that of the king Yarim-Lim, was found and was partly excavated. Its original depth was probably originally about 50 ft. The lowest shaft was reached and partly excavated but the diggers were by now some 14 ft below water level and when the pumps broke down further excavation was abandoned. Although the funerary urn was not discovered much was learnt about the burial rites of a Hittite king and the way that his tomb was built. Very briefly, this was the method. First a pit 30 ft deep was dug, measuring about 150 × 60 ft—in other words, the width of a football field by the length of a cricket pitch. In the bottom of this a 20-ft-deep shaft was dug. In this the urn was set and the shaft filled with large stones. On top was built a mastaba-like building (with perhaps a second chamber) a small courtyard and a passage. After certain ceremonies, these were all filled in, the passage with mud-bricks, the courtyard with soil mixed with quantities of pottery which was even then ancient. Stones, clay, soil and mud-brick were added in layers and on the new floor that these made, another mastaba-like building was made, with passages and small chambers. These were then unroofed and soil and ancient pottery poured in. On this layer were laid course upon course of mud-bricks to roof-level. The roof was then replaced. A brushwood fire was then lit all round this subterranean block of building; and the space all round it filled in with mud-brick and the building was covered with brick, until within 5 ft of ground level. As if this were not sufficient, another building was erected on top, fires lit round, the walls were reduced and filled with mud-brick and all around it was poured concrete to form the foundations for the walls of the Chapel Royal in which stood the statue of the king, Yarim-Lim (Plate 46a).

In the seventeenth century B.C. a popular rising put an end to the dynasty of Yarim-Lim and this Chapel Royal was destroyed and looted and the statuary smashed. Nevertheless several pieces of the statuary have survived, including the very fine head of a king, who is most probably Yarim-Lim himself. This is probably the finest Hittite sculpture yet known. It is of diorite and might almost be the work of a Sumerian artist. It shows a youngish-mature face, full of character and individuality, proud but not without humour, with large eyes and heavily moulded lips and eyebrows and wearing a curious wig-like head-dress which approximates to a small flat turban. It seems likely that a separate stone beard was attached to the smooth-shaven face and indeed such loose stone beard elements were found during the excavations. Although the nose is slightly battered, the head is in excellent preservation and as a work of art and portraiture it stands secure on its merits without the need for any historical or artistic imagination on the part of those who look upon it now.

In view of the fate of the statue and the violent end of the dynasty in a popular uprising, well over 3,500 years ago, there is a certain irony in the fact that this Hittite portrait bears a considerable likeness to the late King Faisal II of Iraq.

At the eastern end of the Anti-Taurus Mountains, where the upper Euphrates rises, there stands as the dominant landmark a conical topped mountain called Nemrud Dagh, some 7,500 ft high. In 1881 a road engineer discovered that the top of the peak was man-made; and in 1882 and 1883 Karl Humann and Otto Puchstein investigated the site and discovered the elaborate temples, courts and colossal statuary which crown this summit with battered and fantastic majesty. On this naked mountain top three terraces had been cut into the rock, and the broken stone had been piled on the summit to make a tumulus or monster cairn 150 ft high. On two of the terraces stood five colossal enthroned statues, mostly headless—though the heads still lay below—and rising each to an approximate original 24 ft. On the back of the thrones were long inscriptions in a most beautiful Greek script. This was the last resting place, the *hierothesion* or "heavenly home" of Antiochus I, King of Commagene (*c* 69–34 B.C.).

In 1953 Miss Theresa Goell began excavations and surveys and associated with her was Dr F. K. Doerner, while not far away at another mountain shrine, of which the name was later discovered to be Arsameia-on-the-Nymphaeos Dr Doerner was directing excavations with Miss Goell in association.

Commagene was a small but strategically-placed state which is identified with a Late Hittite city-state called Kummuhi which was finally conquered by the Assyrians in the eighth century B.C. It then disappears from history until late Hellenistic times; and it makes its mark on western history in 62 B.C. when its king, Antiochus I, made a treaty with Pompey the Great and thenceforward it survived with success as a convenient buffer-state between the Romans and the Parthians until A.D. 72 when Vespasian became weary of the intrigues of Antiochus IV and removed him, incorporating the country into a Roman province as part of North Syria. Whoever they were—and Antiochus claims so many ancestors in the reliefs which adorn his last resting-place, from the Seleucids to the Achaemenians and the Parthians that it is tempting to think he was entitled to none of them—the Commagenian dynasty, rather like the Herods, seem, at any rate for a century or so, to have had a genius for enjoying the best of both worlds, politically, religiously and artistically. They held the balance between Rome and Parthia, they combined Roman and Parthian deities and religions, their art is a combination, lively and piquant of Hellenistic and Oriental and they seem to have shown the way to the Roman Emperors by deifying themselves posthumously or even earlier.

The outstanding features of this funeral monument of Antiochus I, who seems to have been the most successful of their kings, are the seated gods. In each case these are five, seated in a line, looking outwards from the mountain top. On the left, as one faces them, is Apollo-Mithras-Helios-Hermes; next, the only female, Fortuna-Tyche, tutelary goddess of Commagene; in the centre and somewhat larger than the rest, Zeus-Orosmasdes; on his left hand, the king, Antiochus I; and last Heracles-Artagnes-Ares. On either flank and in the same line are a guardian lion and an eagle. These statues stand on a base which rises from a court some 20 ft below; and on either side of this court are walls about 10 ft high with reliefs showing a variety of ancestors of the king, Macedonian, Persian and Commagenian, with an altar in front of each ancestor. On the back of the bases of the five seated statues is a long inscription in Greek describing the ritual and providing for the perpetuation of the cult (Plates 1 and 45a).

The smaller court, on the west terrace of the mountain top, is similar but less spacious and the five seated statues are not set so high; but it contains a long platform composed of *stelae* with reliefs of Antiochus being greeted by his deities; and this terrace also contains a famous Lion Horoscope relief, a lion, that is with nineteen stars, three planets and a crescent moon, which have been variously interpreted as representing some specific auspicious date in Antiochus' life.

It was hoped that perhaps the huge mound of broken stone which tops the summit of the mountain had been erected over the actual tomb of Antiochus and a trench was attempted into this scree-like mass. In the valley below the main terrace a large *stela* was discovered with an inscription in Greek, which, by order of Antiochus, shows the processional way to the sanctuary and warns all who come unknowingly or with evil intent to flee or terrible things will overtake them.

Two streams rising on Nemrud Dagh combine to form the Khata Chai and on its way to join the Euphrates this stream has cut a deep chasm in the limestone with two steep and isolated hills on either side. One of these, called Yeni Kale or New Castle, is crowned with the ruins of a castle of the Arab-Armenian period; the other, Eski Kale or Old Castle is the site of the other Commagenian *hierothesion*, the sanctuary which Antiochus I built for his father Mithradates of Commagene. Harsh and wild though this site is, it is nothing like so remote and inaccessible as Nemrud Dagh and the visible remains are much fewer, rock and earth falls having destroyed much of what had been built. Towards the summit, however, is a large rock-cut portico, of generally apsidal shape, with beside it a tunnel leading downwards by steps to an empty subterranean chamber. In front of this was a platform with two square sockets which most probably held standing reliefs. On two other sites, lower down, were other stepped platforms with sockets and below these were found fragments of reliefs showing Mithras and various royal personages.

But the most remarkable thing which Dr Doerner found on his first exploration of the site was a rock-cut inscription in Greek. In later seasons this was cleared and revealed as an artificially levelled rock-face with an inscription in five columns of beautiful Greek type, totalling in all about 23 ft in length, the longest Greek inscription hitherto found in Asia Minor. It begins "The Great King, Antiochus . . ." and is a Royal Decree and Sacred Edict given for the protection of the tomb and sanctuary of his father, Mithradates Kallinikos and for the maintenance of the cult. The inscription identifies the district of Arsameia-on-the-Nymphaios and says that the city derives its name from its founder, Arsames, one of his royal ancestors and that it had always been a favourite residence of the Commagenian royal family. This huge and interesting inscription was recorded in latex by Mr Kermit Goell, using the technique described elsewhere in this book, and this particular latex squeeze is thought to have been the largest made at that date.

About the time that this inscription was uncovered Dr Doerner also discovered a large monumental *stela* about 9 ft high, a superb piece of work in a wonderful state of preservation showing Mithradates, crowned and in elaborate Persian robes, greeting by handclasp Heracles, bearded, naked except for his lion-skin and bearing his knotty club in his left hand—an epitome as it were of Persian and Hellenic styles and ideas (Plate 45*b*).

In the last stages of clearing the great inscription it was discovered that it stood over and around a rock-cut archway leading to a barrel-vaulted stepped tunnel, hewn from the living rock and about 8 ft high and 6½ ft wide; and that this tunnel led downwards at an angle of between 45 and 35 degrees. It was tempting to believe that this led to the tomb of Mithradates and the first part of the tunnel was easily cleared, but with growing dangers further work was postponed to a later season when experts and proper equipment could be organized.

This was done, but there were still many difficulties. In some parts the rock was decomposing; and there was an alternation of hard limestone with softer strata and bands of clay. At various points timber supports were required and apparently had been in ancient times—and timber is rare, costly and hard to acquire in these south Turkish highlands. By the end of the 1954 season this tunnel had been traced about 125 yds into the heart of the mountain to a point some 160 ft below the entrance. At this point a band of thick clay had been reached and the problem of what lay at the end of this tunnel was still unsolved.

Between the rivers Euphrates and Tigris and at about the same latitude as Aleppo stands Harran. This is an ancient city standing on the crossing of two trade routes linking Syria, Asia Minor and Mesopotamia. The first historical reference to it occurs in a tablet found at Mari and datable to about 1750 B.C. It was the city where Abraham's father, Terah, settled after leaving Ur and where he died at the age of 205; and it was to Harran (spelt Haran in the Bible) that Abraham's son Jacob returned to find a wife and met Rachel by the well, which is still the only source of drinking water in the area. It was ruled over in turn by Assyrians, Greeks, Romans—when it was known by the ill-fated name of Carrhae—and Persians. In A.D. 639 the Arabs annexed it and for a brief period, during the eighth century B.C. it was the capital of the Umayyad dynasty and so the metropolis of a Muslim Empire which then stretched from India to Spain; after which it gradually declined, finally ceasing to be inhabited in about the thirteenth century A.D.

Since 1951 it has been the centre of a number of associated excavations under the general aegis of the Turkish Antiquities Department and the British Institute of Archaeology at Ankara. Bay Nuri Gokce, Director of the Archaeological Museum, Ankara and Mr Seton Lloyd, Director of the Institute were concerned with seeking the temple of the famous Moon-god "Sin of Harran"; Dr D. Storm Rice of London University was investigating the Great Mosque of Harran; Dr J. B. Segal, also of London University, was on the track of the Sabians in the Tektek Hills to the east and in the neighbourhood of Urfa (ancient Edessa); and Mr Michael Gough of Edinburgh University investigated the Roman settlement at the foot of the mound of Sultantepe.

In their search for the Temple of Sin, Bay Gokce and Mr Seton Lloyd decided that the main mound of Harran comprised too much classical and Islamic debris to permit them to reach the Assyrian levels; and taking their clue from the existing records of the Sabians, a strange pagan sect who managed to preserve their shrines and their worship of the ancient Mesopotamian gods almost into the Middle Ages, they turned to a neighbouring but subsidiary mound called now Sultantepe.

Almost immediately Assyrian buildings were found, which were later dated to about 648–610 B.C. and though the actual Temple of Sin proved elusive, the nature of the most important discoveries indicates that it is not far away. These two main finds are a collection of tablets; and the house of a priestess. The tablets seem to be the private collection of a priest named Qurdi Nergal; and from the position in which they were found—stacked behind a collection of empty wine jars—it looks as though an attempt was being made to preserve them when the temple was being looted, perhaps when Harran was sacked by the Scythians in 610 B.C. The presence of a human skull near by conjures up a picture of slaughter and looting. The tablets are mostly religious, literary and magical texts and include nearly all the Epic of Creation and an account of the wars of King Shalmaneser III. Near by was what seems to have been the private house of a priestess, if the quantity of cosmetic utensils is any guide. The objects found include an ivory palette, carved with a sphinx wearing the double crown of Upper and Lower Egypt, a number of delicate glass and faience bottles, a delicately coloured bead bag and the lapis lazuli ornament of what must have been a wooden casket. A tablet was found giving the household accounts of the priestess and it lists among other things her regular offerings to the temple. In an adjoining room was a broken stone *stela*, with in relief the pillar crowned with a crescent which was the symbol of "Sin of Harran".

Meanwhile Dr Storm Rice was at work on the ruins of the Great Mosque at Harran itself. When the Arabs took over Harran in the seventh century A.D., the Harranian pagans called themselves Sabians and since this creed was mentioned in the Koran as based on a revelation it secured them a status of equality with Christians and Jews and made them protected subjects of the Caliph. To quote Dr Rice "Under their cloak of respectability, the Harranians continued to worship the planets, though forms of worship probably varied from crude idolatry to the most lofty philosophical systems"—and the same could no doubt be said of most religions.

At all events the Muslims converted the temple into a mosque but gave the Sabians permission to build another temple elsewhere; in the mid-eighth century A.D. the last Umayyad Caliph, Marwan II, built himself a sumptuous palace and presumably enlarged and embellished the Friday Mosque. From A.D. 990 to 1070 a little-known dynasty, the Numairids, established an independent emirate with Harran as their capital and on one of their buildings Dr Rice discovered two dogs carved in relief—probably the only examples of dogs represented in Islamic art. In the early twelfth century, those great leaders of the counter-crusade, Nur ad-din and Saladin restored and embellished the Great Mosque, whose ruins now cover a square of over 100 yds and are of great interest for the student of Islamic architecture, not least for the piquancy of some of the carved stone ornament, which includes acanthus leaves, vines, and, most remarkable of all when one considers that it dates from the height of the wars between the Crusaders and the Saracens, a cross.

From the archaeological point of view, Dr Rice's most remarkable discoveries were made in the three entrances which were excavated. In all of these —in the stairway of one and the pavement of the other two—basalt slabs were noticed. When these were lifted, they were found to be inscribed *stelae* which had been deliberately set face downwards. Two of them still retained their rounded tops and this semicircular expanse in each case showed a bearded male figure in Babylonian dress, wearing a spiked mitre-like headgear, advancing from right to left, holding a ringed staff in one hand and raising the other to the three divine symbols of Sin (the Moon-god), Shamash (the Sun-god) and Ishtar (the Morning Star), that of Sin being nearest to him. The rounded top of the third *stela* had been cut off but enough remains to show the feet of four figures (two of them with the same ringed staffs) moving towards an object on the left which it is impossible to distinguish. Under the reliefs on the first two were three columns of cuneiform script; under the remains of the relief on the third, two columns of script, with a third narrow column of script on the edge of the *stela*. All three are documents of the Babylonian king, Nabonidus (556–539 B.C.). The first two tell the same story: of Nabonidus' attempts to rebuild the Temple of Sin at Harran, his disagreement with his people and, probably, the priests of Marduk, his self-imposed exile in Arabia, where he built a city "like Babylon" at Teima and journeyed as far as Yatribu (i.e. Medina); and his return to rebuild the temple of Sin (E Khul-Khul—"Temple of Rejoicing") as he had been commanded to do in a dream by the god himself. The third *stela* has a different text, part of which was known from a fragment found in 1906, and it is concerned with the mother of Nabonidus, a great devotee of Sin, who died at the age of 104 and it gives a description of the State funeral accorded to her. It also gives a new list of the Assyrian kings (Plates 42b and 44).

This discovery, apart from its intrinsic interest, also suggests that the Great Mosque was built on the site of the Temple of Sin and that these revered *stelae* were deliberately set face downwards in the entrances in such a way that everyone entering was bound to tread in contumely on the backs of the deposed idols. Meanwhile in the Tektek Hills Dr Segal had discovered in a sacred mountain a group of votive records in Aramaic of the second century A.D. and a female bust in relief dedicated to Sin—which is curious as in antiquity the deity is a male. The site seems to be Sabian; and so too does a remarkable and beautiful mosaic which he discovered in a rock-cut tomb near Urfa (ancient Edessa). This mosaic is a family portrait with the names given in Aramaic. It shows a noble of Edessa with his wife and their three sons and one daughter. One of the sons is the Vizier Ma'nu; and his daughter, Shalmath, is also included, presumably because she became a queen. It is suggested that she was the queen of Abgar the Great who reigned in Edessa at the end of the second century A.D. and who adopted Christianity after a visit to Rome. The rest of the group appear however to have been Sabians.

Sultantepe was the scene of one of several discoveries of mosaics made in Turkey by Mr M. R. E. Gough of Edinburgh University. It was here that he excavated the remains of a Roman bath, of which little remained except a mosaic floor, part of a plunge bath and a lavatory. The mosaic was of a complex geometric pattern, like a rich carpet and an inscription in Greek, consisting of five hexameters, is in the form of an address by the bath itself. The last line may be translated "By the good offices of Isaeus I recaptured my youth"—which suggests that it had been restored or rebuilt. It is probably of the fourth or fifth century A.D.

In the next year (1952) Mr Gough uncovered a mosaic in an Early Christian church at Ayas (ancient Elaeusa) which was built over a pagan temple of the first century B.C., much of the masonry of which had been reused. This mosaic was in that favourite form—the *paradeisos*, literally a park but always in this connexion a park packed full of animals, a sort of zoological garden. The idea is thought to derive from the myth of Orpheus taming the animals with his music, but it had been modified to Christian ends, presumably since everyone enjoys pictures of animals and in any case so many of them had acquired specialized Christian symbolisms.

In 1957 Mr Gough discovered another *paradeisos* mosaic likewise in an Early Christian church at a place called Dag Pazari in the mountains of Isauria, some 60 miles west of Mersin. It is possible that Dag Pazari may be the ancient Coropissus. Here was found a mosaic in what had been the *narthex* of a church probably founded at the end of fourth or beginning of the fifth century A.D. The mosaic is in two parts, each with an inscription and the later part probably dates from a rebuilding in the late fifth century. After about a century the church seems to have been destroyed. The earlier part of the mosaic is an arrangement of interlinking circles framing birds, beasts, vases and fruit; while the latter consists of a vine emerging from a vase with branches straying over the whole area, with birds and animals set in and out among these branches—including a pelican, an ibis, a hare, a heron, a hen with her chicks and a pair of fat-tailed sheep. It is indeed a very lively mosaic, much more accomplished than the Ayas *paradeisos*, and Mr Gough suggests that it should not be associated with the mosaic art of Constantinople or Antioch, but with the Early Christian centres of the southern plateau, such as Iconium.

CHAPTER EIGHTEEN

PERSIA

MORE markedly perhaps than in most countries post-war archaeological discovery in Persia has fallen into two sharply distinguished kinds: controlled scientific excavation; and the clandestine digging of treasure hunters—and both have been richly successful. Museums and private collections have benefited by the latter; scientific knowledge by the former.

The most splendid and valuable forms in which the treasures of ancient Persia are found are Achaemenian gold (sixth to fourth century B.C.) and Sassanian silver (third to sixth century A.D.) and a number of splendid objects of both kinds have been added since the war to the collections of the Metropolitan Museum, New York and the Teheran Archaeological Museum. They are generally described as "from Hamadan" which is both likely and convenient. Hamadan is ancient Ecbatana, which was the summer palace of the Achaemenian kings Darius and Xerxes and which was also the place to which Alexander the Great reputedly transferred the treasures of Persepolis after his conquest of Persia. Unfortunately for archaeology Ecbatana lies deep under modern Hamadan; and it is clear that only accidental or clandestine finds can come to light there and the circumstances of their discovery are rarely known and even more infrequently published.

Nevertheless both the New York and Teheran museums have acquired four pieces each of superb Achaemenian gold, which are so alike that they must originally have been very closely associated. In each case there is a gold ceremonial dagger with animal decoration on the hilt; a bowl in the form of a half-open lotus blossom, bearing the inscription "Xerxes the Great King" in Babylonian, Old Persian and Elamite; an armlet with multiple lion decoration; and a superb *rhyton* in the form of a crouching winged lion, the cup part of the vessel arising from the hindquarters of the beast. All eight of these objects are splendid, but the Teheran set are perhaps a little more sumptuous than the New York set.

Equally splendid, much more interesting from the new light it throws and even more romantic in its origins is the Gold Treasure of Ziwiye. The principal item of this is the great gold pectoral—a large kidney-shaped breast plate of sheet gold, covered all over with scenes and ornament in *repoussé* and considered to be Mannean work of the eighth century B.C. The story of its discovery as originally told by Mme Yedda Godard, the wife of Dr André Godard, the Director-General at that time of the Archaeological Services of Iran, was briefly as follows.

It started probably in 1947. A shepherd boy was with his flocks on a hill near Ziwiye, which is in Persian Azerbaijan, south-east of Lake Urmia, and he noticed a gleam of gold near some ancient ruins. A friend of his was collecting astragalus roots near by; and the two of them together hunted about and found certain objects. Now on the hillside there was also a Jew who had come out to collect a special earth for scouring his pots; and he came up to the boys and offered to buy what they had found. To this they agreed, were paid and handed over their finds; and they parted, all agreeing on the need to keep the matter secret. That night the Jew buried the treasure in his garden and climbed the hill to make a further search in private; and the boys not unnaturally boasted to their friends and neighbours of their good fortune; and, it need hardly be added, the friends and neighbours went and threatened the Jew, handled him roughly and robbed him of the treasure; and likewise went up the hill and throughly searched the whole area of the original find. When they had found all that was to be found, they assembled the treasure and quarrelled violently about its ownership and being quite incapable of reconciling their violent differences took King Solomon's advice and cut this priceless treasure into small pieces and shared it out among all the claimants.

The treasure did eventually reach the Teheran Museum—perhaps all of it, perhaps not—and it has been possible to reassemble the pectoral.

The ornament of the pectoral is in two registers, an upper and a lower, and the general design is the same in both cases—a number of creatures, real or fabulous, facing inwards to a central tree of life. In the lower section the tree of life is crowned with a cauldron of fire, the symbol of the sun and the god Marduk. Among the creatures worshipping these central symbols are: ibexes, that favourite subject of Achaemenian art; winged bulls; rams wearing the Phoenician kilt; the sort of winged gryphons which are common in archaic Greek art, but here wearing the Phoenician kilt; winged sphinxes, also kilted; Assyrian-style bearded man-headed bulls; and bearded and winged genii, with animal legs like satyrs and with both arms raised in the attitude of adoration. Among other objects of the treasure is a gold lion-head with the "warts of strength" between the eyes; a gryphon head of the Archaic Greek type; and a plaque with an all-over pattern of interlacing ribbons and lion heads, with various animals in the intervening spaces—and one of the animals is the typically Scythian galloping stag, with fantastically elaborated antlers.

M. Godard has suggested that the probable history of the pectoral is that it was buried by the Mannaeans when Sargon II attacked them toward the end of the eighth century B.C. and (as he boasts in an inscription at Khorsabad) destroyed their capital Izirtu and their fortresses Zibie and Armaid. The Mannaeans were powerful vassals of the Assyrians and they normally attempted to maintain a state of neutrality between their neighbours, Assyria and Urartu. The pectoral, it is suggested, dates from the ninth century B.C.

There has of course been considerable controlled excavation at two long famous Achaemenian sites: Persepolis and Susa; at Persepolis, under Dr André

Godard, and at Susa under Dr R. Ghirshman, Director of the French Archaeo-logical Missions in Persia.

At Persepolis, on the plateau not far from Shiraz, some work was done despite financial and political complications and in 1951 a Royal building was un-covered below the terrace of the Apadana and about half a mile away from it. It consisted of a forecourt and a hall surrounded with living quarters. The roof of the hall had been supported by twelve pillars arranged in three rows of four. The bases of these pillars, which are in traditional style, still survive and on the two central bases of the middle line there is an inscription in cuneiform in the three languages, Old Persian, Babylonian and Elamite, which says: "Xerxes the King has said: I built this Tatchara." Tatchara is the word used to describe the palace of Darius on the terrace; and therefore this building is a palace. Xerxes, in the inscription calls himself King and not King of Kings, as he would do after succeeding Darius; therefore it would seem that he was Crown Prince or Heir Apparent at the time; and therefore again that the building must date from (at the earliest) Darius' accession, or 521 B.C. to (at the latest) the accession of Xerxes, or 486 B.C.

A year or two later some interesting sculpture was found north of the Apa-dana, near the great staircase known as the Portals of Xerxes, on a site which seems to have served as a quarry and workshop for the sculptors of Persepolis. The first piece was a rather stout dog squatting on its haunches, a pleasant though not very distinguished piece which was apparently never finished. The second piece was a double-headed eagle capital. Double animal headed capitals are of course a common and strikingly beautiful feature of the pillars of Achae-menian palaces and indeed are among the most characteristic beauties of Persepolis; but this is the only one with eagle heads—and it is not difficult to see why. From the ground it is a distinguished and attractive piece of sculpture, but seen from below and set on the top of a tall pillar, in the shadow of the roof, it would have gone for nothing and been simply an unidentifiable bulk with an unimpressive point—the beak—at either side; and with this in mind it is not surprising that the architect rejected it. Another rejected capital was—a double-headed lion capital, an excellent piece of design and workmanship, in the highest degree of finish, and rejected because of a flaw running right through the stone, which must have been quite obvious to the masons from the moment they started and which they had at one point tried to patch up with bronze clamps.

Both these rejections throw an interesting light on what one can only describe as the bureaucratic wastefulness of the Achaemenian Ministry of Works. If the architect wanted to try the effect of an eagle-headed capital, surely the simplest and quickest way would have been to have made a small clay model; and surely it was unnecessary to finish a flawed sculpture before deciding that, on account of the flaw, it would never be used. But presumably such a use of common sense would be "agin the regulations" and "you're not paid to think"; and indeed such things have happened in later ages.

Susa, the other Achaemenian capital, lies in the plain among those rivers which descend from the Persian plateau to Mesopotamia and the Persian Gulf and it has been the scene of excavations by the French Archaeological Mission in Persia since 1897. Susa consists of four mounds beside the River Chahur: the acropolis, the Apadana, the Royal town and a fourth which is generally called the Town of the Artisans. In 1946 a large site was opened under the direction of Dr Ghirshman at the northern end of the Royal town. Four successive towns were revealed, the two uppermost Islamic, then one of the sixth–seventh centuries A.D. and finally one which came to a violent end in the time of Shapur II A.D. (309–379). There is considerable evidence of the suddenness and savagery of this catastrophe; everywhere there are children buried in jars, adults buried on the surface, with a few stones erected round them and a mound of soil placed over the body; and massive wall elements overturned. It is known that Shapur II, a contemporary of Constantine, was a great persecutor of the Christians, whom he suspected of being pro-Roman; and a surviving text of the Acts of the Christian Martyrs relates that he sent an army to suppress a revolt of the Christians at Susa and that he had the whole town levelled by 300 elephants; and it is almost certainly this town that Dr Ghirshman has uncovered.

In the "Town of the Artisans" a very large Partho-Seleucid necropolis was uncovered, dating from about 300 B.C. to the third century A.D. The tombs for the most part are shafts leading to underground funerary chambers cut out of the hard compacted earth of the virgin soil; and the dead are usually placed in terracotta sarcophagi. The lids often have a dotted stylized outline of a human figure, the features of the face occasionally being lightly moulded in a shallow relief. These sarcophagi were sometimes used almost as family tombs and the bones of the previous occupant were either pushed to one end or else taken out and heaped round the base on which the sarcophagus stands. The commonest type of funeral furniture was a simple alabastron; and protective female figurines, usually rather clumsy steatopygous terracottas, are quite often found. They include also some Hellenistic objects, figurines usually in the Alexandrine grotesque style.

"And the whole earth was of one language, and of one speech. And it came to pass, as they journeyed from the east, that they found a plain in the land of Shinar; and they dwelt there. And they said one to another, Go to, let us make brick and burn them thoroughly. And they had brick for stone, and slime had they for mortar. And they said, Go to, let us build us a city and a tower, whose top may reach unto heaven; and let us make us a name, lest we be scattered abroad upon the face of the whole earth" (Gen. 11.1–4). And from this act of presumption—the planning of the Tower of Babel—there came (the Bible goes on) the separation of races, the confusion of tongues, and all the misunderstandings which have derived therefrom.

The plain of Shinar is southern Mesopotamia, the Tower of Babel is a *ziggurat*, that massive roughly pyramidal tower of brick which was such a usual feature of the cities of ancient Sumer. A number of these are known from their foundations, but none has survived to any considerable extent except the most easterly of them, the *ziggurat* of Tchoga-Zanbil, which stands about 18½ miles south-east of Susa and which is the most easterly survival of the Sumero-Elamite religion.

Tchoga-Zanbil is the modern name for the remains of a city called Dur-Untashi, which was built in the mid-thirteenth century B.C. during one of the most brilliant periods of Elamite history, when after a series of conquests the Elamites had much extended their territories both to the west and the north. It survived until 640 B.C. when it was destroyed at the triumphant conclusion of the Assyrian king, Assurbanipal's campaign against the Elamites; and it was apparently never again inhabited. The town survives as two concentric en-closures, the outer one being about 1,300 × 875 yds, the inner being roughly a square of 437 yds. In the centre of this stands the *ziggurat*, a square of about 350 ft, with sacred enclosures on all four sides. Originally it must have risen to about 174 ft; and even today the great mass of brick still stands to about 82 ft. Practically every element of it bears the name, in cuneiform, of its builder "I, Untash-Huban", who seems to have been as determined as the builders of Babel to "make him a name" and who indeed seems to have succeeded, thanks to the efforts of Dr Ghirshman (Plate 47).

It was in 1952 that the French Archaeological Mission in Persia, under the direction of Dr R. Ghirshman began the enormous project of excavating and partly restoring this huge *ziggurat*; and by steady annual work this task was virtually completed during the winter season of 1956–7. Before going into any of the details of this work, it would perhaps be better to describe the final result of Dr Ghirshman's labours and to explain what the *ziggurat* originally was like and how it was built.

It was in essence a square pyramid, on a base of rather over 110 ft, with the sides facing north-west, north-east, south-east and south-west, rising in five massive steps and crowned, almost certainly, with a temple at a height of 174 ft. On all four sides of the first stage there are entrances, vaulted over and with stairs leading to small chapels inside the mass and also to the wide terrace which is the top of the first stage. From this terrace rises the next stage; and in this there is only one entrance and stair—on the south-west face—leading to the terrace which is the top of the second stage. From this rises the third stage and here again there is only one entrance and stair—in the south-east face. So much survives, but also enough to show that this stair on the south-east face led straight onwards through the fourth stage; and it seems probable that the final stair in the fifth stage, leading direct to the temple, was on the north-east face.

All of this was built of brick, sun-dried brick and baked brick, and the method of construction seems to have been very curious. The first stage seems to have been built as a hollow quadrangle. In the sides of this quadrangle were a number of chambers, the majority of which have an interior stair and they had been filled with offerings before being sealed from above. Five chambers, however on the north-east side had originally been empty but with doorways leading into the interior quadrangle. These doorways had however been filled in and the chambers filled with brick from above.

It seems clear, therefore, that when this first stage quadrangle had been built, a second quadrangle, small but about twice the height, was built immediately inside it, thus making the second stage. This completed, a third quadrangle, even smaller, but three times the height of the first, was then built immediately inside the second, making the third stage—and so on, rather like building a set of Chinese boxes, from the outside inwards.

No trace of the temple which is presumed to have stood on the summit of the *ziggurat* remains; but on the upper slopes of the mass was found the head of a lioness carved in black stone, which is believed to have been part of the adornments of such a temple; and lower down, a considerable number of terracotta elements which Dr Ghirshman calls "nails", which are plaques, round or square, of enamelled terracotta, with shafts on one side which were presumably used to secure them into the face of a wall as decorative units. These all bear the inscription "I Untash-Gal", Untash-Gal being the same person as Untash-Huban, the builder of the *ziggurat*. There are also baked bricks with the inscription to the effect that Untash-Gal dedicated the monument to the great god Inshushinak.

It was earlier mentioned that there is a monumental entry and stair at the first stage level of all four faces of the *ziggurat*; but it is also quite clear that the entry on the south-east face of the *ziggurat* is an especially important one, as the walled precinct which lies in front of it contains a number of installations which give some idea of the ritual. The precinct wall is pierced by three gates. One of these, a simple gateway architecturally, is the only one to be paved with stone set in bitumen and this pavement shows the light marks of chariot wheels; and was perhaps the gate through which the sacrificial animals were driven. Near it is a larger gate, the largest of all the entries to the precincts. Four towers, possibly more than 30 ft high flanked the gateway, which would probably have bronze double doors, though these would naturally be melted down when the town was sacked; but the bolt-holding stones, into which the bolt would be shot when the gate was locked, still remain, characteristically inscribed with the name of Untash-Huban.

Inside the gate there is a vast brick-paved forecourt and in front of the entrance to the *ziggurat* and at right angles to its face is a double line of seven low sacrificial tables in the form of truncated pyramids (fourteen in all). Between the two nearest to the *ziggurat* was a pit linked with a pottery drain, presumably to take the blood from the sacrificial animals. A few yards farther off was another pit, linked to a bowl, which was probably for libations. In the line of these tables, but against the inner side of the precinct wall, stand two tribunes, where presumably King Untash-Huban and his Queen Napir Asu, sat during the ceremony. Near by was a great jar for ablutions and three offering tables, convenient for the royal rites before entering the *ziggurat*. Near the actual entrance was another offering table, made of bricks enamelled in green, blue and white; and from this it was but a brief ascent to the tiny temple inside the first stage of the huge massif. It consists of cella and antecella, with two small rooms in front and is presumably the counterpart of the temple which crowned the complete monument. The upper temple however would be the dwelling-place of the god; the lower that in which he made his occasional appearances to his worshippers. The small size of this lower shrine, however, indicate that only a very small number of worshippers were ever allowed to enter therein.

The courtyard of the north-east precinct is the largest courtyard and this has three entrances, each leading by a paved way to a vast ramp. It was here, Dr Ghirshman suggests, that three processions, perhaps of nobles or lesser clergy, gathered to take a somewhat remote part in the ceremonies taking part in the south-east precinct. The north-east precinct also contained a number of sanctuaries dedicated to various deities of the Elamite pantheon, notably Ishniqarab, Nabu, Huban and Inshushinak.

Outside the wall of the north-west precinct was a group of large sanctuaries, dedicated to Ishniqarab, Huban and the goddess Kiririsha; and in the sanctuary of the last, an important group of objects was found. This comprised more than 100 mace-heads in bronze, marble, haematite, and alabaster; daggers, knives and axes of bronze, one of the axes being especially interesting, with the blade emerging from the jaws of a lion and with a crouching boar on the other side of the haft; other small animal figures in bronze and a bronze disk showing two human figures hand in hand; and a number of cylinder seals. This group of objects had obviously been collected together from many sources, presumably by robbers, who perhaps perished before they could carry off their loot.

Although work on the *ziggurat* and its immediate surroundings is now finished in its essentials, it is after all only the central feature of a huge site; and much may yet be found there. Some excavations have been made in the outer parts and these are promising. The site represents about 600 years of Elamite culture; and with the downfall of the Elamites, it ceases to be inhabited. A concise and unusual history for a great city.

An extremely interesting excavation was made in 1948 by Mr T. Burton Brown in Persian Azerbaijan, about $4\frac{1}{2}$ miles south-east of Rezaiyeh. This took the form of a *sondage* at an ancient site known as Geoy Tepe. The main shaft of the *sondage* was about 11 yds square and reached a level about 62 ft below the summit of the mound. This meant that about 18 ft remained unexplored between the bottom and the original ground level, but there was no time to dig farther—and even so, a level parallel with the al Ubaid epoch of Mesopotamia (*c* 3000 B.C.) was reached. Following the al Ubaid period came a people who made polished grey ware, with stamped designs including—what is rare for this part of the world as early as this—spiral patterns. Gaming pieces, knucklebones, are found at this level and little clay figurines of animals. Next followed a people who made black polished pots, usually with a silvery grey rim, which seems to be an effect of the firing; and among their remains were found bronze racquet pins of the type which are found in gold in the Royal Tombs at Ur (of *c* 2500 B.C.). After a disturbed period, marked by several big fires, the city was fortified strongly and polychrome pottery appears. Some tombs of this period were found, the skulls therein being long-headed of the type associated with Indo-Europeans and this is of course the time (*c* 2000 B.C.) of the arrival of the Hyksos people, who probably also included some Indo-European stock.

New civilizations appeared frequently at this site, which seems to have lain in the path of the movements of many peoples. About 1600 B.C. there came a people with black or red or grey polished ware in a variety of distinctive shapes including tall collared cups and teapot-like vessels with long beaked spouts. They were superseded fairly soon by a people the centre of whose period appears to have been about 1200 B.C. and these seem to have been a very interesting people since the designs of their plain red or grey polished ware contain parallels to types found in a great number of places: jugs, alabastra, ring-stands and little cups similar to types found elsewhere in Iran and farther west; vases similar to the *bucchero* ware of Lesbos and elsewhere in the Aegean; vessels with knobbed handles like those found in the South Russia and Cyprus of about 1200 B.C.; and pots with handles in the form of animal heads, of a type also found in Cyprus and Greece.

It is perhaps worth remembering that the classic name of this district is Atropatene, part of which was called Parsua and that it was from this district that the forbears of the Achaemenian family moved southward towards Susa in about 800 B.C.

Also found at this site and probably dating from 1000 B.C. or perhaps a little earlier are three curiously impressive animals of massive character carved from a grey stone. One represents a tiger, crude, massive and battered but with a sort of sinister power. Two others show fat-tailed rams and these are highly stylized, the forelegs and the hind legs being shown as two unseparated masses of stone, the horns and eyes being represented as a single massive spiral in relief. This spiral is the sole adornment of one, but the other besides wearing a collar also carries on the flank a panel of relief inscription, consisting of three circles (one of them double) and a flask-shape, uncommonly like an old-fashioned bed-side carafe. There are three other reliefs—rectangular panels of stone, with simple borders. All three show circles and flask-shapes and two of them show stocky human figures. What these hieroglyphs—for such they seem to be—signify is not known; and indeed they seem to have no parallel elsewhere.

In 1957 an interesting and important series of excavations was undertaken by a joint Persian-American expedition, from the Teheran Archaeological Museum and the University Museum of the University of Pennsylvania under the direction of Mr Robert Harris Dyson, Jnr. The scene of the excavation has been the village of Hassanlou in Persian Azerbaijan, near Lake Rezaiyeh—mnch the same area as Geoy Tepe. At the time of writing nothing had been published about this work; but it was understood that a Mannaean settle-

ment of the eighth century B.C. had been found; and it was known that a
most important gold bucket-shaped vase had been found. It was understood to
have a height of nearly 9 in, a diameter of about 25 in and a weight of $30\frac{1}{2}$ oz
Troy. Although crushed it was otherwise very well preserved and it carries on
the outside two registers of figures in relief, including chariots drawn by oxen
and by mules (or onagers), tribute bearers, a flying two-headed creature, one
head being an eagle, the other human; and other remarkable objects and
creatures.

CHAPTER NINETEEN

IRAQ—I

IRAQ, Mesopotamia, the Garden of Eden, the Biblical land of Shinar, has been at all ages a germinal land for mankind; and so many things have had their beginnings there that it is impossible, even if it were desirable, to list them all. In the northern Fertile Crescent it would seem that agriculture and settled communities first arose; in the southern delta, urban organization (*pace* Miss Kenyon and Jericho) first came into being, with writing, literature and medicine in its train. It was the birthplace of religions which survived intact into the Middle Ages; and the origin of myths which still hold their validity in what may be called the religious poetry of man's nature. It has seen the growth and passing of many great Empires: the Sumerians, the Akkadians, the Babylonians, the Assyrians; the Achaemenians became its masters, until Alexander the Great drove eastwards through it and the refreshing breath of Hellenism swept through it; the Romans and the Parthians fought over it; and in the fulness of time it became the political heart of Islam with the great Caliphate of Baghdad; until recent times it was an essential part of the Ottoman Empire; and with the new nationalism which had its birth under the protection of Great Britain after the 1914–18 War, came the wealth of oil and the opportunity to do all those things which, it seemed, could once again create the Garden of Eden in the plains between the two great rivers, Euphrates and Tigris.

Practically all aspects of this great, prolonged and rich history—especially as it falls in those eras with which what we call archaeology is concerned—have been illustrated by discoveries made since the war: in the hilly north Professor Braidwood and his team from the Oriental Institute of the University of Chicago have been uncovering those first farming villages, of which the type is perhaps Jarmo; in the level south, many excavators have been at work on the cities of Sumer and the like—Sayyid Fuad Safar and Seton Lloyd at Eridu, the Oriental Institute of Chicago under Donald McCown and Richard Haines at Nippur, the Danes under Professor Glob in Bahrein, to mention only the most prominent; in the Mosul area, the high prosperity of the Assyrians has been revealed in a long and rewarding series of excavations at Calah-Nimrud by the British School in Iraq under Professor Mallowan; and farther west and later in time the strange, brief and rich history of Hatra has come to life under the spade of Dr Naji Al Asil, Director-General of the Antiquities of Iraq.

Starting from a pilot exploration in 1948, there has been a series of excavations at a site called Qalat-Jarmo, or simply Jarmo, in the grassy uplands between Kirkuk and Sulimaniyah by the Iraq Project of the Oriental Institute of Chicago University under the field direction of Professor Robert J. Braidwood, and these excavations have been linked with others at three earlier sites, Karim Shahir, Palegawra and Barda Balka, in which the Iraq Directorate-General of Antiquities and the American Schools of Oriental Research have collaborated.

These sites together throw a great deal of light on the origins of Mesopotamian civilization, as between them they cover the full transitional period from cave-dwelling to established village life in what is generally considered as the heart land of the world's civilization; and their dating, which is naturally of the greatest interest and importance, will be discussed below. Barda Balka was marked by Acheulean-type hand-axes, pebble tools and flake tools in Pleistocene gravels. Palegawra is a cave site with industries of the extended Gravettian-like type, including microliths; and Karim Shahir is an open site, probably occupied for a short time only and producing stone blade tools, microliths and some ground stone objects; and Jarmo, the most interesting of all is an established early village assembly, in which pottery appears in the later phases and a microlith industry persists.

Jarmo originally, it seems, covered over three acres on a hill-top overlooking a stream; but the stream has cut into the hill, making a steep escarpment and part of the settlement has disappeared. After the initial digging which revealed the lines of some buildings, the whole site was covered with a grid of metre-square pits—as shown in the dramatic aerial photograph—a technique which is employed to show where more detailed digging would be worth while (Plate 36b).

The village had lasted long enough for about 23 ft of occupational debris to be built up and about fifteen levels were noted, although the site is really a "one period" site. The houses were of several straight-sided rooms with walls of pressed mud and the floors were of mud, often packed on to a layer of reeds. In the later stages the mud walls sometimes had stone foundations. These houses had ovens and some of the earlier houses had baked-in-place floor-basins. Some of these had stones lying in them and it is suggested that they were used for boiling liquids by means of heated stones. Pottery appears during the topmost five levels; and the earliest potsherds are of relatively well-made vessels with painted and burnished exteriors. It is probable that these were not locally made, since the later pottery is much coarser and poorly fired; and it looks, therefore, as if the villagers of Jarmo were beginning to make their own pots but were not particularly good at it.

At all stages of the site little clay figurines of animals and humans (especially steatopygous "mother goddess" figures) are found and none of these has been baked, from which one could argue that they were not intended to last but were made for a single particular purpose, tools of a cult in fact, not works of art. Flint and obsidian tools were found in quantity, many of them being microliths, while the most impressive and significant was a sickle, which had been made by setting four flint units in bitumen in a curved wooden handle. This is not only an example of ingenuity, but it argues the existence of a regularly harvested grain crop.

Softer stones were used in a variety of ways. To produce celts, querns, mortars and pestles; spindle-whorls, beads, ear and nose plugs, paint-grinding palettes and the like. The most advanced products of this industry, however, were door-socket elements; and bracelets of marble, of which there are so many fragments as to suggest that these were usual objects of adornment.

Bone was likewise much used; and hafts, awls, spoons, needles and beads of bone are all found.

Early in the course of the excavations some interesting light was thrown on the agriculture of Jarmo. Two varieties of wheat were discovered and also a legume. The animal bones included sheep, goat, pig, cattle, dog and an equid, together with a small quantity of wild types. The highest proportion was of sheep-goat bones and an examination revealed that nearly all of these were yearlings—which suggests husbandry rather than hunting.

The dating of this great period of human development, from food gathering to incipient cultivation to settled farming communities like Jarmo—a period which must have seen the first general domestication of animals and the first evolution of what Mr Edward Hyams has called the most enduring of man's artefacts, the food-plants—is naturally of great interest. There are now many Carbon-14 dates and many complications arising from them. In the early days —the honeymoon period of the technique—these dates were regarded as sacrosanct; they have latterly been distrusted and perhaps undervalued. It is realized that not all carbon samples give reliable reactions; that the possibilities of contamination in samples are greater than was at first thought; and that there are "geobiochemical" complications which are not fully understood. This handy portmanteau word "geobiochemical" covers a wide variety of possibilities from earth movements to chemical penetrations and the activities of bacteria and earthworms and the deep delvings of such beasts as the Mesopotamian mole-rat. (Incidentally, it should be remembered that Carbon-14 dates are given as, for example, 6570 ±175, B.P. which means that the central date is 6,570 years "before present", i.e. the date of testing with a margin of error of 175 years on either side. This B.P. convention is unfortunate, as it tends to confusion with B.C. and is moreover not a constant; logically all such published dates ought to be adjusted annually.)

However all these factors have been argued and adjusted by the experts; and it is now reasonably asserted that the period of "food gathering"—to which the Palegawra site belongs—was roughly between 10,000 B.C. to 8700 B.C. in this part of the world; the open sites of incipient cultivation, like Karim Shahir are between 9000 and 8000 B.C.; and that the central date for Jarmo is about 7000 B.C.

Linking these in time with Eridu and the urban civilization of Sumer are the village site of Hassuna, for which a Carbon-14 date of about 5000 B.C. is given; and the "Ubaid" town of Warka, with a Carbon-14 date of about 4000 B.C.

A bridge, although a tenuous one, from the cave dwellers to the first makers of recorded history.

Traditionally the oldest of the cities of Mesopotamia is Eridu. The Babylonian Legend of Creation says: "All the lands were sea: then Eridu was made"; and Eridu was the city of the god Enki, the god of the abyss and the source of human wisdom. The site of Eridu was identified over 100 years ago by J. E. Taylor (then British Vice-Consul at Basrah) in Tell Abu Shahrain, an isolated mound standing in uncultivatable desert, 14 miles south of Ur. For various reasons it baffled his attempts (and those of later excavators) and late in 1946 the Iraq Directorate of Antiquities planned a large-scale attempt under the direction of Sayyid Fuad Safar.

Now it is generally believed that Mesopotamian civilization began as the result of three waves of migrants; and that it was the second wave (that associated with Uruk) which introduced writing, monumental architecture and sculpture. The first wave was associated with the people whose type settlement was Al Ubaid, a reed-hut village found by Sir Leonard Woolley, about 20 miles from Eridu. Traces of a considerable settlement of al Ubaid period were found in the immediate neighbourhood of the Eridu mound; and it was thought that possibly a temple for the god of this settlement might be found in the mound. In fact seven such temples were found.

The majority of the mound consists of the ruins of a colossal *ziggurat* built by the Kings of Ur at the end of the Third Millennium B.C. and as a foundation to this the seven temples of Enki had been levelled. At the southern corner of the *ziggurat* the Iraqi excavators found the remains of a temple, dated undisputably by its painted pottery to the al Ubaid period of the settlement, to the early part that is of the Fourth Millennium B.C. It stood on a raised platform round a central sanctuary and it was built of mud-brick and it manifested many of the attributes of later Sumerian religious buildings—and it appeared to overlie an even earlier temple. This earlier temple, called later Temple VII was accordingly excavated. It was a surprisingly elaborate affair, oriented south-west–north-east, a courtyard surrounded by a number of small rooms and approached on the long south-east side by a flight of at least ten long steps—probably the earliest formal staircase in the history of architecture. At the south-west end was an altar of about 4×11 ft; and at the other end, but standing away from the wall, an offering table somewhat larger. Covering the offering table and the floor was a layer of fish bones, nearly 6 in deep—presumably the remains of offerings to Enki, the god of the deep. This would certainly seem to establish the al Ubaid migrants as the originators of monumental architecture. The temple as a whole measured about 60×48 ft.

Five other temples had been built on this site, of increasing elaboration, the last one before the raising of the *ziggurat* being of limestone set in gypsum mortar, and there are traces of mosaic decoration and ornaments of polished copper.

Beside the mound, covered by about 6 ft of sand, a massive black basalt lion statue was found. It probably belonged to the Third Dynasty of Ur and it is about 5½ ft high and weighs rather more than 1 ton. This was seen by Taylor in 1855 on the surface and it had presumably been buried again by sandstorms. It is now in the Iraq Museum at Baghdad.

With the full urban development of Mesopotamia in the Third Millennium B.C. the chief holy city is Nippur, now a 180-acre complex of deserted sandy mounds about 100 miles south of Baghdad and formerly the site of a succession of temples from about the twenty-fourth century B.C. to the second century A.D. It was the seat of Enlil, the chief deity of the Sumerian pantheon, considered as the creator and source of all existence until about the beginning of the First Millennium when he was superseded in this role by Marduk, the Babylonian god. Associated with Enlil was Inanna, the goddess of love and war. Inanna's city lay farther south, at Urk, but there are several key references to her in mythological tablets found at Nippur. One text records that Enlil had given her the title "Queen of Nippur"; and one of the myths tells how when Enlil lay sick unto death Inanna came to Ekur (the name of the inner court with *ziggurat* at Nippur) and succeeded in reviving him. And another tablet describes the marriage of Inanna to Ama-ushumgalanna (which is another name for Tammuz, the popular god of natural fertility) and her coming to him at Ekur for the ceremony.

Now Nippur was excavated in the last decade of the last century by an expedition of the University Museum of Pennsylvania and it was as a result of this that it became famous not only as a holy, great and ancient city but also as the source of about 80 per cent of the known literary and mythological texts in Sumerian cuneiform and so the fountainhead of the world's oldest literature. But since then the site had remained untouched, until 1948, when there began a series of excavations mounted by the Oriental Institute of Chicago, directed at first by Donald E. McCown and later by Richard C. Haines.

The first point of attack was a mound which had been identified by the original Pennsylvania expedition as a scribal quarter and the principal source of the literary tablets; and two of the earlier digs were taken much farther. The Upper Dig which fifty years previously had revealed seven cities from the Achaemenian to the Kassite period (fifth to thirteenth centuries B.C.) was taken deeper and five earlier cities revealed back to the Isin-Larsa period (nineteenth century B.C.). In the Lower Dig, six cities were known from the First Dynasty of Babylon (eighteenth century) to the end of the Third Dynasty of Ur (twentieth century; and this was now extended back through the Third Dynasty of Ur to the Agade period (twenty-fourth century B.C.). And in this way no fewer than twenty superimposed cities covering a period of 2,300 years were revealed like a layer-cake of history.

During these excavations many valuable finds of seals, pottery and business documents were made; a group of magic or religious baked clay plaques, showing demons, gods and rulers was found; and, principally in one particular room, some 300 complete tablets or large sections of tablets with quantities of smaller tablets, were discovered, of which over 200 were literary tablets. This last discovery, which took place within a fortnight, added about 10 per cent to the known total of Sumerian literary texts at a single stroke, as it were.

At about the same time that this great haul of tablets was made, the site of the Temple of Inanna was identified with the discovery of a door-socket with an inscription recording the rebuilding of the Temple of Inanna by Shulgi, second king of the Third Dynasty of Ur. This site, which was to prove of the greatest interest in later seasons, lies a little over 50 yds south-west of the *ziggurat* which stands with the Temple of Enlil in the courtyard called Ekur. Another temple was discovered at the north of the site and this dated from Early Dynastic Period (first half of the Third Millennium B.C.).

Among the interesting objects found in the Inanna Temple were two miniature chair-backs of baked clay with figures in relief, one showing two shaggy-haired guardians on either side of a door, the other a male and female goddess formally embracing. The latter may represent the marriage of Inanna and Tammuz; and it also carries the following symbols—a bird, a fish and an amphora-shaped pot standing on the back of a bird with two heads, the second head being where one would expect to find the tail. In addition, some seated figurines were found; and this combination suggests a probably accidental parallel for the little bronze seated deities of the twelfth–eleventh centuries B.C. which Professor Schaeffer found at Enkomi in Cyprus.

In the north Early Dynastic temple a cache of statuettes was found. The two outstanding ones were both of gypsum. One which stands about $2\frac{1}{2}$ ft high is well preserved and shows a bearded male figure, wearing a straight skirt and with the hands clasped on the breast. The eye-sockets are filled with bitumen, but the eyes, presumably of shell and lapis, are missing. In the double-arched recess of the eyebrows there are traces of green steatite mosaic. The other, which is smaller, headless, and less well-preserved, is wearing the characteristic Sumerian tiered skirt. On the back of the larger statue is a three-columned inscription, which is however badly preserved but seems to record gifts to the temple.

In the later seasons work has been mainly concentrated on the Temple of Inanna. As already stated there are several superimposed temples on this site, and the one which first attracted attention, through the discovery of a door socket, was that built about 2000 B.C. by Shulgi, the second king of the Third Dynasty of Ur. This temple, built with massive walls of mud-brick, appears to have been a planned complex of rooms and courts with a ground area of about 190×330 ft—somewhat larger than a large football field. Some more inscribed door sockets were found and no fewer than seven untouched foundation deposits. These were in neat brick pits with inside measurements of $6\frac{1}{2} \times 12\frac{1}{2} \times 17\frac{1}{2}$ in deep. Inside each box was set a stone model of a brick and a bronze figure between 10 and 12 in high showing a beardless male figure with both arms lifted to steady a basket or bowl carried on the head. These figures are naturalistically modelled above the waist, but below the waist taper in a sort of blunt shaft. The conditions for preservation in the boxes were excellent and traces of the fabric with which these figures were wrapped still survive. After the offerings had been placed in the box the aperture was covered with a reed mat, which was liberally spread with bitumen and capped with three inscribed bricks, the third brick being set on top of the other two.

Somewhat similar foundation boxes were found under the gateway to Ekur, the courtyard containing the *ziggurat* and the Enlil Temple. Here the capping bricks were inscribed with the name of Urnammu, the first king of the Third Dynasty of Ur. The bronze figures in these cases were the same as the later Shulgi figures, but were complete below the waist, with feet standing on an oval pedestal. On the skirt was an inscription similar to those on the capping bricks. Buried with each figure, was a stone model brick, with the same inscription, a number of beads and many stone chips of various colours; and, with one of them, a group of date stones.

While the Third Dynasty Inanna Temple (*c* 2000 B.C.) was being excavated, three others were found below it, of which the best was the earliest, that of the Early Dynastic Period (*c* 2800 B.C.)—although there are very probably still earlier temples lying below this.

The extent, the plan and the relative areas of this Early Dynastic temple are so curious and so interesting for the light which they throw on early formal religion that they perhaps deserve a detailed description. The whole complex is roughly kite-shaped with the entrance at the narrow north-west end and the sanctuary lying in the heart of the widest end which is at the south-east. Its total length is about 275 ft, its greatest width 80 ft. The route from the entrance to the sanctuary, which is roughly axial, is as follows.

From the single entrance, the worshipper enters a vestibule, from which he has a choice of two doors, side by side, leading into a large simple courtyard, whose walls are regularly recessed in a sort of rectangular pilaster formation. At the far end he ascends a monumental stair leading to a small vestibule, from which a single doorway takes him into another courtyard, about half the size of the first, but with two rooms leading off it. The worshipper however goes straightforward to a small recessed doorway at the far end which takes him into a maze of small rooms, whose purpose is obscure. Persevering he goes straight forward and emerges in a large portico with two massive circular pillars. These by the way were made of segment-shaped bricks as the core, and a plaster exterior. Beyond this portico lay the third courtyard, nearly as large as the first. Standing in this courtyard, he would see immediately on his right a small entrance leading to a large room, from which two different series of rooms developed. Ahead of him, on the far side of the court lay another two-pillared portico; and if he ignored two rooms which lay to the left and passed through the portico he would find himself—confronted by a blank wall and standing in a narrow corridor. This corridor runs round all four sides of a centrally placed building, in the south-west wall of which he would find the only entrance, a doorway 18 in wide. This led into the antecella, a room about 11 ft square, with brick benches against three walls and a circular offering table just off centre. In the fourth wall, that facing the narrow entrance, was an opening, 4 ft 9 in wide, leading to the holy of holies, another room about 11 ft square with a very large brick-built altar, standing opposite the doorway and taking up a large proportion of the total area.

Beyond this sanctuary and likewise entered from the narrow corridor was another sanctuary, secondary and rather larger. In this the entrance was in the long side and the worshipper entering would turn left to face the altar. This was a larger undivided room, likewise supplied with a circular offering table, but the benches for the worshippers were grouped near the altar.

Also opening off the narrow corridor is a door leading to another series of rooms, which we may regard as vestries, priests' rooms and the like; and at the farther end of the building, built outside its perimeter but entered from it is a brick-built bitumen-lined tank, and beside this a large oval oven which could only be approached from outside the temple walls.

This complex of buildings had obviously been very well kept and the mud-plastered floors had been re-coated many times; and hardly any objects were found in any of the rooms. Of those that were may be mentioned: a stone statue base showing only two feet, standing side by side (in the second Sanctuary); an alabaster bowl with an inscription recording that it was presented to Inanna by the wife of one of the temple officials (from the main sanctuary); and two objects from the second sanctuary—a stone stamp seal in the form of a crouching calf of about 3200 B.C., and an alabaster statuette of two ox-like creatures, seated side by side but facing different ways, one of which has lost its head, but the other has a female human head, with curls on either side of the face and a curiously beaming drowsy expression.

The uppermost levels of this site had been thought to be Seleucian, but a series of coins after cleaning were discovered to be Parthian and dating from the second century B.C. to the second century A.D. During this period the temple was rebuilt several times and although there is nothing to show to whom it was dedicated, it seems likely that the worship of Inanna continued, the name changing but the nature of the goddess persisting.

Other news from Nippur has recently come—but from the study, not the field. Professor Samuel N. Kramer of the University of Pennsylvania has been deciphering some of the mass of tablets which were found at Nippur in the Pennsylvania University excavations of the 'nineties. These include a number of "firsts", among them the first street-plan and the oldest medical text. The latter is a double-sided three-columned tablet, about $3\frac{3}{4} \times 6\frac{1}{4}$ in and it lists more than a dozen prescriptions. The prescriptions are for salves, lotions and internal doses; and the *materia medica* sound no more outlandish than most prescriptions. They include salt and saltpetre; milk, snake-skin and turtle-shell; and a wide range of herbs including cassia, assafoetida, myrtle, alkali (*Salicornia fruticosa*), thyme and a number of trees—presumably powders made from the root, bark, seeds, leaves or gum. Fluids used were milk, "kushumma" wine, tree oil and river oil, and beer. Various draughts seem to have been taken in beer; and several prescriptions after listing the ingredients end with the phrases, "pulverize, dissolve in beer, let the man drink". This last phrase—a useful one at parties—is *lu al-nag-nag*. Unfortunately the text gives no quantities and does not indicate what diseases the medicines are intended to cure. There would seem to be here a field of research open to volunteers.

About 300 miles south of the present mouth of the delta and close to the Arabian coast lies the desert island of Bahrein, which the discovery of oil has made into one of the fantastically oil-rich states of the Persian Gulf. For many years it has appeared as a sort of archaeologist's nightmare as its surface is diversified with something like 100,000 burial mounds. A few of these had been examined, but no settlement had been discovered; and it had been assumed that the island was simply a burial ground for peoples living on the mainland of Arabia, probably during the Second Millennium B.C. In 1953 however a Danish Archaeological Mission, directed by Professor P. V. Glob of Aarhus University (and accompanied by Messrs Geoffrey Bibby and Kristian Jeppesen) began a systematic examination of the island and in the first season alone discovered twelve palaeolithic and neolithic sites, two temples of Third Millennium date near the villages of Diraz and Barbar and a city mound covering some 250,000 sq yds—presumably the island's prehistoric capital—near Qala'at al-Bahrein.

Annual work has since gone forward and probably the most interesting discoveries have been made at Barbar and the city mound.

The temples of Barbar—for there are three of them, one on top of the other—were discovered in a mound of 4,000 yds square by about 16 ft high. All the three temples had been demolished to foundation level and the mound above them was not a natural growth of centuries of drifting sand but a deliberately piled heap of gravel, with gypsum layers at several points. All three temples were built of worked and squared stone, the lowest of an extremely hard grey stone quarried on Bahrein, the two later ones of a fine-grained white limestone, which had been quarried on the small island of Jida, which lies about 6 miles from Barbar. In early Islamic times there had been considerable robbery of stone from the mound, but much remained and it was possible to work out the plan of all three temples. All consisted of outer courtyard, temple and inner building, each rising in height above the other, so that the total effect must have been like a small Mesopotamian *ziggurat* of three steps. The same architectural idea was found repeated in some of the tombs in burial mounds which were excavated.

Although, as stated above, all three had been demolished to foundation level, in the last temple the altar complex had been allowed to remain untouched before the gravel was heaped above it and even the stone-robbers seem to have respected it to some degree; and its principal features remain virtually intact. In the centre of the inner shrine are two adjacent circles of fine masonry and it would appear that these were sheathed with copper. Between them and the eastern wall were two tall altar stones, each with a depression in the top; and in front of them a small square stone altar. Near by was a copper-lined gutter and in front of the gutter a small but deep pit in which were a number of votives, alabaster jars, ornaments of lapis lazuli, fragments of drinking goblets and two figurines, one a naked male figure in copper, the other a bird. These objects together recall a scene which appears on Mesopotamian cylinder seals of the same period—offerings being laid on an altar before a deity seated on a high throne, the suggestion being that the two tall altar stones were the supports of such a ceremonial throne.

In the second temple were several large blocks of stone, each with a pair of large square sockets in it; and it may well be that these originally supported wooden cult statues. In this same temple a large quantity of copper sheathing was found together with a really magnificent bull's head in copper which is very like similar heads found in the Royal Tombs of Ur. In the earliest temple of all a number of pottery drinking vessels were found, cone-shaped but spreading into a small moulded foot, some fragments of copper and a narrow gold ribbon; and all these things had been deposited during the building of the temple. Many of the objects and the lay-out show a close relation with Pre-dynastic and Early Dynastic Sumer.

In the city mound at Qala'at al-Bahrein a huge building with walls still standing to a height of 15 ft and made of squared limestone blocks of about 3 ft long by 12–18 in high was found; and even by 1957 this building had not been cleared and the plan could not yet be understood. It was however quite clear that it had been built in the Third Millennium B.C. In the First Millennium it was used as a temple or mortuary chapel; and in about 900 B.C. the upper parts of the walls, still projecting from the soil, had been incorporated in Islamic buildings. During the time that it was used as a mortuary chapel—which was round about 700 B.C.—children were buried there in large bowls and adults in pottery sarcophagi, either oval or bath-tub shaped. Only one sarcophagus had escaped robbery and this contained notably a bronze ewer with a bucket-handle, a bronze strainer and a bronze dipper or ladle. Beside another sarcophagus stood an altar in the form of a cube of the same imported limestone as that used in the later Barbar temples and to the west of this altar were buried, in a semicircle, a number of votive deposits. These were mostly covered bowls; and in four of these were the still neatly coiled skeletons of snakes. Also among the offerings was a necklace of precious and semi-precious stones; and Mr Bibby suggests that since the deity was presumably female these unique snake offerings hint at a link with the snake-goddess of Minoan Crete and Bronze Age Europe.

Nearly 100 yds from the sea the wall of the prehistoric city was found, a wall which though robbed of its shaped stone facing nevertheless still survived to a height in some places of 15 ft with a rubble core about 12 ft wide. On the outer side of the wall were remains of the "Parthian" and Greek periods; on the inside layer upon layer of the same Third Millennium pottery as was being found at the Barbar temples; and it was this area which provided what is probably the most significant find in Bahrein: three small round seals.

These are stamp seals made of steatite, or soapstone; and from above they look like buttons, embossed with one or two straight lines crossing the boss, while on the "working" side they are covered with crowded all-over designs identical with those found on the normal type of Indus Valley seal. This type of seal was already known both in Mesopotamia and in the Indus Valley, but is extremely rare in both places and anomalous in both places also. In Sumer cylinder seals predominate; in the Indus Valley nearly all seals are square; and in both places seals are found in large quantities. Of these round stamp seals, however, only twenty-four examples were known at the time of the discovery of these last three: seventeen from Mesopotamia (thirteen of them from Ur), three from Mohenjo-Daro; and now four from Bahrein (for a fourth was found on the surface there a few years ago). The suggestion is therefore that this is a Bahrein type; and that its presence in the three places indicates a state of sea trade between Sumer and the Indus Valley with Bahrein as the *entrepot*. It was already known from Mesopotamian records that the Sumerian cities were trading down the Gulf with three named places, Dilmun, Magan and Meluhha; and it now seems fairly certain that Bahrein can be identified with Dilmun. Magan was perhaps in the Muscat area, possibly somewhere near Sohar; and Meluhha, it is suggested, may well be the ancient name for the Indus Valley civilization.

CHAPTER TWENTY

IRAQ—II

Of all post-war excavations in Iraq, those mounted at Nimrud by the British School of Archaeology in Iraq and directed by Professor M. E. L. Mallowan have been the most protracted, probably the most interesting and certainly the most rewarding in the nature, quantity and quality of the works of art discovered.

Nimrud is an enormous Assyrian site lying on the east bank of the Tigris about 20 miles south of Mosul. Its ancient name was Calah (or Kalhu) and with Nineveh and Assur it was one of the three capitals of the Assyrian Empire, especially during the ninth, eighth and seventh centuries B.C. It was especially the military capital and here the Assyrian armies were garrisoned, trained and equipped for their annual summer campaigns of conquest. It was founded by Shalmaneser I in the thirteenth century, but it reached its greatest glory after it had been rebuilt from the ruins by Assurnasirpal II in 883 B.C. At the height of its splendour it consisted of an acropolis, comprising royal palaces, governors' buildings, administrative offices and temples, an enormous *ziggurat*, about a square mile of city and within the circuit of the walls, parks and zoological gardens. It has been estimated that some 10 million bricks were used in building it. The total area of the outer city was probably more than two square miles; and its greatest population was probably about 70,000. Many of these would be foreigners—artists, craftsmen and captives held as labouring slaves. This mixed population may well have been the source of the revolution which did so much damage in 705 B.C. and of a number of other outbreaks and disasters. Nimrud now stands at some distance from the Tigris, but in the ninth century B.C. its walls were washed by the river and indeed this riverine wall consisted of a massive quay at least half a mile long and made of huge blocks of limestone, waterproofed with bitumen joints—a tremendous feat of public works engineering.

The importance of the site was first realized by the great Sir Henry Layard who excavated there during the years 1845–51 and discovered quantities of ivories and impressive monumental sculpture—the cream of which is now in the British Museum; and he was followed later in the last century by Loftus and Rassam.

Nevertheless Professor Mallowan judged that the site merited another full-scale excavation: in the first place, because it is such an enormous site; and in the second, because the aims and the techniques of archaeology have changed so much in the last hundred years. The Victorian excavators were primarily concerned with furnishing museums and carrying off material for the scholars to work on; and they had not mastered the technique of excavating mud-brick walls. As a result, like Kipling's Chuchundra, the musk-rat, they hugged close to stone-faced walls, both because it was the straightforward method and because it paid dividends in revealing statuary, reliefs and inscriptions. Modern excavators can cope with much more delicate remains and are in any case more concerned in discovering from the evidence *in situ* the historic sequence of events and cultures.

Professor Mallowan's first (and exploratory) season was in 1949 and in that year and 1950, work was concentrated on the administrative buildings in the eastern sector and the southern wing of the North-West Palace. During these seasons some enormous sculpture and reliefs which Layard had seen but covered over were uncovered once more and photographed for the first time. Among these was a huge gypsum bull-man and a portal sculpture, part winged lion, part human. This latter was designed to be seen from in front and from one side and by an extremely bold (and successful) convention, so that it should appear to have four feet when seen from the side and two when seen from the front, was actually equipped with five legs. In the administrative building quantities of cuneiform tablets were found—which was very satisfactory as previously no tablets had been found in Nimrud and it had been assumed that the archives had either been removed elsewhere in antiquity or had been entirely destroyed.

The North-West Palace had been the scene of some of Layard's most rewarding work, but the southern wing, which had housed officials and soldiers, being of mud-brick was untouched. Here an interesting grave was found, that of a noblewoman of the time of Sargon (722–705 B.C.), which had been covered with three stone slabs inscribed with the history of the campaigns of Assurnasirpal of 150 years previous—as if a duchess of today were to be buried with an account of the Napoleonic wars.

Among all the discoveries of the archaeologists some seem to speak with an especial direct and personal message; some perhaps with a beauty which puts one immediately *en rapport* with the creator of thousands of years ago; some with a flash of humour or affection; some with a lightning-flash of intellectual revelation—even so, such and such a Greek was moved, even so an Egyptian laughed, even so a Sumerian scribe thought. But a small pink limestone tablet, about $3\frac{1}{2}$ in square, found at Nimrud in these opening seasons, carries with it a direct impact of evil. It is a magical incantation against sickness, a little larger than a twenty-packet of cigarettes, surmounted at the top by a savagely grinning skull-like head of a male demon, *Pazuzu*—with a curiously Central American look. On one side of the tablet, this demon is continued as a carving in relief, with a human trunk but the legs and spread wings of a bird of prey and the curling tail of a scorpion. The other large side of the tablet is covered with crowded reliefs—again Central American in general effect—and the central figure is a *lamashtu*, a female demon with a lion's head which is pierced by a weapon. This *lamashtu* has a writhing snake in either hand, a pig is seizing one of her breasts and a dog the other, and she is kneeling on the back of a donkey which is carrying her towards a boat. Beside her the sick man is lying on a couch and two grinning bearded men stand by. Here and there wherever convenient in the crowded composition are such objects as might propitiate the demon, bundles of linen, a brooch and the like; and in an upper register, across the top of this face, a line of priests, reciting the incantations which are engraved on the narrow sides of the tablet.

An interesting small object found was a bowl of grey and white marble in the form of a hand, with the fingers clearly shown in relief and above the finger-tips a frieze (unfortunately broken) of animals. It makes an interesting parallel with a stone incense scoop, also in the form of a hand, which was recently found in the Israelite citadel of Hazor and which is dated to the eighth century B.C.

The first two seasons also yielded a few ivories, the first of that astonishing harvest which was to make the later seasons at Nimrud so outstanding. Among them was a large relief of a bull, a beautiful example of a cow turning to lick her calf, a panel showing Astarte plucking a branch, an Astarte head badly broken but with a great deal of the gold sheet which had originally covered it; and two small plaques with the designs roughed out but not completed, so showing that there were artists in ivory working in Nimrud—and among all these was a tablet which could be firmly dated to 715 B.C.

The third season was in the spring of 1951 and about 200 workmen were engaged in the task of exploring the North-West Palace, especially those parts of it which Layard had left untouched. Near the north entrance to the palace was found the season's most important single item. This was an erect and still perfectly preserved sandstone *stele*, about $4\frac{1}{2}$ ft high and just over 3 ft wide. In the upper part of the front face—that which would immediately meet the gaze of all those entering the palace—is a panel, which repeats the proportions of the whole *stele* and shows in relief Assurnasirpal II himself, standing with the right foot advanced, robed and crowned with a mitre and armed with two daggers. In his right hand is a long staff, in his left a mace. Round about his head are the symbols of the Assyrian gods, Sin, Assur, Ishtar, Enlil, Adad and the seven stars. On the remainder of the *stele* is an inscription of 154 lines. This inscription is a record of the glories of the first five years of Assurnasirpal's reign and can therefore be dated to 879 B.C. It tells of the building of the palace, names the principal gods, records the countries which the king has conquered, the buildings he has built and the canals he has dug. The list of the temples is recited, together with the gold, bronze and various stones which adorn them; and an account given of the king's lion and elephant hunts and also of his tree planting—some of these trees being imports from abroad. A list of animals and plants to be found within the city's boundaries is also given. And in conclusion the monument records that Assurnasirpal celebrated the completion of the palace with a great feast—with food, wine and baths for no fewer than 69,574 persons—and that this festival lasted ten days and was attended by a number of foreign notables, who are all enumerated. In fact, a sort of Festival of Assyria, 879 B.C.

At the foot of the *stele* was found another portrait of Assurnasirpal—in ivory this time: a narrow plaque about $10\frac{1}{2}$ in high showing the king robed and raising a wine-cup in his right hand and holding in his left a curious sickle of which the handle ends in a bird's head. Near by another group of ivories was found, plaques showing processions of animals and also a line of captives under escort and with their hands tied behind their backs.

In the great audience hall—which is nearly 150 yds long and over 30 yds wide—where the enormous foundation table (which gives an account of the king's campaigns during the first five years of his reign) stands, the remains of wall frescoes, showing chariot scenes in polychrome were found and a number of fragmentary ivories were found. In the most interesting of these, a naked bearded man is shown felling a tree with an axe and it is suggested that he is perhaps an Assyrian equivalent of Hercules.

In a nearby room a number of pottery storage jars was found and one of these had its capacity given as two *imeru* or homers, the homer being the standard load for a donkey. It is of course extremely useful to know exactly what is meant by even one ancient standard measurement, as others can then often be arrived at by analogy; and what have hitherto been merely interesting lists can be transformed into statistics which throw light on a whole economy.

In another chamber was found a well-preserved well, made of burnt bricks inscribed with the king's name and 255 courses deep. This was excavated to a depth of nearly 60 ft and at this stage there was over 12 ft of water in it. In the sludge at the bottom were found oak beams, an ivory figure of a stag and an ivory comb; and these were so well preserved that it seemed as if the sludge had some preservative effect. Accordingly it was decided that during the next season this well should be pumped out and the sludge fully investigated. It seemed a promising line of research—but no one could have foreseen what incredible riches were to come of it.

During this season another area was opened up which was later to pay rich dividends. This lay in the south-east corner and it was one which had been excavated by Loftus in the last century and had yielded many ivories. It was now however encumbered with the spoil heaps left behind by Loftus and these would have presented a tiresome problem but for the Iraq Petroleum Company who lent a bulldozer to cope with them. The area contains a Nabu temple and a palace which had been so thoroughly devastated by fire—perhaps in the revolution at the end of Sargon's reign—that it has become generally known as the "Burnt Palace". In it were found a very great number of burnt and damaged ivories, some totally burnt, but others preserved by the heat, although changed in colour, some being grey, some almost black and others a dark brown. Among them were a great number of female heads and figures, miniature sculptures as it were, usually naked and with elaborate hair-styles and head-dresses. Most of them have noses far too massive to delight a European taste, but it is quite clear that they represent ideals of sensuous beauty to the ancient Assyrians and that they were made to please a king's fancy, rather than to tell a story or to impress subjects or vassals. Egyptian motifs are not uncommon, but some of the ivories have Phoenician characters on the back; and it is fairly safe to assume that they are the work of Phoenician craftsmen, who were serving as the transmitters of a number of ideas, including especially Egyptian ideas. One of the most interesting pieces found at this time was part of the ornament of a circular cosmetic box (or *pyxis*), showing a frieze in ivory of musicians in procession—a male lyre-player followed by two girls, one playing the cymbals the other a pipe.

In 1952, therefore, the first task was the pumping out of the well and this was found to be even deeper than had been thought, being 83½ ft deep and with 330 courses of brickwork. At the bottom was a belt of fine sludge, which had evidently been refined and cleaned by the steady rise and fall of water through the centuries. This sludge had had an extraordinary preservative effect—in fact one of the first objects extracted from it was a broken length of old rope, which was at first assumed to be modern, but later turned out to be Assyrian. A number of pieces of the wooden gear of the well were also found, in good condition; likewise a great assortment of small objects; and a number of ivories, all of them interesting, many of them beautiful, but three of such outstanding beauty that they must rank among the masterpieces of ivory carving of all time—a piece which has become known as "The Lady of the Well" and a pair of pieces showing a lioness killing a Nubian in a field of lotus blossom, all of which had been units of some piece or pieces of furniture of incredible splendour, thrones perhaps, adorned with polychrome ivories encrusted with gold and precious stones.

"The Lady of the Well" is a maiden's head, 6½ in high, carved from near the base of an exceptionally big elephant's tusk. It shows a face of great beauty, modelled with great sensitivity, smiling, with wide-set almond eyes and wearing a flat crown which had originally been decorated with ivory studs. The hair is parted in the centre and had been stained black, as were the pupils of the eyes; the lips have a faint tinge of red; the eyebrows are strongly marked. The stand which is studded like the crown, the crown itself and the fillets which run between the hair and the crown are a somewhat darker brown than the warm brown of the features as a whole. In the cheeks, the carver has most ingeniously used the circular graining of the ivory to give a very delicate modelling—and this is a trick of technique which appears in the two other outstanding pieces.

These are identical and almost equally well preserved, one being now in Baghdad, the other in London; and they have already become world-famous. To describe one is to describe both. Visualize therefore a single piece of warm brown ivory, about 4 in wide at the base, a little more than 4 in high, and narrowing to a rounded top about 2¾ in wide. At the base a repeated diamond pattern has been cut into the ivory and filled with lapis lazuli. On this is based the subject, a completely naturalistic portrayal of a lioness tearing the throat

of a Nubian. The Nubian is lying on the ground, but pressing up from it with
his arms behind him. His head is thrown back—it has been suggested, in the
ecstasy of sacrifice—and the lioness is standing over him, her left fore-paw thrown
round his neck and she is biting his throat. The Nubian is naked except for
a kilt-like garment of gold sheet; and his curly hair is simulated with tiny gilded
pegs. In the centre of the brow of the lioness is an inserted circle of lapis—the
"wart of strength" presumably. In both figures the grain of the ivory has been
most ingeniously used to bring out the roundness of the limbs—just as in the
cheeks of "The Lady of the Well". As a background to this scene is a field of
lotus blossoms and buds, one row bending this way, the one above the other
way, and so on, and so they seem to sway in the breeze. Flowers and buds
alternate; and each bud is an encrusted hemisphere of carnelian, while each
flower consists of three inlaid panels of lapis; and the stalks and calyces of both
flowers and buds are overlaid with gold. Not all this enrichment survives, but
there is enough to complete the picture in the imagination if not in the eye, and
where the lapis is missing there still remains a trace of blue from the blue frit
which was an ingredient of the original adhesive. The more one considers it, the
more astonishing it appears: a scene of savage violence, conceived however with
a sort of dreaming hieratic calm, set in an idyllic scene and carried out with
consummate artistry and complete sophistication. The artist has no fear, no
horror, no sense of religion, no feelings of humane sympathy; lotuses are beautiful, he seems to say, so are lionesses, so are Nubians—all is for the best in the
best of all possible worlds.

These ivory masterworks tend to overshadow the other ivories found during
this season which would otherwise have been considered outstanding. Both from
the well and "Burnt Palace" came a number of heads, mostly female and representing the various types of beauty to be observed at the Assyrian court. The
court of a conqueror is usually cosmopolitan and these little female heads
are fortunately not always in the Assyrian style but represent a variety of
beauties, some of which are pleasing to the modern eye. Some of the ivories are
in the form of "swimming maidens"—naked girls floating on their backs and
pushing a bowl, the whole object probably being used as a cosmetic spoon.

In the North-West Palace of Assurnasirpal II part of the wall near the second
main gate was dug to reveal again the reliefs which Layard had exposed a
hundred years before and these were discovered to be very fine and for the most
part represent a procession of captives, escorted by Assyrian officers and bringing gifts and doing homage. Among the figures is the King's Vizier, who is
followed by a youthful attendant with a staff tucked under his arm rather in
the manner of an officer's "swagger stick". Many of the eyes in these reliefs are
still encrusted with white and black, which gives the captives in particular a
striking air of apprehension—probably justified.

Another excavation was made beside the *ziggurat* and here was found a complex of administrative units, containing large numbers of accurately dated
commercial documents. In one chamber was found a raised brick bench which
must have been used by the scribes, and built against it a number of low brick

compartments, a foot or two square which must have been used for filing the inscribed tablets which were the documents and records of the period. The most interesting document though was one which was presumably brought to Nimrud as a trophy. This was a fine clay barrel cylinder bearing a long inscription of King Merodach-Baladan of Babylon, and designed as a foundation inscription for the Temple of Ishtar in Erech in Babylonia; and it was probably brought to Nimrud as a trophy of war after the campaign of 710 B.C. The inscription refers to an earlier war with the Assyrian king Sargon and claims a complete victory (c 720 B.C.) for the Babylonians and the end of Subaraean domination over Babylonia. Merodach-Baladan (otherwise known as Marduk-apaliddina II) is mentioned in the Bible. While gathering allies for a later revolt against the Assyrians he made overtures to a number of neighbouring kings, including Hezekiah; and Hezekiah earned the rebukes of Isaiah for toying with the idea of such an alliance.

Oddly enough when excavations were continued on the same site in 1953 still more light was thrown on the crafty Merodach-Baladan, for the discovery of fragments additional to those found previously made possible the almost complete reconstruction of a large clay tablet in the form of an eight-sided prism. This gives a detailed account of Sargon's victorious campaigns and recounts among other things how he had completely defeated Merodach-Baladan.

A residential quarter on the north-east side of the Acropolis was examined and among the interesting discoveries made there was the store-room of a wealthy merchant and a number of tablets which were the records of his transactions over a period of about forty years. Some of these were concerned with the supply of expensive birds, which were perhaps used in temple ceremonies. In this area also, which dates to the reign of Assurbanipal (668–630 B.C.) or later, a number of fragmentary but beautiful ivories were found hidden, all of which date to some eighty years before and which must have been kept as antiquities or, possibly heirlooms. The finest of these are five ivory bulls, charging. One of them bears on its back a fragment of a circular ivory tray; and it is probable that the complete object was a circular tray supported by pairs of fighting bulls.

An excavation in the north-west corner of the outer city led to the discovery of another palace, covering about an acre and with its walls standing in some places to 12 ft. It is built of bricks inscribed with the name of the king, Adad-Nirari III (810–782 B.C.). This king was the son of the famous Queen Summuramat (better known in the Hellenized form of Semiramis) who acted as the young king's Regent for two years. The palace, which seems to have been destroyed and sacked, shows traces of brilliant wall decoration. Among the rooms discovered was the king's bathroom, complete with slabs on which the bather would stand, a drain to carry away the waste water, and large water jars, some turned mouth downwards after use, others still standing the right way up—a vivid preservation of the scene after the last bath was taken there before the disaster.

Deeper excavations in the "Burnt Palace" revealed the floors of an earlier palace; and in these floors were a number of sunken brick boxes containing protective figures. Sometimes these are single figures—the bearded male warriors who are known as "weapon-bearers" or "fish-men"; and sometimes a box contains a group of seven similar figures. These last are the *Apkalle*, the seven sages whose task was the expelling of devils from the sick and the protection and purification of houses. They are also of course the "seven devils" referred to in the Scriptures. They are represented as devils with pinched bird-like faces, they are winged, the right hand (which holds some object) is pressed to the breast and the left (which holds a bucket) is extended. They were originally coated with white plaster and there are traces of black paint on the wings.

The principal objective of the sixth season (in the spring of 1955) was the Temple of Nabu. Nabu is the god of writing and learning generally and his worship at Nimrud was an innovation during about the time of Adad-nirari III (808–782 B.C.). His sanctuary was found, together with an adjacent palace, separated by a road from the "Burnt Palace". The walls were well preserved and were of mud-brick on limestone bases and in some parts were still standing to 14 ft. The sanctuaries were approached from a large oblong hall, about $52\frac{1}{2}$ ft long leading into a courtyard. This contained a portal flanked by basalt statues showing a servant of the god holding in front of him a box. What this box contained is not known but it is suggested that perhaps it was a container for the god's personal tablets. Four corridors led to an inner gate giving access to the antecella. This room was $42\frac{1}{2}$ ft long by 23 ft wide and probably afforded standing room to 100–150 people. At the farther end is a massive podium of stone over 3 ft high, which probably originally carried the statue of the god. Against the front face of this podium are two sets of steps, one at each end and one set is broad and the other narrow; and this distinction is probably related to the importance or numbers of the persons to whose use they were reserved. Alongside the Nabu sanctuary is another sanctuary on precisely the same lines, but smaller; and this was presumably for Tashmetum, the wife of Nabu. The temple had been thoroughly looted and there were few remaining contents.

The adjacent palace however was more rewarding. In it was found a throne-room, with a dais for the throne and the characteristic stone "tram-lines" leading to it—not unlike the two strips of concrete laid in the gravel leading up to the garage in suburban gardens—and indeed probably serving the same purpose, namely to support a wheeled vehicle which, in the case of the throne-room, would carry tributes or gifts for the king's inspection.

The most interesting finds however were the ivories and huge tablets, the record of a treaty made with a number of vassals. The ivories were very burnt and badly damaged and were mainly elements of furniture and they seem, at an early stage in their useful life, to have been handled with considerable vandalism. One long and beautiful strip had been attached to the wood beneath by means of copper nails driven, regardless, through the design. It has however been possible to recover their subject matter and this is of very great interest.

They are mostly long panels, either upright or horizontal and they were probably made in the reign of Esarhaddon. Many show processions of Median captives; and it is very interesting to see that not only are they shown in clothes which would seem outlandish to the Assyrians, but these captives of Iranian origin are shown with features entirely different from the Assyrian type—they have thin pointed noses and small beards, not unlike the faces we are accustomed to thinking of as Archaic Greek.

One long thin panel forms a fascinating frieze and shows (from left to right) a formalized pavilion, the King's tent, and standing in it, the King's squire, a young Assyrian carrying a bow; the King's chariot, drawn by two horses driven by the charioteer and led by a groom; another squire with a bow; an attendant carrying an umbrella which he holds over the King; then walking backwards in front of the King, an attendant with a fly-whisk; and then three Assyrian officers leading to the King six Median captives bearing tribute. A number of tall upright panels—some of which might have been the arms of chairs—show protective deities, winged bearded men holding in one hand a pine-cone and in the other a bucket; or else "Nisrochs", similar but eagle-headed figures, likewise holding a cone and a bucket. Another ivory fragment shows what seems to be a procession of priests of Nabu leading animals: a large bird, a bull-calf, a bull and a horse.

In the Nabu Temple, a fascinating object was found, a clay model of an internal organ of a sheep, with cuneiform inscriptions on various parts of it relating to divination from animals' entrails; and it was presumably used either for training diviners or as a convenient reference for the benefit of a priest confronted with some condition of the entrails which baffled him.

The huge tablets, referred to above, which were found in the Nabu Temple, when examined and read by Mr D. J. Wiseman of the British Museum, were found to be parts of nine "file copies" of a treaty imposed by Esarhaddon on Ramataia, the Median ruler of Urakazabarna and other vassals who had been summoned to Nineveh in May 672 B.C. to acknowledge Esarhaddon's son Assurbanipal as Crown Prince and successor to the throne. In the document the vassals agree to thirty-three clauses, swearing loyalty to Assurbanipal on his succession, that they would never revolt against him and that they would report any such attempt or any defamatory statements made. Rebels were to be seized or killed or assistance was to be given to Assyrian troops in this task. A list of persons to whom Royal powers were forbidden was given. "Assurbanipal alone is your lord. You will die for him and never do anything to him which is not good." "If Assurbanipal is murdered you swear that you will await the birth of a son by his pregnant wife . . . and avenge his death." The treaty was to be eternal and was to endure "for ever"; and if transgressed "You will lose your lives and give your houses to be smashed up and your peoples to be carried off as prisoners"—pretty much as Sargon of Assyria had dealt with the Northern Israelites in 721 B.C. and as Nebuchadnezzar of Babylon was to treat Judah and the inhabitants of Jerusalem in 586 B.C.

The signatories were made to swear by the names of the six planets and of seventeen leading gods and goddesses of Assyria, headed by Assur who was henceforth to be treated as their own god; and these oaths were reinforced with an extraordinary and hair-raising series of curses. "As rain does not fall from a brazen heaven, so may the rain and dew not come upon your fields and your meadows. May it rain burning coals instead of dew on your land. . . . May your insides be empty. . . . As a hinny is sterile so may you, your wives, your daughters and your sons be sterile. . . . As a snake and a mongoose do not enter and lie down together in the same hole without thinking of cutting short each other's lives, so may you and your women folk not enter the same room without thinking of cutting off each other's lives. . . . May your enemy squash you like a fly caught in the hand. . . . Just as those who sin against a god are cursed and their arms and legs become stiff and their eyelids twitch, may the gods annihilate you in like manner. . . . May your enemy wring you out like blood from a bandage. . . ."

But all this was of no avail; the fathers assented; and sixty years later the sons of the Iranian princes broke the Assyrian power and sacked Nimrud; and it was perhaps they who smashed the "file copies" of the treaties which had marked their fathers' submission.

Perhaps the most interesting aspect of this great treaty tablet was the seals with which it was sealed. One and one only was nearly contemporary with the document and was the seal of Sennacherib, the father of Esarhaddon. The second dated from about 1260 B.C. and is about 600 years older than the treaty. Its history is known. It bears the name of Tukulti-Ninurta, King of Assyria and it was taken to Babylon by Shagarakti-Shuriash, who added his name to it. It was found in Babylon in 689 B.C. by Sennacherib when he sacked the city and so brought back to its original home and used by Esarhaddon, son of Sennacherib. The third seal is unique, being the seal of a god and bears the inscription "Belonging to the god Assur of the Temple of the City" and it is more than 1,500 years older than the treaty. The form of this last seal is interesting; it shows a worshipper with hand raised in adoration, behind him a goddess, and in front of them, where the god should appear—a blank. Why the god should be invisible on his own seal can not be definitely stated—but most probably it is because it is after all *his own* seal.

The eighth season (1957) began with a tentative exploration of a large palace on the highest part of the acropolis which was thought to be that of Assur-etil-ilani (633–629 B.C.) the next to last king of Assyria. Although an immense palace and one whose complete excavation would be a gigantic operation, it represents Assyria in decline; and although some of the walls were faced with stone slabs, the king could evidently not afford to have reliefs carved upon them. One wall however of the great hall had evidently been panelled in ivory, but plain uncarved ivory nailed to a wooden backing—a sort of Assyrian version of the "Ivory House which Ahab made". Two Hellenistic graves were found, cist graves which had been sunk in the ruins of the Assyrian city; and one of these contained a set of Assyrian cylinder seals and amulets, immensely older than the grave itself, buried there either because the dead man was a collector of antiques or because they were considered to have magical properties. One of these is a Babylonian cylinder seal of about 2400 B.C. and since the grave dates from about 200 B.C., the dead man is nearer to us in time than to the Babylonian who originally carved the seal. In this area were found the remains of six successive mean settlements, built upon the ruins of the Assyrian city between the years 220–120 B.C.

The principal event of the season was the discovery and part excavation of "Fort Shalmaneser". This is a massive fortified building in the outer city, with an area of about 12 acres. It was built (as was later discovered) by King Shalmaneser III in 844 B.C. as a military store-house and armoury; and it was extensively repaired by Esarhaddon; and it seems, from the quantity of weapons and armour scattered in various parts and the number of iron arrowheads found about its wall and gates that it perhaps saw the last stand of the Assyrian army when Nimrud finally fell in 612 B.C.

In shape it is essentially a square, consisting of four quarters each consisting of a central courtyard surrounded by store-houses and barracks. The barracks are well equipped and contain bathrooms for the troops; and the courtyards seem to have been used for the evolutions of troops and their drill and training and as reception centres for stores and the centres for their withdrawal or receipt. One of the store-rooms was still full of large wine jars and these contained the rations for the King's Kassite choir, a group of specially trained male singers from the Persian hills, who were each entitled to a quart of wine a day. Remains were found of a throne-room with walls still standing 12 ft high and painted with murals of troops. In the floor of this room were the customary stone "tram lines" leading to the throne, but the dais had been removed and re-erected in a corner of one of the great courtyards; and we can suppose that it was there used by the king when he reviewed troops in "Fort Shalmaneser".

But the fantastic riches of this building lay in the store-rooms; and it soon became clear that in its later days, at least, "Fort Shalmaneser" had been used as a repository for royal furniture that was perhaps out-of-date by later standards or maybe requiring repair; and in fact it has proved the richest by far of all the sources of Assyrian ivories yet discovered; and those discovered in 1957 and 1958—not all of which have yet been published—are extremely numerous, of the greatest intrinsic interest, many being unique, and of great beauty and the finest craftsmanship (Plate 48).

It is of course impossible to describe them adequately here; but some indication of their types must be attempted. In the first place there are a number of a favourite Assyrian subject: the "courtesan at the window", a square plaque, showing a square window, divided about half way up by a pillared balustrade and looking out above this, a female head with a very elaborate coiffure, a symbol presumably of feminine wiles and seductions, and one frequently used as a motif in palace furniture. Next and intrinsically much more interesting are two types, which seem to be related with the fertility and vegetation cults asso-ciated with Tammuz and Ishtar. One type shows a bearded man, elaborately and elegantly dressed, who strides vigorously forward to grasp the branches of a tree or a flowering lotus; the other shows a woman, most richly dressed and with a complicated hair-do, one long tress being brought right across the top of the head to hang down on the the other side of the face. She is seated on a throne on a tasselled seat, under which sometimes crouches a little winged sphinx like a pet dog. In front of her is a tree; and perched in the tree, in front of her, is a small table with X-legs and bulls' feet; and on this table are dishes and, perhaps loaves; and these mysterious ladies sometimes pluck a fruit from the tree and nearly always rest a hand on the food on the little table. Next are a group of animals: two panels, for example, of highly accomplished open work showing, one a stag, the other an oryx, browsing amid papyrus stems and palm trees; a beautiful and tender panel of a cow, against a background of lotus, turning to lick the calf she is suckling; and a most engaging lion, a double-sided plaque, resting a fore-paw in the branches of a magical tree and wearing a sun-disk and an Egyptian-style pectoral. Next a group of figures, sphinxes, griffins and a winged Horus of ultimately Egyptian inspiration but Phoenician or Syrian in origin and Egyptian only at second hand. And two master-works of which a more detailed description must be attempted.

One of these is a winged boy, a youthful angel, probably originally one of a pair watching the birth of Horus, holding in one hand a lotus bud, beside which stands a hawk. The wings, both of the angel and the hawk; the angel's hair; and the necklaces he wears; are all cut in for inlays and traces of blue frit and carnelian still remain, and the hair, like that of the Nubian in the Nubian and Lioness plaque, was probably originally encrusted with gold. The ivory of the body is beautifully moulded and of a clean warm tone; and the original com-plete object must obviously have been a brilliant fantasy of polychrome ivory.

The other is in the shape of half a lunette and was obviously originally one of a pair of confronted figures. The frame of the lunette is simple with an engraved guilloche pattern, on which parts of the original gold incrustation still remain. The figure is a winged sphinx, magnificently naturalistic and three-dimen-sional. The style is Egyptian as seen through Phoenician eyes. The head, which is turned to gaze forwards is perhaps a stylized portrait and it wears a high Egyptian crown and double ostrich feathers, a pectoral ornamented with a papyrus-lotus design; and from the front of the apron projects the head of a cobra. The tail is strongly curled and here and there in the composition are branches ending in palmettes. It was probably made about 700 B.C.; and its Egyptian flavour may be connected with Esarhaddon's invasion of Egypt and the tribute sent to him by the Pharaoh Taharqa—the taste of the conquered not infrequently conquering the conqueror.

Although the excavations were not continued in 1959, it is to be hoped that they will be resumed before long, since as these post-war excavations have proved, the treasures of Nimrud seem inexhaustible.

The latest in historic time of the outstanding excavations since 1945 in Iraq is the series conducted under the general direction of the then Director-General of Antiquities, Dr Naji al Asil, and the field direction of Sayid Fuad Safar at Hatra.

Hatra, which lies some 93 miles south-west of Mosul, had a brief and brilliant history. It seems to have had its origin about the beginning of the Christian era, when it was inhabited by a community of Mesopotamian Arabs and became the capital of a province known as Araba. Early in its history it gained control over the trade routes from the Parthian capital Ctesiphon to Singara and Nisibis and other cities to the north; and also became a sort of western bastion of the Parthian Empire. The semi-desert in which it stands is potentially very fertile and with proper management and some luck with the rainfall produces rich crops. In addition it was a religious centre, with a great complex of temples, and so acquired great wealth and influence. This prosperity was however brief and in about A.D. 240 Hatra was destroyed by the Sassanians.

The excavations began in 1951 and in the first four years no fewer than ten temples were discovered and found to be positive mines of sculptures. In general each temple was dedicated to a single god and his spouse; but as time went on other deities were added and also statues of kings, queens and other notables, as it might be after being deemed worthy of permanent commemoration in a sort of national pantheon.

The deities were of the kind usually called syncretic—like those at Nemrud Dagh and Arsameia in Commagene—that is to say compounds or reconciliations of gods from different sources. Thus the sun-god Shamash is equated with Zeus (not Apollo, since Shamash is the chief god); the goddess Allat with Athene; Nergal with Pluto or Dis; and Malak with Hercules. The artistic style is likewise "syncretic" and is a remarkable blend of Hellenistic or even Roman styles with Parthian and sometimes, it seems, even Indian influences.

Perhaps the oddest of these blends is a statue of the paramount Assyrian god, known at Hatra as Ashur-Bel or Bel. The head is broken off at the neck, but the characteristic square-ended Assyrian beard with its parallel curls survives. From the front the god is seen to be dressed as a Roman emperor, with a long cloak over a breast-plate on which is the rayed head of the sun-god, the typical kilt-like armoured skirt and the legs concealed by the figure of Fortuna or Tyche kneeling on one knee. On either side of the legs and appearing as supporters to Fortuna are a pair of eagles. Seen from behind the statue is strikingly mono-lithic in effect. The cloak falls without fold and bears an all-over pattern, repre-senting feathers or perhaps scales; and the wings of the two eagles meet at the back to form a sort of rearguard to the god's legs. Between the shoulder-blades is the head of Medusa (Plate 50).

The eagle, which is nearly always a symbol of power and conquest, had a special association with Hatra, one of the temples being dedicated to Samya, the eagle-god; and the eagle is a curious feature of one of the most interesting statues. This represents Sanatruq, Hatra's most famous king. It shows a long, thin, rather hollow-profiled face, with a spade beard, a full-lipped mouth, elegantly curving moustaches, the hair dressed in the Parthian style, that is to say in two masses of curls, rather like bunches of grapes, one beside either temple —and, crowning the head, rather like a modish hat, an eagle with wings outspread. This perhaps makes Sanatruq sound like a figure of fun; but such is not the effect. The nearest analogy is perhaps with the buccaneer-poets of Elizabethan England; and it may well be a natural analogy, both being *nouveau riche* expanding states, open to new influences from every side and grasping at every source of wealth, vitality and excitement

Nearly all the male heads have this thin-faced bearded elegance—as though they were friends of George Meredith and Cunninghame Graham—with well-barbered spade beards and downward curling moustaches. One is a military commander who stands relaxedly with his right hand lifted in greeting, his left resting on the pommel of a sword of almost medieval proportions, which has a double sword belt. He is dressed in Parthian style in tunic and cloak with Parthian trousers with drooping parallel pleats. There is another bearded limestone head in the same style, elegant, even more stylized, but individual and with lines of worry on the forehead. These are both of limestone. There is however a marble life-size statue of a king of Hatra, Uthal, who appears older and more senatorial. He is wearing Parthian costume of great richness with an all-over diamond pattern, a cloak which is perhaps meant to be of fur, the same pleated Parthian trousers and a tall steeple-like crown, a type of head-dress also worn by Antiochus of Commagene (Plate 49).

The female statues are different and also very interesting. One relief shows the most celebrated pre-Islamic deity of Arabia, Allat, here shown as a rather dumpy woman with a spear in her right hand and a shield in her left and wearing a helmet like a sun-bonnet over a mass of curls. The Medusa-head on her breast equates her with Athene and she is standing on the back of a lion, with two minor goddesses, one on either side and these may be Al-Uzza and Menat. The most beautiful female statue is that of the Princess Washfari, daughter of King Sanatruq. This is somewhat over life size, made of Mosul marble and shows her standing on a pedestal with an Aramaic inscription. She wears a towering head-dress with draperies falling from it on to her shoulders. Her right hand is raised in formal greeting, her left slightly lifts the long and seemingly diaphanous robe which covers nearly all her body. She wears two heavy necklaces. One lies at the base of her neck and it has a number of pendants attached to it; the other is much longer and narrows from the shoulders to fall between the breasts and end in a circular pendant resting on the navel. The folds of the long robe build up into a generally concentric pattern around the navel; and this, together with the supple pose, the slightly thrust-out right hip and the bland, rounded and somewhat abstracted features of the face, gives the whole statue a strongly Indian feeling. And this feeling, though less marked, is present in a seated limestone statue of a Princess Ubal, daughter of Jabal, a pleasant but less accomplished work.

With all this wealth of deities and personalities, it is interesting to learn that the tenth temple excavated was originally built for the worship of an abstract deity called Alaha, of whom no representation has been found; and it was in this temple that the statue of Sanatruq, mentioned above, was found.

Iraq has recently shown a most interesting example of how archaeology can be the helpmate of modern large-scale planning in the best use of a country's natural resources.

All civilizations have an economic basis; and the urban prosperity in which civilization flowers depends on a fertile and continuing agricultural prosperity. Unless the farmer can produce more than he needs *and can go on doing so,* there is no leisure, no art, no learning, no development. But man, although a great developer, is also the greatest of devastators and persistently takes away from the land more than he puts back; to succeed and go on succeeding he needs a prodigious stroke of luck, something which is constantly paying off the overdrafts he is equally constantly incurring on the bank of natural fertility. The Incas were fortunate in the number of plants, notably maize and the potato, which presented themselves and which they developed a high degree of skill in exploiting. The Mayas by contrast, though they had the blessing of maize, never appear to have had a higher idea of farming than working out one area and moving on to the next—an imbecile notion which is however still practised in some countries. But the great civilizations were those of the three great river valleys, the Indus Valley, the Euphrates-Tigris Valley, and the Nile Valley; and in each of these the annual floods, with their rich deposits from the mountains, each year paid off the overdraft; and this is a blessing which it is impossible to overestimate.

Consequently when in recent years the Iraq Government decided to set aside 70 per cent of the immense oil revenues for projects of capital development, especially in irrigation schemes to reclaim the desert, drainage schemes to reclaim the marshes and on the spread of more advanced agricultural techniques generally, the prospects seemed to be unbounded. But in semi-arid and subtropical and tropical countries there are complications to this sort of thing; and the greatest of these is salinity—salt.

All fresh water contains some salt; and the saltness of the sea is simply the sum of the salt which the rivers have brought down to it and which evaporation has left behind there. The sun draws up salt-free water vapour from the sea (thereby making the sea an infinitesimally little bit saltier than it was before) and deposits this absolutely fresh water in the form of rain on hills and mountains. This rain leeches a variety of minerals, including salt, from the soil over and through which it passes; and in a general way carries this fresh supply of salt to the sea, which continues to get a little saltier. The sea is vast however and can stand it—or so we presume.

Not so with land-locked lakes, which grow progressively saltier with the years; and this is even more so in hot countries where the rate of evaporation is the greater. The freshwater Jordan has built up the ancient Dead Sea to an appalling degree of salinity.

Very well. But, it would seem that a great river, running through a hot country, would nevertheless take its salt with it to the safety of the sea. True, unless it dawdles so long that it evaporates before it gets there; and irrigation, which traps the swift running river into slower moving canals, tends to do this; and if the canals are neglected and silt up, they are converted into stagnant water, evaporate in the sun and deposit their salt with eventually fatal results.

It would seem then that irrigation, unless it is efficiently carried out, is a source of danger; but that regular care can successfully protect against this danger. And this, in general, is true—for a number of centuries, at least.

But not all the water runs to the sea or even into the irrigation canals. Some seeps down through the soil to form what is termed the water-table, the level of water under the ground; and here in general it is perfectly safe, provided it has eventual means of drainage. But if your water-table is virtually a land-locked underground lake it is in danger of turning as saline as the Dead Sea, given time and salt enough.

Need this matter? For a short time perhaps not. But it is a sort of creeping and progressive paralysis. As a result of bad drainage, water gets saltier; and the saltier the water gets the worse the drainage gets as one of the effects of salt is to destroy the texture of soil, to "deflocculate" it and turn it into an impenetrable hard-pan—as every gardener knows who has been so misguided as to use sea-sand in his garden.

And furthermore—and this is Iraq's problem—the effect of good cultivation is to raise the level of the water-table and, in fact, the better the cultivation and the more intensive the irrigation, the nearer is brought that creeping death in the basement, the saline water-table; and it would seem as if it is exactly this menace which has provided the tide and, so to speak, the pulse of the great civilizations which have waxed and waned in the great river plains of Meso-potamia.

However, as every modern problem can perhaps carry its solution in its history, the Government of Iraq Development Board asked the Oriental Insti-tute of Chicago to make a comprehensive assessment of ancient agriculture in Mesopotamia; and the Diyala Basin Archaeological Project came into being under the direction of Dr Thorkild Jacobsen and Dr Robert M. Adams. Their programme as well as utilizing ancient textual sources scattered throughout the world's museums and libraries, included field-work designed to elucidate the history of irrigation and settlement of a part of the flood plain watered by the Diyala—which is a tributary of the Tigris. Their task has been one of the greatest complexity and consists basically in attempting to build up out of thousands of tiny facts, gathered from literature, aerial photography and large-scale maps, and from the examination and dating of all ancient remains in the area—to build up a succession of pictures giving the population, economy and techniques at all periods in the history of this ancient land; and to endeavour to wrest, if possible, any general principles from it which might emerge.

Work of this nature is, of course, impossible to summarize here; and one can only admire such devoted labours and call attention, almost at random, to two striking facts. The count of grain imprints in the pottery has revealed a gradual supersession of wheat by barley as salinity rises, barley being more tolerant of salt than wheat is; and the Mongols under Hulagu Khan, who have generally been charged with turning Mesopotamia into a desert in the thirteenth century A.D., can be in part acquitted. Salinity had preceded them by a hundred years.

CHAPTER TWENTY-ONE

PAKISTAN AND AFGHANISTAN

PAKISTAN and Afghanistan may conveniently be taken together for a variety of reasons: because they are most closely related at three great germinal periods in the history of this part of the world—the beginnings of the Indus Valley civilization, the spread of Hellenistic culture after the conquests of Alexander the Great, and the entry of Islam into India; because the discoveries made in them since the war illustrate the history of both; and because both hold immense possibilities for the further development of knowledge on these same lines.

It was in the 'twenties of this century that the late Sir John Marshall discovered and announced the existence of a great civilization which had flourished in the Indus Valley from at least the middle of the Third Millennium, a riverine civilization comparable with, though perhaps a little later than those of Mesopotamia and Egypt; and in the years that followed, his excavations and later those of Dr R. E. M. (now Sir Mortimer) Wheeler uncovered the great and complex cities of Harappa and Mohenjo-Daro. Both cities were characterized by a high degree of planning, revealed not only in the lay-out of their streets and the thoroughness of their drainage and sewerage but also in the huge brick-built granaries which from their very nature argue a sort of bureaucratic autocracy designed to regulate a controlled prosperity. Before the war two interesting and rather teasing features had emerged. First, in all the mass of brick construction which had been revealed there seemed to be no trace of any considerable defensive work; and it was suggested that the Indus Valley civilization had realized that dream of Utopia, a world successfully dedicated to peace and prosperity, none of whose resources were dispersed on the provision of armaments, defensive or offensive—a paradise of the reasonable man. The second feature was in the nature of a problem—what were the beginnings of this civilization. It was possible to work back to about 2500 B.C. but no farther. At Mohenjo-Daro, cultivation and irrigation of the district over the centuries had raised the water-table to such an extent that it was impossible to dig down to virgin soil and examine the unknown number of strata which were now submerged. Harappa was indeed in drier land, but here the mass of later constructions had reached such a bulk and height that although excavation down to virgin soil was theoretically possible it was nevertheless quite impracticable at this stage of the excavations.

The two outstanding questions, therefore, were: was the Indus Valley civilization a paradise of peace? and what were its origins and early history?

In 1946, the first question was answered with a categorical no, when Sir Mortimer Wheeler's excavations at Harappa revealed a citadel, of several ages and of the same massive style of construction as the other buildings. What progress has been made towards answering the second question will appear in the course of this chapter.

Soon after the partition of the Indian sub-continent into the two states of India and Pakistan, the newly created Archaeological Department of Pakistan, to which Sir Mortimer Wheeler was Adviser, resumed excavations at Mohenjo-Daro, under his direction. Mohenjo-Daro, like Harappa, consists of an Upper and a Lower City and at the highest point of the former lie some of the principal religious and administrative buildings, including two pillared halls, a collegiate building and a Great Bath, or tank. In this district, near the ruins of a Buddhist shrine of the second century A.D. was a brick-strewn sandy mound, some 30 ft high, the contents of which were quite unknown. A trench was made in its outer side to see whether perhaps it concealed some fortifications of the citadel; and a high sloping brick wall was revealed. This may have had a secondary use as a fortification; but further excavation revealed that it was built as part of a podium of a granary, with an area of about 150 × 75 ft, later enlarged. The original height of the podium was about 25 ft; the upper stages were pierced with ventilation passages; and the actual granary would be built of wood on top of this podium. On the northern side, the sloping brick face was broken, at about half the height with a terrace, something like a dry-land wharf, and in this terrace there was a perpendicularly-sided bay—in other words, a loading-bay where the wagons would draw in to discharge their freight of sacks of grain.

An architectural feature of this granary is the use of long beams of wood to reinforce the mass of bricks—a technique, not uncommon in ancient buildings of widely differing civilizations, which has obvious short-term advantages and, at all events to posterity, equally obvious disadvantages on a long-term basis.

In 1955 and 1957, Dr Fazal Ahmad Khan, now Director of the Archaeological Department of Pakistan, conducted excavations at Kot Diji, near Khairpur in Sind, about 25 miles east of Mohenjo-Daro. The site is a mound about 40 ft high and some 600 ft long; and cuttings revealed between eighteen and twenty successive occupational layers. The uppermost six layers revealed a normal Indus Valley civilization agricultural village, a reasonably prosperous but quite simple community, without any of the beautiful Indus Valley seals and with no trace of the usual drainage system. There was however the appearance of a town plan and the utensils and equipment were those which one would expect in a village of this civilization which originated a hundred or so years before 2000 B.C. and which was renewed several times.

Beneath this level, however, was a universal deep layer of burnt material which vividly suggests that the preceding settlement came to a violent end; and under this layer of destruction down to the virgin rock are the strata of an entirely different civilization. Above, Kot Diji is an open farming village; below, it is a strongly fortified citadel, with 10-ft stone walls crowned with mud-brick fortifications and with part of the town lying outside the fortifications. Copper was seemingly unknown, there are no seals and no hint of a script, there are quantities of leaf-shaped chert arrowheads of a type unknown in the Indus Valley towns (but reminiscent of material found in upland Baluchistan) and the pottery is quite distinct. It is wheel-turned, fine, hard ware usually consisting of small goblets, globular bowls, open dishes and "fruit stands". Some of it is buff, but the majority is red or pinkish with a simple decoration of horizontal bands on the upper part, cleanly drawn in a fugitive paint which may be red, sepia or black. Sometimes the bands of paint have a fringe of pendent loops. Animal designs are very rare.

In the upper layers of this pre-Indus Valley culture, which is now called Kot-Dijian after the site, there are a few pots decorated with the intersecting circles or scale-pattern typical of the Indus civilization; and there was one deep brown globular jar, decorated in black and white and showing the head of a horned deity, with boldly curved horns within whose curves are rosettes of the normal Indus type. The horned god, which has been described as a sort of proto-Siva, is also well known in Indus Valley seals.

The suggestion therefore is that towards the end of this Kot-Dijian civilization either the Kot-Dijians were beginning to evolve towards the Indus Valley civilization, were in fact its ancestors; or that for a time they were in contact with it and influenced by it before being either overwhelmed or absorbed by it, and, in view of the thick layer of burnt material, it seems more likely that they were overwhelmed. It is perhaps dangerous, though, to deduce a wide scale revolution from what may have been only a local incident.

Light on events over much the same period of time has been thrown by excavations at Mundigak in Afghanistan, conducted by Jean-Marie Casal, Head of the French *Mission Archéologique des Indes* during the period 1950–54.

Mundigak—the word means "small mound"—is a now much eroded cone-shaped mound, standing in a valley parallel with that of the Arghandab and about twenty miles north-east of Kandahar. It stands a few hundred yards from a river bed which seems to have been dry for centuries except for occasional spates after thunderstorms in the surrounding hills. It is a desolate area, uninhabited now except for the seasonal passage of the nomadic tribes; and the mound itself seems to have been unoccupied for about 3,000 years. But the mound is about 60 ft high and a preliminary *sondage* revealed that it was made up of about thirteen different levels of construction dating from about the end of the Fourth Millennium to the beginning of the First—after which it was abandoned.

The deep *sondage* and the excavation of the upper levels have enabled the history of Mundigak to be summarized as follows.

The lowest nine levels are known only from the *sondage*. The earliest is of semi-nomadic occupation and it is followed by a settlement with *pisé* walls.

After this comes mud-brick and buff-coloured pottery, at first rather coarse, but getting finer with the passage of time, as painted pottery appears and becomes more and more important. This is related to Quetta ware and has a rather elegant decoration of painted lines, by the time that the ninth level from the bottom is reached. A Carbon-14 date for the fifth level was 2625 B.C. ±300 years. At the sixth level metal (copper or bronze) appeared.

By the time the ninth level was reached, the mound had risen 30 ft from the plain and the inhabitants moved down from the mound, and, using it as a pedestal, built on it a huge monument with massive colonnades of half-columns of mud-brick, plastered and several times whitewashed, and pierced with a red-painted doorway. Associated with this pillared monument was a network of rectangular cells, which seem to have been used as store-rooms, two of them containing carefully sorted pottery of different types. In all this nexus of northern rooms there is not a single hearth and since there appear to be no defensive works, it seems certain that the monument was a public building and most probably a religious one. The typical vessel of this period is a truly striking one: a footed cup in the shape of a *verre de dégustation* or "brandy balloon" in a buff ware elegantly decorated with purple paint. Near the narrowing mouth are four horizontal thin lines and a similar group of lines at the widest part of the belly. Between these two bands and sometimes overlapping them are painted ibexes with sweeping curved horns or partridge-like birds, roughly naturalistic in outline, but with a rather schematic use of lines to diversify the body; or a design of *pipal* leaves—a widely separated trefoil, that is, of heart-shaped leaves. These which recall Kulli and Indus Valley pots are provisionally dated to the second half of the Third Millennium.

This period probably ended with violence and the pillared monument is succeeded by a bigger coarser one, of masonry cubes piled up into a sort of truncated pyramid. Although the purpose of this building may have been the same as the previous one it was certainly erected by newcomers to the site, with an entirely different pottery. Instead of being buff, it is red, and the decorative pattern, though still in purple, is always geometrical only.

There follows a long and undermined period during which this second monumental building slowly deteriorates and is even sometimes used as a camping ground by shepherds. This period eventually ends when newcomers take over the mound, level the summit and build on it granaries of *pisé*, after the style of the Indus Valley people; and these are three times reconstructed, usually on much the same plan. The pottery of this period is plain, dark grey in colour or orange-red and slightly burnished. This appears to have been a period of insecurity however and in the early years of the First Millennium B.C. occupation of the Mundigak mound ceases after an occupation of rather over 2,000 years.

"What's Swat?" said the Victorian poet George Thomas Lanigan. Swat is a beautiful and prosperous country in the north-western part of Pakistan, ruled over by a Wali and adjoined by Azad Kashmir and Dir, which separates it from Afghanistan. Remote in the modern world, in ancient times it was in the track of great events and notable developments. After most probably being under Achaemenian Persian rule, it was in the track of Alexander the Great's invasion of India and, being conquered by him, became a centre of that art which resulted from the blending of Hellenism and Hinduism, which finds its finest expression in Gandhara sculpture. It became one of the great centres of Buddhism in all its schools and the Tibetans still consider it a holy land. It was ruled by Indo-Greek kings, Indo-Scythians, Kushans; overwhelmed by the White Huns and later by the great Ghaznavid Sultan Mahmud when he swept east out of Afghanistan and extended the bounds of Islam into India.

In 1956 excavations in Swat were begun by the Italian Archaeological Mission under the direction of Professor Giuseppe Tucci and sponsored by the Institute for Cultural Relations between Italy and Asia. These excavations, with the agreement of the Archaeological Department of Pakistan and the Wali of Swat, were undertaken at two places, Mingora and Udegram.

Mingora is especially a Buddhist site, with a monastery surrounding a large Buddhist *stupa*, and this for many years has been a source of Gandhara sculpture unearthed by clandestine diggers. During the Italian excavation, some sixty-two minor *stupas* have been examined and in eight of them the relic-casket complete with golden ash-container was found. Apparently these *stupas* were at some time overwhelmed with floods; but sculpture slabs were recovered and reused, new sculptures being carved on the previously unused sides. As can be imagined, this has provided a great deal of convenient evidence for the art historians in the way of establishing the chronological sequence of various features of style. All told some 300 sculptures or fragments of sculpture were recovered. These include: stucco heads of Buddha; a Buddha *stela*; two fine heads of donors, one of whom might well be a moustached "barbarian" of the Pergamene School; a partly equestrian relief of Sakyamuni leaving his home; a winged griffin from a pediment, which combines Greek and "Scythian" styles; and what might be described as an epitome of the wedding of Greek and Buddhist, a column capital in the Corinthian style with the familiar acanthus leaves, but with a Buddhist *deva* emerging from among the leaves.

Udegram was known to the Greeks as Ora and it was one of the places captured by Alexander the Great; and several sites in what has been a very large town were excavated. On a rock face a number of rock carvings of animals were known and a trial trench sunk to between 15 and 20 ft and still not reaching virgin soil has revealed other carvings of the same kind and it seems likely that this is a prehistoric or, at least, proto-historic site. Part of the lower town, which seems to have been a bazaar, was excavated; and here six different levels, the latest being contemporary with the Kushana King Vasudeva III (end of the third century A.D.) when this part of the town was finally destroyed by floods; while the lowest dates back to the Achaemenian period. Other parts of the town climb on to the slopes of the mountains and on one spur stands the remains of a castle. Traditionally this castle was destroyed by Mahmud of Ghazni in the eleventh century A.D. and it seems most likely that Alexander would also have captured it. The massive central buildings on the summit date from the Kushan period and they hold out the prospect of interesting discoveries. A massive stairway leads up to the castle and this appears to be Sassanian work; but it is possible that this and the buildings on the summit overlie earlier constructions. Great quantities of arrowheads have been found during the excavations in the locality; and they tell graphically of fierce battles fought around this stronghold.

Farther south, not far from Peshawar, where the Swat River approaches its junction with the Kabul River on their way to join the Indus lie a number of ancient mounds of which the tallest is the Bala Hisar, or High Fort, of Charsada —the ancient Lotus City, Pushkalavati. This mound rises some 70 ft from the plain and except for some slight exploration by the late Sir John Marshall, when a young man, in 1903, was untouched by the archaeologist. It too lay in the path of Alexander the Great and it is recorded that in 327 B.C. it was able to resist his tried troops for a month before yielding, and that Alexander himself came out of his way to accept its surrender.

In 1958 Sir Mortimer Wheeler was invited to undertake its exploration with the aid of the Pakistan Department of Archaeology and the support of the Stein-Arnold Fund of the British Academy; and this he did in a seven-week campaign, which also served to train and stimulate young Pakistani archaeologists.

The principal operation in this campaign was the cutting of an enormous trench down the face of the mound into the subsoil below, removing about 1,000 tons of earth. This revealed, as it were, a summary of the site's history— in fifty-two layers—and established the points of reference for any future excavations. It would appear that the city's earliest buildings perished in flames in the sixth century B.C. and that the mound had risen to nearly three-quarters of its height before the appearance of Gandhara Buddhist art in the early centuries A.D.

Another trench was cut, at a low level and this uncovered an impressive defensive ditch, most fortunately at a point where parallel lines of post-holes indicated that there had stood there a postern gate and a bridge. A group of houses across the river was examined, and the earliest states of these date from about the fourth century B.C. In two wells near by, one of which was reinforced with terracotta rings, a quantity of pottery and figurines, principally of the third and second centuries B.C., was found and a silver coin (a tetradrachm) of Menander, the Indo-Greek king of the mid-second century B.C.

Of the objects found, perhaps the following are the most interesting: a number of small terracotta goddess figurines—naked steatopygous females with very elaborate, as it were swathed head-dresses, incorporating apparently flowers; a small terracotta dog; and a curious fragment from a pottery bowl, bearing a frieze in relief of women dancers wearing gazelle head-dresses—all these being of the fourth and third centuries B.C. Of the Indo-Greek period and influence are: the battered torso of a marble statuette of Hercules, or more probably Alexander the Great as Hercules; a terracotta relief, part of a jug-handle showing the head of Alexander wearing the lionskin of Hercules; a clay-sealing showing the classical figure of Athena; and, most delightful, a stone carving showing the head and shoulders of Silenus with a can of drink in his left hand—it is right that Silenus should have used the Frothblowers' technique —and in the right a palm-leaf fan to cool him in this Oriental climate.

The Pakistan Air Force had been invited to assist by taking aerial photo-graphs of the mounds; and one set—of a large mound called Shaikhan, lying across the river and about half a mile from the High Fort—produced a most remarkable and striking piece of information. Seen from on foot this mound was just a muddle of heaps and hollows where the villagers of modern times had grubbed out bricks and stones for re-use. Seen from the air the whole summit of the mound was revealed as a rigidly-planned city with a grid-iron system of streets and in their midst, at one end, a huge circular Buddhist temple with a large rectangular courtyard. A rigid street plan like this is a rare thing in India or Pakistan; and it is to be found only in Indus Valley cities like Mohenjo-Daro or Harappa or in Indo-Greek or Indo-Scythian times. This mound is of course of the latter date, the second century B.C. to the early centuries A.D. Its closest parallel is at Taxila, which lies on the same trade route, about 100 miles to the east. At Taxila, a city of the sixth-century foundation was abandoned in Indo-Greek times and a new city on a grid-iron plan built near by; and it seems clear that the same thing happened at Charsada—that the High Fort was abandoned in Indo-Greek times and a new city, laid out by town-planners, was built on the near-by Shaikhan.

No excavation has been done on this newly discovered site, but it is obvious that both Bala Hisar and Shaikhan hold out immense promises for the future and work for many years, if funds and facilities were available.

That Pakistan is an Islamic state is first due to the Ghaznavid Sultans (whose name has been mentioned in connexion with Udegram) and the dynasty which succeeded them, the Ghorids—and both of these conquerors of India came out of Afghanistan.

The nature of Afghanistan, especially its physical nature, and the scantiness of its communications are such that even large surface antiquities can remain unrecorded for hundreds of years; and as it happens the post-war years have seen the discovery of an unknown Ghaznavid group of palaces and an immense and extremely well preserved Ghorid minaret.

The ancestor of the Ghaznavid dynasty was a Turkish adventurer who be-came the master in A.D. 962 of the fortress of Ghazni in eastern Afghanistan, a little south-south-west of Kabul. Some fourteen years later a successor, Subuk-tigin seized Bust in south-west Afghanistan, west of Kandahar; and these two fortresses became the poles of an increasing empire which under the great Mahmud (A.D. 998–1030) and his son and successor Masud, who died in A.D. 1041, stretched from Turkestan to the Indian Ocean and from Hamadan in Persia to Lahore in the Punjab. Little of their splendour was known to remain, except for two brick towers at Ghazni and the seldom visited ruins of Bust. Near Bust however flows a large river, the Helmand, which here joins its great tributary the Arghandab and thence flows south-westwards through the Dasht-i-Margo Desert until it drains into the vast swamps of Seistan, on the borders of Persia and Afghanistan, in years of exceptional flood sometimes continuing into the Gaod-i-Zirreh swamp. Traditionally, in ancient times these swamps were fertile country, with an elaborate system of irrigation canals but since the fourteenth century and the devastations of Tamerlane have been nothing more than a barren waste of salt alluvial levels. However near Bust the Helmand is a splendid broad river and some little distance to the west there was known to stand a group of large ruins, so large in fact that they were assumed to be "modern".

In 1948, however, M Daniel Schlumberger, Director of the French Archaeological Delegation in Afghanistan, examined them a little more closely and wondered whether they might not be the royal residence of Mahmud and Masud referred to by a number of Persian and Arabic authors as al-Askar or Lashkargah. It was certainly an odd coincidence that the modern name of the site was Lashkari-Bazar. In 1949 therefore M Schlumberger and a little later, M Le Berre, the delegation's architect, undertook an excavation of one of the groups of ruins.

The one chosen was found to be the southern palace, an enormous quadrilateral of buildings, standing on the bank of the river and about 550 yds long by about 300 yds wide, with additional garden enclosures. Its chief feature is a very large central courtyard, with an *iwan* (which is a hall with one open side) opening in the centre of each of the four sides of the quadrangle. The majority of the walls still stand to nearly their original height, and on the exterior seem to have been later turned into fortifications with a number of semicircular bastions. A great number of rooms surround the central court; and of these perhaps the most important are a large cross-shaped hall which lies behind the southern *iwan*, and a square banqueting hall which lies behind the northern *iwan*. In the centre of this banqueting hall stands a brick-paved banqueting platform, which would be spread with carpets and cushions for the Sultan and his honoured guests. In Mahmud's time this was a rich and famous court and a centre of culture to which came such distinguished men as the great Arabic scholar, al-Biruni and the greatest of all Persian poets, Firdawsi. Mahmud is known to have been a great admirer of Firdawsi and to have valued his poems at a gold piece a line. Firdawsi was not unnaturally stimulated by such a contract—but some highly complicated financial transactions ensued, which led to a quarrel which led in turn to Firdawsi's flight and eventually to the composition of the violently reproachful *Shahnama*. It is not difficult to fancy that some of the happier meetings of king and poet took place at this banquet platform and that this hall was the first to hear those lines that Mahmud rated so high.

Some thirteen sultans of this dynasty succeeded Masud, the son of Mahmud, until the Ghorid Sultan Alauddin seized Ghazni, and sacked Bust in about A.D. 1150; and it seems likely that at about this time Lashkari-Bazar was abandoned to its long sleep beside the Helmand.

Strangely enough, light has recently been thrown on these same Ghorid Sultans who overcame the Ghaznavids and succeeded them as Empire builders. These great warriors came from, and took their name from, Ghor, the still largely unexplored centre of Afghanistan and like the Ghaznavids had two capitals, Ghazni which they took over from their predecessors and Firuzkoh—which has hitherto not been satisfactorily located.

One of the most famous monuments of the Ghorids is in India, not far from New Delhi, namely the Qutb-minar, the world's largest minaret. The lower part of this was built by the Turkish general Qutb-ud Din Aibak, acting as viceroy for two Ghorid Sultans, brothers called Mu'izz ud-Din and Ghiyath ud-Din and he inscribed their names on this monument—which was completed later under Altamish.

Now, some time prior to the summer of 1957, M André Maricq, a member of the French Archaeological Delegation in Afghanistan, had heard rumours of a large tower in central Afghanistan, in the valley of the Hari-Rud and, with the encouragement of the President of the Afghan Historical Society, M Ahmad Ali Kohzad, paid a visit to those parts in 1957. In general the rough road from Kabul to Herat follows the line of the Hari-Rud, but leaves it to loop southwards to Shahrak, and steep mountains at this point lie between Shahrak and the river. M Maricq negotiated a way at this point back to the Hari-Rud and on 19 August 1957 was astonished to find in the most desolate country at the junction of the Hari-Rud and Jham rivers a large and beautiful golden-coloured tower, rising to about 200 ft and in a remarkable state of preservation, with a band of blue faience encircling it. The three stages of this colossal minaret are adorned with panels of relief ornament and a long winding inscription in Kufic—the whole of the nineteenth *sura* of the Koran (over 1,000 words); while the blue faience band recites the names and titles of Ghiyath ud-Din (1163—1202), whose name is likewise recorded on the Qutb-minar in India.

M Maricq was able to stay only one day, but recorded this astonishing find in photographs and explored in part its interior, coming to the conclusion that its original true entrance had been subterranean, possibly by way of a tunnel under the river. This suggested that somewhere in this neighbourhood might lie the lost capital of the Ghorids, Firuzkoh.

In 1958 the site was again visited, this time by Mr Michael Alexander—who likewise was unable to stay there long. He was however able to climb rather farther up the interior of the minaret and discovered that it contained two spiral staircases. Noticing traces of buildings on the other banks, he made a crossing of the swollen river, but was unable to take a camera. However he was able to identify a number of ruins: the mouths of two sewers; the remnants of a mosque with a circular dome; a large water cistern; walls and towers climbing up the hill-side; and a number of fragments of glazed pre-Mongol pottery lying on the surface. The evidence that this is indeed Firuzkoh appeared to be mounting; and it is to be hoped that a Cambridge expedition which planned to visit the site and spend some time there, is able to establish the point once and for all.

CHAPTER TWENTY-TWO

INDIA AND SOUTH-EAST ASIA

IN INDIA archaeology thrives. The seeds that were sown and cultivated by Sir John Marshall and Sir Mortimer Wheeler have proliferated like the Indian jungle. It has been said, on good authority, that there is at present more archaeological activity in India than anywhere else in the world—but hardly any of it has been published. Excavators dig like terriers; and one excavation completed, are hard at work on a new dig; and all that emerges for the time being is voluminous excavator's notes, a lecture or so and a number of unrelated stories in newspapers in several languages.

This is perhaps an exaggeration, but not by very much; and it is a regrettable necessity that at this stage in time and in this volume at least it is quite impossible to give any summary of this remarkable activity; to attempt to do it would be worse than unsatisfactory, it would be utterly ridiculous.

There are two particularly teasing problems in the Indian past: what were the origins of the Indus Valley civilization? and what happened in that dark age between the end of the Indus Valley civilization somewhere about 1500 B.C. and the arrival of Alexander the Great in the fourth century B.C.? The answer to the first question would seem to lie perhaps rather in Pakistan and Afghanistan on the assumption that, as in Mesopotamia, the origins of a great riverine agricultural urban civilization are to be found in the foothills around the river's origins. But to the second question, some answers are perhaps to be found in excavations at Hastinapura on the Ganges, north-east of Delhi, and at Navda Toli on the River Narbada in Central India.

Hastinapura is a large city mound, rising some 50 ft above the general level and standing about five miles from the Ganges, which was, however, much nearer in ancient times. In 1951 excavations were carried out there by the Excavations Department of the Archaeological Survey of India under its superintendent, Mr B. B. Lal; and these excavations took the form of three trenches cut across the mound to a depth of 30–35 ft reaching the natural soil; and the results of all three were consistent. Four principal levels of occupation were discovered, of which the two earliest were the most interesting.

The first level, which was 8–10 ft deep, was characterized by wheel-turned bowls and dishes of Painted Grey Ware, in which the designs, which are usually in black, include simple lines, groups of vertical, oblique or criss-cross lines, chains of simple spirals and such simple motifs as concentric circles and swastikas; and these are found both inside and outside the vessels. The houses which were poorly preserved seem to have been of mud-brick associated perhaps with bamboo or timber. A few fragments of copper were found and iron was absent. No inscriptions were found, but a number of bone styluses suggest that some sort of writing was practised. This period seems to have begun about 1000 B.C. and to have been ended by a disastrous flood. Indeed a great deal of this layer was obviously completely eroded by water; and fragments of pottery of this same kind have been recovered from the bed of the Ganges, whither they were presumably carried by the floods many hundred years ago.

After this civilization (which is called Hastinapura I) the site seems to have been abandoned for some time, but was later reoccupied by a people who did not use the Painted Grey Ware, but what is known as the Northern Black Polished Ware, which is of a metallic quality, with a jet-black or steel-blue colour and a mirror-like surface. Their houses were well built of baked or mud bricks; and they paid considerable care to drainage. There were for example brick-built drains; separate house drainage consisting of soakaways formed of perforated pottery vessels set vertically one within the other; and there were also wells or deep drainage pits in that fine and remarkable Indian technique, whereby terracotta rings with a diameter of about two feet, are set one within each other, thus making a water-tight pit to any required depth. During this occupation iron was known and a system of coinage, the coins being oblong or square pieces of beaten silver or copper bearing punched designs. Cylindrical weights of stone are also found. This culture, Hastinapura II, came to an end in a great fire, which destroyed nearly all the settlement.

Hastinapura III can be fairly accurately dated from the first levels of the early second century B.C. (with Sunga and Mitra coins) to the end of the reign of King Vasudeva of the Kushan dynasty in the second century A.D.

After a long period of desolation, a low-grade settlement (Hastinapura IV) came into being about the eleventh century A.D. and this lasted until about the middle of the thirteenth century when Hastinapura seems to have been finally abandoned.

Now Hastinapura III and IV seem to be securely dated by coins; and Hastinapura I seems to have begun about 1000 B.C. When did it end and what was the duration of Hastinapura II? The evidence is circumstantial and derives from comparisons with another site (Kausambi) where the Northern Black Polished Ware and punch-marked coins are found and which the Buddha visited about 500 B.C. when King Udayana was reigning. The beginnings of Kausambi are at least as old as the sixth century B.C.; and it seems probable therefore that Hastinapura II dates from the sixth century B.C. to some date before the beginning of the second century B.C. And moreover since Hastinapura I ended in disaster by flood, and since there was a gap of time before the reoccupation of the site, the general bracket for this first occupation seems to be the eleventh century to the seventh century B.C.

Moreover Hastinapura and other sites in the Upper Ganges and Ghaggar basins are associated in literature with the epic story of the Mahabharata,

Hastinapura for example, being the capital of the Kaurava kings, the dispute over whose throne led to the great battle of Kurukshetra. The dating of the events of the epic is disputed but a conservative estimate puts them in the tenth century B.C.; and it may be that when archaeology and literature have come to terms, the makers of the Painted Grey Ware may turn out to be the peoples of the Mahabharata epic.

The Excavations at Navda Toli likewise throw light on the "Aryan gap". Navda Toli is a mound on the southern bank of the River Narbada and lies over against Maheshwar. This point in ancient times was a ferry over the river and seems to have been an arterial crossing from the northern plains to the Deccan. In recent years this Navda Toli mound has been investigated by Dr H. D. Sankalia (Director of the Deccan Postgraduate Research Institute, Poona), Dr B. Subbarao and others. The upper levels were marked by the presence of the Northern Black Polished Ware, which is found in Hastinapura II, and which is characteristic of the Early Iron Age of the Ganges plain and dates forward from about 500 B.C.

Below this level however were four successive occupations of villagers who evidently imported some copper—a number of flat copper axes were found—but who continued to use small tools of the local chalcedony. They were cultivators, and seeds of wheat, rice, lentils, peas and beans have all been found, growing more abundant as time passed. They had square or round houses with walls of close-set posts and their floors were smoothed and hardened with a plastering of lime which was sometimes continued up the daubed walls. A great quantity of interesting pottery has been found. Some of it, large plates and storage jars, is unpainted but decorated either with incised motifs or with appliqué reliefs, animal or human, the latter including a pleasing naturalistic female figure, the former a lively swinging monkey. Of the painted ware, the earliest and rarest is greyish-black painted externally with white. The early and middle levels yield also pottery painted in black on a white or cream surface; and in the uppermost level before the Iron Age is a common black on red pottery. In this last are a number of spouted vessels, rather like teapots or feeding vessels of a type found at Sialk, Hissar and other sites in Iran where they are ascribed to the centuries immediately following 1000 B.C. The painted pottery of this level is very lively, with a great variety of motifs painted on a white or cream slip. They include peacocks and a number of goat-like creatures, simplified in various ways; rather stick-like human figures, sometimes in continuous friezes and perhaps representing dancers, sometimes accompanied with the goat motif; and a few examples of a shock-headed human being, sometimes holding a stick or spear—and there is a suggestion that this may be a prototype of the great god Siva.

There are also some pottery shapes which seem to be Iranian in origin, notably a round-bellied vase with a narrow neck and a wide funnel mouth—in Iran this vessel usually has a tripod stand—and a large number of cups and dishes-on-stand.

All these last therefore, although found in Central India, are parallels with things found in Central Iran; and there seem to be no intermediate links between them. Presumably they will be found however and some logic of the Aryan cultural and linguistic invasion of India may become apparent.

Two of the most interesting post-war activities of the Archaeological Department of Ceylon have been recovery and restoration—one might almost call it excavation from the jungle—of two virtually lost marvels: Mandalagiri Vihara and Sigiri. Both these operations have been under the direction of Dr S. Paranavitana.

Mandalagiri Vihara was for centuries a place of the greatest holiness and its history begins, it seems, in the second century B.C., from various incised bricks found there; it is mentioned in literature from about the second century A.D.; its most notable monument, the Circular Shrine, was built in the seventh century; and the monastic establishment was flourishing in the ninth and tenth centuries; and it featured in the wars of the great twelfth century king, Parakramabahu I. Thereafter it declined and for some five or six centuries it has been losing itself in the jungle, the site, today called Madirigiri, standing some fourteen miles from the nearest road and 6 miles from the nearest habitation; and consisting of two principal monuments, the House of the Images looking like a tumble of menhirs and the Circular Shrine like a Ceylonese Stonehenge—a rather modish one, to be true—before the operations started.

The Circular Shrine, as already stated, was known to date from the seventh century A.D.; but during the restoration discreet excavations were made and it was discovered that the *stupa* which it enclosed was built about the second century B.C. and originally stood open to the sky on a rectangular platform, whose retaining walls were later buried below the pavement of the Circular Shrine. This shrine was built up from a rock and the circular retaining walls which constitute its extreme measurement are about 286 ft in circumference and some 17 ft high, this platform being approached on one side by an impressive monumental stair. On the platform and surrounding the *stupa* are three concentric rows of slender monolithic pillars, octagonal in section with massive typically Sinhalese capitals. In all there are seventy-eight pillars, the inner circle being 17 ft high, the outer 9 ft; and it seems clear that they originally supported a domed roof of wood—of which, naturally, no trace remains. The outermost pillars are linked by a low screen wall of stone simulating railings.

Not far away the House of the Images was also cleared and restored. This is a rectangular building, which is dated by the bricks of which its base is composed to the third or fourth century A.D. Its architecture is simple, consisting of a number of squared monolithic pillars which must have supported a roof. Its glory rests in its images, five standing Buddhas of limestone, three of them being of colossal size. These were in fragments but have now been restored and are massive and impressive figures standing on lotus pedestals. Under each statue pedestal was a stone receptacle containing twenty-five square holes and covered with a stone slab. Presumably each hole originally contained a deposit; most of these have disappeared but a few copper objects were found, including a tiny figure of a deity, a swastika on a pedestal, a wheel on a pedestal and two objects which may be standards, one of them flanked with fishes. Under the stone receptacle under the central Buddha was a brick-lined pit in which lay a single object—a conch shell, part of the widest whorl being cut away so that the shell could be used for a vessel. Now traditionally the ancient kings of Ceylon were consecrated with water poured over them from a right-handed conch shell. Now, the shell discovered is not a right-handed one, but the circumstances of its deposition are so impressive that it is easy to believe that it was used for some ancient and important lustral rite before being deposited deep below the central image in so important and holy a shrine.

Since 1947 somewhat similar operations have been carried out, also under the direction of Dr Paranavitana, on and around the lion rock of Sigiri in Central Ceylon. This lion rock is an immense mass of granite rising precipitously some 600 ft from the surrounding jungle to a full 1,193 ft above sea level. According to the Sinhalese chronicles this rock was fortified by King Kassapa I, who ascended the throne after arranging the murder of his father and attempting that of his brother and who presumably therefore preferred to rule from the top of an inaccessible and impregnable rock. When in later years however the brother returned with an army, Kassapa made no attempt to defend the rock and indeed descended to the plain, and when the battle went against him committed suicide in front of the contending hosts.

When Sigiri is considered rationally it is clear that it was never intended as a stronghold. The summit, which has an area of about three acres, is for the most part laid out with walled gardens, cisterns, an ornamental pond and only two dwelling places. The footpaths cut into the side of the rock and leading to the summit are elaborate and decorative, plastered with polished plaster and adorned in one part to a height of 40 ft with wall paintings of profusely jewelled female figures—*apsaras*—floating among clouds. At one point this approach is cut through the gigantic figure of a lion; and at the base of the rock are a number of huge fantastic boulders, which at the time of the rock's occupation were crowned with various ornamental structures, and among them are a number of caves which six centuries earlier were occupied by Buddhist priests. It is clear in fact that Kassapa built and adapted Sigiri in a spirit of megalomania, seeing himself as Kuvera, the Indian god of wealth who had his paradise, called Alakamanda, on top of the peak called Kailasa; in the same spirit, in fact that Kubla Khan built his "stately pleasure-dome" at Xanadu, where

'twice five miles of fertile ground
With walls and towers were girdled round:
And there were gardens bright with sinuous rills
Where blossomed many an incense-bearing tree;
And here were forests ancient as the hills,
Enfolding sunny spots of greenery.'

And with the clearing and restoration which began in 1947 the resemblances to Xanadu have become even more striking; because a great deal of the level ground at the foot of the rock has been cleared of jungle and it has become apparent that in the time of its glory Sigiri rose from a complex of water-gardens, pavilions and trees. Most of the clearing has been done on the western side where the city wall and a most impressive moat, 80 ft broad and averaging about 14 ft deep, have been restored. In the centre of this stretch of moat it seems that there must have been a drawbridge and this drawbridge led to a walled enclosure, a quadrilateral 660 × 390 ft. In the centre of this was a large square tank, with four causeways leading to a central island 75 ft square and carrying a pavilion on a raised platform. On either side of this enclosure were other enclosures with pavilions and gardens, and small cisterns of water. Leading from this complex to the foot of the rock between two symmetrical kidney-shaped lakes was a long walled enclosure with channels of water, some of them "sinuous rills" and connected one with each other by underground conduits. All these waterways and tanks are brick-walled but floored with limestone and the effect of these gardens, especially as seen looking down from the rock, bright with trees and flowers, sparkling with water and gay with elaborately painted and gilded pavilions of wood, must have been that of an earthly paradise, an excess of *hubris* which invited the fate which befell Kassapa and accounted for the fact that Sigiri was never again occupied.

Southwards and eastwards in Asia political disturbances of many kinds have not produced an atmosphere encouraging to a humanist art and science like archaeology; and—to reverse Cicero's favourite quotation (from his own works) —the toga of the archaeologist has had in many places to yield to the arms of the terrorist. In one odd case however it might almost be claimed that terrorism was a contributing factor to an outstanding discovery—in Kelantan.

Now Malaya was inhabited from Pleistocene times to about the beginning of the Christian era by men of successive Stone Age cultures, who occupied the innumerable caves and rock shelters with which the limestone of northern and central Malaya is riddled. Unfortunately for the archaeologist these caves were also occupied—indeed still are—by innumerable bats. The resultant guano is a valuable fertilizer; and as a result all the caves have been regularly cleared out (or despoiled) ever since the value of guano was realized; and with the guano have gone the remains of Stone Age Man. However untouched rock shelters do still exist in the virgin jungles among the limestone hills of Pahang and Kelantan—an area inhabited by the primitive Temiar aborigines and infested, in 1954, by bands of terrorists. Towards the headwaters of the River Nenggiri at Gua Cha, there was just such a rock-shelter and, fortunately, just across the river from it, a police post. As a result Mr and Mrs G. de G. Sieveking of the National Museum, Kuala Lumpur, and Mr M. W. F. Tweedie were able to maintain a six-weeks' expedition there, with a police escort and headquarters inside the barbed-wire perimeter, and to train a labour force of Temiar aborigines, who did nearly all the work.

This proved a very rewarding excavation. Over 2,400 sq ft of undisturbed deposit was removed and a 30-ft square sounding was taken down to bedrock which for the first time in Malaya gave a clearly stratified succession of Stone Age industries. In the lowest areas were the plentiful remains of a Mesolithic culture of a type first recognized in Tonking and called after the site Hoabinhian. These were a primitive hunting and food-gathering people with simple tools made by flaking river pebbles, which look like inferior Acheulean hand-axes. Bones of this period were very well preserved at this site; and although some of the human bones were dispersed and there is a suspicion of cannibalism, some individual burials were found, with the skeletons in the contracted or foetal position. These Hoabinhians were evidently large, mostly over 5 ft 6 in, with large skulls and powerful limb-bones.

Their Neolithic successors were entirely different: small, fine-boned, never over 5 ft tall and indeed not unlike the Temiar aborigines of today who were assisting in the excavation. Their dead were buried fully extended and their burials were marked by a profusion of grave goods, pottery, beautiful stone tools and stone and shell ornaments. The stone tools are usually adzes or chisels, bevelled with great precision and beautifully polished and in a variety of sizes down to the diminutive; and there also occur stone bark-cloth beaters, rather like massive stamp seals, with the flat face cross-hatched. From the position in which these are found in some burials, it looks as though these beaters were suspended round the waist. The pottery comes in a number of shapes and types. There are shallow rounded-bottom bowls, bag-shaped bowls, footed dishes and bowls, a bucket-shaped vessel with holes in the rim for suspending it, a bulbed vase with flaring mouth and pot-stands for the round-bottomed vessels. The ornament is sometimes simple cord-impression, but incised patterns, chevrons and spirals, are also found. There are also shell pendants and mussel-shells which may have been used as spoons; and this is the more remarkable as Gua Cha is a long way from the sea. The most impressive objects, however, are the stone bracelets, in as much as they are beautiful objects in themselves and also as representing hours of skilled industry devoted to a non-utilitarian purpose. Some of them are made of limestone, some of jadeite, they are exactly symmetrical, they are well polished and some of them are of a curious flanged shape resembling certain Pi bracelets of polished jade known from the Chinese prehistoric period. These Neolithic agriculturalists of Gua Cha had no knowledge of bronze or iron, yet some of their pottery shows a metallic inspiration and there are other indications that they may represent the very end of an ancient cultural tradition from the Far East.

Gua Cha is indeed a striking and important excavation; but some of the most valuable work which has been done by the Malayan and Singapore museums lies in the steady training of local archaeologists and the laying of foundations for native antiquities departments which play so essential a part in linking new nations with the past and establishing and as it were asserting the brotherhood of man both in time and space.

In Sarawak operations on a large scale are being conducted by the Sarawak Museum under Mr Tom Harrisson in a cave site in the Subis Mountain near Niah on the west coast of Borneo. This site is a vast network of dry cathedral-like caves inhabited by thousands of bats and those swiftlets whose nests are the source of the Chinese delicacy "bird's nest soup"; and this network is extremely inaccessible, being approached, first by a boardwalk causeway in swampy jungle and next by a tree ladder up a cliff face. As a result of its inaccessibility, the cave system has not been disturbed by the larger mammals, and the strata of innumerable cultures going back to something like 30,000 B.C. can be found over very wide areas—the known floor of the main cave alone being 26 acres; and as a result of its dryness and of its lying well above flood level since Pleistocene times, the remains which are found in these levels have been astonishingly well preserved, even including fabrics of great delicacy and going back in time to man's earliest use of weaving in these parts. A whole history of mankind has been preserved here; and the vast task of unearthing and codifying it has now been begun.

CHAPTER TWENTY-THREE

EGYPT

According to the historian Manetho, who was an Egyptian priest writing in Greek in the third century B.C. the kings of the First Dynasty of Egypt were: (1) Nama (who reigned in about 3100 B.C.); (2) Aha; (3) Zer; (4) Uadji; (5) Udimu; (6) Anezib; (7) Semerkhet and (8) Ka'a. And Manetho says that the dynasty lasted 253 years but nowadays this is generally thought to be an over-estimate.

A great deal of light has been thrown on these distant and somewhat shadowy monarchs by post-war excavations near Helwan-les-Bains (by Zaki Y Saad Effendi) and in the Archaic Necropolis at Sakkara (by Professor Emery).

The excavations about five miles from Helwan-les-Bains, on a site which during the course of the work was discovered to have been Heliopolis Un, took place on what was royal property and the work was indeed financed and en- couraged by King Farouk. It began in 1942 and continued for a number of years and more than 5,000 tombs of various sizes, all dating from the First and Second Dynasties, were investigated. The most interesting of these tombs was that of an official of King Anezib, the sixth king of the First Dynasty, the name of the official unfortunately being completely illegible; and the remarkable thing about this tomb was the fact that its floor was paved with limestone and its walls were lined with erect limestone slabs. Previously the use of stone in burial chambers as early as this had only been found in the grave of a First Dynasty king (which had a granite floor) and in that of a Second Dynasty king (which had a white limestone burial chamber). But at Helwan the stone-lined tombs are those of officials of the First Dynasty; and it is established that this architectural use was already spreading a good 5,000 years ago.

Among the objects found in these tombs was a large number of large and beautiful flint knives. These were generally of the same type as the famous and beautiful flint knife of the Pitt-Rivers Museum (with its ivory handle carved with innumerable animals) which was recently restored in the British Museum laboratories and exhibited in London for a while in 1955–6. Certainly the Helwan knives can boast no ivory handles, but whereas the blade of the Pitt-Rivers knife was about 19.5 cm long, the largest of the Helwan blades was about 50 cm long (the longest ever found) and there were two others of 48 and 45 cm. Like the Pitt-Rivers blade they were flaked on one side and polished on the other and of beautiful workmanship.

Another object of great interest is a piece of ivory, nearly $1\frac{1}{2}$ ft long in the form of a bundle of lotus buds, with their stalks, tied together. In all it represents eight such buds and stalks, seven of them tied round a central one, the buds together approximating to the capital of a pillar very like the lotus pillars which were to appear in many temples in later periods. The tieing-together of the buds is represented as a rope wrapping just below the buds, very skilfully executed.

The most important work, however, done in this field has been the series of excavations in the Archaic cemetery at North Sakkara directed by Professor W. B. Emery and conducted by the Egypt Exploration Society, working on behalf of the Egyptian Antiquities Service; and these excavations are really a continuation of those conducted by Professor Emery before the war.

In 1953 this expedition working near the site of the tomb of Queen Merneith, which had been discovered in 1946, discovered a crenellated wall of plastered mud-brick. This led to the discovery of a huge tomb, full of examples of the name Uadji, the fourth king of the First Dynasty and in view of the size of the tomb it seems certain that it was the tomb of the Pharaoh himself.

Since it has proved possible to discover pretty exactly what this tomb looked like and since it is the first of four of the same general style which Professor Emery found, it is perhaps worth while describing with some detail the pristine appearance of the tomb.

In the first place it was enormous, the superstructure being a mass of mud-brick about 55¾ yds long by 23 yds wide—about a quarter of a large football field—and it originally stood rather more than 39 ft above ground. The whole of the exterior façades was a succession of redans, i.e. panelled buttresses and re-entrants, rising from a continuous bench running round the foot of the whole of this exterior. On this bench were modelled a series of bulls' heads in sun-dried clay; and in these heads real horns were inserted. (Many of these heads still survive in perfect condition.) The panelling of the walls behind these heads was faced with mud plaster covered with a gypsum stucco and a white limewash, which in turn formed the background for elaborate painted decorations in red, green, yellow and other colours. All round the building ran a plastered corridor, painted green and this in its turn was surrounded by a low enclosure wall, plastered and painted white. Outside this enclosure wall on three sides of the tomb were regular single lines of small identical tombs with rounded tops, sixty-two in all, containing the bodies of the servants who had been killed to accompany their master, the king, into the next world. Nearly all of them were young men, but eight were young women and one was a dwarf with a normally sized torso and small malformed legs—a jester perhaps, a Yorick of 5,000 years ago. In none of these bodies was there any sign of violence and most probably they had died from the administration of poison.

The tomb itself contained above ground forty-five rectangular magazines, packed with supplies and objects for the dead man's use in the next world; and beneath these was a substructure consisting of a large central burial chamber, four subsidiary rooms and sixteen subterranean magazines. The whole building then, despite its painted panels and bull's head frieze was a severely functional building, a slab of brickwork, a sort of bunker, something not unlike a safe deposit building. And that indeed was presumably the intention.

The intention but not the achievement. When the excavators began on it they discovered that all the interior walls were riddled with the tunnels of tomb-robbers and that the whole was like a gigantic Gruyère cheese. Egyptian tomb robbers are an incredibly skilful, determined and ruthless guild of great anti-quity. The tomb of Uadji was robbed while his dynasty was still reigning and probably within a few years of his death. The robbers, as was their usual custom, set fire to the tomb chamber after robbing it; and the slow kiln-like fire caused great destruction and, owing probably to the large size of the tomb chamber, caused the collapse of the central roof of the superstructure. At all events the central burial chamber was rebuilt and remodelled during the reign and probably at the instance of King Ka'a, the last Pharaoh of this dynasty and some of the magazines were refilled with goods bearing his name. It is hardly necessary to add that this rebuilt chamber was likewise robbed in its turn.

Despite these various plunderings, great quantities of objects were found, principally in the magazines. Over 1,000 stone vessels (mostly broken) of alabaster, diorite, schist, crystal and basalt were found and over 3,000 pottery vessels of various types. These last were mainly originally filled with foodstuffs, and packed with them in the magazines were large joints of beef. Many of the jars were sealed and stamped with the seal of the Pharaoh Uadji; and others, in the magazines which were restocked in the restoration of the tomb, with the seal of the Pharaoh Ka'a. A number of gaming pieces, in sets, were found, made from ivory. These include pieces rather like the castles of chess, spheres, crouch-ing lions, tiny balls which may have been counters, and sticks which may have served the same purpose as dice. A box to hold a set of such pieces, made from wood, was found almost perfectly preserved; and also stubby bull's feet in ivory, which probably supported the gaming board. Other miracles of pre-servation were several leather soles of sandals, part of a leather quiver in which the painted decoration is fragile but not the leather, and a number of woven reed baskets still containing the cereals with which they were filled to stock the tomb 5,000 years ago.

In 1954, immediately south of the Uadji tomb, another even larger complex was investigated. This covered an area, 65.5×38 m, consisting of two brick-built and parallel enclosure walls enclosing a funerary temple and a mastaba-like tomb. This tomb superstructure (36×24.5 m), like that of Uadji, was brick-built and rose from a step decorated with clay bull's heads and had the same elaborately panelled façade on three sides, the fourth side being of a much simplified pattern of panelling. These sides had originally risen to about 27 ft and were faced with white lime stucco on which were still preserved consider-able areas of fresco in geometrical patterns imitating matwork and carried out in red, white, black, blue, green and yellow. When excavated this mass was discovered to consist of brick walls some 16 ft thick, the central rectangle consisting of rubble filling; and the whole superstructure was discovered to overlie a large underground rock-cut burial chamber, reached by a dog-legged rock-cut passage, which started in the corridor outside the superstructure and descended beneath at a continuous slope. As it passed under the brick and rubble mass it gave admittance also to two magazines, one on either side; and these were the only two magazines in the whole tomb. The burial chamber had originally been roofed over with wood—and the holes for the beams still survive—and the whole interior (and the magazines likewise) had been completely destroyed by fire, although traces of a large wooden sarcophagus do survive. There are no subsidiary slave burials in the precincts of this tomb; but in the corridor, near the underground passage, is a single stone-lined tomb (which had been rifled) containing the bones of a middle-aged man and a comparatively crude *stela* about $4\frac{1}{4}$ ft long, whose inscription identifies it with a nobleman called Mer-Ka "a Count, a Sem Priest, a Priest of Neith, etc".

Now the main tomb provided many imprints of the seals of the Pharaoh Ka'a (the last king of the First Dynasty) and the question arises: is the tomb that of Ka'a himself, or of the nobleman Mer-Ka, the little tomb in the corridor being that of a servant of Mer-Ka? But the crudity of the *stela* argues against this. The whole tomb and its precincts are so rich and elaborate that they are not consistent with its occupant's having so crude a *stela*; and the probability is that the tomb is that of the Pharaoh Ka'a and the subsidiary tomb that of Mer-Ka, a nobleman who had been awarded the privilege of being buried within the precincts of his master's tomb.

The terrible damage done to the tomb by fire has raised an interesting point. All the great tombs of the First Dynasty have been robbed and burnt; those of the Second Dynasty have been robbed but not burnt. It has been usually thought that the burning was done by the robbers to cover their traces, but it is also suggested that it was officials of the Second Dynasty who arranged the burning in order to obliterate the glories of the preceding Dynasty. This would be a satisfactory explanation but for the fact that the tomb of Uadji was fired during the course of the First Dynasty, as is proved by the fact that the Pharaoh Ka'a restored it; and surely the fact that the tombs of the Second Dynasty were not burnt can be explained on the basis that the "guild of tomb-robbers" had given up firing tombs since they had discovered that far from covering their tracks the firing gave notice that the tomb had been robbed—as is also proved by the fact that the last king of the dynasty had had to restore the tomb of his ancestor Uadji.

Strangely enough the next two Royal tombs to be excavated at Sakkara by Professor Emery had neither of them been burnt, though both had been extensively plundered; and both belong to the reign of Udimu, the fifth Pharaoh of the dynasty and the successor of Uadji.

The first of these was excavated in the winter of 1954–5 and it presented a number of new architectural features together with the oldest substantially intact funerary boat yet found. This last was exceptionally interesting since it was only a few months previously that an intact funerary boat, but of somewhat later date, was found beside the Great Pyramid of Cheops—and this discovery will be described a little later in this chapter (Plate 51*a*).

Superficially the tomb resembled those previously found. It consisted of a very large enclosure measuring 65 ×27 m. More than three-quarters of this area was taken up by a brick-built mastaba, 37 m long and 20 m wide. All round this ran a plastered corridor and at the foot of the panelled sides was a step decorated with clay bull's head decoration. In the corridor on the east and north sides were ten slave burials, attendants killed to accompany their master into the next world. So far the tomb is reasonably like the others. On excavation, however, it proved very different. Inside the mass and below ground level was a great rectangular rock-cut pit 14 ×9 m, approached by a stair which descended from the entrance to the enclosure down through a limestone doorway. All around this pit was a sort of shelf or triforium just below ground level, and this triforium was flanked by buttressed walls of brick. This shelf could be approached either from the main stairway or from a little stair which led to it from ground level. The floor and walls of the pit were covered with white plaster, as was the pavement of the triforium and the access stairways, while the buttressed walls were painted yellow. At this stage the whole building was open to the upper air; and it is presumed that while in this form the pit was used for some purpose or ceremonies connected in some way with its eventual destiny.

At all events, before it was used as a tomb, it was drastically remodelled. The floor of the triforium was raised with brickwork, in which were embedded the great wooden beams and planks which roofed over the entire pit and the triforium itself was divided up by short walls into a series of small magazines for funerary offerings and these magazines were roofed over with wood at floor level, while the small stair leading to the triforium was bricked up. Meanwhile the size of the pit was much reduced by the building of deeply recessed brick walls against the original plastered rock sides; the plastered rock floor was covered with a wooden floor, on which rested a wooden construction containing the burial; and the whole thing was roofed over and covered with the huge rubble and brick superstructure of the mastaba.

This pit had of course been robbed many times and it is not possible to reconstruct the burial installation. Among the remains were flint knives, ivory arrowheads, fragments of ivory-inlaid furniture, copper tools, many stone vessels of schist, alabaster, marble and the like, and much pottery, including ware which seems to have been imported, perhaps from North Syria. Many of the wine vessels bore the seals of King Udimu and also the names of principal officials named Hemaka, Ankhka, Medjedka and Mesenka. It would seem that these last sealed the funerary goods in some official capacity; and the fact that such important noblemen (their names being known from other tombs in the Archaic necropolis) had taken part in the ceremonial argues that this is most likely the tomb of Pharaoh Udimu himself, or, at the very least, of someone very close to him.

In the other part of the great enclosure, at the northern end of the mastaba and parallel with its shorter side, was a long shallow pit and in this had been set a funerary boat of white plastered wood, about $47\frac{1}{2}$ ft long. The boat had a central cabin and contained a number of pottery vessels which perhaps contained food and drink for the dead man during his voyage with the celestial gods in the after-life.

In the following season, during the winter months of 1955–6, Professor Emery excavated another royal tomb of the reign of King Udimu, that of a Queen Her-Neit who died in that reign. The superstructure of this tomb, which lies about 50 yds south of the previous one, resembles the others very closely—from the outside. It is a very large rectangle, 127×56 ft, with an enclosure wall in some parts preserved to its original height of $4\frac{1}{2}$ ft and pierced by one gateway in the long east side. The walls are of the usual panelled pattern rising from a step decorated with clay bull's heads (of which a few survive). The east façade was exceptionally well preserved, rising in some parts still to more than 8 ft and retaining much of the original painted decoration in red and pale yellow. The corridor between the façade and the enclosure wall was plastered and painted green. Indeed the state of preservation was such that the Egyptian Government Service of Antiquities announced its intention of restoring part of the walls to their original height and roofing over the east corridor to preserve it as a monument.

The interior of this brick-built superstructure or mastaba appeared also to be like the others, being divided up into about thirty rectangular magazines filled with funerary goods.

But beneath all this was something entirely different: a deep rectangular pit cut 14 ft down into the rock, divided into an upper and a lower chamber and covered over with a brick-domed square tumulus. Now this burial pit is like the burial pits of the archaic kings which had been discovered at Abydos by Petrie and Amelineau in the nineteenth century—although these lacked the domed brick tumulus, which had evidently been destroyed; and so this tomb of Queen Her-Neit combines the burial pit of Upper Egypt with the panelled mastaba of Lower Egypt.

The pit itself is interesting. It has a stairway leading down the north side and the lower chamber, which was the scene of the burial, was divided from the upper with a stone and timber ceiling, the stone part of which rested on a stone lintel carved with a design of crouching lions, the earliest known example of architectural sculpture in Egypt. The tomb had been thoroughly plundered, but not burnt, and traces of a large wooden sarcophagus still remained together with the scattered bones of the queen. Of the funeral goods which had survived the robbers the most interesting were a necklace of gold and carnelian beads (rare for this period) some perfectly simple but exquisitely delicate rock crystal saucer-like dishes and the queen's drinking vessel, a trumpet-shaped vessel of dark schist with a pink limestone foot.

There are no burials of slaves or attendants associated with this tomb, but near the entrance was buried the queen's pet dog, the curled-up skeleton of a Saluki-like animal, destined, no doubt, to be his mistress's sole companion into the next world.

There are still a number of unexplored tombs in this Archaic necropolis, but the political troubles of 1956 and after put an end to this series of excavations; and Professor Emery's activities were transferred to the Sudan, as will appear in a later chapter.

Meanwhile, also at Sakkara, and indeed within sight of Professor Emery's diggings, the extraordinary drama of a hitherto unknown second Step Pyramid was being played out.

During the autumn of 1951, the late Dr Zakaria Goneim, one of the best known and respected Egyptian Egyptologists of this generation, had been making some trial pits near the Pyramid of Unas at Sakkara and hit on a vast artificial terrace and eventually the massive remains of a panelled limestone wall very like the enclosure wall of the Step Pyramid of Zoser. This wall, of which a very considerable length was found in excellent condition standing to a height of over 10 ft, had never been completed, as the bed of the uppermost course had never been levelled in preparation for the next course. Furthermore while this wall was extremely like that of Zoser's enclosure, the blocks were larger and the limestone had been used much more thriftily in the casing—the building technique was in fact more advanced—and this enclosure wall was almost certainly later than Zoser and might perhaps be ascribed to his successor, Sanakht.

The construction of the enclosure seems to have been subject to alteration and addition and the situation is complicated by the fact that at some later date it was used as a quarry for dressed stone. Nevertheless it was discovered to be of great size, having a north-south axis of 601 yds and an east-west axis of 186 yds. (The dimensions of the enclosure surrounding the Step Pyramid of Zoser are 597 yds from north to south and 304 yds from east to west.) What was the central edifice in this huge quadrilateral? A trial pit was sunk in the geometrical centre and in 1952 Dr Goneim found the characteristic walls of a stepped pyramid, which had been discontinued when it reached a height of between 26 and 29 ft above ground level. Here then was a unique discovery, a second Step Pyramid, later than that of Zoser, which had never been completed. But the fact that it had never been completed did not necessarily mean that the burial had not taken place. Wars, political troubles and the like could have interrupted the completion of the monument; and indeed it was conceivable that this truncated mass could contain an indisturbed royal burial.

Work went on and by the early part of 1954 it was reported that the approach to the tomb had been discovered, and it was established that the pyramid was not Sanakht's, but Sekhem-Khet's. By 1 June an entrance to an untouched royal tomb was reached and some thousands of stone and alabaster bowls were found in the store-rooms near the central chamber. On 3 June Dr Goneim

crawled into the burial chamber and found therein an intact alabaster sarcophagus. On 7 June Dr Mustapha Amar, Director-General of the Department
of Antiquities confirmed the discovery and gave the dimensions of the sarco-
phagus as 7 ft $9\frac{1}{4}$ in long, 3 ft $8\frac{7}{8}$ in broad and 3 ft $6\frac{1}{2}$ in high. Furthermore it was
described as being unique in having a sliding panel at one end instead of a lid.
Photographs showed the sarcophagus lying among tumbled blocks of stone in
a chamber whose walls were unfinished and completely unadorned. On
9 June it was announced that a box of jewellery, including gold and precious
stones had been found outside the chamber. A few days later the sarcophagus
was ceremonially opened and found to contain—nothing.

The acute disappointment of this event was however modified by a most
important and indeed for a time unique discovery made at about the same time.
During May of the same year work was in hand which consisted of clearing
ground immediately to the south of the Great Pyramid of Cheops to allow the
free movement of visitors; and this work had been entrusted to Zaki Nour, one
of the departmental directors, with Kamal el-Malakh in charge of works. While
a wall parallel with the face of the pyramid was being cleared two rows of
massive limestone blocks were revealed in the ground, one consisting of forty-
one blocks, the other of forty-two, and each block was estimated as being of
about 18–20 tons' weight. One block was bored and photographs were taken
which revealed that the blocks covered a rock-cut trough and that lying in this
trough was a virtually intact funerary boat. This was a discovery of the utmost
importance. Troughs to contain funerary boats were of course already known:
there are three in front of the Great Pyramid; and five beside the Pyramid of
Cephren. But all of these were empty; and indeed until a little less than a year
later when Professor Emery (as reported earlier in this chapter) found a funerary
boat in the Sakkara tomb which is almost certainly that of the Pharaoh Udimu,
this funerary boat of Cheops was absolutely unique; and as it transpired later,
although Udimu's boat is several centuries earlier, that of Cheops was far better
preserved.

It was decided to uncover one trough, leaving the other (which, it was presumed, also contained an intact funerary boat) untouched for the present; and
it was also announced that a permanent museum would be built on the spot to
house both boats when they had been lifted and restored; and a large temporary
working shelter was erected over the trough which had already been pierced.

From the first glimpses into the trough it was established that the boat was
rather more than 115 ft long and about 10 ft wide, that it was covered over with
a number of deckboards on which lay the remains of reed-matting and beneath
which was a quantity of cordage. On top lay a long spear-shaped steering oar
and at one end, or rather to the side of one end, was a finial of the "reed-
bundle" type. The wood was stated to be mainly cedar with some acacia; and
it was announced that hieroglyphics recorded that the boat had been placed
there by the successor of Cheops, but it was not clear if this successor was named
Tet-F-Ra.

The first of the limestone blocks was lifted in November 1954; and by mid-February 1955 the great majority had been raised; and the extremely ticklish task of raising from the bottom of the pit the presumably fragile timbers of a boat nearly 5,000 years old was being planned.

By this time practically the whole length was visible and the general aspect was interesting, with some teasing features. In general shape it is a simple long slender shell. It appears that it was a little too long for the trough and that one end (with a "reed-bundle" finial) had to be cut off and tucked in at the side. It also looks as though the hull was lowered into the trough and that funerary goods (whatever they may have been) were then lowered into the hull. These were then covered over with the deck boards, in a curiously higgledy-piggledy way—they are in no particular order, they are not in alignment and, judging from the fact that the cross battens of some can be seen, some are upside down—and then presumably the whole surface was made decent and shipshape with a covering of matting. Some of those who saw the trough at this stage suggested that when the remains were lifted they would prove to be not a completed boat but rather an assortment of component parts arranged to look like a boat.

This was in 1955. At the time of writing this (summer 1959) nothing further had been published on the progress of the work—doubtless owing to the tensions of the Egyptian revolution and Near Eastern political developments—but it was rumoured that the restoration and lifting had been completed and that an American diplomat had actually seen the complete boat.

In 1947 some important work was done by Abd Essallam M. Hussein on the Bent Pyramid at Dahshur. This is a large pyramid previously attributed to Huni, a Pharaoh of the Third Dynasty who died about fifty years before the Great Pyramid of Cheops was built. Its most striking feature (and the origin of its name) lies in the fact that rather less than half way up the angle of its sides changes from 54 to 43 degrees. Beside it is a small pyramid.

Its interior had been investigated on a number of occasions since 1837 but without finding any indication of the occupant, the burial chamber, or any evidence that it had been successfully robbed. One entrance was known and one apartment, below ground level and largely blocked by masonry. During the present investigations this lower apartment was cleared and a way was forced into an upper apartment, which was likewise mainly blocked with masonry. There was evidence to show that there had been a connecting passage from the upper to the lower apartment but this was not found. The upper apartment was cleared and in its walls were found cracks which had been filled with ancient gypsum. From this it was argued that the original builder had discovered this stress while the pyramid was still being built and had therefore altered the exterior angle of the sides (thus producing the "bent" effect) with a view of reducing the weight the chamber would eventually have to bear. This upper chamber was also cleared, but no indication was found as to where a third chamber might lie. Since all the traces of the tomb robbers have now been found and since they seem to have been completely unsuccessful, it still seems likely that somewhere in all this mass of masonry there is a third chamber and that this contains the untouched burial of a Fourth Dynasty Pharaoh.

Furthermore the identity of this Pharaoh is now known. On the north-east cornerstone of the pyramid was found the Horus-name of Senefru, the first king of the Fourth Dynasty, a discovery which upset all the previous theories. In addition the entrance to the small pyramid alongside was also found and this was discovered to be that of Hetepheres, the wife of Senefru. The chamber was empty, as was to be expected, as all the grave goods were removed by Hetepheres' son Cheops, when he transferred the remains of his mother to the burial place he prepared for her beside his own pyramid, the Great Pyramid, and where they were discovered in modern times.

CHAPTER TWENTY-FOUR

SUDAN

THE SUDAN has had a long, complicated and still largely obscure history; and although it has in the past been the subject of considerable archaeological investigation, the interest has for the most part been confined to the remains of three periods: the years between say 2000 and 1700 B.C.—the Egyptian Middle Kingdom—when the northern Sudan was an Egyptian province and which ended when the Egyptians were overpowered by the Hyksos; the Egyptian New Kingdom period (1580–1100 B.C.) when Egyptian power returned to the Sudan and which was followed by the growth of the Kushite power, the Kushite kings even becoming the rulers of Egypt in the eighth and seventh centuries B.C. before they were driven out by the Assyrians in 661 B.C.; and finally the period —500 B.C. to A.D. 350—when these Kushites moved south and established the Kingdom of Meroe.

In the period after the war and before the Sudan became an independent kingdom, what was to be the new kingdom's Department of Antiquities was being developed and trained under Commissioners from Great Britain, first Mr A. J. Arkell and later Mr P. L. Shinnie; and under them the archaeology of the Sudan was extended, respectively backwards and forwards.

As a result of being confined by work during the war to Khartoum itself and to the accident of finding very near by the richest Acheulean site in the Sudan, Mr Arkell concentrated on the study of the palaeolithic inhabitants of this part of the Nile Valley, supplemented by later discoveries on the Atbara and much farther north. At the Khor Abu Anga site no fewer than 1,139 stone artifacts from pre-Chellean to Tumbian, but principally Acheulean and late Acheulean, were found and classified by Mr Arkell.

Mesolithic and Neolithic remains have also been found, notably at Early Khartoum and a picture of the Stone Age inhabitants of the Nile Valley near Khartoum has begun to emerge. In the Old Stone Age, the makers of the Acheulean hand-axes, primitive hunters, appear to have lived during a climate pretty much resembling that of today; but later, in Mesolithic times, the climate grew much wetter and the massive-headed negroes (unlike any now in the Sudan) who were the inhabitants lived by hunting and fishing in a swampy country, a prominent feature of their diet being a large water-snail, thousands of whose shells have been found. They used bows and arrows tipped with small stone crescents and fish-spears with barbed heads of bone. They seem to have done little or no cooking, but they used fire to bake pottery, mostly large brown pots decorated with patterns scratched on with the spine of the little catfish known in the Sudan as the *gargur*. They had no domesticated animals, not even dogs.

These Middle Stone Age negroes were superseded by, most probably, a brown Mediterranean-type race; and it is suggested that this change is linked with the progressive desiccation of the Sahara and that these new peoples may have come from Tibesti, to the west. It is probable also that these newcomers amalgamated with the older inhabitants but, bringing in new ideas, adapted them to existing ones. It is significant, for example, that, although they burnished their pottery, they took over the shapes and patterns of their predecessors on the site. They also were hunters and fishers but they had begun to domesticate animals —small goats, and perhaps also sheep and dogs. They made an improved type of bone harpoon and they also made fish-hooks (though without barbs) from shells. Their stone tools show a great advance and they also made bone axes, which may have been used as meat choppers. They made beads of ostrich shell and also blue beads of a stone called amazon stone, one of the two known localities for which is the northern part of the mountains of Tibesti.

At the other end of the Sudan's ancient history, the researches of Mr P. L. Shinnie, literary, historical and archaeological, have done much to sort out the history of the three Christian kingdoms which arose out of the ruins of the Meroitic power and which became Christian as the result of two missions sent out from Constantinople about A.D. 540, one orthodox or Melkite under the patronage of the Emperor Justinian and the other monophysite and supported by the Empress Theodora. The three kingdoms were Nobatia, in the north, with its capital at Faras (near Wadi Halfa); Makuria, in the centre, with Old Dongola as its capital; and, farther south, Alwah or Alodia, with Soba as its capital, near modern Khartoum. Some time round about A.D. 700 Nobatia and Makuria became one as the kingdom of Dongola; and despite the fact that the Arab conquest of Egypt in A.D. 640 had cut them off from all contact with Byzantium and Christendom, this kingdom remained Christian (monophysite) in religion, Byzantine in art and Greek continued to be used at all events until A.D. 1181. Arab penetration was resisted, indeed at two different periods the Nubian armies of Dongola successfully invaded Egypt; and Dongola maintained its religion and identity until A.D. 1323 after which it was rapidly Islamized.

Very little is known of Alwah, but it appeared to reach its greatest prosperity between the tenth and sixteenth centuries; but some excavations carried out in 1950–2 revealed a town of large mud-brick buildings, but simple and of a rather poor culture; and they are reported to have been in ruins by A.D. 1523.

Before the war an expedition of the Egypt Exploration Society, directed by Mr H. W. Fairman, had been excavating a site at Amarah West on the north bank of the Nile about 113 miles south of Wadi Halfa in the desolate region between the Second and Third Cataracts; and these excavations were continued, likewise under Mr Fairman, in the winter of 1947–8. They have revealed that Amarah was originally an island in the middle of the Nile, but that

ferocious sandstorms and the violent north winds which are a feature of this
district filled in the north channel of the Nile, and so destroyed the security of
the town, made it uninhabitable and also covered over and preserved its
remains.

Excavations in three parts of the site, a temple built by Rameses II, a workshop area and the governor's palace have revealed something of the town's
history. It was founded about 1306 B.C. in the reign of Seti I, most probably to
exploit gold mines in the area—in one of the workshops a jar bearing lumps of
rich gold-bearing quartz was found under the floor. This town rapidly fell into
ruins, most probably as a result of jerry-building and a failure to understand
the destructive nature of the local climate. A second town was planned and built
by Rameses II about 1266 B.C. and some fifty years later it was entirely rebuilt
in the early part of the reign of Rameses III; and this third town lasted about
120 years until the silting up of the north branch of the Nile caused it to be
abandoned. Several hundred years later a small town came into being, inhabited
by a poor community whose main interest seems to have been fishing.

In the temple of Rameses II, on the walls of the Hypostyle Hall, are inscriptions giving long lists of African and Asian towns and peoples whom
Rameses II claimed to have defeated. Most of this list is mere empty boasting
and the greater part of the list is simply a copy of an inscription which Amenophis III set up at Soleb about 100 years before. Part of the list is new, however,
and it contains the earliest mention in hieroglyphics of Jericho and Jehovah.
This is of course an important and interesting inscription, which gains in interest
and indeed in piquancy when it is realized that the "Jehovah" here is a place-
name, the literal translation of the hieroglyphs being "Jehovah in Edom".

Only about a third of the site was excavated; and it may well be further work
here would prove very rewarding. The more that is learnt about Northern
Sudan, the more interesting the district appears, the excavations at Buhen,
which will be described later in this chapter, being a case in point. Furthermore, if ever the High Dam at Aswan is built, many important sites in the
northern part of the country will disappear below the water and consequently
those which, like Amarah West, will probably be unaffected, will gain an
added importance, in as much as it will still be possible to excavate and study
them at leisure, instead of in the haste of a "last chance" excavation.

The threat of the High Dam materialized at about the time of the ending of
the Anglo-Egyptian Condominium of the Sudan and the coming into existence
of the Republic of the Sudan. Under the terms of this change no positions of
political influence could be held by either British or Egyptian nationals; and
it is a measure of the status and significance of archaeology in these days that
the post of Commissioner for Archaeology was judged to be one of political influence. In consequence in June 1955, Mr Shinnie left the service and was succeeded by M Jean Vercoutter—a "neutral" foreigner—since there was no
suitable Sudanese candidate.

M Vercoutter, who had previously been directing the French excavations at

Sai Island, was immediately confronted with establishing what would be the effect of a High Dam on the antiquities of Northern Sudan and what measures should be taken to offset it.

The effect of raising the dam at Aswan is basically of course quite simple—it would raise the height of the Nile upstream proportionately to the height of the barrage and this effect would be felt x miles upstream. Now since Northern Sudan consists (and has consisted for many centuries) of a narrow strip along the banks of the Nile with desolate deserts on either side, it was quite clear that any considerable raising of the Nile as it runs through this area would result in all the fertile ground, all the towns and villages (including of course Wadi Halfa, which is the fourth largest town in Sudan, with a population of 10,600) and all the antiquities, which are all beside the river, disappearing under the waters—the chief and indeed, so far as could be seen, the only beneficiary of the plan being Egypt.

In a grim desperate sort of way this threat was immediately beneficial to Sudanese archaeology. It pin-pointed the situation, it called for immediate action and it involved questions of national prestige.

In his first report M Vercoutter stated that between Faras in the extreme north and Merowe lay one of the richest parts of the Sudan for archaeological remains—including temples, fortresses, churches (some of them 4,000 years old) which are still standing and also buried towns, graves, rock inscriptions and drawings (some of them much older) which still await excavation. With the completion of the High Dam, nearly half this area would be submerged and as a result about sixty Sudanese historical monuments would disappear for ever. Of these sixty about seven had already been excavated or surveyed in the past. Since each site would require on an average two months' work, and since work in this area is only possible during six months of the year, it was obvious that the Antiquities Department would need something like twenty years, working intensively, to complete the task. At the time of the report (February 1956) it appeared that the High Dam Project was going through immediately and that, as a result, only six years remained for the task; and accordingly it was agreed to ask foreign archaeological missions to co-operate. As well as the business of excavation and survey, there was also the question of dismantling and re-erecting in a safe place three temples and two churches of great artistic interest.

Although almost immediately the world political situation postponed indefinitely the construction of the High Dam, the threat and the stimulus remained—and were indeed intensified in 1959 when the Russians offered to undertake the work—and the Antiquities Department began a systematic survey and some foreign archaeological missions began to work.

During the first year the west bank was surveyed by M Vercoutter and the east bank by Senior Inspector Thabit Hassan; and about twenty-five new sites of widely differing periods and varying interest were discovered and it was found that the first immediate need was a topographical map on a sufficiently

large scale. Accordingly in 1957 a systematic aerial survey from Kosha in the
south to Faras in the north was put in hand and completed by March. On this
a provisional archaeological map could be based as the first really essential tool
for a thorough survey of the threatened area.

Perhaps the most interesting discovery during the survey work was that made
during the clearing of the tomb of Djehuty-hetep at Debeira East. This tomb
had been found in 1938 but had never been cleared and the work was now entrusted to Thabit Hassan. It was found to be a tomb of the usual Egyptian
plan, belonging to a local ruler of the New Kingdom, apparently of the reign
of Queen Hatshepsut, but re-used as a funeral vault during Roman times and
later as a Christian chapel (which had been built as a mud-brick structure
inside the hall). The original tomb consisted of a hall and a shrine. With the
removal of the Christian chapel, the painted walls of the hall were revealed:
the north wall shows a banquet, musicians, attendants and the deceased and his
wife; part of this wall and part of the west show the dead man watching agricultural work in progress on his estate, fruit being gathered and plants being
watered, four different species of tree being shown and two different races of
labourers, one black, one red, and in the trees monkeys are playing. On the
other part of the west wall are traces of a battle scene. In the shrine are four
seated statues, larger than life size and carved from the rock. They are probably
plastered and painted, but the faces have been badly smashed. Inscriptions
identify them as Djehuty-hetep, his wife, Tentnub, his father Ruiu and his
mother Runa. The principal tomb chamber had been completely robbed and
terribly disturbed.

In 1957 the Michela Schiff Giorgini expedition began excavations at Soleb
(or Sulb) to the south of Wadi Halfa, between the second and third cataracts.
This mission, which was sponsored by Pisa University, was led by Mrs Schiff
Giorgini, while the excavations were directed by M. Clément Robichon of the
French Archaeological Institute at Cairo. Soleb is quite a well-known site and
is especially famous for the temple, the largest in the Sudan, which was built
by Amenophis III at the beginning of the fourteenth century B.C.; but although
it had been visited by a number of archaeological parties since the 1820's, it
had never been excavated. Two famous lions from it are in the British Museum.
Part of this temple was cleared and a number of interesting discoveries were
made. It was found, for example, that a large hall had been repaired several
times; and in the plaster of one of these repairs a short Meroitic inscription was
found, which strongly suggested that this building was still substantially intact
during the last centuries B.C.—a considerable life for an exposed structure in
desert surroundings.

The most interesting and teasing discovery, however, was made in the necropolis, which lies in a depression about 1,000 yds from the temple. One of the
tombs there took the apparent form of a small step pyramid of black stones,
surviving in some parts to the second step. This being the largest of the tombs,
it was excavated and in the remains of a chapel on the east side of the pyramid

a shaft covered with five large slabs of slate was found. This shaft was filled with black stones, in among which were found several human skulls, some pottery, and a very fine New Kingdom vase in the form of a seated monkey holding a sack. When this shaft was cleared, it was found that the stone walling which closed the entrance to the tomb had been pushed backwards into the tomb intact by the weight of water in successive floodings of the shaft during the course of some 3,400 years. The tomb itself was empty—but it had not been robbed but had been deliberately emptied.

Careful examination of the remains revealed quite clearly the odd and teasing history of this tomb, of which it is almost certain the occupant died in the reign of Amenophis III. In its first form a vaulted chapel was built over the shaft tomb, with behind it a brick-built pyramid containing the *stela* of the deceased within it. In the second phase, this brick pyramid is demolished and the *stela* is brought forward to a niche in the wall of the chapel and an open courtyard is built on to one end of the chapel. In the third phase, the doorway of the burial chamber is removed and an outer wall is built sealing in the chapel and the open courtyard. In the fourth phase, the remains are brought up from the tomb to the surface, the entrance to the tomb chamber is walled up with stone, the shaft is filled up with black stones; on the site of the original brick pyramid, a much larger pyramid of black stones is built in the step form, the courtyard is completely demolished and a massive wall of black stones is built up, sealing off what was left of the chapel, which now contained the remains of the deceased. In other words, the original tomb was discarded and the chapel above, now completely sealed in, had taken over the functions of the tomb. The remains which had been underground had now been brought up to the surface. Why? No answer can be given which is completely satisfactory; but it has been suggested that there is a parallel in the empty sarcophagus which Dr Goneim found in the unfinished step pyramid of King Sekhem-khet at Sakkara. The occupant of the Soleb tomb was certainly moved about of set purpose while his tomb was drastically altered around him. King Sekhem-khet's apparently untouched sarcophagus was empty and his pyramid was incomplete and its enclosure altered in plan. Perhaps war or revolution interrupted for Sekhem-khet's remains a removal as purposive (though enigmatic) as that of the unknown occupant of the Soleb tomb.

In the extreme north of the Sudan, over against Wadi Halfa—and therefore in the heart of the most important area threatened with inundation if the High Dam is built—stands Buhen. This very large site has a long history. It was established in about 1900 B.C. by the Egyptians of the Twelfth Dynasty as a trading station and as a fortress to protect their southern frontier, one of a number of such strongholds. It was known to have been strong, important and rich and it remained so until the Hyksos invasions of 1675 B.C. weakened the Egyptians power. After this it stood as a deserted and partly burnt out ruin until the coming of the warrior kings of the New Kingdom who ended the domination of the Hyksos and of the Kushites in the south. Buhen was rebuilt, refortified and grew in size and prosperity until the eclipse of the Egyptian power about 1085 B.C. In the beginning of the fifteenth century Queen Hatshepsut built there a fine temple, which has been famous in modern times since about the beginning of the last century. In 1892 it was realized that the temple was surrounded by the remains of a town and extensive fortifications; and the outline of these fortifications was traced in 1902 by an expedition of the University of Pennsylvania which was excavating tombs and cemeteries in the vicinity. After this the site was untouched until 1958 when, with the permission of the Sudanese Government, an expedition of the Egypt Exploration Society began operations under the direction of Professor W. B. Emery.

The site as a whole consists of a square walled town backing on the Nile and this area contains Hatshepsut's temple. Likewise anchored on the Nile but much farther out and of much greater extent is a line of outer defences, which with its salients and re-entrants probably amounts to a perimeter of about a mile. It is a happy accident of the site that through the centuries sand has been *deposited* on it and in consequence mud-brick buildings and defences are buried and preserved instead of being rapidly eroded by cutting sand-laden winds as is usually the case in the Sudan. A small section of the outer defences was excavated and was discovered to consist of a 17-ft thick wall, which was probably originally about 32 ft high, fronted with a dry ditch 22½ ft wide, cut to a depth of 11 ft into the rock and sand and faced with brick and stone.

After this, operations were transferred to the north-west corner and west front of the square inner walled town; and here and during the following season an astonishing and indeed uniquely well preserved example of Egyptian military architecture in the Middle and New Kingdoms was discovered; and of these, strangely enough, the earlier phase is the better preserved in as much as the later was built on top of and around it.

It will perhaps be more comprehensible if the results rather than the process of the investigation are described. By the end of the second season the whole of the west front was cleared and found to be 188 yds long, symmetrical and with a massive fortified gate in the centre. In Middle Kingdom times, the main wall was a massive affair, probably about 34 ft high, with massive buttresses at either end and with the whole façade as it were panelled with broad shallow buttresses and narrow shallow re-entrants. At the outer foot of this wall was a wide brick-paved terrace with a rampart, pierced with loopholes at two levels, regularly diversified with round bastions. Each loophole had a single opening on the defender's side opening into three slots on the outer side, so that the archer had three fields of fire; and these loopholes were set one above the other, so that they could be used simultaneously by kneeling and standing archers. On the outer side this rampart descended in a steep scarp to a rock-cut dry ditch, which rose again in a counterscarp, crowned with a wall and a covered way. And beyond this again was an outer glacis. All these fortifications had been plastered and painted white; and it is still possible to see in some parts how the white paint had been regularly renewed to the best standards of military maintenance. The purpose of the white paint was no doubt to make it very difficult to mount a surprise night attack (Plate 51*b*).

These defences must have presented a frightful problem to attackers without artillery. First they would have to scale the outer glacis under fire from the walls and the covered way. Having overcome the defenders in the covered way, they would then be confronted with the steep, deep and slippery dry ditch under the full fire of the ramparts, bastions and the summit of the inner wall. After this they would have to scale the ramparts and destroy their defenders; and even then would find themselves only in command of a narrow enclosed terrace, dominated by a towering and perpendicular wall, crowded with the main body of the defending force.

In the centre of this west wall was the massive gateway, protected with two huge and towering buttresses, the full height of the inner wall, which projected over the ramparts, dry ditch, counterscarp and glacis on either side of the narrow way of entry; and in this alley between towering featureless walls was a dry ditch with a drawbridge, in front of the inner gate. This gateway is most impressive and, at first sight, apparently impregnable; and yet the evidence shows that it was taken and burnt towards the end of the Middle Kingdom. In a sense its weakness lies in its strength. The two huge buttresses are solid brick and the only places for defenders on them are the (presumably) battlemented summits. As a result, once attackers had forced their way into the narrow alley between the buttresses, they could only be attacked (with arrows, spears, missiles, flame and boiling liquids) *from above*, i.e. from the summit of the buttresses and the main wall, or, in a last state of desperation, through the opened main gate. Therefore if the attackers had the wits to use some form of *testudo* or armoured canopy, under which to mount their attack on the gate, they would be in a position to attack without possibility of effective reply by the defenders; and we can only suppose that it was in some way like this that the Kushites stormed the fortress some time in the mid-seventeenth century B.C.

When the armies of the New Kingdom returned in strength to Buhen some 200 years later, they enlarged the town and modified the defences on another plan. In the first place they built the long perimeter of outer defences, consisting, as described earlier, of a massive wall, fronted with a dry ditch, and with many salients and re-entrants. Between these outer defences and the old walled town, a new town grew up; and the Middle Kingdom walls were considerably modified. In the first place the great projecting gateway was cut back almost to the level of the main wall—and it is possible to see in this change a recognition of its weakness. The main wall was strengthened and thickened with the addition of buttresses. The dry ditch was partly filled in and converted into a sunken way leading to the gate and the buttresses of the ramparts were done away with and covered over in the course of these operations. These New Kingdom defences had become simpler, plainer and much less impressive; but the problem was after all different. They were no longer outer defences fronting on the desert; they had become the inner keep of a growing town, no longer the first defences against an enemy army, but simply the last stronghold or a daily threat to a perhaps restive populace.

In the second season some excavation was done inside the Middle Kingdom defences; and the headquarters buildings of the Commander were found immediately inside the north-western buttress and with a stairway leading to the summit thereof, from which the Commander would be able to watch the progress of an attack and direct the operations of the defence. In a space under a staircase in the headquarters was found a quantity of carefully torn up papyrus, which after treatment at the British Museum was found to be covered with Middle Kingdom hieratic. It is a pleasant thought that if and when the jigsaw is completed and read these may be military secret documents of some 3,800 years ago, carefully destroyed and as carefully stored away by the eternal staff sergeant.

A most interesting, and surprising, discovery was made when the New Kingdom additions to the main wall were being removed between two bastions. Here below the New Kingdom brickwork and underneath a stratified deposit which included a layer of cinders from the burning of the fortress when it was stormed around 1675 B.C. was found the skeleton of a horse. This was so unusual that the skeleton was at first thought to have been an ass, but a scientific examination has definitely established that the bones are those of a horse. Now although the horse was known in Mesopotamia around 2000 B.C. it does not make its general appearance in Egypt until the Eighteenth Dynasty, around 1570 B.C. and it has been generally assumed that it was introduced into the Valley of the Nile by the Hyksos invaders. This skeleton can be dated on sound archaeological evidence to something like 200 years earlier than that.

In May 1958, a brief exploratory excavation was made near Omdurman Bridge by Thabit Hassan. This was a site where two proto-dynastic graves (c 3000 B.C.) were found in 1940. The recent excavation did not touch the proto-dynastic cemetery but uncovered instead a Neolithic occupation site in which were found pottery sherds of the Shaheinab type and fine fish-hooks cut the mother-of-pearl of Nile shells. In among this site were a number of ancient burials of the Meroitic period (400 B.C.–A.D. 350), others perhaps of the Jebel Moya culture and in the top layer a few burials which may be Christian or Early Muslim. The significance of these finds lies in the evidence they provide of the long occupation of the area near the confluence of the Blue and White Niles; and it is suggested that the site may repay further excavation.

PLATE 45. Eastern Turkey. (*a*) The peak of Nemrud Dagh (7,500 ft). Against a background of an enormous man-made tumulus are 24 ft-high seated statues of Antiochus I of Commagene and his fellow deities, some of whose detached heads can be seen in the foreground—see also Plate 1. (Left to right) Apollo-Mithras-Helios-Hermes; Fortuna of Commagene; Zeus-Oromasdes; Antiochus I; Heracles-Artagnes-Ares; and a guardian lion. (*b*) Mithradates, King of Commagene, father of Antiochus I, being greeted by Heracles, in a magnificent relief, some 9 ft high, found at Arsameia, the mountain-top tomb-sanctuary of Mithradates.

PLATE 46. Alalakh, Syria, and Amman, Jordan. (*a*) The diorite head of a Hittite king, probably Yarim-Lim—perhaps the finest Hittite sculpture known, 17th century B.C. (*b* and *c*) Two strange and possibly unique sculptures, found in Amman, probably of the 9th century B.C., and presumably indigenous Jordanian work.

PLATE 47. The Elamite "Tower of Babel", built in the 13th century B.C.: the *ziggurat* of Tchoga-Zanbil, not far from Susa, Iran. (*a*) The south-west face, cleared and partly reconstructed. (*b*) Looking down on the south-west entry, with, left background, altar built by Untash Huban, Elamite king who built the *ziggurat*.

PLATE 48. A bearded prince, priest or god, plucking the lotus: a splendid ivory found in "Fort Shalmaneser", Nimrud, and typical of many of the great treasure of ivories found in the Assyrian military capital. Possibly booty from north-west Syria. The garments may represent armour.

PLATE 49. The splendid syncretic statuary of Hatra, an autonomous city-state of Hellenized Arabs, nearly 100 miles south-west of Mosul. (*a*) A military commander of the Hatra army, in full uniform, his hand raised in greeting to the god of the temple; limestone, life-size. (*b*) The Princess Washfari, daughter of King Sanatruq: a life-size statue in Mosul marble, curiously Indian in feeling.

PLATE 50. The chief deity of Hatra and the paramount Assyrian god: Ashur-Bel, garbed as a Roman Emperor. These back and front views of this small marble statue show, at his feet, the goddess Tyche or Fortuna; on his breast, the sun-god, Shamash; between his shoulder-blades, Medusa; and, on either side, protective eagles.

PLATE 51. (*a*) The world's oldest substantially intact funerary boat: the vessel lying in the boat grave, at the northern end of the mastaba-tomb of the Pharaoh Udimu, fifth king of the First Dynasty (*c.* 3000 B.C.)— in the archaic necropolis of Sakkara, Egypt. (*b*) Military architecture of some 3,900 years ago: the west face of the Middle Kingdom fortifications of Buhen, just south of Wadi Halfa, Sudan. The loopholes in the bastions are most ingenious, three of them meeting in a single interior embrasure, so that each archer had three fields of fire.

PLATE 52. "The White Lady of the Brandberg": the most impressive and astonishing figure of all southern African cave art—from the transcription by the Abbé Breuil.

PLATE 53. One of the finest of the "big heads" of La Venta; a colossal Olmec sculpture of about 2,000 years ago, now transferred to open parkland at Villahermosa, in the Mexican state of Tabasco.

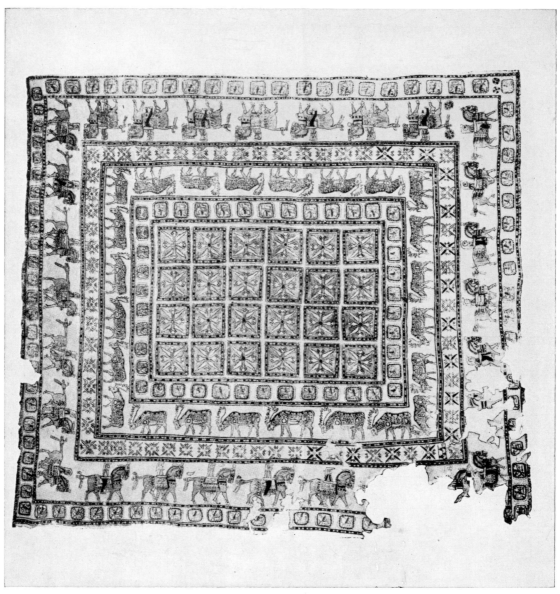

PLATE 54. The world's oldest Persian carpet. Found almost perfectly preserved in perpetual ice in a tomb chamber at Pazyryk, in the Altai Mountains in southern Siberia, it measured 6 by 6½ ft and is about 2,400 years old. The central feature is of quatrefoils of basically Assyrian origin and is surrounded by griffins. In the next row are grazing elks with a row of quatrefoils dividing them from horses alternately led and ridden by grooms; and the final row is again of griffins. The colours are red, pale blue, greenish yellow and orange.

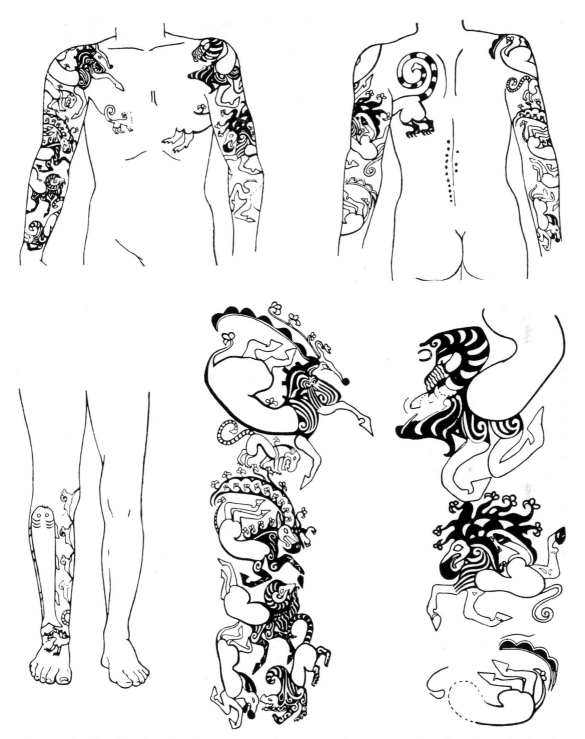

PLATE 55. "Scythian" animal art in tattooing. Fantastic tattoo designs found on the bodies of men of 2,400 years ago, preserved in perpetual ice in the tomb chambers of Pazyryk, southern Siberia.

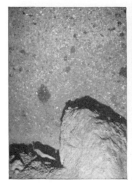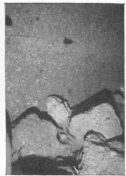

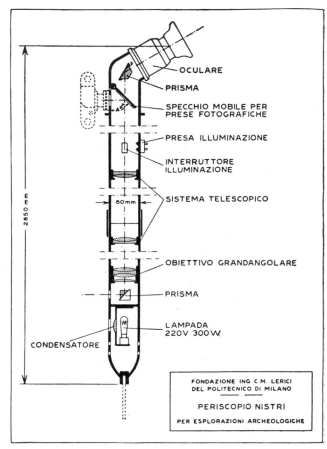

OCULARE

PRISMA

SPECCHIO MOBILE PER PRESE FOTOGRAFICHE

PRESA ILLUMINAZIONE

INTERRUTTORE ILLUMINAZIONE

SISTEMA TELESCOPICO

60mm

OBIETTIVO GRANDANGOLARE

PRISMA

LAMPADA 220V 300W

CONDENSATORE

2850 mm

FONDAZIONE ING. C.M. LERICI
DEL POLITECNICO DI MILANO

PERISCOPIO NISTRI

PER ESPLORAZIONI ARCHEOLOGICHE

PLATE 56. "Periscope photography" among the Etruscan tombs. (*a* i–iv) A sequence of exposures taken of an unexcavated tomb by means of the periscope camera, which gives a complete all-round picture. (*b*) A hole has been drilled in the top of a tomb and the periscope is inserted. The tall man is King Gustav Adolf of Sweden with Signor Lerici on his left. (*c*) Signor Lerici using the eyepiece of the Nistri periscope. (*d*) A diagram explaining the working of the Nistri periscope, which can be used either with the eyepiece or with a camera attached as in (*e*). (*f*) Athletes from a painted tomb at Tarquinia, discovered by periscope photography. (*g*) A relief from an Etruscan sarcophagus, discovered by the same means at Vulci.

PLATE 57. Technology to the aid of archaeology. (*a*) Peeling a latex "squeeze" from the huge Greek inscription at Arsameia in eastern Turkey. (*b*) Transporting a tomb which had been lifted entire in plaster and crated for detailed examination in the museum at Stockholm. (c) Latex "squeezes" are tough, permanent, light and can easily be rolled for transport, even on the back of a donkey like the one Mr Kermit Goell is leading.

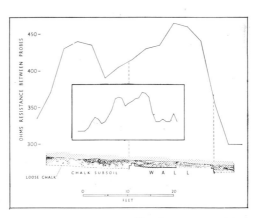

PLATE 58. Two methods of exploring under the surface without digging. (*a*) Making an underground electrical resistivity traverse with transportable transistorized device. (*c*) Result of a series of readings with this machine. In the centre box is a graph of the whole traverse; above is the interesting section with its peaks of high resistance; and, below, a diagram of the result of the excavation which followed, the peaks of resistance being equated with a buried wall and a dyke of loose chalk. In (*b*) a light oil-drill is used to probe the summit of the largest tumulus at Gordion in Phrygia. With a series of drillings the stone capping of the buried tomb was accurately located and economically reached by a tunnel.

CHAPTER TWENTY-FIVE

NORTH AFRICA

THE North African littoral has seen the passage of many civilizations, many centres reaching a high degree of prosperity and sophistication before the coming of the Vandals and the Moslem invasion; and it is rich in remains Greek, Phoenician, Roman and Byzantine. In the two great provinces of Cyrenaica and Tripolitania which make up the new kingdom of Libya, there have been many years of Italian excavation and preservation with splendid results in the way of the discovery of great works of art and architecture. Although the last war brought an end to this, steps were immediately afterwards taken, first under the temporary British administration and later under the independent government, to build up an Antiquities Department, staffed almost entirely with Libyan personnel. At first the Department was short of funds, but this has been to some extent remedied by financial agreements made with Great Britain and the United States, new work has been begun of great interest in itself and yet calculated to attract tourists to a little-known country which is nevertheless easy of access from Europe. UNESCO has also supplied some special tuition.

In Cyrenaica, the principal interest has centred round Cyrene, where Mr R. G. Goodchild, the Controller of Antiquities of Cyrenaica has been engaged on a number of operations, intrinsically important and also designed to exercise and train the new Department in as many branches as possible.

Cyrene was founded by Greek colonists, probably from the island of Thera, towards the end of the seventh century B.C. and its early prosperity was founded on the silphium plant, which appears on all its coinage where it resembles a sort of stylized leek. As to what silphium was, there is no agreement; and since the plant is now apparently extinct, its dying out being a grievous blow to the Greek colony, there seems to be little chance of finding out. Cyrene was famous as a seat and school of philosophers and Christianity seems to have taken an early root there—it was Simon of Cyrene, it will be recalled, who carried Christ's cross—and it experienced a fresh burst of prosperity under the Romans. This suffered a setback after the massacres of the Jewish Revolt of A.D. 115 from which it recovered, especially under the patronage of the Emperor Septimius Severus, who was born, not so very far away, at Leptis Magna in Tripolitania. Its final setback was the great earthquake of A.D. 365. Even so a recovery was made and one of the first tasks directed by Mr Goodchild was the clearance of a Roman Theatre which had been built after the earthquake and which is indeed one of the latest Theatres to be built under the Roman Emperors. It contained little in the way of works of art, but was found to overlie in part a market, with marble floors of the Severan period, which in its turn overlies an even earlier market. Leading to the upper part of the city from this district is a broad flight of stairs, in front of which had stood an impressive propylaeum of the time of Septimius Severus. This had crashed to the ground, with its massive architrave, in the great earthquake; and afterwards the citizens of Cyrene had felt incapable of coping with these huge blocks and had simply raised the street level to pass over them.

They came to light however in 1955 and provided an excellent exercise in technique (and effort) for the Department. They were accordingly lifted, consisting of three blocks each of 10 tons, and it was discovered that they made up a sculptured frieze, which had fortunately fallen face downwards, of the time of Septimius Severus. It is a long scene, in bold relief, showing a vigorous battle scene of horsemen and foot soldiers in hand-to-hand combat. It carries a fragmentary inscription in Greek which indicates that it was erected by an unnamed donor in honour of the Emperors Septimius and Pertinax and it refers to a chariot—but whether this was a trophy or a piece of sculpture is not clear.

Excavations were also begun on the site of the Cathedral which was built about A.D. 450. Among the early discoveries there was the Baptistery, in which a pagan marble sarcophagus had been fitted with interior steps to serve as a baptismal tank, set under a canopy supported by six marble Corinthian columns. In a chapel near the eastern apse a fine mosaic floor was found, with an inscription stating that it was given by "our holy bishop and lover of building". It contains a number of animal subjects, including lions and elephants as well as hares, stags and the like, some enclosed by vine tendrils, others by guilloche borders. There is also a scene of a Nile fisherman hauling in a net; and in the central panel a very odd scene: in front of a background of sea monsters, two animals are fighting, one apparently a crocodile (but with a curiously humped back which makes it look more like an armadillo) the other perhaps a cow, as a man is trying to pull it away by its tail. A parallel to this strange scene was later found at Qasr el-Lebia, some 50 miles away, as will be described later in this chapter.

Other interesting work in Cyrene was the continuation by Mr G. R. H. Wright of pre-war Italian researches in the underground ritual baths beside the Sacred Way leading down to the Sanctuary Area of Cyrene. These are a row of grottos cut into the scarp of the rock and separated from the Sacred Way by a Roman retaining wall. Some of these are apparently service chambers but three of them form a sort of nymphaeum and their walls are made up of chair-like baths, sedilia as it were, cut out of the rock, in which the bather sat in a niche with her feet in a footbath. Each niche contains a small recess for a lamp and, above, a larger recess, perhaps for a vase, perhaps for the bather's clothes. Their purpose has fortunately been revealed by some *stelae* which have been discovered (by the Italians) and which bear the "Sacred Laws" of the city of the fourth century B.C. At one point in these laws, dealing with the worship of

Artemis, girls are enjoined to "go down to the nymphaeum of Artemis"; for, presumably, rites of purification and the renunciation of the ritual garment on the eve of marriage. One of the main forms of Artemis ritual centres round the identification with a bear of the goddess, her priestesses and, on occasions, the girl celebrants; and these rites are referred to in the Cyrene laws.

In 1957, some labourers engaged on an American-sponsored development project at Qasr el-Lebia accidentally uncovered a mosaic floor and the American engineer reported this to the Department of Antiquities; and the Department under Mr R. G. Goodchild investigated the site.

Qasr el-Lebia, which lies about 50 miles west of Cyrene, near the Libyan Federal Highway, is probably ancient Olbia, a small community which was the seat of a Bishopric in the Byzantine period. In the first season, three mosaics were found; and despite the fact that the church is of no great pretensions one of these (in the eastern part of the nave) measures 35 × 20 ft, is in an excellent state of preservation, probably the finest Christian mosaic in Libya and has at least one feature which is probably unique. It is divided into fifty square panels, in ten rows of five and these panels are separated by a guilloche design. The central panel is a Greek inscription recording that the floor was laid in the third year of an Indiction by Bishop Makarios. At the top of the design is a city gateway with the inscription "the new city, Theodorias" and this is flanked by female personifications of *Kosmesis* (adornment), *Ktisis* (foundation) and *Ananeosis* (renewal). And this presumably all refers to a programme of embellishment associated with the renaming of Olbia in honour of Theodora, wife of the Emperor Justinian—which would make the date A.D. 539. There are also four panels of naked river gods, Tigris, Euphrates, Geon (the Nile) and Physon (probably the Danube)—not pagan demigods, but the Four Rivers of Paradise. There is also a panel of the nymph Kastalia, the spring of Delphi. A pillared church façade appears in one panel, a small castle with a single gate (not unlike the fortified farms of Ghirza) in another. Of human figures there is a horseman, a musician with his dog under a tree and two men working a sailing boat. A lively satyr is an unusual figure on a Christian mosaic; as is a merman with a tiller and a trident, spearing a fish. Crab's claws rather oddly protrude from his stomach. There are two other sea monsters with animal forelegs and fishy tails. There are many panels of water-fowl, fish and sea creatures generally. Other birds include an eagle, doves, a pair of ostriches and the inevitable peacock in his glory. Among the four-footed creatures are stags of various types, lions, an odd humped crocodile with a duck perched on its hump, bulls, two striped animals which may be zebras, a horse, a leopard and a ram. And in the centre of the bottom row, the panel of the greatest intrinsic interest, one of the Seven Wonders of the Ancient World, the Pharos of Alexandria. This is identified in Greek as the Pharos and it shows the lighthouse foreshortened to include the colossal bronze statue of Helios on the summit, with his sword pointing downwards to a semicircular object which may be the famous iron mirror which reflected the light of the fire on the summit. In the background, presumably across the waters of the harbour, is another tower, also crowned with a colossal bronze statue—which may perhaps represent the statue which stood on Pompey's Pillar in the Serapeum. The significance of the Pharos in this mosaic is a little baffling but it seems at all events to confirm that Alexandria is the source of the mosaic as would also be suggested by the frequency of Nilotic subjects among the panels.

Of the other two mosaics found in this little rural bishopric one is of minor interest; but the other contains three inscriptions, one of which, while of the same date as the Makarios inscription, refers to "our new bishop, Theodore" and this seems to imply that Makarios died while the work was not yet complete. Most of this mosaic is given over to lively hunting scenes; and one of the subjects repeats that odd scene which had just previously been found in the Cathedral at Cyrene—namely a crocodile pulling a cow into the water, while the cow's owner vigorously pulls on the cow's tail.

As in Cyrenaica, so in Tripolitania. During the period between the war and the establishment of the independent kingdom of Libya, the Antiquities branch of the British military government, under, first, Mr J. B. Ward-Perkins and, later, Mr R. G. Goodchild, continued the admirable care of the antiquities of the country which the Italians had begun. Much of this work naturally lay in conservation and making up for the neglect which had been the inevitable result of the war, but, as will be seen later in this chapter, much original work, particularly in the fields of exploration and survey, was also done.

When Mr Ward-Perkins left the military administration to become the Director of the British School at Rome he returned with an expedition of that School to carry out a series of excavations at Sabratha.

The province of Tripolitania took its name from the three cities, originally Phoenician trading centres, which were the focal points of its prosperity: Oea, Lepcis and Sabratha. Oea lies beneath modern Tripoli, but Lepcis and Sabratha have been deserted since the Arab invasions and in modern times these two cities have been the subject of large-scale excavation, restoration and conservation by the Italian Antiquities Service.

The splendid ruins of Sabratha, including temples, forum and a magnificent theatre, record for the most part the Roman period, the time of the city's greatest extent and prosperity, and also, in some parts, the short Byzantine renaissance which lay between the invasions of the Vandals and the final darkness which the Arab invasions brought. The British School concentrated on elucidating the pre-Roman history of the port.

Underneath the earliest buildings beside the harbour was found a considerable accumulation of material in layers separated by thin layers of sand. There were no signs of any buildings in this except for an occasional post-hole, but there were considerable quantities of pottery, mainly Phoenician but including some Greek sherds which may date from the sixth century B.C. And from these remains it seems quite clear that the Phoenician paid seasonal trading visits to the place, set up his tents and stores on or near the beach and traded with the natives for a few weeks perhaps, packed up his tents, left his litter to be covered over by the drifting sand (like any modern tourist) and sailed away to return in following years to repeat the process. Like in fact Matthew Arnold's "grave Tyrian trader" who under the pressure of Greek competition "held on indignantly

'O'er the blue Midland waters with the gale,
   Betwixt the Syrtes and soft Sicily,
      To where the Atlantic raves
Outside the western straits, and unbent sails
   There, where down cloudy cliffs, through sheets of foam,
      Shy traffickers, the dark Iberians come;
And on the beach undid his corded bales."

But towards the end of the fifth century B.C. the Phoenicians began to make permanent settlements and to build small mainly mud-brick houses on the seaward side of a massive wall. Quantities of pottery have been found and coins, but nothing to suggest a great deal of prosperity or artistic development. But the town must have prospered and during the next two centuries it continued to spread outside the perimeter wall, and there are traces of larger and more impressive buildings and perhaps a market square, but this is overlaid by the drastic Roman developments which took place at the end of the first century B.C.

After this Sabratha's history is known and for the most part visible on the surface. Part of the Phoenician town was rebuilt on Roman lines, part was swept away and levelled and graded to accommodate a group of large public buildings—a forum, a basilica, a curia, a large Corinthian temple dedicated to Liber Pater, another temple, perhaps a Serapeum. The continued progress of these public works has been worked out by the British School and they were found to increase in magnificence until about A.D. 200; by which time a massive Capitolium had been built facing the temple of Liber Pater and two other temples were built. A whole new quarter had also come into being, centred on a splendid Theatre. But this was the city's zenith and by the end of the third century A.D. the province was suffering from barbarian invasions and the Basilica was destroyed, to be rebuilt at the time of Constantine. Disaster came again with the Vandal invasions of the middle of the fifth century and this was the end of Roman Sabratha. A century later however the Byzantine Empire recovered the province and the Basilica was converted into a Christian church, the forum being used as a graveyard. The houses of this period are built on top of the 6 ft of rubble which had accumulated on top of the Roman city; and much of the building of this time incorporates worked stones and architectural elements of the earlier buildings. As always, however, in Byzantine cities, there were fine mosaics. This final prosperity lasted about 100 years and with the Arab invasions Sabratha ceased to be an inhabited town.

In 1948 and onwards the presence of the expedition of the British School at Rome under its Director Mr Ward-Perkins at Sabratha, and also the presence of numerous units of the British Army and the R.A.F. in Tripolitania enabled Mr R. G. Goodchild (who had succeeded Mr Ward-Perkins as Antiquities Officer under the British Military Administration) to make a number of wide-spread and interesting discoveries in terrains normally very difficult of access. The normal procedure of troops in training in desert and near-desert areas in the hinterland naturally led to many places being discovered that were never normally visited—in 1946, for example, a British officer discovered by accident an early Christian church at Gasr el-Suq in a remarkable state of preservation —and aerial photography is undoubtedly the best way of surveying an empty and mainly roadless country. This back area of Tripolitania is especially interesting as it formed part of the *limes*, the Roman Empire's frontier; and it has provided much evidence of their method of settling and protecting such a tract. As various fortified farmhouses and the like were recorded it became apparent that some systematic work, while the troops and their transport and the aircraft were available, would be desirable and rewarding; and in the summer of 1949 a programme of "archaeological reconnaissance" was carried out in the zone of the Roman frontier with the fullest co-operation of the Army and the Royal Air Force authorities.

In the course of military schemes designed to exercise the desert rescue organization of the 1st Infantry Division over 600 miles were covered and this was linked with aerial survey and photography. One of the most interesting sites examined was a Romano-Libyan necropolis at Bir el-Dreder. This contained over forty tombs marked with inscriptions in Latin characters but in the still unknown Libyan language. It is thought that the tribesmen whom the Romans recruited to serve on these frontier posts were analphabetic; and that the use of the Roman script to write their own language was a first step in Romanization. The names given on these *stelae* are usually a Roman name, like "Julius" followed by a barbarous one, one for example being Julius Nasif, described as a "tribune", a rank generally applied in the later Roman Empire to the leaders of irregular detachments incorporated in the army. At Mselletin a small Roman fort was discovered; but it seems that as the country grew more settled, so regular defences were abandoned in favour of a sort of Home Guard of Romano-Libyan farmer-soldiers. The 3rd Augustan Legion was disbanded in A.D. 238 and the system of *limitanei*, soldier-farmers, receiving grants of lands on the frontier and occupying fortified farmsteads besides the wadis they cultivated, worked very well for a number of years. Economically it was a great success and survived into the Islamic period; but as a military protection it broke down with the Vandal invasion and in the sixth century the Byzantine generals found themselves engaged in bitter combat with the descendants of those who a few centuries before had been the sentinels of the Roman Empire.

One of the most interesting of these soldier-farmer settlements is Ghirza, which was the subject of considerable study in 1952 and 1953 by Mrs Olwen Brogan and Dr E. Vergara-Caffarelli, Superintendent of Antiquities for Tripolitania. Ghirza lies on the Wadi Ghirza, which is a tributary (if that word can be used, without creating a false impression, of a valley which rarely holds any water) of the Wadi Zemzem and it is about 156 miles south-south-east of Tripoli, in the zone of isolated Roman farms, which lies behind the outermost forts of the *limes*. It stands astride one of the ancient routes leading from the coast to the Sahara; and it consists at present of the massive ruins of at least eighteen large fortified farm houses with very many smaller buildings standing on the higher ground on either side of a small wadi which opens off the main wadi; and, within the distance of a mile, two groups of remarkable mausolea.

The farmhouses, some of which still stand to a height of about 20–30 ft, are two- or three-storey buildings, for the most part enclosing a central courtyard and entered by a single well-fortified gate. The walls consist of a rubble core, cemented together with mud, and faced with a workmanlike ashlar of stone in rough courses. They have loop-hole-like windows and in some cases doorways at first floor level which must have opened on to balconies overlooking the courtyard. Two wells were found, one dry, the other still giving a copious supply of water which though brackish can still be taken by sheep or camels. Cisterns had also been built with prepared catchment areas to catch the rare rainfall of this zone. In both the wadis low walls had been built from side to side to prevent the soil washing away and also to hold up for as long as possible whatever rain fell and drained from the neighbouring slopes. Also in the wadi bottoms were circular walls, which were presumably built to retain the soil round palm-trees and—what is most surprising—olive trees. There are no palms or olives in the wadis now, nor within many miles; but palm-trees frequently appear in the sculptures in the mausolea and though they may be symbolical palm-trees, there seems no real reason why, with the continuous care these farms obviously received, palms should not have grown there. Olives are much more surprising and no olive trees have been found in the sculptures; but in one of the farms the remains of a standard North African olive-press have been found and surely no one would have gone to the trouble of importing the fruit of the olive to such a remote spot when the expressed oil could have been imported with much less trouble and expense.

But for the life of the Romano-Libyan farmers of Ghirza, the tombs of the dead are the best evidence. These tombs, the two groups of mausolea referred to above, are of a richness, variety and oddity difficult to parallel outside Brompton Cemetery. Like the farmhouses they are built of the local limestone but a fantastic amount of care, craftsmanship and imagination must have been spent on them. The stones are exactly squared and dressed, classical columns, pillars and pilasters in various developments are used, with arches, stairs, trabeations and capitals, the whole ornamented with friezes, rosettes (in infininte variety) and quantities of sculptured reliefs, naturalistic, symbolic and fantastic. The basic idea of the mausolea, which survives completely in the largest of the tombs, seems to have been a Doric temple, without pediments but with colonnades of a sort of bastard Ionic surrounding the cella, which contains the tomb. This idea is then, as it were, compressed, and the "temple" which rises from a square podium containing the actual burial, is square with four columns on each side surrounding a central "cella" which is in fact solid and ornamented with a false door in relief, symbolizing the entry into the after-life. The four columns on each side, however, do not support the classical horizontal trabeations but serve as the bases for springing Romanesque arches covered with reliefs, which in their turn support broad cornices, richly adorned with sculpture. This compressed design, in some tombs, suffers a further compression; and a small square podium supports four pillars only, surrounding a central dummy "cella" and supporting four arches beneath a sculptured cornice. Finally the design shrinks even farther and approximates to an obelisk, the four pillars having become rectangular shallow pilasters in a Corinthian style applied to the dummy cella and supporting a horizontal cornice. When this last tomb was first photographed (in 1931) it was crowned with a tall pyramid, but this has since fallen as a result of an earthquake. This extraordinary architectural progression—which calls to mind (though at a very distant remove) the developing fantasies in which Wren indulged in the spires of his City churches—was carried out in the second–fourth centuries, in their spare time, by Romano-Libyan soldier-farmers, miles from any urban settlement, and while engaged in wresting a living from singularly infertile land and under threat of hostile nomadic tribes from the near-by desert.

As though this was not enough this do-it-yourself architecture is restlessly adorned with do-it-yourself sculpture; and although these reliefs are without exception clumsy and naïve—rather like the sculptures in the Jewish necropolis at Beth Shearim—they are nevertheless sincere, rather endearing and packed with information. It is not difficult to visualize those soldier-farmers filling in the long frustrated periods which are characteristic alike of desert farming and garrison soldiering by chipping away at the local stone and producing after a fashion representations of the people and animals which were familiar to them, and symbols of their hopes and beliefs and, wherever there seemed likely to be a blank space, yet another variation of the rosette which is the almost invariable concomitant of every composition.

North Africa was the great supply source of wild animals for Imperial Rome; and as a result hunting scenes are very frequent, with hunters on foot and horseback pursuing lion, leopard, antelope, and such small game as hares. Bows and arrows are used and there are hunting dogs. A great variety of birds appear; and for that matter fishes, although it seems likely that these are considered symbolically as the souls of the departed. In one relief four fish are seen in various positions round a central rosette and seem to evoke a small fish-pond seen from above. Ostriches are also portrayed; and it is worth remembering that ostriches, antelope, lions were still common in North Africa in the last century and that cheetahs were shot in Tripolitania as recently as 1938. Date-palms, as mentioned above, are represented: in one a man is seen climbing the trunk; in another a date-palm in fruit is shown beside a naked giant with a staff and a leaping dog. There are a few ceremonial scenes. In one, perhaps a funeral banquet, a chief is sitting on a curule chair; one servitor carries a wine-jug and a bow and arrows, another a bowl, another a staff of office; while the chieftain holds the scroll of destiny which is not uncommon on Roman tombs. In another, part of the same frieze, the chief is shown standing with his wife and children, one of them on horseback; and here and there in this composition are rosettes, grapes, pomegranates and the case containing bow and arrows. Perhaps the most interesting reliefs are those showing farming scenes: in one, men are sowing and ploughing with simple ploughs drawn by mules and camels; in another harvesters are reaping barley with sickles, the heads of corn being stacked together at one side; and in a third a group of men are threshing and winnowing the heads of barley.

In general the country round Ghirza is so arid and inhospitable that it is difficult to imagine such pastoral scenes taking place or indeed that any settled community could have maintained itself. But when Mrs Brogan visited Ghirza briefly in April 1954 she was rewarded with the sight of the main wadi filled for several miles with good crops of barley and bearded wheat. There had been a single good rainstorm in the preceding winter and the local tribe had immediately set to work ploughing and sowing. Some of the crop was ripe and it was being harvested with sickles in precisely the same manner (and with the same gestures) as shown in the relief of 1,600 years before. Furthermore, camels are still sometimes used in ploughing in Libya; and the plough which they draw is the same as that used by the soldier-farmers of Roman Ghirza.

In 1951 and 1952 some remarkable discoveries were made by Mlle Marguerite van Berchem in the heart of the Sahara, at the site of Sedrata, the lost city of the Sahara and the medieval capital of the Ibadites. The Ibadites, who were Islamic schismatics of Berber origin, left their capital and kingdom in the province of Oran about A.D. 909 as the result of attacks by rival Arab tribes and made their way far southwards under the guidance of a holy man and built a city after very great hardships; and the site of this city was the result of their discovery 200 ft below the surface of the "Sea of the Deluge"—an underground supply of water. Their city prospered until about the thirteenth century, when they were attacked by orthodox persecutors and withdrew to the plateau of the Mzab. There the sect still survives, usually known as Mozabites; and every year they still make a pilgrimage to the ruins of their ancient mosque.

Sand rapidly covered the ancient city, which now survives as a tract of tumbled hummocks in endless dunes; but Mlle Van Berchem had the valuable support of the French Air and Ground Commands of the area; and aerial photography proved absolutely invaluable in providing a sort of ghostly plan of an enormous city which could not have been achieved by ground survey without enormous labour—and so indicated in considerable detail sites which might repay excavation. Aerial photography also revealed the ruined buildings on the top of the great rock of Gara Krima, a near-by stronghold—a sort of acropolis of the Ibadites—which rises up like a black Gibraltar in the endless sea of sand.

Orthodox excavation was impossible in these circumstances, but with the aid of Arab labourers with baskets it was possible to shift many tons of sand to a depth of 10 ft in some parts. In this manner a spacious dwelling house was uncovered. This consisted of a number of communicating rooms opening on a central court, with thin elegant pillars supporting horseshoe arches. One room was a date store with two huge storage jars built into a counter of solid masonry. The material of these buildings was rubble faced with grey plaster. At the eastern side of the city a large building which was probably a palace was explored; and in this was found a wealth of sculptured plaster panels which had decorated the walls. This carved plaster is of great intricacy and beauty, giving an almost lace-like effect. The decoration, which includes several Kufic inscriptions which enable it to be dated to the later eleventh century A.D., is in some places characteristically Berber in inspiration, but elsewhere recalls the Ommayyad art of Spain and other Oriental elements, including some Persian motifs. Underlying it likewise can be traced some faint Hellenistic elements, the last vestiges of Christian (and classical) art in North Africa.

At the extreme west end of the North African coast some interesting excavations have been conducted by Princess Martha de Chambrun Ruspoli, in Tangier itself and also at Rass Achaqqar on the slopes of Cape Spartel—which might be described as the extreme north-west corner of Africa.

On the Marshan cliff above Tangier and facing the Straits are a number of tombs cut downwards into the rock summit of the cliff. These, which are now open and empty, are part of the Phoenician necropolis. During the Lisbon earthquake of 1755, part of this cliff split off and fell away into the sea, taking with it part of the necropolis. Princess Ruspoli thought that part of the cemetery might lie somewhat inland, where sand and soil had begun to overlie the rock level of the cliff top. This turned out to be correct and a number of burials at three different levels were found. Most of these were quite simple inhumations, but there were also some incinerations in small urns, both types of burial being contemporaneous. The most remarkable of these was a lead urn inside which was a second urn of very thin pale blue glass containing the charred bones of a child of about ten years old. This was probably late Punic of perhaps the first century B.C. At a lower (Phoenician) level, there was a basin cut to collect the water of a spring, possibly for purification rites.

The other excavation may perhaps be connected with one of the oldest documents of classical geography, the Periplus of Hanno. Hanno was a Carthaginian of about 500 B.C. who made a voyage of discovery along the west coast of Africa as far as Senegal or thereabouts. On his return he erected in the temple of Bel at Carthage a tablet describing his voyage, in the Phoenician language. This does not survive, but a Greek translation (of uncertain date) does and it includes a passage describing his emerging from the Mediterranean, passing between the Pillars of Hercules (Gibraltar and Jebel Musa) and founding the city of Thymaterion. "Then, towards evening we assembled on the thickly wooded Cape Soloeis. There we raised an altar to Poseidon"; and the text describes the sacrifices made to the sea-god. Now it seems almost certain that Cape Soloeis is Cape Spartel, from references in Herodotus and from the description "thickly-wooded" and from its locality. Now part of the Cape Spartel range is the hill, Rass Achaqqar, which dominates the first convenient landing place after rounding Cape Spartel; and here, after clearing thick scrub, Princess Ruspoli began excavations. More than thirty sacrificial pits were found, cut into the hard red earth, each about 10–12 ft deep and 6–7 ft in diameter. Each of these pits seems to have been used for a single sacrifice, filled with earth and stones, capped with flat stones and marked with one or more upright triangular blocks of stone. At the bottom of each a mill-stone was found on which the fire had been kindled and on it were thrown sacrificial meats and animals and a great variety of offerings. The principal animals sacrificed were cattle, sheep and goats, but bones have been found also of elephant, horse, various felines and rodents, quantities of birds, dolphins, tunny and swordfish; the stones of olive, plum, apricot and peach; oddments of metal, tools, bracelets, ear-rings, nails, fish-hooks and lamps; various stone tools and quantities of pottery. Of this last some is of a coarse and primitive ware, which was doubtless local (and is indeed still made by the Berbers); but the majority is good wheel-turned pottery, sometimes corded and decorated in various colours in stripes and geometric patterns. Some of the pieces are marked with Carthaginian letters, but a few fragments appear to be of Greek origin.

Oddly enough, until a few years ago, when the festival was abolished, the Berbers used to assemble near this site at the summer solstice to sacrifice a bull, the ceremony being followed by three days of feasting and dancing. The rites included ritual baths; and the feast was popular with young brides and had the name of ensuring happy motherhood within a year.

On the slopes above the sacrificial pits Princess Ruspoli found a rock-cut reservoir, now filled with sand and stones. It appears to have been built in Carthaginian times to supply a factory for salting and preparing fish on the sea shore below. This factory which was brought to light and excavated by Don Cesar Luis de Montalban in 1950–4, was almost certainly originally Carthaginian, but it was reconstructed and developed by the Romans, who built baths and villas near by.

CHAPTER TWENTY-SIX

AFRICA—THE SAHARA AND SOUTH

TO PAINT, to doodle, to write on walls has been the practice of man from the earliest times to today; and in time and in quality his works range from the great bulls of Altamira and Lascaux to the Chads and "Kilroy was here" of the last war and to the extraordinarily limited propositions and pieces of advice which every innkeeper scrubs off his walls week after week. They are perhaps a function of despair; attempts to snatch a little personal immortality in the darkness of eternity; and are the products of desolation—loneliness, whether physical or psychological, exile, hardship and fear. The happy and prosperous man makes no *graffiti*; the places where they are found are the caves in which prehistoric man sought some shelter, railway stations, stopping places along the ancient caravan routes—and the desert places of Arabia and Africa are full of them. The stones are clamorous with human cries, every doodle a *cri de coeur* and no doubt to the god-like creature who could and would interpret them are packed with new and fascinating information as well as containing a sort of Lowest Common Multiple of human hopes and aspirations. But so much of it is an L.C.M., so uniform, so strident, so confused that it seems like that ceaseless uniform mutter that the gods of Olympus heard as a background to their eccentric lives and that was in fact the sum total of human prayer—to which little attention need be paid: but for art—which wings prayers, crystallizes perception, immortalizes momentary delight, and makes the invisible visible and which is fortunately sufficiently common in ancient cave drawings and paintings to make their study a means to that increase of pleasure which is the true object of all learning.

Soon after the war, in the three years that her husband, Brigadier F. G. Drew, was chief administrator of Eritrea, Mrs Sannie Drew, an adventurous and inquiring artist, collected a great number of rock carvings and paintings in the Highlands of that country, in the ravines and on the crags along the ancient routes which lie between Adulis on the sea and Axum on the plateau. Much of this material consists of rock faces and even great boulders covered— almost like a textile pattern—with scratched and hammered letters, symbols and doodles, sometimes seeming to hint at significant inscriptions perhaps Coptic, perhaps early Ethiopic, almost Greek but always elusive, evasive, petering out as perhaps the idle traveller sheltering for the night became tired or bored or the rock became too hard or the tool he was using broke in his hand. But there are, too, crude pictures of animals, lions, elephants, cattle, hunting and herding scenes—the sort of things that primitive peoples have drawn through the centuries—and are still drawing. And then, among all this, there are suddenly things that impress with their power and their strangeness; and two of these discoveries of Mrs Drew are quite outstanding.

One was at Meallaui, in a rock shelter overlooking the Hagamo plain from a great height. The rock face was much weathered, with lichen growing over a black and grey rock; and on it had been carved, or rather hammered, a frieze of human figures of about half life size. It is a warlike scene of square shouldered men armed with lances. One seemingly has taken a woman prisoner, others are stabbing at a trussed up captive. It is an intaglio technique of sculpture, the figures being hammered in recess to show the lighter coloured stone below the surface—but large masses in the trunk and heads and thighs have been left unhammered and so still dark; and as a result the figures look strangely like the "hollow" men of many modern sculptors; and share with them the same uneasy menace.

The other remarkable frieze was found low down in the entrance to a cave at Dahro Caulos in the Hamasien division of Eritrea; and here the figures are carved in a fairly bold relief in pink sandstone. They are all roughly alike, small, varying in height between 7 and 10 in and all nightmarish females. They are somewhat tadpole-like, with round large featureless heads, thin necks, broad shoulders with thin limply hanging arms, the hands fringed with fingers, long rather tubular bodies with short massive legs usually ending in a fringe of toes. There are about thirty of them, crowded close together; and they have the same sort of horrible threat as John Wyndham's "Trifids".

Far to the west in the "Red Desert" of Tripolitania, about 217 miles south of Tripoli in 1954 an Italian expedition consisting of Professor Paolo Graziosi, Professor Vergara-Caffarelli and Dr Paradisi found a rich collection of animal carvings in a number of rock shelters opening off the Wadi el Kel. In 1874 the explorer Rohlfs, passing through this district, had noticed a grotto in which he had seen carvings of elephants, camels, antelopes and a female human figure; and this gave the expedition their clue. They were fortunately able to find a guide, an old Arab woman of the Oasis of Mizda, who knew the site of the Wadi el Kel and she led the expedition there after a difficult journey far from all roads and tracks. Here they found a number of rock shelters containing hundreds of carvings ranged like friezes on the walls of the shelters and representing many different ages.

The oldest phase of these consists of large and fine naturalistic carvings, some deeply carved, others in low relief, of both wild and domestic animals: elephants, ostriches, lions and giraffes; and of the domestic animals, especially bulls, some of which are almost life-size. In some of the oxen, the horns apparently join together in a circle in a manner which recalls the solar disks so frequent in Egyptian art; and this question of Egyptian influences in Saharan art arises even more strongly in the Tassili sites to be mentioned below. In later phases in the Wadi el Kel oxen and antelope begin to predominate and there is an artistic deterioration, the animal pictures being smaller, stiffer and less careful. This is followed by a phase when horses are frequently represented; and as Professor Emery's discovery at Buhen (discussed in the chapter on Sudan) has shown, the earliest ascertainable date for the presence of the horse in northern Sudan is about 1770 B.C. and this is about 200 years earlier than was previously believed. The last phase at Wadi el Kel is the phase of very poor drawings of camels; and as these animals were late comers to the Sahara, this period can probably be equated with the first centuries of the Christian era.

The succession of animal carvings then gives a sequence (vague in the earlier stages, but increasingly definite in the later) for the history in the Sahara of men, animals and the climate. In the late Palaeolithic or early Neolithic the climate, in parts at all events, was damp enough and the vegetation rich enough for hippopotami, elephants and rhinoceroses, and man seems to have been a hunter of animals and gatherer of food; later, in the Neolithic, cattle and antelopes appear as the predominant animals with man, the herdsman; about the time, probably of the Egyptian New Kingdom, horses appear and in some places chariots; and we can suppose that armies are beginning to move in, the Age of the Conquerors is beginning. Cattle steadily become rarer, the desiccation of the Sahara accelerates (perhaps as the result of over-grazing); and finally, as the Christian era dawns, the second "beast from the east" (the horse having been the first) moves in as the sole practicable draught animal in what has now become the desert.

Not all the carvings at Wadi el Kel are, however, of animals. There are numerous representations of female figures, which from their style, placing and careful execution can perhaps be dated to the end of the first phase. They can most probably be linked with a sexual cult; and it seems certain that some of the shelters were used at one time as sanctuaries for the practice of fertility rites.

In 1957 even more striking proof of the Sahara's great climatic change was found, much farther south and somewhat east, in the neighbourhood of the Tibesti highlands which rise in the desert, at about the level of Wadi Halfa, some 900 miles west of the Nile. The British Ennedi Expedition under Captain B. D. McD. Booth, and with Mr A. J. Arkell as its archaeologist, had crossed the Libyan Desert to study the natural history and archaeology of the Wanyanga Lake area in Northern Borkou and of the Basso in the plateau of Ennedi. On their return journey they visited the ancient amazon-stone quarries of Eghei Zumma in north-east Tibesti and while they were in that neighbourhood Captain Booth discovered an important series of rock engravings in the Wadi Zirmei. These range from what appears to be the Upper Palaeolithic; but there are no drawings of either horse or camel so that it seems likely that the latest considerably antedate the Christian era. Nowadays in this area rain falls only very occasionally and there is no mammalian life whatsoever, large or small, wild or domesticated. The carvings in the rock shelters however show dogs, domesticated cattle, both long- and short-horned, wild cattle, hyenas, giraffe, mountain sheep, kudu, sable or roan antelope, elephant, rhinoceros and ostrich. All this is of course in accordance with the repertory of the ancient Saharan artists: what is new is the discovery of several representations of an elk—and these are quite unmistakable. Fossils of such an animal (*Megaceroides algericus*) are known from the Atlas Mountains, and they appear to have reached there from Eurasia, together with the bear and Merck's rhinoceros during the Wurm Ice Age; but no trace of such an animal has been found so far east (and south of the Tropic of Cancer) as Tibesti before and its presence there is proof positive, if any more were wanted, that the climate of the Sahara was formerly much less hot and dry than it has been for some thousands of years.

However it was in 1956 that the *locus classicus* of Saharan rock art was discovered and recorded in an expedition led by Henri Lhote (a pupil of the great Abbé Breuil) under the aegis of the Musée de l'Homme, Paris, in the savagely eroded massif of Tassili n'Ajjer, just north of the Hoggar and about 900 miles south-south-east of Algiers. A vast collection of life-size transcriptions of these rock paintings has now been exhibited in the Musée de l'Homme and the story of the expedition has been told by M. Lhote in his book *A la Decouverte des Fresques du Tassil* (of which an English translation by Mr Alan Houghton Broderick with the title *The Search for the Tassili Frescoes* appeared in the autumn of 1959). But some brief summary of the nature of the discoveries must be made here to set the other discoveries of Saharan art in a true perspective.

The Tassili is a rocky massif of sandstone, violently eroded on a roughly chequerboard pattern. It is very difficult of access, indeed in the latter part of the expedition, supplies had to be parachuted in by courtesy of the French Air Force; but it is not yet quite so completely dessicated as the area where the elk carving was found. Heavy thunderstorms do occur, there is some vegetation, hares, lizards and mouflon are still found and there are a few human inhabitants, a dwindling remnant of somewhat wretched Touareg. And in a great number of places, usually in the water-eroded hollows at the foot of great cliffs, were innumerable rock paintings and carvings, so abundant as to give the impression of townships and immensely varied in style and subject and in size, some of the human figures being nearly 18 ft high, one feline about 12 ft long.

As elsewhere in the Sahara the material falls in four main phases: (1) an ancient period, probably early Neolithic, and associated with hunters of the *bubalus*, an extinct wild buffalo; (2) a Neolithic period of herdsmen of cattle, which perhaps begins about 3500 B.C. and to which the name Bovidian is given; (3) a protohistoric period of pastoralists who are acquainted with horses and chariots; and (4) the cameline period at the beginning of the Christian era. But so rich is the material that M Lhote has been able to subdivide the earlier periods into a succession of art styles. The earliest paintings are small human figures painted in violaceous ochre, with stick-like arms and legs and with horns or feathers sprouting from their heads. Somewhat later these figures are somewhat evolved and both red and yellow ochre are used; and this period leads into the period of the "round headed men". In this phase the especial feature is, as the name implies, a sort of neckless round-headedness, the figures shown being like divers or the popular idea of "Martians", and the faces usually have no features or else highly schematized ones; and this is the period of the giant figures. The period has about four main phases, becoming more elaborate and "decadent" as time goes on and in its latest stages (at Aouanrhet) is marked by an extraordinary running horned goddess in yellow and white, wearing elaborate flounces at the elbows, knees and waist, with patterns on the body, legs, shoulders and the long pointed breasts, which perhaps represent scarifications and with a design around the horned headdress which, it is suggested, represents a field of corn, with grains of corn falling from it. This strange figure, also, is amazingly like the Abbé Breuil's "White Lady of the Brandberg" in south-west Africa at the other end of the continent. Also appearing in paintings of this phase are what are clearly recognizable as African masks of a kind familiar from modern West Africa; and there seems little doubt that the artists of the "round-headed men" were Negroid.

They were followed by immigrant pastoralists, the Bovidians whose paintings are mainly human and animal figures of small size and naturalistic in, usually, red, yellow and white. Oxen, of two different species, are their favourite subject and these are shown in great herds, sometimes in a rich polychrome. But a great variety of wild animals appear: elephants, rhinoceros, hippopotami, giraffes, large antelopes like the sable, roan, addax and the like, gazelles, aardvarks, lions, wild asses, ostriches and fish; and there are scenes of pastoral life. In one case there is a scene of hippopotami pursued by hunters in a canoe. There are various Egyptian influences visible—for example, Egyptian boats and an extraordinary small picture (at Jabbaren) of a group of four bird-headed goddesses, slim, formalized and of great elegance, which are tentatively assigned to the eighteenth dynasty; and the later and post-Bovidian period is outstanding for a number of figures of remarkable beauty. These include: a dancing female figure of "European" profile, which M Lhote nicknamed "Antinea"; two girls of singular beauty with profiles like the Fulani women of today: and (at Sefar) a man and woman seated, facing each other, again with the "Fulani" profile and drawn with a masterly appreciation of perspective.

These are followed by drawings which include chariots drawn by horses in the "flying gallop" convention, and these by mounted horsemen and men drawn in what M Lhote calls a bitriangular style—that is to say broad shoulders narrow to a fine waist and spread out to a balancing width at the hips.

In the rest of Africa it is difficult to know quite what falls within the heading of archaeology. In general, I suppose, it means the study of man, by means of the excavation of his cult or living sites, from the earliest times up to the period of known history; and in the framework of Western civilization and its origins it is fairly clear what this means. Outside that framework, it is not so straightforward. What is man? *Homo sapiens?* Neanderthal Man? Apeman? And what is known history? For some parts of Africa it hasn't yet started; in other parts the New Stone Age is still in existence. In Africa below the Tropic of Cancer, for the most part, archaeology proper seems to dwindle between, on the one side, palaeolontology, the study of fossil bones and, on the other, historical research and anthropology, the study of living man as a social animal; and none of these are our concern in this book. But a number of most important discoveries have been made in this continent on the origins of man and it seems right that they should at all events be mentioned *en passant*; and, likewise, archaeological methods have been used to lay bare what on a simple time scale is relatively recent history—and again it seems right that some mention should be made of this.

In 1951 Father Gervase Mathew undertook on behalf of the Tanganyika Government an archaeological survey of the mainly Arab ruins of a group of coral islands, Kilwa, Songo Mnara and Sanje ya Kato, off the Tanganyika coast, about halfway between Dar-es-Salaam and the Mozambique border. These had been the centre of the Islamic Empire of Kilwa, which was at its most powerful between the fourteenth and fifteenth centuries A.D. It was occupied later by the Portuguese and is mentioned by the great Portuguese poet, Camoens, and, in consequence of this connexion, by Milton. This empire was of considerable importance in its time and its people were in close cultural contact with the Mamelukes in Egypt and the Bahamani in India; and its prosperity derived from its success as a commercial *entrepot* in the trade between India and China and the Mediterranean.

On Kilwa itself the principal remains excavated were: the castle, which is on the site of an earlier building but which is mainly Portuguese with later Arab additions, including modernization by the Sultans of Oman in the eighteenth century; the huge Friday mosque, the largest in East Africa; another, smaller, mosque; a large palace; a pavilion, and a number of houses.

On Songo Mnara island a whole deserted city was found, the most complete specimen of a mediaeval Islamic town yet discovered on any of the Indian Ocean islands. The principal buildings examined were a large mosque, with a splendid (and surviving) demidome of a fluted praying niche; and a large palace with the Sultan's Hamman, which was remarkable for an elaborate system of sanitation and a vault inset with a hundred glazed bowls as ornaments.

Finally on the neighbouring island of Sanje ya Kato earlier remains were found, comprising what is probably the first pre-Islamic town to be found off the East Africa coast—small coral houses inhabited by people who smelted iron and used a thin red pottery of a "Samian" type.

The great glory and the still living and continuing art of West Africa is its sculpture, principally in wood and especially in the form of ritual masks; and when it was realized that these objects were not merely quaint or grotesque but that their distortions and elaborations were concerned with presenting ideas and abstractions and not simply failing to present naturalistic likenesses, they became a potent and still major influence in modern Western European art.

But in the nature of the material, particularly in tropical countries, wood is not very permanent and for the ancient aspects of West African sculpture it is necessary to turn to the bronzes. Of these for a number of years the Benin bronzes were the best known and the most famous; and these are of course much more representational than the wooden sculpture and they were obviously much influenced by the first Europeans to frequent West Africa, the Portuguese. They contain much that is in the nature of portraiture, but even so it is portraiture abstracted, the *idea* of the person represented, whether majesty, strength, richness or some other attribute, being obviously much more important to the sculptor and the patron than any mere temporal physical characteristics. Consequently the discovery at Wunmonje in 1938 of the now world-famous Ife bronze heads and their exhibition in the British Museum after the war, by courtesy of the Oni of Ife, was a complete and startling revelation. For, quite simply, these heads are extraordinarily beautiful portrait heads, quite naturalistic—in the same tradition as Greek, Egyptian and indeed Renaissance sculpture. The sculptor they brought to mind to many people was Donatello. Their date has been the subject of intense disagreement and suggestions have ranged as wildly as 1500 B.C. to A.D. 1500. It seems clear, however, that they are earlier than the bronzes of Benin, but a discovery made in 1957 seems to suggest that they are not so very much earlier.

In that year a workman was clearing a site at Ita Yemoo for new buildings of the Ife Co-operative Union when he hit upon a group of buried bronzes, which were deeply patinated and had evidently been undisturbed for a long time. Some were broken during excavation. The finest of the figures is a magnificently preserved standing figure (about 1½ ft high) of an Oni of Ife in the regalia which is still used for coronations. The head is a portrait and the figure is wearing a three-tier tarboosh-like crown, on the front of which is a rosette and plume in a familiar form. The next most important figure is somewhat damaged but it shows a man and woman, perhaps arm in arm, and probably a king and queen; at all events the man wears the same plumed crown as the first figure, while the female's head-dress is one of receding flanges. This same female head-dress is also worn by a reclining royal figure which is incorporated in a small heavy cup, which is of brass, not bronze. Two very strange objects are in the forms of eggs of bronze, to the bigger end of which are attached two naturalistic human heads; and there are also two bronze ceremonial staffs which end in very similar human heads. Now, although all the heads in these objects are naturalistic, the objects themselves are not and the human figures are squat and compressed, as Benin figures usually are; and it seems as if these are relatively late Ife bronzes when the classical, naturalistic style of Ife (wherever it derives from) was beginning to succumb to the general West African tendency to abstract or reduce reality to idea.

As stated above, West African sculpture is usually of wood or, as at Benin and Ife, of bronze. In 1946 and 1947, however, some interesting pottery sculptures turned up in the central plateau tin-fields of Nigeria. One was a life-size head of a man, hollow, with open mouth and pierced eyes, naturalistic but skilfully simplified. This was collected by a mining engineer from an African workman who had found it in tin-bearing gravels and had used it for about a year as a scarecrow. Twenty-five miles away, in the tin workings at Nok, there were found two heads of what is obviously the same culture and the same material, a tan clay mixed with tiny granite chips; a lively naturalistic monkey; and an elongated and extremely sophisticated bearded head, rather less than life-size. A characteristic of all these three heads is that they are much more of the same family as the Ife bronzes than of the Benin work. Though simplified or stylized they remain portraits, representations of living things and not symbols or representations of ideas. It has been suggested that from their position in the tin gravels they could date from the First Millennium B.C.; but West African dates are difficult and it is perhaps sufficient to say that the Nok culture was a Neolithic one.

In 1948 and 1949, in French Equatorial Africa, in the Lake Chad area adjacent to eastern Nigeria, M. Jean-Paul Leboeuf and his wife, Mme Annie Masson Detourbet, found a rich source of terracotta sculpture, in the form of great quantities of statuettes, during their investigation of the mounds and sanctuaries of the enigmatic Sao people, a race of negroes who settled round Lake Chad in the period of the ninth to sixteenth centuries A.D. These Sao seem to have arrived from the north and later to have been dispersed by Muslim arrivals also from the north. The great majority of these statuettes, which seem to be funerary offerings, are of human figures, sometimes furnished with stumpy bow legs, but in other cases cut off at the waists. They are for the most part clumsy and grotesque, but filled with a certain disquieting power. The complete figures are usually between 9 and 15 in high and they fall into two groups: ram- or goat-headed figures who may be called masked dancers; and more nearly human figures who are considered to represent deified ancestors. These latter have broad square shoulders, short vestigial arms, duck-billed mouths open in a wide gape. Massive and clumsily modelled necklaces and huge beads adorn their necks; their eyes are usually shown as slits, sometimes upright slits like the irises of goats' eyes; sometimes they are bearded; and their hair is apparently worked up into a topknot.

Despite their use of terracotta for these statuettes, the Sao were skilled workers in bronze, which they used, in the cire-perdue technique, to make a great variety of personal ornaments. Of these the commonest were rings and bracelets, pins, ear-clips, studs and buttons; a number of tiny animal figurines and the like. The most impressive objects in this material which were found, were a libation bowl; a phyllactery; a pectoral ornament; and some curious massive objects which are puzzling and best described as ritual objects. The principal motifs used in adorning these objects are the spiral and the plait.

The existence of another cryptic culture in the Katanga province of the Belgian Congo has been recently tested and proved. For a number of years now specimens of pottery have been coming from the area of Lake Kisale, through which the young Congo River (called at this point Lualaba) runs; and in 1957 an expedition, sponsored by the Congo State University at Elisabethville and the Musée Royal du Congo Belge of Tervuren, Belgium and consisting of Professor J. Hiernaux, M de Buyst and M Jacques A. E. Nenquin conducted excavations at Sanga on the north bank of Lake Kisale. Although no settlement site was found, part of a necropolis was and about sixty graves of what is now called the Kisalian culture were excavated. Generally these graves have a number of common characteristics. The skeletons are generally lying on their sides, in a flexed position, on a north-south axis with the skull to the north and with one hand placed under the head. With the bodies are quantities of grave goods, copper necklaces, bracelets, chains and the so-called "croisettes" (H-shaped copper money) and iron bracelets, anklets and belts; and very large numbers of pots. One grave, for example, had thirty-two pots; another, thirty-three; one, only two, but this contained eleven "croisettes"; and another, a child's grave, sixteen pots. All these pots are new and unused, very well made without the help of the wheel, in colour varying from pinkish-grey to grey-red. Most of these are round bowls, sometimes with a contracted neck and flaring mouth, sometimes set on a foot, and sometimes the bowl is carinated and occasionally handles link the carination and the flaring mouth. The decoration is both incised and impressed, sometimes taking the form of repeated half-moons or cross-hatchings, zigzags or chevrons. The copper money is especially interesting. In several graves this is found in the skeleton's hand and it is natural to think of it in the same way as the obol which the Greeks placed beneath the tongue of their dead to serve as a fee for Charon, the ferryman who took the souls of the dead across the River Lethe. Stone casting moulds for H-shaped money like this were found at Zimbabwe, but there the ingots were much larger than those found at Sanga. Still this forms a link between Sanga and Zimbabwe and is indeed probably the only link between the Kisalian culture and any other African protohistoric culture. But as the date of Zimbabwe is itself much disputed, this link is very little help towards dating these "Kisalians" who were buried at Sanga. It is hoped that Carbon-14 will throw some light on this.

Farther east, where the Belgian Congo, Northern Rhodesia and Tanganyika draw together at the southern end of Lake Tanganyika, an extraordinarily rich site of a far earlier man was discovered in 1953 by Dr J. Desmond Clark, Curator of the Rhodes-Livingstone Museum, Livingstone, during fieldwork undertaken by that museum and the Northern Rhodesia National Monuments Commission. The site lies in the valley of the Kalambo River, which is in those parts the boundary between Northern Rhodesia and Tanganyika and which is famous for the Kalambo Falls, among the world's highest waterfalls, whose waters fall in a sheer drop of 702 ft into the Great Rift Valley. They did not so fall in the distant Upper Pleistocene but formed a lake on the upper side of the escarpment. During the wetter Gamblian Pluvial Period the waters rose more than 70 ft and cut through the retaining ridge. The lake was suddenly drained, the Kalambo Falls came into being and as a result the Kalambo River above the falls cut through the old lake levels and revealed a series of five living or camping floors of Early Man, exceptionally rich in stone tools from say 100,000 years ago to perhaps 41,000 years ago. The lowest three floors show industries which may be described as final or transitional Chelles-Acheul; the fourth floor is a local form of Fauresmith; while the fifth may be a final Fauresmith or else the beginning of the local Middle Stone Age proper. One peculiarity of the site lies in the fact that the lake peat has preserved wood in association with the stone tools; and it is believed that some of these wood remains were in fact used as tools themselves.

Stone tools of the same periods and also of the later Still Bay culture of the Middle Stone Age, associated with fossil remains of a wide and interesting selection of animals extinct and still surviving and—most important—a fossil skull of a new type of human, were found during the years 1951–3 in an area of undeveloped sandy veldt near Saldanha Bay about 90 miles north of Cape Town. The site is a very interesting one inasmuch as, following the destruction of the vegetation, wind erosion has started white sand dunes moving and these have revealed the fossiliferous brown quartz sands below. The process is still in operation and the dunes are still in movement, covering one part of the fossiliferous layer and at the same time uncovering another. There appear to have been lakes at one time in the area and it is in the layer of silt which they left and which lies between the white sand and the brown, that an exceptionally rich record of fossil bones and human artefacts has been found. The artefacts are principally hand-axes and cleavers, but there are also some later fossilized bone chisels. There is no sign that the use of fire was known. The animal remains are abundant and well-preserved. Some of these are of animals still existing and they include antelope, rhinoceros, hippopotamus, tortoise and hyena (one of the very few carnivores found). The extinct animals have a general resemblance to the fossil fauna of the Olduvai Gorge, Tanganyika—of which more, later— and these include extinct horses (in great quantity) giant warthog (*Mesochaerus*) extinct buffalo (*Homoioceros bainii*) and an extinct giraffe (*Griquatherium*).

The most important find however was a number of fragments of fossilized human skull, which, although scattered, clearly build up into the skull of a single individual. There are no fragments of the facial or jaw bones; but what does remain is the whole of the top of the skull from the brow ridge to the occiput. There are of course some fragments missing but these do not prevent a complete reconstruction of these areas. It is in general extremely like the famous Rhodesian (or Broken Hill) skull and also very like Solo Man from Java. It is very thick and somewhat smaller than Rhodesian Man; and as a result the brain box is about 10 per cent smaller than that of Rhodesian Man and 20 per cent smaller than the average Neanderthal Man. The Saldanha Man is more primitive it seems than Rhodesian Man and he may be an earlier variety of this extinct African race. Fluorine tests suggests that the skull is of the same era as the giant warthog remains; and this would seem to support the theory that he was an earlier variety of this extinct African race; and that he was contemporary with the hand-axe industry.

During the second quarter of this century Africa (and especially South Africa) has been the scene of the most important discoveries of all relating to the possible first origins of the human races—the extraordinarily rich material relating to a related group of tool-using "apemen" of upright posture, who are now known as the Australopithecines. In many ways this is an unfortunate name as it simply means "southern apes", and the general tendency nowadays is to think of them as "apemen" or "man-apes" or even "near-men". Their central date is taken to be about 1,000,000 years ago.

The first of them was the Taungs skull which was found by Professor Raymond Dart as long ago as 1925; and in 1936 Dr Robert Broom found another Australopithecine at Sterkfontein; and in 1938 a somewhat more advanced type at Kromdraai. In 1947 Dr Broom and his assistant Dr Robinson found a perfect skull of an elderly female at Sterkfontein and this was at one time given the name of *Plesianthropus transvaalensis* and through all the changes of formal nomenclature acquired and retained the much more convenient nickname of "Mrs Ples". In 1948 the same pair found at Swartkrans a fossil lower jaw of a different and more man-like type of Australopithecine which was at one time known as *Paranthropus crassidens* and is now known also as *Australopithecus paranthropus*. In the following year they found another, larger and more complete Paranthropus fossil—a boy's skull, at this time the first male Australopithecine to be found. This had a much larger brain capacity than any previous skull and if allowance were made for an increase in the size of the brain box when maturity would have been reached, it was considered that this type might in some specimens have reached a brain capacity of something like 900 cc.—or, in other words, within the lower ranges of human brain capacity.

Meanwhile since 1945 the Makapansgat Limeworks in the Central Transvaal has proved to be an incredibly rich source of fossil bones; and the grey bone-brecchia there has provided Professor Dart with ample material for further studies of the Australopithecines and their tools. These are of bone, horn and tooth and the majority of them come from antelopes, armbones, thighbones and shin bones providing clubs and daggers, upper jaws scrapers, horns making picks, the lower jaws blades, saws and knives and shoulder and pelvic bones chopping tools. Cannon-bones in particular were split and shaped to form points, chisels and blades; and, what is most extraordinary, the same types of bone tools, produced in the same way, also from antelope cannon-bones, were found in the *Homo sapiens* Middle Stone Age site at Kalksbank (70 miles away). In other words the true man of 15,000 years ago had inherited a tool-making technique from the ape-men, or man-apes or near-men of 1,000,000 years ago. The conditions under which they lived, says Professor Dart, were "grim and formidable. They hunted what they could; they contested 'kills' with other scavengers of the veld like vultures and hyenas; they murdered one another and were cannibals." Two skulls have been found which had been crushed in with blows from double-ridged bone clubs (antelope arm- or thigh-bones). A number of Australopithecine pelvic bones have been found; and from these it would appear that they varied very considerably in size—from the pygmy to the most robust type of present-day South African Negro.

Meanwhile in Kenya and Tanganyika, Dr L. S. B. Leakey had been making a number of important discoveries which in the most recent years began to relate to man and near-man.

Shortly after the war—in 1946—he first published a discovery which he made during a brief leave in 1942, the skull of a Miocene ape, now famous under the name *Proconsul*. The first fossil fragments of this type were found in 1931 by Hopwood at Ruisinga near Lake Victoria in Kenya and so named; in the same neighbourhood in 1942 Dr Leakey found a complete skull of the same species. It dates from about 6 million years ago and while undoubtedly an ape, it has a number of non-simian characteristics, notably in the absence of the simian shelf and in the form of the chin, which is after a fashion beginning to resemble that of man. It has been suggested that it is ancestral to man and that it bears some resemblance to Heidelberg Man, who is ancestral to Neanderthal Man; on the other hand it is also held that *Proconsul* represents a dead end in the evolution of the apes, just as the Neanderthalers represent a dead end in the evolution of man.

Dr Leakey also investigated and excavated exposed sites near Olorgesaile in Kenya, which were positively littered with hundreds of stone axes, cleavers and bolas stones, and found a series of Acheulean camp sites of about 125,000 years ago. This site was also rich in fossil remains of a number of extinct animals of the same general type as those found at Olduvai, including a number of giant animals, giant baboons and giant pig, the sivatherium or giraffe with elk-like horns, *Elephas antiquus*, *Hippopotamus gorgops* (a kind of hippo with periscope eyes), and a variety of equines.

In 1952–3 he moved to the Olduvai Gorge in Tanganyika and found a living site of Chellean Man and what seemed to have been his hunting and killing ground. It seemed to have been a lake margin where the hunters had driven their prey into swampy or clayey ground in which it was helpless and could be killed at leisure. At all events nearly all the skulls found here had been smashed to get at the brain, nearly all the bones had been split to reach the marrow. Some of the larger animals had been driven too far into the lake and had drowned and made perfect fossils. Among these were gigantic sheep and oxen, giant pigs and warthogs, Sivatherium giraffe and pygmy horses.

Dr Leakey's work in the Olduvai Gorge continued and in 1958 he was able to announce the discovery there of two living sites of Chellean Man—the first ever to be found, although the culture was first identified as long ago as 1947. This culture dates from about 500,000 years ago and it had hitherto produced no human remains. It was associated in this case with the fossils of still more gigantic animals. Three different forms of giant pig were found, two of them being about the size of hippopotami, and with immense and formidable tusks.

A female baboon jaw was found of such a size as to suggest that the males of this genus would be the largest African primates. Of the remains closely associated with man, two were especially interesting: the first being a hand-axe made from a huge flake of hippo ivory for which the nearest parallel is to be found in the Upper Palaeolithic about 470,000 years later; and some pieces of red ochre, which must have been brought from a site some 50 miles away. This suggests that Chellean Man was already interested in colour; and, since the area of these living sites is very remote from rock faces, it suggests that the ochre was used by the Chelleans of Olduvai for painting their own bodies, as the Ancient Britons used woad.

All these discoveries however were overshadowed by the finding of two human milk teeth, an upper milk molar and a milk canine, apparently the teeth of a child of $2\frac{1}{2}$–3. These are remarkable in themselves as the first physical remains of Chellean Man; but the story becomes really strange when it is realized that they are about four times the size of those of a modern infant. Now this does not necessarily mean that Chellean Man was a giant like the animals among which he lived, but it does mean that he must have had an extraordinarily massive jaw; and, bearing in mind the gigantism of so much of the local fauna, it is very tempting to think that the Chellean Man of Olduvai must also have been on a giant scale.

In July 1959, perhaps the most important discovery yet to be made in the Olduvai Gorge was made by Mrs Leakey. Dr and Mrs Leakey had been working on two levels, the Chellean level on which the giant milk teeth had been found and where they hoped to find other human remains; and on a lower level, which was marked by the presence of hand-axes, choppers and hammerstones and which preceded and led up to the Chellean-Acheul hand-axe culture. This earlier culture of the Lower Pleistocene Dr Leakey had called the Oldowan and its date is perhaps 600,000 years ago. Mrs Leakey was working alone in this Oldowan level when she uncovered what looked like a human jaw. Dr Leakey was summoned from his tent and together they extracted with dental probes what proved to be an almost perfect palate, with all its teeth, and almost the whole of the skull and facial bones. This newly discovered creature has been named *Zinjanthropus boisei* by Dr Leakey; and he seems, while related to the Australopithecines, to be a much advanced form and, of course, he is immediately associated with a stone tool industry and must therefore rank as the oldest fully-established maker and user of stone tools. The most obvious feature of the palate is the immense size of the molar teeth (which have earned him the nickname "Nutcracker Man") and the reduced size and straight line of the incisors and canine teeth. He was not of course very like modern man and much more resembled, it seems, the Australopithecines. He had a crest of bone on the top of his skull like them and also like the gorilla; and he also had a unique feature, a massive "nuchal crest" a ridge of bone running round the back of the skull between the mastoids, which were quite well developed. The facial structure is rather more like man's than that of the Australopithecines and indeed this part of the skull seems to be in line of development towards *Homo sapiens* rather than towards Neanderthal or Rhodesian Man. Whether this newly-found creature is indeed ancestral to man is of course highly debatable and the discovery of further material from this site or this culture at other sites is now extremely desirable. Still, as perhaps this chapter has shown, *ex Africa semper aliquid novi*—there is always something new coming from Africa.

A great deal of work has been done on discovering and recording the rock-paintings of Southern Africa. A good deal has been published on this subject and much of it has been the centre of a good deal of argument. However the recording of the "White Lady" of the Brandberg by the doyen of cave art, the Abbé Henri Breuil, not only presents the most beautiful and striking of the cave paintings, but his deductions from it and his dating of it provide a historical framework which seems reasonable and which (whether or not it is accepted) gives some "bone" to an otherwise elusive subject (Plate 52).

The "White Lady" painting is a panoramic, but unitary, panel in a rock shelter about 7 ft high and 18 ft long in Tsisab ravine in the Brandberg mountain in South West Africa, north-north-east of Walvis Bay. It had been discovered in 1917, by accident by Herr Reinhardt Maack, who made a rough copy of it; and it was copied again by Fraulein Weyerberg in 1928; and in 1937 Mrs Alice Bowler Kelley and Dr Scherz photographed it. In 1942 the Abbé Breuil in response to the invitation of Field Marshal Smuts began a six-year study of the rock paintings of South Africa, South-East Africa, Basutoland, South-West Africa and Southern Rhodesia; and in connexion with this made a special expedition to the Brandberg accompanied by his assistant, Miss Mary Boyle, Dr Martin and Dr Scherz. His results and deductions were published in *The White Lady of the Brandberg* (1955, The Trianon Press, for the Abbé Breuil Trust) the first of a series planned to record the Rock Paintings of South Africa.

This shelter has been painted by many artists at many different ages, but the eleventh layer completely dominates the rest and is quite distinct from them. It consists of a procession of human, part human, and animal figures moving from right to left across the panel, the human figures varying in height from 19 to 8¾ in—and the paintings are polychrome.

The first two figures in the procession (starting on the left) are two musicians playing on musical bows and facing the remainder of the procession, either to welcome it or walking (or dancing) backwards before it. Both wear elaborate head-dresses. Advancing towards them is a steatopygous woman carrying a split wand and wearing red-and-white slippers; next a sexless figure with red hair in a page-boy cut wearing a red coat—all the features and exposed limbs being painted white; and then comes a large male figure, painted in white, orange-red and black and wearing an enormous mask on his head, resembling the head of a giraffe with the teeth of a crocodile. This creature carries a curved object in his right hand, and in his left, a bow, two arrows and a knife. The next figure is much smaller, walking briskly, with white features and body, except where covered with a red coat and a red head-dress like a

Roman helmet. Next comes a most attractively painted figure—a youth, perhaps an attendant, painted in red. The face is lighter and seems "European".
He wears a number of bracelets and other ornaments and carries two bows in
his left hand, two blade-shaped objects which may be castanets in his right.
Behind him is a musician dancing backwards, blowing a round-ended pipe
which is held in the left hand, while the right holds two blade-shaped objects.
The next group consists of a zebra (red stripes on white), a very faint human
figure seemingly clearing sweat from his brow with a strigil-like scraper, a roan
antelope with human hind-legs (or else a human being wearing the antelope
skin) who may represent a ghostly character; and a horned devil. This last
figure is bent forward and presumably running. He is painted in dark brown,
is masked and wearing two short curved horns. The original brown "European"
profile has been overpainted with a white African profile. Round his body are
white and orange bands and orange bands round the knees. In one hand he has
a switch with eleven strands, in the other a long double rod.

Next comes the centre of the composition: the White Lady and her immediate attendants. In front of her walk two pages: one is dark skinned, painted
in brown-red with white strokes on various parts of the body; he is wearing a
tasselled helmet, a gauntlet on his left hand and he carries a rod in his right
hand; the other attendant is painted mainly in black with orange ornaments and
he looks very Egyptian. The White Lady is springing forward with a dancing
stride, her right shoulder advanced as her left leg comes forward. Her right hand
carries, level with her face, a large white chalice, or perhaps, flower, her left
hand, which trails behind her carries a bow and four arrows, one of which
seems to have a longer point. Her hair is adorned with strings of beads; her
profile is straight-nosed and Mediterranean, painted in pink outlined with
white while under her chin is a white fold of cloth. Her body is covered to the
waist with a short-sleeved brown-red jerkin. Her legs and thighs appear to be
clothed in flesh-pink tights with red diagonal stripes. She wears arm-bands,
knee-bands and a belt in orange with white decoration and her shoes are
moccasin-like and white. Above her on the frieze is a gemsbok with human
hind legs and buttocks, white with black stripes, perhaps another ghost figure;
behind is the sinister skeleton-man, the tallest figure of the frieze. This is a very
emaciated man striding forward immediately behind the White Lady and as it
were lunging forward with a long barbed pole, which passes behind the body
of the lady. Down the centre of his thin body runs a black line like a backbone.
He wears an elaborate helmet with either a mask or a visor. In his left hand he
carries four fans, two of them black, the other two coppery; and a couple of
long blade-shaped objects.

After this impressive group come two hartebeest, one of which has white
human hind legs; a faded male figure leading a group of archers, whose face
has been overpainted in white with a Negro profile; a walking youth, apparently tired, and behind him a magnificent polychrome painting of a gemsbok
with its head turned to face the beholder. Above the tired boy is a group of

small pink dancers; and above and below at the extreme right of the frieze are a number of smaller figures, faint or altered at a later date and a quantity of animals.

Now this White Lady frieze, although the most beautiful and remarkable of its kind yet known, is not unique; and a dating framework for such paintings has come into being, supported by a Carbon-14 date for the Philipp cave, also in South-West Africa and bearing paintings of the same period; and this date is 1300 B.C. ±200 years. The White Lady paintings, as already stated are the eleventh to have been made on that particular rock shelter and they are preceded, accompanied and succeeded by simpler forms of art, which is probably Bushman. The characteristic racial types portrayed in the White Lady frieze are "European" or "Mediterranean" or Semitic; and a number of features are shown which are variously interpreted as Libyan, Cretan or Egyptian. It seems likely therefore that the people of this culture were immigrants from North Africa, perhaps driven by the increasing desiccation of the Sahara, kinsmen in art at all events with the ancient inhabitants of the Tassili, who eventually reached southern Africa, lived apparently in amity with Bushmen in the Brandberg, later moved to south-east Africa and there lost their identity, "crossed out of existence", many centuries before the arrival of the Bantu.

CHAPTER TWENTY-SEVEN

THE AMERICAS

ARCHAEOLOGY in the Americas is curiously different from archaeology in the Old World. To begin with all the dominant and learned races in the Americas are of European origin—and from all the races. of Europe; and that greatest of spurs towards archaeological investigation—the desire to know something of *one's own* past, however remote—would naturally tend to make them archaeologists in the Old World countries, and indeed some of the most distinguished classic archaeologists of yesterday and today are Americans. Again, America before Columbus was out on its own, with no contact with the rest of the world and its Siberian origins quite forgotten and indeed still in dispute, presenting to its masters from the Old World nothing but its humanity, its riches and the fabulous wealth of economic plants which its inhabitants had created—maize, tobacco, the potato, the tomato, quinine and a whole range of beans. And finally the creators of pre-Columbian America still survive in a changed, vanquished, suppressed, decadent form—a submerged fraction in deserts, jungles, villages, reservations and slums—and archaeology turns into a sort of social anthropology or, at the worst, a tourist attraction, something quaint or fascinating.

This is of course an overstatement but it does perhaps indicate a danger—curiosity without sympathy, a temptation to regard the subjects of one's inquiry as "funny little monkey people", a turning of archaeology into a mere science instead of that far richer thing, a humane art using scientific method.

But, of course, classic archaeology of the most interesting description does exist in the Americas and principally in Central America—and principally in connexion with the Mayas.

In 1947 an expedition of the Carnegie Institution of Washington under Mr A. Ledyard Smith excavated a Maya burial mound near Nebaj in the northern highlands of Guatemala. It is presumed that these mounds were originally crowned with temples and shrines; but that since this is an area frequently disturbed by earthquakes these structures would have been of wood and so have not survived. At the edge of the mound was found an altar stone and underneath it an arrangement of human skulls. One, upside down and with a number of jades piled on it, stood in the centre of a circle of eleven others, the right way up. In a tomb of about A.D. 1200 a splendid fluted alabaster vase, some 10 in high was found. Made entirely by hand, with stone tools and without the assistance of any form of lathe, this is an exquisite piece of work, the creamy white stone having been worked with such skill and delicacy that the walls are only about ⅜ in thick and are softly translucent if a light is placed inside. Other graves were earlier and in one which can be dated to about A.D. 500 was a large pottery urn, with a lid crowned with the representation of a human head, in which two splendid jades were found. One, the smaller, was a plaque about 4½ in wide which was probably used as a breast ornament and this shows a seated god (or perhaps priest) wearing a jaguar face head-dress. The other, about half as large again is of apple-green and white jadeite and it shows a priest, seated and leaning over to his right to address an inferior (and therefore much smaller) human being. As a sort of decoration to this scene is a border incorporating the profiles of various Maya deities. This breast-plate is a remarkable work of art and craft and it has also supplied an exact parallel to a discovery at Bonampak in Chiapas.

In Chiapas, the southernmost state of Mexico, live the Lancandones, a small and dwindling group of Indians who are considered to be the purest descendants of the ancient Maya. These Lancandones led Mr Giles Greville Healey of Yale University to a hitherto unknown group of temples of the Mayan Old Empire. The site has no known ancient, or indeed modern, name, but has now been called Bonampak (Mayan for "Painted Walls") from the most remarkable discovery made there. Mr Healey's discovery was made in 1946 and in 1947 an expedition was mounted to explore the site, financed by the United Fruit Company and directed by the Carnegie Institution of Washington.

Three very large *stelae* were found, one being 18 ft high, 30 in wide and weighing at least 4 tons. The dating glyphs of these appeared to cover a period between A.D. 495 and 672, that is to say the Mayan Old Empire, before the appearance of Toltec influences. There were also two finely carved altar stones and one of these showed a god seated on a dais, in exactly the attitude of the figure in the jadeite breast-plate mentioned above, leaning over to his right, to lend his attention to three kneeling supplicants on a lower level.

The most astonishing discoveries, however, are the murals, amounting to some 1,200 ft, and, considering the terrible vicissitudes of the jungle, extremely well preserved; and the principal objective of the expedition was to preserve and record these paintings. This was done photographically (infra-red, ultra-violet, black-and-white and colour) and by transcriptions by two artists, Señor Antonio Tejeda and Señor Augustin Villagra, working direct and from the combined photographic results. Three rooms were known to contain murals; and one, the most outstanding, was immediately recorded. The task was complicated by the fact that large trees had grown on the top of the building and the action of the roots had led to three things. Water had entered the rooms from above and in some parts had coated the paintings with calcite, sometimes clouded with bubbles and sometimes making a white sheet; fungal growth, both green and black, had developed; and in some parts the roots had displaced the plaster which carries the paintings and fragments had fallen to the ground and shattered there. Despite these difficulties, the results were remarkable and a number of scenes with human figures portrayed in brilliant colour and nearly

life-size throw a vivid light on Maya life and ceremonial. The principal room
has a coffered ceiling and the paintings fall into three registers. The topmost
panels show seven masks of gods of the soil, in profile. The middle panels show
the preparations for a ceremony, on a tan ground, above panels of cursive
glyphs; and the lowest register, the perpendicular walls of the room that is,
shows the ceremony taking place—on a blue ground. In the upper panels, in
one section three personages are seen seated on a dais, presumably discussing
the ceremony to come, since they appear to be conversing; in two other sections
a number of notables in white robes are gathered together, all wearing elaborate
head-dresses and apparently ready to play their allotted parts. At one end of
this scene a servant is holding up a child, presumably to see what is going on.
A suggestion that the child is about to be sacrificed may probably be discounted
as human sacrifice was rare among the Maya. In the fourth section of this
register, the three principal personages are being garbed with huge head and
back structures of green quetzal feathers, the elaborate head-dresses consisting
each of a large water-lily which is being nibbled by a leaping white fish. Beside
this group are several men obviously engaged in vigorous discussion.

The lowest register—the ceremony itself—is a single panoramic picture
covering all the four perpendicular walls of the chamber. The three principal
personages, in all the splendour of their green quetzal feather accoutrements,
occupy the centre of the composition. On one side of them is a group of thirteen
characters, who seem to be taking part in the ceremony. Two of them carry
parasols, some are dressed in jaguar-skins and from their gestures and the way
in which some are turned to speak to the man behind it would appear that they
are engaged in an argument of some kind. The group on the other side is rather
larger and is entirely composed of musicians or dancers. At one end is a youth
blowing on an ocarina; and next to him are two men blowing long trumpets of
the kind believed to have been used by the Maya in the Oxtun dance. Next to
these are some masked dancers, costumed to represent deities of the surface or
interior of the earth. They are garbed with vegetation, and the water-lily and
leaping fish motif occurs several times. One wears a crocodile mask on his head,
another is dressed to resemble a crab or lobster with huge claws. One represents
the old god of the interior of the earth with a water-lily on his head and a *tun*-
glyph under one arm; while another has a "T" sign in one eye, which usually
signifies the rain and storm gods. Next to these dancers there are some more
musicians: a number of men beating on turtle carapaces with pronged sticks; a
drummer beating on a tall upright drum; and five men with pairs of gourd-
rattles, as it might be maracas. Two of the musicians also carry parasols.
Despite the odd shape of this picture—in which the length is more than eleven
times the height—it contrives to be a single unitary composition of great
vivacity with all the individual figures, no matter which way they are turned,
contributing to the interest of the three central figures in their splendid green
accoutrements.

In another chamber was found a scene of the greatest intrinsic and artistic interest. It shows a group of figures on three different levels—the steps of a pyramid, it has been suggested—and it seems to be a scene of sacrifice. On the top step are six figures, splendidly attired: four of them wear jaguar-skins and two of these have enormous quetzal feather head-dresses; and three of the figures have jaguar-head head-dresses. The central figure holds a sort of standard and wears a jade jaguar-mask pectoral; and before him kneels a naked man, with hands raised apparently imploringly. On the two lower levels are other naked kneeling men, one of them with his hands seemingly dripping with blood; and one lying across two steps and shown in perspective—a thing hitherto unknown in Maya art. At his feet lies a decapitated head.

In 1949 Dr Alberto Ruz, who had been appointed Director of Research at Palenque made a most amazing discovery there. Palenque is an already known Mayan site of great importance and beauty deep in the dense vegetation of Chiapas. Arguing that the Mayans tended to build on top of already existing monuments he judged that the tallest existing monument, the Temple of the Inscriptions, would bear further investigations. And so it did—though not in accordance with his argument. This temple crowns a stone pyramid and is approached by a long steep flight of steps. Mayan pyramids, it should be explained, have always been considered to be entirely different from Egyptian pyramids and to have been built not as tombs, but rather to bring the temple at the summit more conveniently near to the god and to serve as a platform for astronomical observations—in fact, more like the Towers of Babel, the *ziggurats* of Mesopotamia.

The temple on the summit of the Palenque pyramid consists of a portico leading to a sanctuary and to lateral cells. The flooring is made of large slabs of stone instead of the more usual levelled plaster; and one of the slabs in the sanctuary was distinguished by two rows of holes provided with plugs. Dr Ruz decided that the answer to this anomaly lay below; and accordingly lifted the slab. Underneath was a packing of large stones. When these were removed, a descending stair was disclosed, which led downwards for forty-five steps to a landing. At this landing there was a U-turn, and a further descending staircase of twenty-one steps. Two sets of small offerings, ear-plugs, beads and the like were found; and in a corridor an obstruction some yards thick of stone and lime. When this was demolished, the skeletons of six young persons, of whom at least one was female, were found, lying in front of a triangular slab of stone, about 6 ft high, which had been used to block an entrance. When this slab had been displaced sufficiently for a man to enter, a large crypt was disclosed, whose walls sparkled with a veiling of stalagmites and calcite; and on the walls, partly hidden by the calcite, were stucco figures of priests, rather larger than life size. Almost the whole of the crypt was taken up with a single massive monument, like a colossal altar. Its top consisted of a single huge stone slab, with an area of nearly 9 sq yds. This rested on a colossal monolith, which in its turn was supported on six great blocks of chiselled stone. All of these elements carried complex reliefs. The top slab was carved with a symbolic scene, surrounded by astronomical signs, while its four edges carried hieroglyphical inscriptions giving thirteen abbreviated dates corresponding to the beginning of the seventh century A.D.

Was this an altar; or was the monolith below the slab hollow? Dr Ruz had borings made at two corners; the drill reached a hollow space; a wire was poked through the hole and it came out covered with red cinnabar. This was most promising as red in the Maya cosmogony signifies the East, resurrection and immortality and it is often found in tombs.

It was decided to lift the slab, a difficult task since its estimated weight was 5 tons, it was in itself a most valuable piece of Maya sculpture and working conditions in the crypt were far from convenient. However with the aid of four jacks and an assortment of pieces of hard wood, the slab was eventually lifted about 7 ft above the monolith. It was then discovered that a huge cavity in the shape of a capital Omega (closed at the base) had been carved out of this block and then sealed with an exactly-fitting slab of the same shape. When this was lifted, the interior was revealed.

This was a blaze of vermilion and jade. The walls and base of the cavity were brilliant with cinnabar; and in the cavity lay the skeleton of a man unusually tall for a Maya and so covered in jewels, principally of jade, that the form seemed to be filled out and there was an illusion of life. The teeth of the skeleton were not filed or incrusted with jade or pyrites—as would be customary in a high-born Maya—and although it was not possible, owing to the state of the skull, to tell if this had been artificially deformed—as would also be customary in a Maya of high social rank, nevertheless the great size of the dead man and the condition of his teeth led to the belief that here was a non-Mayan stranger who had nevertheless made himself a rich and powerful king in Palenque. He had been buried in the most extraordinary tomb yet to be discovered in the Americas; and he was decked with a positive treasure-house of jewellery. On his head was a diadem made of tiny disks of jade and his hair was divided into separate strands by means of small jade tubes. Around his neck was a collar of jade beads of many forms—cylinders and spheres, buds and open flowers, pumpkins and melons and a snake's head. The ear-plugs were of various elements together making up a flower and counterpoised by what at first appeared to be a pearl of fabulous size but proved to consist of two pieces of mother-of-pearl exactly fitted together. On his breast was a pectoral formed by nine concentric rings of twenty-one tubular beads in each. Round both wrists were large bracelets of jade and on each finger of either hand a great ring of jade, one carved in the form of a crouching man. The right hand held a huge cubical bead of jade, the left hand a spherical one; and beside the feet were two other great beads of jade, one hollow and with two plugs in the form of flowers. There were two small jade idols, one by the left foot, the other by the waist; and in the mouth cavity, according to the Mayan custom, there was a beautiful bead of dark jade, so that the dead man should have the means to obtain food in the next world. And, most splendid of all, partly still over the face but partly fallen to one side a complete facial mask of jade mosaic, made of hundreds of small pieces of jade, with eyes of shell and obsidian. This mask originally fitted completely over the dead man's face, the elements being fitted into a base of thin stucco. It is possible that it was prepared beforehand and kept fitted on to a stucco dummy head. It is perfectly realistic in treatment and may well represent the actual features of this powerful prince and stranger. It is worth noting that the six young persons who were sacrificed outside the crypt to act as the dead man's companions all had the characteristic deformed skulls of the Mayan upper-class families.

A serpent, modelled in plaster, seems to emerge from the sarcophagus, and ascend the steps leading to the threshold of the room; here it becomes a tube which runs as far as the corridor and then leads on into the temple in the form of a hollow moulding superimposed on the steps. This amounts, one must suppose, to a conduit for the spirit of the dead man and a means whereby the priests of the temple could maintain contact with his departed spirit and so interpret his wishes from this splendid, elaborate and, as far as is known, unique tomb.

Another most important Maya site (or rather group of sites) came to light as the result of accident. Some 17 miles south of Guatemala City lies a beautiful lake, Lake Amatitlan, some 7½ miles long, surrounded by lava hills and dominated by the four-peaked cone of the volcano, Pacaya. This has become a resort centre for Guatemala City, with hotels featuring thermal baths, and much frequented by those interested in motor-boats, sailing and water-ski-ing. Amateur skin-diving also became popular; and its purpose in the first place was to locate good underwater fishing-grounds. In 1955 however these divers began finding Maya pottery vessels in large quantities—and they had very soon collected more than 400 virtually intact vessels, incense-burners and stone sculptures.

Now, to set this in context, it should be mentioned that between 1905 and 1908 a Harvard expedition had dredged the Sacrificial *cenote* (or ceremonial well) at the great Maya city of Chichen Itza; and had found there great quantities of objects thrown into the water by pilgrims visiting the city: objects of gold and copper, jade jewellery, obsidian knives and also, the skeletons of of men and women. In 1956 aqualung divers of an expedition of the Middle American Research Institute of Tulane University, under Dr E. Wyllys Andrews, explored the principal *cenote* at the Maya centre of Dzibilchaltun in Yucatan; and they brought to the surface from depths of 100–140 ft some thousands of potsherds including whole vessels and a number of other artefacts.

In 1957, therefore, Dr Stephan F. de Borhegyi, of the University of Oklahoma, busy in the Guatemala Highlands with a group of students of the San Carlos University of Guatemala Summer School, heard of the activities of the Lake Amatitlan skin-divers and decided to examine their collections and to undertake a survey of the lake-side sites.

This consisted of plotting as far as possible the location of each object found and preparing maps of the lake-sides where these objects were found; and also examining certain near-by Mayan sites on the southern shore of the lake.

These were found to cover a very considerable period of time and consisted of:
the oldest, Contreras, with continuous occupation from about 1000–200 B.C.;
the Early Classic site of Mejicanos, A.D. 300–600; the Late Classic site of
Amatitlan (A.D. 600–900); and a few uninvestigated hill-top sites, believed to be
Post Classic and dating from about A.D. 1000 to the Spanish Occupation in
1524. The objects found in the lake appeared to correspond in date and type to
the site nearest to the point where they were found.

The objects themselves may be numbered in hundreds and are for the most
part complete or nearly so and in excellent condition. They consist for the most
part of offering bowls or incense burners with covers and they range in height
from a few inches to 4½ ft. They bear a great variety of designs, mostly in high
relief; and some of these designs are unusual, rare or even unknown for the
Maya Highlands, including the cacao tree, beans, quetzal birds, jaguar heads,
bats and human skulls. One splendid drum-shaped offering vessel has four large
human skulls in high relief at the cardinal points half-way down the side, while
on the upper rim, immediately above each skull, is a human face in such high
relief that it looks like a medieval gargoyle—wearing a feather head-dress and
with mouth open and eyes closed. This combination of closed eyes and open
mouth, which is found also in other examples, may be intended to suggest death;
and on one incense burner there is a figure in low relief holding a sacrificial
knife; and these things may suggest the possibility of human sacrifice as at
Chichen Itza. Some of the objects were found underwater still stacked, with
four or five incense burners one on top of the other; and here it is possible that
these offerings were deposited by the lakeside and submerged only by an alteration of the water level. Others however, were scattered at very much greater
depths and here it looks as though they were purposely thrown into the waters
of the lake. It is quite easy to see why the lake should have been considered as
a sacred place, as there are a number of spots on the south shore where geysers
appear periodically and very hot sulphurous water in several places bubbles up
from the floor of the lake; and these phenomena, together with the presence of
an active volcano in the neighbourhood could well have given rise to the belief
that the lake was the haunt of very powerful and potentially dangerous spirits.
Furthermore to this day, every year on May 3, the Festival of the Cross, a
wooden figure of the Holy Child is taken across the lake in a procession of boats,
and flowers and fruit are thrown into the lake by the pilgrims—and it is not
uncommon, especially in Central America, to find ancient pagan customs preserved in vestigial form in Christianized festivals and rituals.

In 1938, a group of mahogany cutters stumbled on a group of caves deep in
the Chiqubul Forest, in British Honduras, south-west of Belize and Mr A. H.
Anderson, the present Archaeological Commissioner, briefly investigated the
site but was not able to do any digging. Early in February 1957, however, Mr
Adrian Digby, Keeper of Ethnography, British Museum and Mr A. H. Anderson, at the expense of the British Museum and the British Academy, mounted a
small expedition to examine this site and find out what it was. Severe flooding

made the site even less accessible than usual and their digging time was cut down to little more than half what they had planned. Nevertheless they were able to make some very interesting discoveries of a quite unusual kind. On their arrival at what is now known as Awe's Caves or more simply as Las Cuevas, they found a pyramid and a low mound completely overgrown with vegetation beside a deep natural depression, roughly circular in shape and with a diameter of about 260 ft; and in the cliff-like side of this depression the mouth of a cave could be seen. They made a preliminary reconnaissance of this cave with the aid of hurricane lamps and they discovered that it went back about 400 yds but that at about 100 yds in there was a stone wall dividing the outer from the inner chambers. Beyond this wall the cave was everywhere littered with broken bowls and urns.

They decided to divide their forces, Mr Anderson working on the monuments above, Mr Digby concentrating on the cave.

Above, the bush was extremely dense and it was not so much a question of excavating as clearing with axe and machete, but, in all, seven mounds or pyramids were disclosed. Two of these were long and close together and may prove to be the sides of a ball-court. The two tallest probably originally carried temples on their summits and two others may have been priestly dwellings. An unusual architectural feature was a pair of long low banks of stone-work facing each other across an open space and each built with two levels or steps running the whole length. Possibly they were reviewing stands for people watching ceremonies in the space between them. No inscribed *stelae* were found, and although three altars were uncovered these were quite without carving or inscription.

Meanwhile, in the cave, Mr Digby had been excavating one of three platforms in the outer chamber of the cave. This had been considerably disrupted, probably as the result of an earthquake and the consequent fall of boulders from the roof of the cave. The platform had been built and rebuilt several times, with stone and mortar and a staircase was its principal surviving feature. It was soon clear that it had been used as a mortuary chapel for cremation burials; and also that the inner chambers of the cave had been used for the depositing of cinerary urns—all of which had been smashed, presumably by chicle-gatherers who had hoped to find treasure. The most remarkable feature was however the desperate poverty of the site. There were no inscriptions, there were no jades, there were only a few crude ornaments made from shell or bird bone; a beautiful cylindrical ceremonial vase had been used for cooking—to quote Mr Digby "It was as if somebody had used a piece of Sevres porcelain to boil potatoes in". The date of the site was revealed as being of the end of the late Classic Period, when the Maya civilization was breaking up.

Perhaps the Mayan populace had revolted against the tyranny of the literate hierarchy; and had violently freed themselves from their masters—and from all the crafts, skills and knowledge which had built so elaborate a civilization on, in the last resort, the cultivation of the maize plant—and were now paying a terrible price for their freedom, a price of misery, incompetence, ignorance, starvation and barbarism, lapsing into a Dark Age, for which there are parallels in the past and warnings for the future.

A curious, if somewhat oblique light is thrown on this possibility by the discovery of several curious lids of pottery. These were dish-like but with a domed centre and the underside was deeply scored. This scoring was presumably functional (since it could not be seen from above) and its probable use was to "key" some substance to the lid. One of the lids still had a partly carbonized substance still adhering to it; and a small fragment when held in a flame gave off an aromatic odour. Now scored lids of a similar type had been discovered by Dr de Borhegyi at various sites in Guatemala associated with three pronged incense burners and were considered to be lids for the incense burners. At the Las Cuevas site the lids were associated with cinerary urns; and the suggestion is that the lids were smeared with an aromatic pitch or resin, heated on the incense burner and then transferred to the cinerary urn, where they would serve a dual purpose, both purifying the contents and sealing the urn. Now the three-pronged braziers or incense burners have been shown by de Borhegyi to go back to pre-Classic times, or about 300 B.C. It is well-known that cremation was practised by the Maya in their late period. If the braziers were used in the manner suggested, it would seem that they also practised cremation in very early times; and it would then appear that these "Dark Age" Maya of Las Cuevas, having thrown off the hierarchy, were also reverting to "the old gods". Whether this can be proved still remains to be seen, but it is not inconsistent with what happens in other periods of national disaster or racial decline.

In the Old World archaeological sites seem modern unless they are over 1,500 years old; and, unless they happen to be in the Indies or central Africa, it is soil and the debris of the hungry generations which cover them over. Amurath succeedeth Amurath and one occupation layer imperceptibly deposits itself on another. In Central America the tale of history is shorter, but the jungle buries the past with remorseless speed and, as was mentioned in connexion with Las Cuevas, the axe and the machete replace the trowel and the brush as the archaeologist's tools. A Mayan city, for example, can be perfectly well known to exist in such and such a place; but no one can get to it without an elaborate expedition and having got there can hardly see it, much less gain any comprehensive view of it. In the case of Las Cuevas, Digby and Anderson were three days before they even saw a considerable mound which was only three or four yards from their principal trail to the camp.

Tikal, one of the great Maya cities in Guatemala was a case in point and this was the chief goal of an expedition of the University Museum of the University of Pennsylvania which began operations in 1956, with the object of freeing five great temples from the overwhelming jungle.

An even more drastic procedure has been followed in the Mexican state of Tabasco. Here in 1942 Mathew Sterling, Miguel Covarrubias and others had discovered in the jungle at La Venta a large number of colossal sculptures in basalt and andesite. These are the work of the Olmecs, Central America's first great culture and they date from about the beginning of the Christian era or, and perhaps more probably, from some 200 years earlier. These are very large monolithic sculptures of various types, and in their original positions stood a considerable number of miles (of very difficult country) from the nearest sources of such stone. Parenthetically, it may be mentioned that cultures and peoples with a taste for megalithic architecture and sculpture seem almost to find a merit in hauling their huge blocks of stone great distances. The various builders of Stonehenge fetched their stones from south-west Wales and Marlborough; the sculptors of the great statues of Easter Island lugged their colossal portraits relatively great distances from the quarry; and the Egyptians hauled the great blocks of Imperial porphyry from the most inhospitable fastnesses of the Eastern Desert.

However this may be, on the instance of Carlos Pellicer, a poet who is also the organizer of the museums in the provinces of Mexico, twenty-seven of the finest of these Olmec sculptures have been transplanted from the jungle and set in a 15-acre parkland site at Villahermosa. The smallest of the monoliths weighs 6 tons and the largest 37 tons and this last one still remains at La Venta, because although the machinery lent by the Mexican Petroleum Co was capable of lifting and transporting it, the highway bridges leading into Villahermosa were not strong enough to carry such a load (Plate 53).

For the most part, these sculptures are typically Olmec in character. That is to say that when they portray the human face—and most of the subjects are, or contain, human figures—those faces are not in the least like the savage Aztec face or the nosey rather chinless Mayan profile, but are broad, brooding, short-nosed, rather blubber-mouthed, muscular but fat—in fact not unlike a certain type of modern American athlete run to seed. This last feature is particularly noticeable in the most striking type of sculpture—the "big heads". These are simply colossal male heads, executed in the round and some of them about 10 ft high. They have no necks and were never part of larger sculptures. They simply rest on the ground, complete in themselves, endlessly brooding, and usually portrayed as wearing what looks uncommonly like the head-harness of an American footballer. There are other types of human figure in the collection: one kneels and holds some indefinite object, rather like a box, in front of his chest; one clasps his hands behind his head which is thrown back to gaze at the sun with an expression of complete self-dedication; one stands impassively on a *stele*, wearing a short kilt; and others appear in what may be altars. These last are curious massive blocks, not unlike knee-hole desks in shape; and in the kneehole crouches a human figure. One simply relaxes there, as if this were the perfectly natural thing to do (rather like Mr Darling in Nana's kennel in the last act of *Peter Pan*); another holds out a child across his arms—perhaps a sacrifice, perhaps an emblem of motherhood, perhaps a dedication.

Finally, reference must be made to two extremely interesting series of excavations at approximately the inhabited poles of the Western Hemisphere, both by Scandinavian expeditions: in Greenland, under the Danish C. L. Vebaek; and in Easter Island, under the Norwegian, Thor Heyerdahl.

It is widely believed that the Norsemen discovered the mainland of America long before Columbus—but that nothing came of their discovery. It is quite certain that they reached southern Greenland about 1,000 years ago. It is believed that the actual discovery was made by the Norwegian Gunnbjorn early in the tenth century and it is known that in A.D. 986 Eric the Red started a colony near Julianehaab. A few years later Leif Ericson brought Christianity to Greenland. At its zenith the colony had a population of some 3,000 settlers; but it had completely died out by A.D. 1585.

Its especial interest, oddly, lies in the fact that it is the best source of information on the medieval agriculture of the Norsemen. Their farms there, for the most part, have not been disturbed or worked over since they were abandoned; and in the severe climate all sorts of objects in a variety of materials are exceptionally well preserved. In the 1920's excavations were carried out under Dr Norlund; and in 1939 an expedition was headed by Mr C. L. Vebaek of the Danish National Museum, Copenhagen. This last expedition's work was resumed after the war in 1945 and 1946 under the same direction, and then continuously for some years from 1948. The principal districts investigated were Vatnahverfi (between Igaliko and Agdluitsoq Fjords) and the Unartoq Fjord area.

A considerable number of farms were discovered and examined. Some of these contained quite elaborate buildings, the dwelling-houses being usually built of a mixture of stone and turf, while the other buildings were of stone alone. In some the walls were standing to a height of 6–7 ft, in other words almost completely intact; but many were completely ruined and the footings alone survived in position. One of the farms contained a bath-room—a characteristic Scandinavian steam bath-room—with a stone-built stove on whose outer walls water was thrown to produce a copious steam. Examination of the bones from kitchen middens revealed that a number of domestic animals had been kept—horses, cattle, sheep and goats—and the remains of wild animals included polar bear, reindeer, hares, Arctic foxes, many different birds and fishes, and especially walrus, and several species of whale and seal. Quantities of medieval objects of many kinds were found—of wood, iron, walrus ivory, bone and steatite (or soap-stone)—and they included two small crucifixes of steatite, a hammer, an axe, wool-shears and some sickles, all of iron, and gaming pieces and chessmen together with bone combs and bodkins.

The most evocative discovery however was the quite large Benedictine nunnery and church, discovered beside the Unartoq Fjord. A nunnery in a hitherto unknown continent, close up against the Arctic Circle, years before the austere Cistercians founded Fountains Abbey in Yorkshire and considered that they were pioneering in the wilderness by doing so—it is impossible to withhold one's astonishment and admiration at the courage and devotion of this community of Benedictine nuns. Their church was oriented east-west and its interior measurements were about 43 × 17 ft. Three of the walls were of stone about 3 ft thick and the fourth wall was most probably of wood, as was not uncommon in Greenland. There is a fireplace hearth near the middle and there were burials of about twenty persons inside the church, towards the west end, and this apparently establishes quite definitely that it was a nunnery church. There were many burials also outside the church, including some mass burials of both young and old, evidence, it is thought, of some plague or epidemic. A large building, in a very poor state of preservation, but which had been built of large stone blocks and originally a building of some dignity, was very probably the nunnery itself and the dwelling-place of the community. In one of the rooms of this building the remains were found of seven large wooden tubs (with a base diameter of about 4 ft) set side by side and into the floor. The staves of these tubs were fastened with whalebone and they had probably been used to contain milk. At some point in time, however, the purpose of the room had been altered and the remains of the tubs were filled in and the floor level raised to cover them. Three somewhat similar tubs were found in a farm in the Vatna-hverfi district; and in these were discovered—the bones of about a hundred mice. A curiously dramatic scene in miniature is evoked; in the last state of despair and resignation, this northern settlement is abandoned, all is silent in the deserted farmhouse except for the squeaking of the mice who take over undisturbed, swarm into the tubs for the last drains of the last milking, glut themselves, fail to climb the overhang of the staves and perish of starvation and cannibalism—the logical fate of all successful parasites.

The discoveries made by Mr Thor Heyerdahl's expedition in Easter Island have of course been most vividly and fully described in his book *Aku-Aku: The Secret of Easter Island* (George Allen and Unwin) and it only remains to summarize here some of the more striking discoveries made. Some of these were artefacts; others historical and sociological findings.

The famous feature for which Easter Island is so well known is the quantity of colossal human statues—of which there is a striking example in the British Museum—carved out of a dark compressed volcanic ash and showing abnormally long heads with long ears and a sort of dished profile quite un-Polynesian in effect. It was known from the early voyagers that these statues had originally been crowned with massive head-dresses of an entirely different stone, a red tuff. The carving of these statues had been entirely discontinued and it was assumed that the modern Easter Islanders knew nothing about them and were incapable of such art, skill and engineering competence; and were indeed a different race.

By a combination of excavation, experiment, interpretation of legends and by gaining the confidence of the Easter Islanders, who were very much impressed by his feats with the *Kon-Tiki* raft, Mr Heyerdahl has been able to put forward what seems a very consistent history for the island. One of the most striking made features of the island is a deep defensive ditch—Iko's Ditch—which cuts off the eastern extremity of the island from the rest. A radio-carbon reading from the bottom of this ditch gave a date something like A.D. 400 (which is the oldest established date in Polynesia). Traditionally this ditch made this end of the island a stronghold for the dominant race, the Long Ears, against possible uprising by a subject race, the Short Ears, who provided the helot population of the island and the labour force for carving, moving and erecting the huge statues. Sometime about A.D. 1600 a rising of the Short Ears resulted in the capture of the ditch and the wholesale massacre of the Long Ears. Traditionally, there was only one survivor and certain families of Easter Islanders today claim descent from this survivor; and support this claim by their possession of certain esoteric knowledge, certain secret possessions and by the not infrequent physical trait of having red hair.

By appealing to this racial pride, Mr Heyerdahl was able to persuade men of these families to demonstrate how these huge statues could be moved across country and erected on their bases by traditional methods and using only traditional means; and they also demonstrated how the statues were carved out of the wall of the volcanic quarry in which numbers of uncompleted statues can still be seen. Later, men of these same families led him to their secret family caves underground and showed him quantities of small stone statuary of a hitherto unknown type, but with a strong South and Central American flavour.

Excavations also revealed many things. Of these the most important is a huge human figure in a kneeling position carved out of the red stone, from which the head-dresses were normally made; and this is believed to be much earlier than the dark stone figures. One of these latter was cleared below ground; and on his belly was discovered carved a large reed boat with three tall masts for sails. Others were similarly cleared below ground; a considerable amount of anomalous sculpture was found; and temple platforms, or Ahus, were cleared. In all, a great quantity of material was found which is still to be interpreted; but which seems almost certainly to link Easter Island and various other Polynesian islands very firmly with the American continent.

CHAPTER TWENTY-EIGHT

RUSSIA

As WAS stated in an earlier chapter, it is known that an immense amount of archaeological activity has taken place in all parts of the Soviet Union since the war. Unfortunately very little information about this is readily available in English. Perhaps this will not always be the case; perhaps the increasing cultural exchanges between the Communist and non-Communist countries will lead to a flow of information, which must obviously be of the greatest interest and use to archaeologists, amateurs of archaeology and the general public throughout the world. Possibly a book in succession to this one may be of help in spreading such information.

In the meanwhile a description can be given of a truly astonishing series of discoveries made over a period of years at Pazyryk in the Altai Mountains in southern Siberia, which are of the greatest intrinsic interest and importance and which will also give some idea of the richness of the archaeological treasure still waiting to be disclosed. For what follows on this subject I am indebted to what has been published in English by Dr R. D. Barnett and Dr William Watson, both of the British Museum, but a book on these finds, in Russian, by the excavator, S. I. Rudenko, is available in this country.

What was found was a series of burial mounds or *kurgans* of nomadic peoples living in the region now called the Gorny Altai about 50 miles from the Outer Mongolian frontier. These were excavated by S. I. Rudenko first in 1927 and 1929 and later in 1947–9, when the most important tomb, *Kurgan* 5, was found. The typical form is a cairn of stones covering a timber-lined pit, which in its turn contains a smaller burial chamber. For some reason which is not quite clear these pits had in every case become filled with perpetual ice. Soon after the burials had taken place robbers had entered and apparently removed all objects of gold, except for gold foil decoration of clothes and equipment. Perhaps as a result of this breaking in, water seems to have filled the pits and permanent frost developed which has had the effect of perfectly preserving the contents of the tombs in "deep freeze" conditions for some 2,400 years.

The typical tomb contains a man and a woman, embalmed, supplied for the after world with precisely those things they had used and needed in this one: wooden bowls, full of food, tables, cushions, clothes and harness with elaborate decoration, weapons, and musical instruments. In the outer chamber of each tomb were a number of horses, between seven and sixteen, all of which had been killed with an axe-blow on the head and in each tomb, with the horses, was a cart. In *Kurgan* 5, there was also a light four-wheeled chariot with thin, many-spoked wheels, made to be drawn by two horses on either side of a central shaft, with two others, out-runners, attached by traces. This chariot seems somewhat Chinese in style and may indeed have been acquired from China either by capture or as a diplomatic gift. Each burial chamber also contained a bundle of poles, which are interpreted as the framework for a tent in which the intoxicating fumes of hemp could be inhaled. In one of the tombs a flask of hemp-seeds was found.

As will be described later a great many of the objects found at Pazyryk show strong influences from both east and west, China and Persia; but a very great number are obviously of local origin and show most markedly that fantastic style of Scythian animal art in which a great variety of animals appear, treated in a fantastic formalizing way. Among the animals found so treated in these tombs are horses, eagles, falcons, cats, elk, deer, panthers, bird-griffins and lion-griffins—and these animal forms are treated by the artist as a basis for the wildest fantasy, in which, for example, antlers may develop into a wild series of curlicues, tails prolong themselves into endless flowering branches and any limb may be turned in any direction to suit the requirements of the composition of the picture or the disordered fancy of the artist. As it has been said "instead of the relatively ordered, objective and natural world of the Near East, the 'animal style' expresses the wild and bewildering dream world of the visionary, the ecstasy of hemp-smokers, the mysticism of shamans."

Oddly enough perhaps the most perfect examples of this animal art were found on a human body—for the bodies of the dead were as perfectly preserved as the other objects in the tomb, despite the fact that the tomb robbers had in some cases severed the heads or cut off limbs, presumably in order to remove gold necklets and bracelets. One of the males found was elaborately tattoed about the arms and shoulders and on one leg; and although the leg tattoos were relatively simple representations of a fish and a frieze of running ibex, the animals on the arms and shoulders (as shown in the transcript on Plate 55) are the purest phantasmagoria. While mentioning the bodies of the dead, it should also be recorded that these were of mixed physical type, some of them being Near Eastern in physique and appearance, others purely Mongol.

The most beautiful and astonishing object to be found at Pazyryk was an almost perfectly preserved Persian carpet, $6 \times 6\frac{1}{2}$ ft, which was discovered lying as a saddle on one of the dead horses in *Kurgan* 5. It is of a sheared pile, made on a loom, with thirty-six knots to the square centimetre. It was made with a knot which represents the Turkish tradition in carpet making, which would suggest, since the Turks came from Central Asia, that it was made locally; but the motifs, as will appear, are almost entirely Persian or Near Eastern, so that again it would appear that either the Persians used the Turkish knot in antiquity or else that, if the carpet was made in Siberia, it was a local copy of a Persian model (Plate 54).

Its design is rich but straightforward, not in the least like anything a Scythian "animal artist" would produce. The centre is a quadrilateral of four rows of six square designs of a quatrefoil derived from Assyrian palmettes (and exactly paralleled in a carpet sculptured in stone in the Assyrian palace at Nineveh). Round this quadrilateral runs a border of forty-four plaques each showing a sphinx. Outside this is a wider border showing twenty-four grazing elks, all nose to tail. Next comes a narrow border of sixty-nine quatrefoils with outside this a border of twenty-eight horses, also nose to tail, but proceeding in the opposite direction to the elks and alternately ridden and led by a Persian cavalier, wearing the characteristic Persian head-dress; and the final border repeats the sphinx-plaques. The colours of this carpet are red, pale blue, greenish-yellow and orange.

It is known that carpets were made as long ago as the eighth century B.C. at such places as Babylon and Sardis, and Xenophon says that there was a Royal factory at Sardis which made carpets exclusively for the Persian king; and they were regarded by the Greeks as Oriental luxuries—but nothing even distantly approaching the antiquity of this Pazyryk carpet has ever been found in such wonderful preservation.

Two other beautiful Persian textiles, both of them tapestries and almost certainly Persian royal fabrics of about 450 B.C. were found in the same tomb; and these may have been booty or perhaps royal gifts. One of these is of fine wool and it is made up from a number of squares joined together and it had been cut up to form the edges of a horse cloth. Each square bears a similar but not identical design, showing two crowned queens sacrificing at a central incense altar and behind each queen is a smaller similar queen, but the taller queens wear veils. The backgrounds are either light brown or blue. On the brown background the queens wear yellow and red; on the blue, their clothes are yellow and brown; and their flesh is white. The other tapestry had also been used on the chest cloth of the same set of horse trappings and is of the same manufacture as the preceding one. It shows a frieze of roaring lions *passant* in a considerable variety of colours, blue, brown, red, white and yellow on a pale blue ground between a border of brown and blue triangles.

There was also a fine Chinese textile of a silk rather like tussore silk and this had been embroidered with pheasants either perched on flowering branches or running among them.

The local materials are felt and leather and both had been used in an appliqué technique. The most elaborate piece of appliqué felt was a tomb wall hanging with two repeated designs. One of these designs shows an elegant moustached horseman with a flying cape, mounted on a tall lightly built horse (of the same sort as the slaughtered geldings found in the tombs); and this rider has brought his horse to a halt before a bald-headed seated figure, dressed in a long robe and wearing what appears to be a felt turban-like cap perched on his bald head. One of this figure's hands is raised to his mouth or nose—rather as though he were taking snuff—while the other clasps the stem of a highly formalized "tree of life" which grows beside him. The chair on which he is seated is odd. No chairs are found in the tombs; its legs look to be lathe-turned; and its back turns over and points downwards in a positively *art nouveau* manner. What this scene represents it is difficult to say; but, since of late what were usually thought of as Herodotus' "tall tales" are now considered to contain a great deal more fact than they were previously credited with, it is possible that the seated figure is one of Herodotus' Agrippaeans. These were a tribe of Scythians who were said to be bald and who lived as judges under trees acting as arbiters between their neighbours and offering sanctuary to fugitives who came to them. This being so the horseman with his flying cape could well be such a fugitive riding up in search of sanctuary.

Between these scenes ran borders made up of squares bearing a formal design based on elk antlers, alternating with crosses, the four legs of which end in fleur-de-lis. And as a margin to this hanging is the repeated figure of an extraordinary sphinx or perhaps a shaman dressed as a sphinx. The stance of this creature is the rampant position of heraldry. The feet are those of a lion; the arms and hands are human, but with only three fingers; the face is human, realistic and wearing a moustache rather like that of the horseman. The body is slim, pale blue and decorated with rosettes. A striped tail curls forward between the legs and ends in an elaborate flourish of leaves and flowers. The head is covered with what looks like a lightly twisted turban and the hair hangs down in a short thick, up-curled pigtail. From out of the turban sprouts a complex set of antlers—a "head" to gratify the greediest of Goerings. From the small of the back shoots out a highly formalized wing: three long straight feathers, four richly curly ones. Despite the oddity of the units of this figure, the final effect is neat and balanced and the colouring is immensely gay.

Other felt hangings and horse-clothes were equally gay, but less elaborate and sometimes show repeated motifs such as whirligigs usually derived from formalized antlers—antlers being a priestly attribute in Siberia and being taken to indicate an ability to pass rapidly through the sky—which sounds almost like a distant ancestral origin for Santa Claus' team of reindeer. One felt hanging shows swan-like birds of Chinese origin but it was quite obviously of local execution and may be considered as an example of Chinese influence.

CHAPTER TWENTY-NINE

CHINA

As HAS been the case in many countries, archaeology in China has seen a great surge in activity and interest since the war. This is partly due to the organization of the Archaeological Institute of the Peking Academy of Sciences in 1950; partly to the increased tempo in opening up the country and in large-scale industrial development; and also very largely to a growth of national feeling about the monuments of the past. Also, no doubt, with the change from being one of the great international trading countries to becoming one of the great enclosed self-developers, there has been less scope for "dealers in antiquities" and clandestine digs. For example in the past when such things as rock-cut Buddhist shrines were discovered it was not uncommon for the heads of statues to be cut off as in this form they became negotiable objects of commerce; and similarly the treasures of a tomb would be quietly dispersed to appear, eventually and irregularly and after considerable trading processes, as objects in collections and museums all over the world.

Interest in this increased activity has been aroused in this country by the exhibitions of photographs which have been arranged by the Chinese People's Association for Cultural Relations with Foreign Countries and staged by the Britain–China Friendship Association*; and these exhibitions have been interpreted by, among others, Dr William Watson of the British Museum and Mr William Y. Willetts. Archaeological pictures and articles have also appeared in such sponsored publications as *China Pictorial* and *China Reconstructs*. What follows is an attempt to give some slight idea of the scope of this activity.

For many years Chang Shu-hung had been working on the famous Buddhist caves in Tun-huang, in far north-west Kansu and a programme of conservation and restoration of the murals there developed out of this work. In 1951 an exhibition of this work was staged at the Historical Museum, Peking, the main exhibits being reproductions of the murals, hand-painted by, among others, Chang and his daughter. Such was the interest aroused that since 1952 a number of postage stamps have been issued bearing motifs and decorative borders based on these murals—servants and musicians, a battle scene, a hunting scene, horses and carts and the like.

Other Buddhist shrines, also in Kansu, but much farther south, also came to light and were the subjects of scientific survey. Notable among these are the cave shrines of P'ing-ling Ssu, which probably date from the hundred years

---

* Some of these have been recently published with the title *Archaeology in China: a survey of some recent discoveries, from the Palaeolithic to the end of the Han dynasty* with text and commentary by Dr William Watson.

after A.D. 650. The most interesting features of these are the rock-cut sculptures, in very high relief, usually of a Buddha between Bodhisattvas. They show a very strong Indian Gupta influence and indeed many of them seem far more Indian than Chinese. The carving is sensuous and indeed voluptuous and a frequent use is made of the pose called *tribhanga*. In this the weight of the body is on one leg, with the hip to one side, the trunk slopes the other way in counterpoise, while the head and neck tilt in the same line as the legs. A most striking example of this is given in a relief of Avalokitesvara, Saviour deity of Mahayana Buddhism (who is better known in his later female guise of Kuan-yin, goddess of mercy). This Indian style eventually offended Chinese taste and about the middle of the seventh century A.D. one famous Buddhist said that sculptors now made images so like dancing girls that every Court wanton imagined herself to be a Bodhisattva.

Work was also done farther north but also in Kansu, on the Yellow River at Mai-chi Shan, "the paradise of woods and springs" where there are 158 caves in a towering rock-face, dating from the mid-fifth century A.D. The outstanding feature is a huge recess in the rock with a great canopy carved above it, of Northern Chou date (A.D. 557–581). In this niche are seven caves symbolizing the Seven Buddhas of the Past, the last seven, that is to say to attain Buddha-hood on earth, the last being the historical Buddha, Sakyamuni or, in Chinese, Shih-chia. Also at Mai-chi Shan are murals very much in the manner of those, mentioned above, at Tun-huang. One of these shows a man, perhaps a donor, riding in a light two-wheeled cart drawn by a single horse and accompanied by grooms and mounted attendants. The wheels of this cart are light and thin-spoked and are indeed very much like those found with the chariot in *Kurgan* 5 of the Pazyryk tombs in Siberia. Another mural shows a Buddhist heaven, with horses, musicians, *apsaros* and even an elephant in violent eddying flight across the sky.

In 1954 or 1955 a large haul of curious Christian relics of the China of Kublai Khan came to light and were interpreted by Professor John Foster of Glasgow. They come from Ch'uan-chou (the Zaitun of Marco Polo's narrative) and from its medieval walls. During the Japanese war these walls were pulled down, but later a Chinese schoolmaster collected together from the rubble all the stones with inscriptions or carvings, dividing them into Buddhist, Muslim and Christian. These Christian stones are grave-stones and they date from the time that Kublai Khan (whose mother was a Christian Kerait princess) was taking a great interest in Christianity and indeed in 1269 asked the Pope to send him a hundred missionaries. Actually one Franciscan, Brother John of Monte Corvino, arrived in Peking twenty-five years later in the year that Kublai died. Seven other Franciscans came about thirteen years later and communities of Chinese Christians did come into existence, some Roman Catholics with Latin as their liturgical language, others Nestorians with Syriac. The gravestones are of both communities, the not-very-legible inscriptions being sometimes in Syriac, sometimes in Latin, sometimes in unidentified scripts and in one case in Chinese written in the Tibetan Phagspa script. The signature of these stones, however, is the cross, usually, however, somewhat exotically mounted on the lotus, sometimes on a symbolical cloud (which is a Taoist symbol) sometimes on a combination of lotus and cloud. In some cases the cross stands between flying angels—but strange angels, with Mongolian features, moustaches, and flying draperies which serve them as wings. In the more elaborate examples these angels wear trousers and three-pointed caps in the Persian style.

Chinese history gradually changes from legend and tradition into recorded history during the "Three Dynasties"—Hsia, Shang and Chou—and excavations at two sites in central Honan, just south and north of the Yellow River have thrown considerable light on both the early Shang period (fifteenth–twelfth centuries B.C.) and the late Shang period (c 1300–1027 B.C.).

The earlier site is at Chengchow, near the junction of two railways, the Peking-Hankow line and the Lunghai which runs east to west from the coast to Lanchow and which both follow routes which have been the main thoroughfares of central China since remote antiquity. In this plain the Shang capital changed its location several times, according to tradition; and although the date has been much disputed, it is now thought that it was around 1300 B.C. that one of the Shang kings, Pan Keng, moved his capital from the south side of the Yellow River and built a new city, Anyang—which has been the scene of archaeological activity since 1928.

In 1950 however an ancient town site was discovered at Chengchow at which under characteristic Anyang remains cultural layers were found which clearly belong to the earlier Shang dynasty; and from these it seems clear that this period marks an important phase in China's history, the phase during which bronze-working, writing and, in general, an urban civilization came into being. In 1955 more extensive excavations were conducted and town-walls of beaten earth were discovered which seem to enclose a rectangle of about $1\frac{1}{4} \times 1$ mile, rather larger in fact than the present walled city of Chengchow. Unfortunately most of this early city lies under the modern town; but nevertheless some interesting finds have been made in the western suburbs. This must have been a potters' quarter and some fourteen kilns were found in the area. These are of a vertical type (about 4 ft in diameter) with a central wall supporting a perforated clay shelf on which the pots were fired. A number of potters' tools were found. These include clay stamps for impressing standard decorations on the surface of pots; and these standard patterns were such things as an "ogre-mask", dragon, trellis and squared spiral designs. A clay mushroom-shaped tool—rather like the wooden object used in darning socks—was probably held against the inside of the pot while the outside was beaten smooth with a wooden bat. Most of the pottery was hand-turned, but some vessels show the marks of the wheel. The ware is usually grey, having been fired in reducing conditions. Among the typical shapes are the li-tripod—rather like a goat's udder—whose bulging hollow legs would bring the food being cooked in close contact with the heat of the fire; a tulip-shaped beaker, again probably a cooking vessel though also used with a clay cover as a crucible for melting bronze; a hollow-pedestalled cup, a *ting*-tripod with solid legs and wine vessels which imitate the shape of contemporary bronze vessels.

On two sides of the ancient city bronze casting workshops were discovered. Two kinds of crucibles were found: the tulip vessel already mentioned and a bucket-shaped vessel of coarse sandy ware. Quantities of earthenware moulds for bronze casting were found, among them one for a socketed axe and many for arrowheads, arranged like the elements of a feather on either side of a central spine from which they could be broken off. There were also sectional moulds for ritual vessels. Small bronze objects like arrowheads, knives, fish-hooks and awls were found near the foundries; and bronze vessels in graves. Among these last, mostly rather thin and crude compared with later Shang bronzes, are *ting*-tripods, *ku*-beakers and *chueh*-cups. There was also a considerable bone industry, for the making of awls, arrowheads and hair-pins. A somewhat unexpected and gruesome discovery was that about half the raw material used in these workshops was human thigh-bones.

Gruesome also, but in the grand manner, was the royal tomb which was discovered at Wu Kuan village near the later Shang capital at Anyang. This was probably discovered in the 'thirties but a systematic account only became available in the 'fifties. This was a large rectangular pit, about 46 × 40 ft, approached by long ramps on the northern and the southern sides. Its walls went down straight for 15½ ft; and then, after a step, a coffin pit of the same shape, but about half the size, went down another 8 ft or more. In the centre of the bottom of this pit was a small cavity in which was found a single funeral victim, armed with a bronze halberd and presumably intended to protect the coffin from attack from beneath. Above this nether guard, the lower pit formed a burial chamber lined with roughly-trimmed logs to form floor, walls and roof. This chamber had been rifled of all except a few funeral offerings which had escaped the robbers. On the step, which was level with the roof of the burial chamber was an ordered array of grave-goods and, on the east side, the skeletons of seventeen men, and, on the west side, those of twenty-four women. None of these skeletons showed signs of violent death. On the northern ramp were the skeletons of sixteen horses (four chariot teams) some dogs and two men. These men are kneeling and looking outwards, one holding a halberd, one a bell. On the southern ramp was a similar collection of skeleton guardians. In the earth fill of the main pit were the skeletons of monkeys, dogs and deer and, piled in the corners and facing inwards, thirty-four human skulls. Some 50 yds from the tomb were four rows of graves containing the head-less skeletons of those who had been executed to provide the thirty-four skulls.

Strangely enough, among all this carnage the most important object found was a musical stone. In later times suspended stones, graded in appropriate notes, were a prominent feature of Chinese music, but this is quite easily the earliest found. It is very large, a piece of white marble with green mottlings,

$33\frac{1}{8}$ in long, $16\frac{1}{2}$ in high and about 1 in thick. It is roughly the shape of a trimmed pork-chop and it has a hole for suspending it and on one face is carved a stylized tiger, *passant*. It is not only the oldest musical stone but also the largest and the most strikingly decorated.

At another village near the later Shang capital, Ta Ssu K'ung Ts'un, a splendidly preserved chariot burial was found in 1953. Great care had been taken with this 3,000-year-old burial. A pit large enough to take the chariot with its horses complete was dug; and then a series of smaller pits were dug in the bottom of it to take the lower halves of the two wheels, the axle and the shaft between the two horses. Then the chariot had been lowered carefully in position; the two horses were killed and laid on either side of the shaft, on their sides but symmetrically back to back; and the dead man was laid at full length crosswise in the body of the chariot. All the wood had perished, but the pattern of the thin-spoked chariot wheel (very like that preserved in the Pazyryk *kurgan*) survived as an impression on the side of the pit in which it had stood. All the bronze fittings of the chariot and of the harness survived in the appropriate positions, including two bronze bow-shaped objects with U-shaped ends terminating in jingles. These are sometimes said to be ornaments for bows, sometimes only cautiously described as "bow-shaped objects"; and although at first glance they would look uncommonly like chariot fitments for guiding the reins and their position in the tomb would support this, it is generally agreed by the pundits that they can be nothing of the sort.

Similar chariots, but 600 years later in date, were found in excavations conducted by Mr Hsia Nai near the town of Hui Hsien, also in Honan, some 30 miles north of the Yellow River. Here a number of tombs were found dating from the period of the Warring States (fourth and earlier third centuries B.C.). One tomb, or rather burial pit was 23 yds long, 26 ft wide and nearly 15 ft deep. In this had been buried nineteen chariots in two rows, close together, with the shaft of each resting on the body of the one in front. With them were no human remains at all but at one end of the pit, but separated from the chariots, were the skeletons of the horses. The wood of the chariots had entirely decayed, but in place of each timber was compacted earth different in texture from the surrounding soil and extremely careful excavation resulted in laying bare the "ghosts" as it were of all the chariots. One of these "ghosts" was detailed enough to allow of a reconstruction being made. They are light two-horsed chariots with a central shaft and wheels with twenty-six spokes. In one case these spokes are in the same plane as the felloe, but the others are conical in profile, the hub being set inwards in relation to the felloe; and one of this latter type even has two members crossing direct from edge to edge of the wheel in complete disregard of the hub—a very arbitrary piece of reinforcement.

By an odd coincidence this reconstructed chariot looks very like Sir Cyril Fox's reconstruction of the Ancient British chariot, whose remains were found at Llyn Cerrig Bach in Anglesey.

In 1953 and 1954 two large intact tombs of the Han Dynasty, both dating from the second century A.D. were found. One of these, at Wang-tu in Hopei, was excavated in 1954 and is of brick construction and is outstanding for its murals, the largest group of Han paintings known. The other, at I-nan, in Shantung was excavated in 1953–4, is of massive stone construction, and its remarkable feature is the bas-relief carvings.

These tombs are completely underground structures, on a north-south axis, with three main axial chambers, the plinth for the coffin being in the northernmost chamber. Opening off these main chambers are subsidiary rooms and in both these cases these numbered five.

In the brick-built Wang-tu tomb three walls of the south chamber and part of the corridor leading to the central chamber were covered with murals painted in red, blue and yellow outlined with black and disposed in two registers, an upper and a lower. In the upper register the paintings show a frieze of minor court officials, all presumably concerned with the funeral arrangements, since they all look in the same direction—towards the north chamber, in which the coffin would lie. The lower register shows a variety of auspicious objects, birds, beasts and plants, all belonging to the world of magical Taoism and popular myth.

Architecturally the I-nan tomb is more impressive and its chambers are formed by a sort of corbelling, with massive stone slabs, successively projecting farther outwards and supported in the centre of the roof by a boat-shaped bracket of stone carried on the top of a pillar—which is really a method of wood construction carried out in stone.

These columns, walls and entablatures are covered with bas-relief carvings of the greatest intricacy and their subjects are drawn from popular mythology and scenes of daily life. They include a detailed representation of the battle between the mythical Yellow Emperor, Huang Ti and the rebel Ch'ih-yu; other battles; the Scarlet Bird of the South Quarter and the Sombre Warrior, the Tortoise of the North; enthroned and accompanied by musicians are Hsi Wang Mu, the Queen Mother of the West and her male counterpart of the East, Tung Wang Kung; a man bending a compound cross-bow, with an arrow in his mouth; the mythical Fu Hsi with his consort Nu Kua with, behind them, a mason's square and compasses; and many others.

In 1956 and 1957 an enormous Imperial tomb on much the same lines was discovered north-west of Peking; but this is of much later date, being about contemporary with the last years of Elizabeth I. It is the tomb of one of the last Ming Emperors, Wan-Li, who reigned from 1573 to 1619. It is completely underground, reputedly some 60 ft or more down and it is about 90 yds long. The principal chambers are oriented north-north-west by south-south-east. It is entirely of vaulted construction without any pillars and a square entrance hall leads to a long chamber, which leads to another long chamber (the sacrificial chamber) which leads to the long burial chamber which is at right angles to the axis of the preceding two. There are also two other long chambers, one on either side of the sacrificial chamber and connected with it by longish corridors. The principal chambers are separated from each other by massive double doors of stone, sometimes described as being of white marble, sometimes of "sweat-white jade". They are decorated simply with nine rows of circular bosses with two carved animal heads to hold the door-rings. Each door weighs several tons, but they are so well engineered that they can still be pushed back by a single person. The floors are made of "gold brick", bricks, that is, made of very fine clay mixed with tung-oil, which give a highly polished long-lasting surface.

In the sacrificial chamber, just in front of the doors leading to the burial chamber were three massive thrones, facing inwards, of white marble with their backs carved in a design of coiling dragons. In front of them were incense sticks and candles still in perfect condition; and three "eternal lamps", very large drum-shaped vases of blue Chia-ching ware with dragon designs. Presumably lack of oxygen had extinguished these lamps untimely, as they were still half full of oil in liquid condition.

On a plinth in the burial chamber stood three very large red-lacquered coffins of nanmu wood, each with an inner coffin, also red-lacquered, containing the skeletons of the Emperor and two Empresses, with only the hair intact—and the Emperor's reddish-brown moustache. Each was crowned with a crown of black and gold and beside the Emperor lay another crown. This last was entirely of filigree of gold wire and was in the form of a domed skull-cap with a raised part at the back adorned with a pair of gold dragons playing with a pearl.

The tomb as a whole was packed with treasures of every description in the elaborate late Ming style, vases, bowls, coins, precious stones, gold, silver, porcelain and brocades. It is the last which are the most valuable from the archaeological point of view, as hitherto only small pieces of Ming embroidery existed. This tomb has provided an immense quantity, whole 14-yd bolts of them, uncut, and with the maker's name still on them, woven of silver and gold with dragons, rabbits, fish, birds and flowers. Naturally there is much jade of the finest workmanship—there is for example a wine jug (rather like a modern coffee-jug) complete with lid and a chain attaching it to the handle, carved from a single block of jade, chain and all—and there are many combinations of gold and jade of the most exquisite craftsmanship and an oppressively opulent taste. With the Emperor's coffin were the remains of helmets, armour and swords, encrusted with pearls and inlaid with jade, a book recording the Emperor's merits and posthumous title, his seals, wooden figures of horses and men, most complex bridal head-dresses and tiny models of houses.

An exhibition of these treasures was staged in the Palace Museum, Peking.

CHAPTER THIRTY

NEW TECHNIQUES—IN THE FIELD

In the high old days of archaeology, when the practice of that science in the field bore a suspicious resemblance to tomb robbing, standards were low and labour was cheap and statuary and the like could be ripped out of the unprotesting earth expeditiously and in quantity.

All that is changed; not only have standards gone up—witness Sir Mortimer Wheeler's book, *Still Digging*—but the object of the operation has changed. The idea is to discover what went on at each level of the site or each phase in the cultures (which is more or less the same thing); and this calls for ceaseless vigilance and ordered documentation—almost as every trowelful of soil is lifted. And all costs have gone up and, notably, the cost of labour. Many many more sites are being excavated, much more meticulously and at much greater expense.

Sometimes it would almost seem that if every butterfly has to be broken on a wheel, it is hardly worth while to swat a fly. But things have not, in fact, reached this pass. There is much more money available; not enough perhaps, but there are innumerable universities, institutes, schools and societies active in the field and they all have some money to devote to the work and there are certain notable foundations and some industries which have given generous help; and in one interesting case, that of Iraq (which has been dealt with in the appropriate chapter), the Government has actually employed the archaeologists in solving irrigation problems. And of course science and engineering have lent the archaeologist massive assistance—in the field and in the laboratory.

To deal first with developments in the field; and to mention only the most striking of these.

Labour being the largest single item of expense, it is essential to use the labour force to the best advantage and in the least wasteful manner. If hundreds of tons of soil have to be shifted, it is important that it should be the right soil; and, furthermore, that it should not be dumped in a place where it will have to be moved all over again. In other words, first find your site. . . .

Of all the modern detection methods, aerial photography is the most striking and the most generally useful. It has now been developed and used, of course, for a considerable number of years; and in consequence is outside the scope of this work. It will be sufficient perhaps to mention the continuous archaeological survey which is going on in the British Isles, principally under the direction of Dr J. K. St Joseph of Cambridge; and to refer to its valuable use in recording the innumerable Etruscan tombs to the north of Rome and to the part it has played in identifying the part-submerged site of Etruscan Spina, not far from the delta of the Po. Very briefly indeed what aerial photography does is to reveal the "ghosts" of buried buildings, earthworks and the like by showing inequalities in the ground which can not be seen at ground level; or by recording what are called cropmarks. These last are regular variations in the height or colour of a growing crop; and from the air they are clearly discernible at certain stages of the crop's growth. To put the phenomenon at its simplest: the well-being of a crop of grain depends on the depth of the topsoil. If that has been deepened by an ancient ditch, the crop along that line, will tend to be stronger-growing than elsewhere; whereas a buried wall will tend to produce a line of poor soil or drought, and so a line of inferior growth. From such data as these plans of buried buildings can often be drawn in surprisingly accurate detail, before a spade is put in the ground.

With an aerial photograph of the site to work from, a rough working plan can be made on the ground, with a reasonable degree of accuracy. Still even so a good deal of time, labour and money can be expended on trial trenches and the like; and it is here that electrical resistivity methods can supply the answer.

All soil resists an electrical current, the drier the soil the greater being the resistance, the wetter the less. This principle is made use of in the following way. A buried feature is suspected to exist (perhaps as the result of aerial photography). Along the lines of this feature a number of traverses are made by inserting a pair of steel probes and passing an electrical current between them. The resistance is recorded on a suitable meter and transferred to a graph and this graph shows with considerable refinement where the topsoil is wetter (and therefore deeper) and where drier (and therefore shallower); and when a sufficient number of traverses and readings have been made, the lines of buried ditches or walls begin to appear on the plan with remarkable precision; and the archaeologist knows exactly where to dig with the minimum of wasted labour.

This method has been employed with great success in a number of places since the war; and especially in the huge Etruscan cemeteries north of Rome, where aerial photography had revealed literally thousands of tombs, stone-walled chambers below ground level; and resistivity traverses have proved invaluable in translating aerial photographs into working plans for the actual diggers.

The ordinary resistivity apparatus however is large and cumbersome, requiring a truck to itself to carry a generator and the ancillary gear. The transistor, however, that seemingly magical germanium valve which operates on a minimal current of electricity has changed all that; and Mr John Martin, working in the Instrumentation Laboratory of the Distillers' Company, Ltd for Messrs F. A. Hughes, Ltd, has produced a remarkably simplified and completely hand-portable instrument, which makes use of the properties of the transistor, and which was used by Mr Anthony Clark with great success in the excavations of the Roman site of Cunetio near Mildenhall in Wiltshire (directed by Mr F. K. Annable and Miss Ilid Anthony). This instrument in use and a diagram typical of its findings are shown in the illustration on Plate 58a and c. Mr John Martin is also developing a four-terminal apparatus of similar compactness, which will be independent of probe contact resistance. This, as a result, will require less careful probe insertion and will be effective for a wider variety of soil conditions.

Both these techniques—aerial photography and electrical resistivity—are then extremely valuable and economical; and both were used with great success in the huge Etruscan necropolises at such places as Cerveteri and Monte Abbatone. But they revealed such a wealth of tombs that the archaeologist was at once delighted and embarrassed. It was well-known that many of these tombs had been clandestinely dug and robbed in all periods since antiquity. What a pity if, after all the trouble of excavation, the cupboard was bare. Now it was also well-known that these Etruscan tombs were all pretty similar—underground stone-lined chambers with an entrance at one end, sometimes with painted walls, sometimes with carved sarcophagi, always with an assortment of grave goods, usually pottery. If only it were possible only to excavate intact tombs; if only it were possible to see inside the buried chamber before digging. . . . A delightful dream.

Signor Carlo M. Lerici and his technicians in the Lerici Foundation made this possible with remarkable success. First of all they used a powered light drill to take soundings in the soil above the chamber and by plotting on a chart the points where the drill struck rock they obtained a plan of the roof of the tomb chamber. This done, they then drilled right through the roof of the tomb and lowered through the hole a long tube of metal, containing an electronic flash apparatus and a tiny camera, of the sort used by secret agents during the war, controllable from the surface. This tube was rotated through 360 degrees and twelve exposures were made; the tube was hauled up, the camera taken out, the film developed and a complete all-round picture of the interior of the tomb was obtained, without ever putting a spade in the earth. This "periscope photography" (as it was called by Mr John Bradford who was the first to publish the technique in this country) had truly worked a miracle (Plate 56).

The perfectionists of the Lerici Foundation, however, were not content. There was the delay of developing and perhaps printing the film (which might show nothing) and there was the waste of time, labour and film, if the tomb proved to be empty. And so, perhaps inspired by those words "periscope photography", they produced a somewhat larger tube, with a $2\frac{3}{8}$-in diameter, with a telescopic system and a pair of prisms, an eye-piece at the top and, at the bottom, a light bulb and a condenser lens to illuminate the tomb. Once this was inserted in the tomb roof, the operator could switch on the light and examine the interior of the tomb and see what lay inside. Furthermore, this ingenious tube also contained an adjustable mirror in phase with an aperture in the side which could be opened to allow a good-sized camera to be attached and so photographs could be taken without the necessity of using microfilm—and only if they were necessary.

The results obtained by this method are quite outstanding and include the first painted tomb to be found in Etruria since 1892—the "Olympic Games" tomb; but the logistic and economic aspects are even more remarkable. In only 120 working days between February and September 1957, using these methods, 450 tombs were recorded, 280 were photographed, 340 were excavated, and about 3,000 objects were found; at a total cost for prospecting, photographing and excavating, of about £6,000.

Not all problems, however, are so straightforward and uniform as the Etruscan necropolises; and the periscopic methods of the Lerici Foundation were the solution to a particular problem. But the mechanical drill has proved useful elsewhere. When the Mexican archaeologist Carlo Ruz found a huge stone block in the heart of the Palenque pyramid and was doubtful whether it was a sarcophagus—it was the first to be found in a Central American pyramid —he drilled through the side, found that it was hollow and, when the drill came out coated in cinnabar, knew that indeed it contained a burial. In Phrygia more recently the American archaeologist from Pennsylvania University, Professor Rodney S. Young was confronted at Gordion with the task of excavating several large tumuli, which were believed to be artifical burial mounds. Such Phrygian tumuli usually contain in their hearts wood-lined burial chambers, capped with a pile of large stones and a dome of clay, and then heaped over with hundreds of tons of earth; and since these chambers are usually off centre with relation to the circle of the tumulus, the task of finding and excavating them is colossal. The largest of these Gordion tumuli was about 165 ft high with a diameter of nearly 800 ft—incidentally the tomb when found proved to be a rectangle of 17 × 20 ft.

How to lessen the work—and cost—of excavation was the problem. A light oil rig was used at a number of points on the top of the mound—the first year on a smaller tumulus, later, when that proved successful, on the great tumulus —and a planned series of drillings were made. Whenever the drill struck stone, the point was plotted and the drill moved until a complete picture of the cap of stones over the tomb was obtained. Incidentally this had a diameter of 100 ft, lay at about 130 ft below the peak and was somewhat to the south-west of the centre. The tomb lay below the centre of the cap of stones; and although the task of reaching it was still one of very great labour, it was very much less than it would have been without the reconnaissance by oil-drill (Plate 58b).

Two other techniques of detection may perhaps be mentioned here and more fully described where the discoveries with which they were concerned are related in the appropriate chapters. In Denmark ordinary army mine detectors were used to discover metal objects below the surface in what was now a peat bog but had been the edge of a lake in antiquity. The other technique is the use of photography coupled with strong oblique lighting to reveal shallow or battered reliefs or engravings in rock; and examples of this use that come to mind are the

Magdalenian sculptures in the rock-shelter at Angles-sur-l'Anglin in France, and the "Mycenaean" weapons and symbols discovered a few years ago on some of the stones of Stonehenge.

Not all archaeology however is excavation; it is not only land which covers the past; it can also be water and diving may be as useful as digging. There was the case of that positive museum of a Roman ship which had foundered off the Tunisian coast near Mahdia and from which a whole treasury of Greek works of art of all kinds—marble statues, bronzes, pottery, and architectural elements—was recovered by divers during the years 1907–13. Of recent years Turkish sponge fishers found by accident not far from Halicarnassus a singularly beautiful fifth-century B.C. bronze Demeter. And to this sort of archaeology, the sort of underwater swimming developed by the frogmen during the war and the invention of the aqualung, which has given the diver almost the freedom of a fish, have given a new impetus.

At Baiae, near Naples, part of the old pleasure resort of Imperial Rome, a sort of "Brighton of the Emperors", now lies under the sea and a number of statues and fragments of sculpture have been recovered from the shallow water at various times; and here Signor Raimondo Bucher, one of Italy's foremost underwater explorers, has been reconnoitring the plan of the ancient town, which has been revealed fairly clearly by aerial photography. At Emporio, a small Greek city of Homeric times and later, in the isle of Chios, English skin-divers have worked with the British School of Archaeology in Athens to explore the ancient harbour. But of course the classic feat of underwater archaeology since the war has been the work of Commandant Cousteau in exploring the wreck of a Greek merchantman lying in 18–21 fathoms off the French coast, not far from Marseilles. This ship, his divers have discovered, was laden with a full cargo of wine packed in hundreds upon hundreds of amphorae, some so well packed and sealed, that their liquid contents were still well preserved, completely untainted by salt, but also, alas, after all these years, quite innocent of alcohol. In exploring this ship Commandant Cousteau made use of a gigantic suction pump, to clear the wreck section by section of the centuries' deposits of mud, thick, deep and almost concreted.

And this brings us to the great snag in underwater archaeology. If the wreck or the submerged buildings are in water with a regular current or tide, they may well have remained clear and easy to discover; but they are almost certain to have been broken up and dispersed. If, however, they lie on a still bottom, they stand a good chance of being very well preserved and static; but it is virtually certain that they will be covered with such deep mud, ooze or sand that they will be extremely difficult to find and impossible to explore and recover, without the use of such elaborate and powerful pumping apparatus as that used by Commandant Cousteau.

Not all archaeology's new techniques, however, are concerned with discovery; and one of the most interesting of these is the use of rubber latex for the recording of inscriptions and shallow reliefs. It should perhaps be mentioned that the old method of making facsimile records of such things was by making a series of papiermâché "squeezes", which although light were cumbersome, fragile, far from permanent and tiresome to prepare. Latex records have none of these faults and they have been made by a number of archaeologists, especially Americans and the most elaborate and certainly the largest latex records were those made by Mr Kermit Goell during excavations at Nemrud Dagh and Arsameia in ancient Commagene conducted by his sister, Miss Theresa Goell and Dr F. K. Doerner. These mountain top sites contained a number of very long, excellently preserved inscriptions in a singularly beautiful Greek script. The method briefly was as follows: the inscription was brushed and washed, sprayed with polyvinyl-acetate, and painted very lightly with talc suspended in water; then a thin coat of latex was applied all over the surface, the latex being a pre-vulcanized latex with an added white fill to give it opacity. Three coats were applied and then a grid of gauze bandages was added to give strength, and a final coat of latex painted on. This was usually left overnight to dry; and the whole thing pealed off in the following morning. When thoroughly dried and powdered the sheet of latex, recording the inscription in the completest detail, could be rolled up on a rod and packed for transport. These squeezes are light, survive endless rough treatment, folding and handling and plaster casts can be made of them. When it is stated that one of the squeezes made at Arsameia was of an inscription $7\frac{1}{2}$ ft high by 23 ft long and that this could be rolled on a pole and carried away on donkey-back the advantages and practicability of this method are immediately obvious. Furthermore unlike Rawlinson's papiermâché squeezes of the Behistun inscriptions—which mice ate in the British Museum—latex squeezes are inedible (Plate 57a and c).

These then are some of the principal new techniques which have been developed or extended since the war to help the archaeologist in the field. Archaeology at home, however, has also received substantial technical assistance; but since these are techniques of the laboratory or of the study it seems appropriate to reserve them to another chapter.

CHAPTER THIRTY-ONE

NEW TECHNIQUES—IN THE LABORATORY

IT WOULD be foolish to suggest even for a moment that any new scientific discoveries or newly developed techniques can solve all the problems of the archaeologist; as foolish in fact as to imagine that the problem of catching the criminal was solved by the development of "finger-printing". Yet there is no doubt the "finger-printing" system does help in catching the criminal and more especially in *proving* his guilt; and similarly in archaeology—which often has much in common with a detective story—scientific means are often invaluable in establishing a theory which has been arrived by more subjective means. Or disproving one—as in the case of the Piltdown Man hoax.

This extraordinary story, which in the first place seemed to set a great portion of the scientific world in a ludicrous light, in the end reflected the greatest credit on the men of that world for the ruthless way in which they re-examined the evidence, tested it in a great variety of ways and published the newly discovered truth at whatever loss of face.

As the result of the discovery over a period of time, apparently in the Piltdown gravels, by a Sussex solicitor and amateur palaeontologist, Mr Charles Dawson, of a cranium, a mandible, a number of flint tools, a "bone implement" and a variety of animal remains, the existence was apparently established of a type of incredibly early man—Piltdown Man (*Eoanthropus dawsoni*)—of a quite anomalous type, with a human type brain but a massive anthropoid jaw. Nevertheless Piltdown Man was accepted by some of the most impressive authorities, became a regular feature of all the text-books, and the crucial remains were an honoured exhibit at the Natural History Museum, South Kensington. But a truly admirable scientific caution remained in some scientists' minds, a germ of suspicion grew and very soon after the war the word was passed round that Piltdown Man might not be all that he seemed to be and that he had better be left out of scientific arguments on the subject of human evolution. A great deal of work was being done on the subject, in which many departments played a part but which is chiefly associated with Dr Kenneth Oakley of the Natural History Museum, South Kensington, and Professor Le Gros Clark of Oxford University; and on 21 November 1953 it was publicly announced that as a result of investigations by the Department of Geology, British Museum (Natural History) and the Department of Anatomy, Oxford, it had been found that the Piltdown mandible was a deliberate hoax, being in fact the jaw of an immature orang-outang, broken and stained to simulate great age and with the molars mechanically ground down in a way and at angles quite impossible in living wear. Furthermore the cranium was much more modern than had been supposed and it was clear that the whole of the Piltdown finds had been deliberately "planted" on the site and actually came from widely differing ages and countries.

Besides the departments named, others who played a part in the investigation were the Department of the Government Chemist, the Geological Survey and the Physics Department of King's College, London University. Actually once it had been accepted that the remains were not sacrosanct and uniquely precious, a great number of the tests applied were simple and obvious. For example, a number of the finds had been artificially stained, principally with iron and in one case with a chromium compound, to simulate the natural colouring of objects "native" to the Piltdown gravels. A drop of acid on the surface of one of the planted flints instantly revealed the white undersurface, whereas similar treatment of a "native" flint revealed that the natural staining was much deeper. As regards the "worked bone implement", experiments with raw and fossil bone revealed that such effects could only be produced with a metal knife in bone that was already fossilized—and that therefore the "bone implement" was a modern production. One of the exhibits was a beaver tooth embedded in a gravel conglomerate. When this was washed, a solution of gum was produced—the gum in fact which had been used to give verisimilitude to the conglomeration of gravel which the hoaxer had produced. Similarly once the finds had been "blown upon", the extraordinary collection of animal remains—"the Piltdown Zoo"—which was something like a representative collection of palaeontologist's swaps—a little of everything and a predominance of no single item, appropriate perhaps to a Noah's Ark but to no other known system of animal ecology—was seen for what it was, the clearest example of the impudence of the hoax.

These were indeed the methods of common sense, but the clinching and most impressive test was something new: the fluorine test, which was developed jointly by the Natural History Museum and the Department of the Government Chemist. Fluorine is a gaseous element, fairly common in different forms nearly everywhere. It has the character of entering into the structure of the material of bones and teeth and becoming locked there, and this process is cumulative. The longer a bone has been lying in gravels which contain fluorine, the more fluorine the bone will contain. Now since gravels, shall we say, do not all contain the same amount of fluorine and indeed can be fluorine-deficient, it is clear that no absolute dating technique can be based on the fluorine content. But it is also clear that if two bones have been lying in the same gravel for the same length of time they will both have the same fluorine content; and this is how the test worked in the Piltdown case. The majority of the animal bones and teeth in the find had considerable though varying quantities of fluorine in their make-up; but the cranium and the mandible, only the slightest traces, the cranium because, though old, it must have come from a fluorine-deficient site, the mandible because it was modern.

A great deal of research into the application of modern scientific discoveries to the purposes of archaeology in the broadest sense has been done at the Oxford University Research Laboratory for Art and Archaeology under its Director, Dr E. T. Hall—an institution which came into being very largely as the result of the interest of the late Lord Cherwell. Here some most ingenious devices have been invented and developed and tried out, their purpose being to give certain specific answers, certain highly particularized data—and nothing else. The machine gives the fact; but not the how, the why and the significance of that fact. The sum has still to be worked out later, but facts are the first essential.

One of the most impressive devices at Oxford is one set up for X-ray spectrum analysis, which is, at any rate theoretically, capable of giving a complete quantitative and qualitative analysis of any object without touching it. It is often of interest and importance, for example, to know what particular metals and what impurities there are in a particular metal object. Such knowledge could for example establish by what method an object was made or where its raw materials derived from. The usual procedure is to break off a small portion and analyse it in the usual way, which naturally destroys it. But this could be extremely undesirable in the case of an object of high art and inestimable value. Here is where the Oxford apparatus comes into action and supplies that analysis by as it were translating the appropriate sections of the spectrum cast by a beam of X-rays. This is an astonishing result, but not without its snags. The analysis when given refers to the outer skin of the metal and although when it was first made that metal was homogeneous, it is not necessarily so after say hundreds of years underground. Corrosion may have altered the surface, some factor of the various metals may have leached out, and there is also the very odd feature that in some alloys, the particles of the various metals tend to sort themselves out separately, some moving towards the surface, others to the centre. And so, however exact the answer, it must nevertheless be treated with reserve.

Another most interesting apparatus has been built around the interesting fact that free iron molecules, such as appear in every handful of soil, are always in alignment with magnetic north at every given moment. If however that soil, in the form of clay, is moulded into a pot and baked, the iron is fixed in the alignment which was inevitable at the moment of baking. But, as every map-reader knows, magnetic north varies slightly each year, moving through a fixed sector over a long period of years and then starting all over again. So if it were possible to build an apparatus which would measure the angle of the iron molecules in a particular pot, it should then be easy to refer to a table of the inclination of magnetic north and state with confidence the exact year in which the pot was fired. Such an apparatus has been built and does indeed work—provided the pot has a flat base and was indeed fired in the kiln with its perpendicular axis perpendicular, a very exacting proviso in the case of the ancient potters.

The most immediately useful and indeed handy apparatus which has emerged from the Oxford Laboratory is Dr M. J. Aitken's proton magnetometer, which promises to be a very useful tool of the archaeologist. Its origins, to quote Dr Aitken, are as follows: "The archaeological possibilities were suggested to me by Mr J. C. Belshé, a Cambridge geophysicist, the basic design had been developed by Mr G. S. Waters and Mr P. D. Francis, both of the Ministry of Supply and the instrument itself was built jointly by the Littlemore Scientific Engineering Company and the staff of the Oxford Archaeological Research Laboratory under the personal supervision of its Director, Dr E. T. Hall." The purpose of the device is to measure the normal magnetism at the earth's surface consistently over a given area and to plot any variation, any magnetic disturbance. Naturally such a disturbance is given by buried iron, but the working of soil, as for example a ditch cut into a gravel subsoil and later filled in with earth would produce a magnetic disturbance, as do filled-in pits, or, most particularly, kilns where the clay heated to red heat has become a weak permanent magnet. In any case however this disturbance is very slight and very difficult to measure; and the recently developed technique of nuclear magnetic resonance has been employed. The detector is a simple bottle of water encircled by an electrical coil. The protons that form the nuclei of the hydrogen atoms contained in the water molecules gyrate at a speed which depends on the strength of the external magnetism in which the water is placed. Over undisturbed ground these protons might gyrate at the speed of 2,000 revolutions a second, but if there were something magnetic in the soil this speed would be increased to say 2,000.2 revolutions a second—and furthermore this gyration only lasts for a few seconds at a time. To do the counting, techniques used in analogue computers and guided weapons are employed and transistors (about 150 of them) are used in the process and enable the whole measuring apparatus to be compressed into a portable box weighing about 23 lb.

In use this complex machine is very simple. The area to be tested is marked off in squares and the recorder's chart marked likewise. The bottle is suspended from a light tripod in the centre of each square and the reading from the four dials in the apparatus read off and marked on the chart. A consistent variation in the chart will usually give the location and even rough plan of any underground disturbance. It gives in fact the same sort of findings as the electrical resistivity method, but no probes have to be inserted and the speed of operation is greater. Measurements can be taken at the rate of about six a minute. There are one or two snags. The first buried antiquity located by the device was a dump of old iron bedsteads; and old tin cans can also complicate the picture. It can not be used within 20 ft of a wire fence and the ground to be examined needs to be clear and fairly level, without bumps and dips. Nevertheless it has now been tried out at a number of sites in England and also at Enkomi in Cyprus and has proved its worth for exploring a site and cutting out the need for laborious, time-wasting and costly trial trenches made simply in accordance with guess or hope.

Other experiments at Oxford have been concerned with a new technique for arriving at Carbon-14 readings; and these, if successful and practicable will be of the greatest importance in view of the present-day importance of Carbon-14 dating.

The radio-carbon method of age determination, or Carbon-14 dating, has now given rise to an immense amount of learned literature of great technical complexity; but the technique derives from a basically simple principal—the fact that one of the three isotypes of the element carbon is radioactive. These three natural isotopes of carbon are known as C-12, C-13 and C-14. They all have six protons to the nucleus, but C-12 has six neutrons, C-13 seven and C-14 eight. It is in fact the total of protons and neutrons which gives the distinguishing number to the isotope. Now C-14 differs from the others in that it is unstable. Its neutrons and protons cannot live happily together and there is a constant tendency to change the configuration. This comes about by the ejection of a beta-particle or electron from the C-14 nucleus which results in the conversion of one of the excess neutrons into a proton thus making the proportion into seven protons and seven neutrons—in other words a nitrogen atom. In other words Carbon-14 eventually ceases to exist, its life before disintegration being about 8,000 years. However there is a constant production of new Carbon-14 in the atmosphere in the form of carbon-dioxide as the result of cosmic radiation. This is changed into carbon by plants and also taken from them by all animals. Once that animal or plant is dead, the process of the disintegration of the Carbon-14 isotope begins and continues on a known curve. Consequently, everything else being equal, the proportion of Carbon-14 atoms remaining in any sample of bone, charcoal, peat, shell or the like should give the time that has elapsed since that particular sample "became dead" or in other words was removed from the carbon dioxide cycle.

And, in fact, so it does. A list of radio-carbon dates was first published (in Chicago) in 1951 and since then a great number of other lists have been published and the system has survived both the first unthinking enthusiasm and the succeeding disillusion as various complications appeared. The laboratory technique is difficult and laborious; samples can be contaminated by radioactive dust and atomic explosions have much increased the quantity of radioactive dust in the atmosphere; it is possible that the nature of the samples may have been altered by various means underground, although this is highly unlikely; and it is also possible that cosmic radiation may have varied through the centuries and that this variation might have affected in some degree the proportions of the three isotopes in, say, wood growing at that time. Parenthetically it may be mentioned that the normal proportions of the three are Carbon-12, 99 per cent, Carbon-13, 1 per cent, while the presence of Carbon-14 is so small that it is demonstrated only by its radioactivity. But these difficulties and anomalies are relatively trifles. The more the technique is used and the more samples are tested, the more accurate (on the law of averages) and useful it becomes. As two scientists, writing on the subject have pointed out, if you spin a coin, you have a 50 per cent chance that it comes down heads. If you spin it ten times, you might conceivably get eight heads and two tails; but if you went on spinning to 500 times, it is extremely likely that you would get something very close to 250 heads and 250 tails. The more tests, the greater the accuracy; and also, naturally the simplification and perfection of the technique for testing.

In conclusion, bearing in mind the mingled delight and distrust with which the method was greeted, it should be said that so far it has generally confirmed the dates reached by the various means known as the historic method. Most archaeologists have had their dating techniques justified by Carbon-14; and the very great majority gladly accept it as a most useful and reassuring check to their own calculations.

INDEX